Wasting Away

The Undermining of Canadian Health Care

Second Edition

Pat Armstrong and Hugh Armstrong

OXFORD
UNIVERSITY PRESS

OXFORD

UNIVERSITY PRESS

70 Wynford Drive, Don Mills, Ontario M3C 1J9
www.oup.com/ca

Oxford University Press is a department of the University of Oxford.
It furthers the University's objective of excellence in research, scholarship,
and education by publishing worldwide in

Oxford New York
Auckland Bangkok Buenos Aires Cape Town Chennai
Dar es Salaam Delhi Hong Kong Istanbul Karachi Kolkata
Kuala Lumpur Madrid Melbourne Mexico City Mumbai Nairobi
São Paulo Shanghai Taipei Tokyo Toronto

Oxford is a trade mark of Oxford University Press
in the UK and in certain other countries

Published in Canada
by Oxford University Press

Copyright © Oxford University Press Canada 2003

The moral rights of the author have been asserted

Database right Oxford University Press (maker)

First published 2003

National Library of Canada Cataloguing in Publication Data

Armstrong, Pat, 1945–
     Wasting away : the undermining of Canadian health care / Pat Armstrong,
Hugh Armstrong. — 2nd ed.

Includes bibliographical references and index.
ISBN 0-19-541715-1

     1. Health care reform—Canada. 2. Medical care—Canada.
I. Armstrong, Hugh, 1943– II. Title

RA449.A75 2002   362.1'0971   C2002-903455-8

1 2 3 4 - 06 05 04 03

Cover Design: Brett Miller
Cover Image: Angela Wyant/getty images

This book is printed on permanent (acid-free) paper ∞.
Printed in Canada

Contents

PREFACE

Since the first edition of *Wasting Away* was published in 1996, the public health-care system in Canada has continued to waste away in increasingly visible ways. Government surpluses and multiple tax cuts have made it more difficult to justify radical reductions in public care primarily in terms of debts and deficits. Indeed, the policies of restraint that characterized the last decade of the twentieth century have been followed in the new millennium by some more public funds for care.

Calls for reforms have not ceased, however; nor has talk of crisis disappeared. Now the main issue is 'sustainability' in the face of an aging population, new technologies, and shortages in health-care personnel. The emphasis has shifted from a focus on removing people from institutional care to primary-care reform and telehealth, strategies intended to keep people out of hospitals and long-term care. Evidence-based everything has also gained prominence as a means of ensuring that the right people provide the right service at the right time, making providers more responsible for the quality of care and managers better able to direct resources to care.

In spite of this new emphasis, many of the strategies now promoted to address sustainability are the same as those promoted a decade ago—markets, users fees, private for-profit delivery, private/public partnerships, business techniques, and more individual responsibility for care. And there are still claims that health care is too expensive. Such claims are based on inflated projections that fail to consider the disastrous effects of past cuts to social programs, changing health patterns, and the possibilities for public reforms.

This new edition of *Wasting Away* takes up these issues. Significant portions remain the same because many of the assumptions, problems, and solutions have not changed. At the same time, emerging and revived techniques may lead to fundamental change and certainly create the need for the additional description and analysis presented here.

As governments across Canada contemplate changes that could transform public care, we intend this book as a contribution to the debate. While it is critical that Canadians know how the system has developed over time, the assumptions that are built into it, and what the research tells us about care, in the end the decisions about solutions must involve fundamental value choices. We would argue that the only sustainable system is a fully public one, based on a notion of the individual right to care and the collective responsibility for care.

Acknowledgements

As always, our work owes an enormous debt both to our research colleagues and to those providing care who have shared their experiences with us. Writing is always a collective project in the sense that it builds on the work and knowledge of others, and we have been particularly privileged to learn from some fine scholars and dedicated providers too numerous to name. We would like to single out Joel Lexchin for special thanks, however, because he provided a careful reading and suggested sources for Chapter 2.

We have also had the privilege to work with supportive, patient, and skilled people at Oxford University Press. We would like to thank Megan Mueller, who began the project with us, Phyllis Wilson, who continued with it, and Richard Tallman, who edited with sensitivity a manuscript turned into a mess by mismatched computer programs. Carleton University provided the funding for us to hire Willow Scobie-Vachon as a research assistant. And once again, our daughter Sarah Armstrong helped with everything from typing to research.

1

The Wasting Away of Care

THE INVISIBLE HAND

Canadians have enjoyed publicly funded health care for over a quarter-century. More than one generation has grown up knowing nothing else. Moreover, many of those over 40 did not come in contact with the previous system because their illnesses happened later in life. And some older Canadians have long forgotten what illness and care before medicare were like. For most Canadians, life without medicare is simply unthinkable.

This inability to imagine what it would be like to pay the full costs of hospitals and doctors, of nursing homes and therapy, of meals-on-wheels and home care, to be restricted to certain doctors, hospitals, or treatments, have wards for the poor and private rooms for the rich, is dangerous. This inability to imagine makes it much easier to dismantle the health-care system because people do not, and will not, know what they are missing until it is too late.

This is not to suggest that Canadians do not value their publicly funded health-care system. Indeed, opinion poll after opinion poll has shown that it is our most popular social program, one supported by more than four out of five Canadians. Unquestionably, the complex array of federal, provincial, municipal, volunteer, religious, lay, and profit-making organizations that constitute our health-care system is understood to be an essential component of Canadian society. 'At a time when other traditional expressions of Canadian values have been placed under demonstrable stress, health and health care have increased in importance and prominence as a shared and common value.'[1]

Recognizing this, politicians from all parties have declared medicare a sacred trust and have avoided frontal attacks on Canada's best-loved social program. Even when Premier Ralph Klein introduced legislation to allow for-profit hospitals in Alberta, he repeatedly declared his commitment to the principles of public care. Most elected officials have avoided this kind of public debate, however. Instead, they have initiated a process that is transforming and undermining the system in ways that are frequently difficult for Canadians to see or oppose. When they become visible, these strategies are justified publicly as the only way to save the system.

Early in the 1990s, debts and deficits provided the major justification for reforms. Health-care costs, Canadians were told, were out of control. We could no longer afford such an expensive system and in order to preserve the sacred trust, we had to reduce expenditures. Not only would these changes save the public system in the long run, but they would improve our overall health as well. The title of a government report, 'When Less is Better', nicely summed up this position.[2]

This seemingly contradictory claim was based on two premises clearly evident in the various provincial reports on health and in a range of documents produced directly or indirectly by governments during that period. The first premise was that health is not primarily determined by our health-care system. The reports pointed out that, in spite of the enormous amounts of money invested in health-care provision, the health of Canadians has not improved significantly in recent years. Agreeing with many of those who have criticized the focus on illness rather than on health, more and more policy-makers argued that prevention and health promotion should be the priority, not treatment and cure. Increasingly, politicians and other decision-makers also critiqued the way care was provided in the health-care system. Referring to the research literature, they argued that many of the procedures carried out in hospitals and doctors' offices have never been proven effective. Thus, putting more money into old treatments was simply inefficient. Instead, evidence-based decision-making, evidence-based medicine, and quality assessment of services should be the order of the day. This emphasis on evidence was echoed later in the decade in a report from the National Forum on Health, a group appointed by the Prime Minister to consider the future of health care in Canada.[3]

The second premise was that the private sector is both more effective and more efficient than the public sector. On the basis of this belief, more and more policy-makers claimed that the application of market principles to the system and a privatization of many services would provide the solution to health-care ills. Using techniques from the profit-making sector would help save the most important parts of the system while maintaining quality, eliminating waste, and expanding choice. In spite of evidence from abroad to the contrary and the negative experience in Canada with privatization strategies, this premise is even more strongly held by many policy-makers today.

In addition, the policy-makers and policy advisers claimed that reforms were a response to 'consumer' preferences. According to various policy documents, many Canadians would prefer to be cared for closer to home rather than in institutions and to rely less on the formal health-care system and more on the community. Furthermore, Canadians were demanding more say in how their health-care system works and in how they are treated. This could best be accomplished, many policy statements maintained, through the decentralization of services and responsibilities.[4]

On this basis, governments across Canada began reforming health-care services in the name of both cost-saving and life-saving, claiming to maintain quality and equity while cutting costs. Contrary to the promises, however, the reforms have not rescued the public system or significantly improved quality, access, and choice. Instead, we hear more talk of a crisis in health care and more emphasis on medical intervention rather than health promotion. With deficits gone, additional causes for concern have been highlighted. Now an aging population, 'consumer' expectations, and new technologies are increasingly blamed for a continuing crisis in costs and care. And this crisis is used to justify yet more reductions in public services and more reliance on the for-profit sector.

THE CRISIS IN CARE

Is the Canadian public health-care system in crisis? There is no simple answer to this question. On the one hand, cutbacks in public financing combined with new approaches to managing health services have created enormous problems for those who provide care. Some have lost their jobs entirely, more work as casual employees, and those who remain in full-time positions have to work much harder, caring for more and sicker patients. Many worry about the quality of care they provide.[5] While some of the public funding has been restored, expenditures have failed to keep up with population growth and much of the spending goes to paying for the consequences of reforms rather than for care.[6] Those who receive care have been protected to some extent from the negative impact of reforms by the extraordinary efforts of care providers to fill the gaps in the system created by these reforms. Indeed, most people who use the system feel they get good care. However, with daily media reports of long waiting lists, patients turned away from emergency rooms, the lack of home care, and the shortage of providers, there is every reason for Canadians to perceive a crisis in care.[7]

On the other hand, there is no crisis in public health-care costs. Canada has spending under control primarily because we have a mainly public health-care system rather than a private one. Although Canadians enjoy better health and longer life than their neighbours to the south, Canada spends about half as much per person on care as the United States.[8] Indeed, the costs that are out of control in Canada are those in the private sector. This is particularly the case with drug expenditures, which are mainly produced and purchased outside the public system.

Nor is there necessarily a crisis looming as a result of the baby boomer population reaching old age.[9] Today's baby boomers are relatively healthy and may not need the kind of care required by their parents. Equally important, the rising health-care costs associated with aging are at least as much a result of health-care practices as they are a consequence of growing old, and thus these costs are not unchangeable forces faced by the health-care system.[10] Other countries such as Germany have handled large elderly populations without either bankrupting their systems or denying care. Similarly, the rising expectations often cited as a cause for concern are frequently the result of advertising by corporations intent on increasing demand.[11] 'Consumer demand' is not an unchangeable force either. Technologies, too, are also frequently about created demands based on untested promises rather than on strong evidence that they result in substantially improved care.

In other words, to the extent that there is a crisis in Canadian health care, it is at least as much a consequence as a cause of reforms.

The purpose of this book is to make these invisible aspects of reform visible. In making these visible, we seek to contribute to a continuing reform process by allowing more people to be part of the debate. From our perspective, there is no single or simple strategy for reform because the issues are complex, because an enormous diversity in needs requires a diversity in solutions, and, most importantly, because strategies are about values as well as about evidence. We do know from the evidence that, although far from perfect, public systems allow cheaper services, better access, and more possibilities for public debate and influence.[12] For-profit strategies are thus more likely to create problems than provide solutions.

ORIGINS, SOURCES, AND METHODS

This book is based on more than a decade of research on Canadian health care. All research reflects a dialogue between theory and evidence, each influenced by the particular experiences and perspectives of the researchers. And this book is no exception. For us, our years of studying women's work and our contact with the health-care system resulting from our daughter's broken leg triggered our interest in the female-dominated health-care sector.

Our survey of existing literature on health care indicated that much of it concentrated on those, primarily men, who make policy decisions, rather than on the women who either do the work or receive the care. When health-care personnel were examined, the stress was on doctors and registered nurses, while the many others working in the system were frequently not even defined as health-care workers.[13] Patients made even fewer appearances in the Canadian literature. Instead, most of the research was based on either numerical data describing health-care resources or on expert opinion about care.

Yet it seemed clear that health care was not only about the work done by doctors and registered nurses but also about cleaning and laundry, about records and food, about volunteers who read, and about families that provide care. The food, cleanliness, control, comfort, and support that have been established as critical determinants of health are even more critical in health care. It also seemed clear that the patients ought to be a subject of concern and that the conditions of work for those employed in the system would have a significant impact on the care patients receive. Moreover, from our perspective, the best sources of information on how policy is practised are the people who do the work and receive the care.

With such issues in mind, we began a series of projects designed to fill in these gaps. Much of this research has been conducted with a team of researchers and in partnership with a variety of unions that represent a range of health-care workers. The primary research strategy is semi-structured group interviews, because such interviews allow participants to stimulate each other, to raise their own issues, and to serve as a verification for each others' claims. Once the interviews are analyzed, we report our findings to an equivalent group of providers. We ask them to assess not only what they think we have appropriately represented but also what we have failed to capture about their work and about policy in practice.

Our research purpose and strategy have evolved in response to concerns raised in interviews as well as to new developments in care. This means that we are continually adjusting our methods and adjusting our interview techniques. We often include interviews with individuals as well as analysis of other primary qualitative data, when these strategies are appropriate in our effort to develop as complete a picture as possible of the impact on care. Documents on particular workplaces, government policy reports, and secondary sources provide the background for this work. Here, these sources are combined with an analysis of primary data collected by such organizations as Statistics Canada and the Canadian Institute for Health Information to set out as fully as possible the complexity and nature of reforms.

THE GUIDING THEORY: POLITICAL ECONOMY

All of this material has been collected and analyzed from a feminist political economy perspective. The political economy refers to the complex of institutions and relations that constitute not only what are conventionally referred to as the political and economic systems but also the social, physical, ideological, and cultural systems.[14] It thus encompasses the private and public sectors of the formal economy as well as households, which themselves have private and public aspects. It provides a more integrated approach to the study of health than one that examines health care as an institution largely separated from the rest. And it is an approach that fits best with our understanding of the determinants of health.

This approach contrasts sharply with both social interaction theory and functional theory, the two most common traditions in social science approaches to health care. In social interaction theory, the emphasis is on what happens within asylums and hospitals. Little attention is paid to the context for these institutions or the relations of power that shape this context. Although functional theory does consider the broader purposes of health care, it assumes a shared set of values and a society differentiated according to socio-economic status that reflects agreed-upon rewards and goals. Profit does not enter the picture, nor is it questioned as a purpose. Biology and technology, assumed to be developed through objective investigation and shared needs, are seen as central to an explanation of what services are provided and how they are provided. Change is understood as primarily a response to developments in technology that reflect innovation and scientific evidence.

From a political economy perspective, the structure of the health-care system is understood within a historically specific context characterized by inequalities in power and economic resources and dominated by the search for profit. It is also characterized by enormous tensions between classes, regions, sexes, cultural groups, and races. In addition to these tensions are those within and among aspects of the system itself that, within the confines of inequality, provide the dynamic aspects of the system and much of the basis for change. Thus, developments in health care are not seen as simply responding to a set of agreed-upon needs, as primarily reflecting technological and other innovations, or as based on scientifically established procedures, although all of these play a role. The developments are also understood to reflect the search for profit, as well as struggles over power and resources. A critical contradiction is that between public and private interests. Some of these systemic tensions cannot, and should not, be resolved, although they must be recognized as central to reform.

States, employers, and others who direct the money markets, employee organizations, and popular groups have all played significant roles in these struggles. The pressure on each employer to increase profits by introducing new technologies, by breaking jobs up into fragments that can be handled quickly by workers who require little training and who can be easily replaced, by making each employee work longer and harder, and by increasing control over the labour process endangers the health of workers.[15] In response to these dangers, people have organized into unions, professional organizations, and popular groups both to limit the actions of individual employers and to demand that governments intervene to provide collective protection, including protection against financial ruin when health care is required.

These efforts to develop collective protection were particularly successful in the period following World War II, when the economy was booming and when those who had made so many sacrifices during the war were demanding something in return. Services such as health care and education were defined as public goods and rights of citizenship, a benefit for both employers and employees. Much of this protection was provided by what came to be known as 'the welfare state', a term used to describe both a set of institutions and a set of social relations. In *The Fiscal Crisis of the State*, James O'Connor maintained that welfare states have two essential roles: accumulation and legitimation. States help create the conditions for private profit-making by providing roads, sewers, highways, utilities, communication services, airports, research, and an educated workforce. They help ensure social harmony by providing a justice system and services for citizens, and by promoting a shared value system. These two roles are intimately linked as states vary their support for businesses and for workers, as well as their stated values, to accommodate changes in the needs of organizations seeking profit. Health care is very much part of such welfare states.

Writing in 1973, O'Connor argued that because states were paying for more and more of the costs of accumulation while continuing to allow the profits to be collected and controlled privately, they were headed for trouble. State expenses increase more rapidly than revenues. The resulting crisis is 'exacerbated by the private appropriation of state power for particularistic ends', with disputes among these particularistic or special interests resolved in the political process rather than in the market. Because the process is a political one reflecting the quite different strengths of these interests, 'there is a great deal of waste, duplication, and overlapping of state projects and services.'[16] This not only means that the costs increase unnecessarily, but also that states are open to attack on the grounds of inefficiency. Increasingly, states are unable to meet citizens' needs or to respond to criticisms from a variety of sources.

Twenty years later, there was little opposition to the notion that states indeed faced a fiscal crisis, that there was waste in the system, and that revenues had not kept up with expenses. The economic boom ended in an economic bust. And the bust was blamed on social spending and used as a justification for cuts in spending as well as for a move towards a 'free market' system. But, as Brendan Martin argues in *In the Public Interest?*, what was called the debt crisis was largely the result of international bank and private investment practices, rather than primarily the result of inefficiencies in public services.[17] This claim is substantiated by figures on the Canadian federal debt. According to a Statistics Canada publication, 'Expenditures on social programs did not contribute significantly to the growth of government spending relative to GDP.'[18] The debt is largely the result of the way debt is financed and the way taxes have been reduced for some corporations and individuals, rather than the result of overspending on public services. It is also related to slow growth in the economy, as the recent expansion in government funds clearly shows, and to a dwindling number of places for investment.

Nevertheless, international organizations such as the World Bank and the International Monetary Fund blamed national states and greedy workers for the debt. They used the debt as a means of demanding that states withdraw from both the ownership of the infrastructure and the provision of services to citizens. These organizations called for the privatization of government-owned enterprises and major cutbacks in the provision of services, on the grounds that not only were they too costly and inefficient but also that they interfered with the free trade necessary for economic development. Their questionable and unproven assumption is that 'free markets' and for-profit companies are more effective and efficient. In the process, the 'ability of nation-states to protect and promote the public interest has been undermined and the authority of their citizens usurped.'[19] As a consequence, the areas previously occupied by states were opened to for-profit concerns.

Although deficits have largely disappeared and debts been reduced, governments still claim they have no choice about limiting the state sector if we are to compete in the global economy. And in spite of much fuller government coffers, social programs such as health care are still under threat, albeit in more covert ways than they were when deficits and debts were the dominant theme. Governments still argue that market mechanisms are the most effective means and that health-care costs are too high. Indeed, some governments in Canada are using the perceived crisis in health care as a justification for further privatization. Unions, professional organizations, and popular groups have lost much of the power they enjoyed in the immediate post-war period, largely as a result of widespread insecurity in employment. Some, such as the unions representing registered nurses, have begun making significant gains in the face of nursing shortages and growing government revenues. Popular groups, too, are gaining strength. But the covert nature of reforms, combined with the undermined system, has begun to erode public support for public care in ways that make it difficult to resist these trends.

O'Connor recognized that the processes he identified work to the disadvantage of women and racial minorities in the formal economy and create large 'surplus populations' outside this market, but he did not examine the impact on households[20] or on actual reductions in necessary work time. Martin acknowledged that cutbacks in the provision of services will 'leave gaps to be filled by private or voluntary organizations or gaps within family or community (usually filled by women)'.[21] But he, too, failed to explore more fully the consequences for households of the attack on state power and provision. And neither of them explored the consequences for health and health care.

Yet it is clear that these developments have enormous implications for households in general and for women in particular. Indeed, the theory needs to be revised to include a third role for the state. In addition to encouraging accumulation and legitimation, states also play a critical part in structuring what is provided for publicly in the market and privately in households, in determining who does the work in these spheres and how it is done.[22] This mediating function of the state is here both made explicit and explored.

Although, as Marilyn Waring makes clear in *If Women Counted*,[23] unpaid work done primarily by women in households is invisible in government accounts, it is not the case that states have failed to take women and their households into account when constructing or destructing policies and programs. Various provincial reports have recognized that people sent home early from hospitals or released from institutions will be cared for primarily by women in the home or by women working as volunteers in community organizations. In general, however, states address these concerns by offering 'interventions that aim to help carers cope with the responsibilities of caring, to improve carer effectiveness with caring tasks, and to provide occasional relief from the responsibilities of caring'.[24] Such interventions primarily reinforce women's work as informal caregivers, rather than challenge it.

At the same time as cutback strategies are transferring the work of caring from female workers paid by the state to unpaid female workers in the home, they are increasing the demand for products produced in the profit-making sector. Many homes now need medical supplies that are purchased individually for individuals. Institutions can buy equipment, such as safety bars for bathtubs, in bulk because the institutions service many people. Private homes cannot benefit from such savings and there is a constantly growing demand as more and more people sent home require special medical equipment or supplies. Thus sales, and profits, increase—sometimes at the expense of individuals and sometimes at the expense of the state.

It is not only the overall structure of health care that is understood here within the context of the social, physical, and ideological environment. It is also patient care. The health of patients is influenced by much more than the efficacy of particular procedures. The entire context and structure of care has a profound impact on patient health. Central to this care are the wide variety of workers within the system and the conditions of their work. Many of the dangers to workers that result from efforts to increase profits and reduce costs in the private sector also are evident in state health care. But here they may risk not only the health of those employed in the system but also that of those cared for.

The importance of physical and social environments to health is now widely acknowledged. The assumption that these environments 'play a major role in creating a healthy society'[25] has been made explicit in a number of provincial commissions and reports. But what is argued here is that air pollution, cleanliness, control, social support, and psychological factors are even more important for those who are ill or disabled. Moreover, employment security, occupational health and safety, and work organization and hierarchy for those employed in health care have an impact on the health of both the workers and those for whom they provide care.

It is this theoretical perspective that initiated and guides our focus on work within the health-care system.

THE BOOK IN OUTLINE

Given this political economy perspective, it is not surprising, then, that our emphasis is on the context for both the overall structure of the system and the particular health-care environment of patients and workers. We begin with an analysis of how formal health care in Canada has developed, offering a critical examination of the ideas and practices that underlie our system. This historical analysis is central to an understanding of the entrenched powers in and the primary assumptions of our current system. It is mostly a story of the successful struggle for domination by a particular group of medical practitioners focused on cures, although their power, too, has come under threat with new market technologies. But prevention, most commonly seen in the form of 'public health', has also been a recurring theme. Moreover, although often invisible in public discussion and in research, most health care and prevention have continued to be provided mainly and informally by women at home and by volunteers in the community. And providers, both in and out of the formal system, as well as patients have fought to shape care delivery in ways that reflect their needs. The purpose of this chapter and the next is to examine the assumptions and relations built into the system. The argument is that the health care we have is the result of power struggles and political choices, because other assumptions and other relations are possible. At issue is not only the structure of the health-care system but also the dominant medical model on which the structure is based.

In the following chapters we are concerned with the institutions and people who provide the care. The determinants of health outlined in the first two chapters are used as a means of evaluating the impact of reforms on the health of both patients and health-care workers. The argument is that reforms are based primarily on the dominant medical model and/or for-profit strategies. Such reforms tend to emphasize the worst aspects of the model and to impede access to quality care. As a result, the health of both providers and patients is at risk.

Directly linked to the risks faced by patients and providers is the structure of decision-making, the topic of Chapter 3. The less control people or providers have, as discussed in Chapter 4, the greater the possibility that their health will deteriorate. Although reforms are frequently described as strategies to increase participation and control, they often do the reverse. In the process, they increase inequality while reducing the quality of care.

Because money is at the centre of the current transformations in health care and at the centre of a political economy approach, it is also not surprising that money is a major issue in this book and the focus of Chapter 5. The assumption at the core of much writing on Canadian health care—that current levels of care are no longer affordable—is challenged. So is the notion that private delivery of services is necessarily more effective and efficient. Effectiveness and efficiency cannot be measured primarily in terms of money spent and people processed. Indeed, many strategies taken from the private sector can serve in the long run to increase costs in terms of both health and government finances, precisely because they are based solely on outcomes defined in terms of output or immediate financial costs.

Money is not the only source of power. Unions and professional organizations have played an important role in the development and structuring of care, as have a variety of other groups. But new managerial strategies, combined with cutbacks in resources, have challenged many of their hard-won gains. So have other state initiatives. At the same time, there is an emphasis on 'consumer' participation—on choice and on a devolution of responsibility to the local level. Although 'empowerment' is frequently used as a way of describing these developments, too often they have the opposite effect. Who decides is the subject of Chapter 6, which explores how power relations are changing within the health-care sector.

Differences in access to financial resources and to power are related to differences in access to services. Public provision of health care has served to reduce inequities in access to care. Although a commitment to equity is often expressed when changes are introduced, reforms that shift responsibility to individuals and households necessarily have a greater impact on those who are the most vulnerable. Moreover, at the same time as states have made this shift in health care, they have also cut back in those areas that are increasingly recognized as critical determinants of health. As a result, not only do more people find themselves without access to services, but more people also find themselves without access to decent housing, stable employment, safe work environments, or adequate food and clothing.

Central to the discussion of all these issues is the notion of tension and contradiction. Questions in health care are often posed in terms of alternatives such as centralization or decentralization, institution or community, cure or prevention, this technology or no technology, these reforms or none at all. And answers are given in terms of one or the other. This book explores the tensions between these alternatives, arguing that in many cases neither alternative should be given priority. Rather, the strengths of each, along with the tensions between them, need to be retained. Indeed, the contradictions inherent in many strategies provide the best hope for the system.

The argument of the book is that reforms are still based mainly on the medical model, now combined with for-profit strategies. The result is an increasing emphasis on the medical model and a movement away from public care. The consequence is likely to be a more uneven distribution of existing kinds of care rather than a reformed system based on our understanding of the determinants of health. And in the long run, the costs are likely to rise, especially if more than government finances are considered in the cost accounting.

No simple solution is offered to reforming the system. Indeed, we believe there is no single or simple solution. Instead, what is required is a new approach that begins from different assumptions and leads to a variety of alternative means of helping the ill and disabled. Such an approach would recognize and build on the tensions within the system rather than seek to eliminate all of them. These alternatives must be based on the determinants that all government reports agree are critical to health but fail to see are also critical to care.

RECOMMENDED READINGS

Pat Armstrong, Hugh Armstrong, and David Coburn, eds, *Unhealthy Times: Political Economy Perspectives on Health and Care in Canada*. Toronto: Oxford University Press, 2001. This collection of articles uses political economy perspectives to locate health-care reforms within global and national forces. It is intended to both reveal the nature of reforms and extend political economy to help understand new developments in health and care.

Lesley Doyal, *What Makes Women Sick: Gender and the Political Economy of Health*. New Brunswick, NJ: Rutgers University Press, 1995. While this British author focuses on an understanding of women's health, the exploration of political economy is relevant to both women and men.

National Forum on Health, *Canada Health Action: Building on the Legacy*, vol. 2, *Synthesis Reports and Issues Papers*. Ottawa: Minister of Public Works and Government Services, 1997. The National Forum on Health was a group of experts from a variety of fields who were appointed by the Prime Minister to make recommendations on the future of health care. Their reports cover a broad range of issues on health care in Canada, issues that are summarized in this volume.

From Cuts and Chemicals to Carrots and Condoms:
The Development of Canadian Health Care

Health is about much more than health-care services. Indeed, as various provincial and federal government reports make clear, health is not primarily determined by health care. What happens outside health-care institutions and services is much more important for the overall health of the population than what happens within them. Recognizing that health is about much more than cuts and chemicals, these reports question the need for additional or even continued government investment in health care. Indeed, until quite recently they recommended less care and more prevention, with prevention defined more in terms of carrots and condoms than secure employment and guaranteed incomes. Although the reports suggested a variety of ways the delivery system could be improved, the main concern was saving money by providing less of the same. They did little to challenge the medical model on which the system is based or to apply research on health determinants to health-care delivery.

In this chapter, we do just that. We argue that the set of assumptions that together constitute the dominant medical model needs to be questioned if health care is to be reformed in a way that takes the established determinants of health into account. We do not argue that the system should be dismantled or that the assumptions should be simply discarded and replaced by their opposites. Rather, we reject the notion of simple choices between such alternatives as prevention and cure, promotion and intervention. We argue for the necessity of recognizing the fundamental contradictions between such assumptions as the doctor as expert and the patient as empowered. At issue is not which side to choose, but how to retain and manage the tension between the two. There is no single or simple solution to reforming the health-care system. Health is determined by social, physical, and psychological environments, interacting with biological factors.

DEFINING HEALTH

In 1947, the World Health Organization (WHO) defined health as 'a state of complete physical, mental, and social well-being and not merely the absence of disease and infirmity'. This definition was repeated again in the *Ottawa Charter for Health Promotion* in 1986, suggesting that ideas about what constitutes health changed little in the intervening years.[1] Although the definition was criticized for being too broad, too much about a condition rather than about a process and impossible to achieve,[2] it nevertheless became a standard way of defining health. The WHO claim that an individual's state of health was influenced by much more than biology and personal practices also became widely accepted.

Variations on this definition of health have been adopted by all the Canadian ministries responsible for health. And there is a broad consensus on what determines a state of physical, social, and mental well-being. As the National Forum on Health concluded in 1997, 'We have known for some time that the better off people are in terms of income, social status, social networks, sense of control over their lives, self-esteem and education, the healthier they are likely to be. . . . We know that there is a gradient in health status, with health improving at each step up the slope of income, education and social status.'[3]

DETERMINING HEALTH

These determinants are critical to the positions taken in various government reports and in the strategies for change. Indeed, they provide the shared framework that justifies a wide range of reforms. An Ontario report, *Nurturing Health: A Framework on the Determinants of Health*, provided details on the research and theory behind the consensus on what determines health.[4] According to this report, health is determined by five factors: social environments, physical environments, psychological environments, productivity and wealth, and, finally, health care. Because they are central to the new health strategies, how these factors are presented is worth examining more closely.

SOCIAL ENVIRONMENTS
As the Ontario report pointed out, study after study has demonstrated that social relations and social support are critical to health. Interpersonal contacts and recognition as a person count in health terms. According to the Ontario report, 'People with more social contacts and friends tend to live longer than those with fewer.'[5]

What the report failed to discuss, however, is the considerable research indicating that social support is even more important to those who are ill or disabled. Comfort and support provided to people undergoing treatment can not only speed recovery but can also make a difference in whether or not recovery happens at all.[6] Social interaction based on knowledge of the person and the particular problems is also essential to the health of the disabled. Providing such comfort to the sick is not simply a reflection of caring for someone, something women do naturally, or an additional frill offered by those with the time. Rather, it is a skill long recognized in nursing as central to what constitutes health care and is increasingly being acknowledged in other areas as well.[7]

As Green-Hernandez makes clear in her discussion of nursing work:

> Professional caring is learned and transmitted with therapeutic intent as a direct nursing intervention. The nurse intentionally used professional nursing as the *modus for* therapeutic means for meeting a client's assessed needs, in order to attain nursing and client health care goals.[8]

Such caring is not a separate activity but is integral to all health-care work, whether administering drugs or giving a bath. And it is critical to helping a patient 'attain or maintain health, or die a peaceful death'.[9] Moreover, the kind of social support people want and need varies with their cultural origins. Cultural sensitivity is particularly important in providing care, given that familiar practices are especially supportive in stressful situations.[10]

Perhaps the most vital ingredient in social support is a sense of security. And nowhere is security more critical than in paid employment. According to the National Forum on Health, 'improving the health of the population depends above all on achieving the lowest possible unemployment rates.'[11] Unemployment contributes significantly to premature cardiovascular deaths in particular. Involuntary job loss also increases the rates of suicide, depression, panic, and substance abuse.[12]

It is not only employment security that is important, however. The nature of the work is also critical to health. According to Ontario's *Nurturing Health* report, 'The lifespan and the health of an individual is linked to his or her location in the job hierarchy and to associated factors such as degree of authority, freedom to make decisions and level of social support in the workplace.' As well, workplace 'social supports, as measured by the number and quality of interactions with co-workers, also have an effect on health', and health is 'affected by the stress related demands of the job.'[13]

What many reports fail to acknowledge, however, is that the nature of the job and employment security are equally important to those providing care. Indeed, it could be argued that employment insecurity and lack of social support and control over their work may be even more important issues in health care because the consequences may be felt by the patients in terms of inadequate or even dangerous care. This may be particularly the case for those many women expected and required to provide care, without pay, for their relatives in an isolated private home.[14]

PHYSICAL ENVIRONMENTS

It has long been recognized that the physical conditions under which people work and live are fundamental to health. In fact, these were the major concern of the public health movement that first appeared towards the end of the nineteenth century.[15] Nutritional food, clean water, clean hands, and clean air are essential to good health. And it is difficult to remain healthy if homes and workplaces are dirty, crowded, noisy, poorly ventilated, or lack toilet facilities. Healthy physical environments are even more critical to those who are ill because their immune systems are weaker, a fact that the Ontario report failed to point out. It also failed to consider the part played by food, crowding, noise, and ventilation in health-care settings.

Nurturing Health recognized that 'It is apparent that important health gains can be achieved in Ontario through improved occupational health and safety measures.'[16] There was, however, no discussion of the health and safety measures that need to be taken within health-care services. The work environments of health-care providers were not considered, even though they face special risks in their workplaces. Yet here, too, the risks to health-care workers may have a significant impact on the care they are able to provide to patients.

PSYCHOLOGICAL ENVIRONMENTS

Nurturing Health drew attention to the importance of mental states in remaining healthy. According to the report:

> There is growing evidence that mental health influences physical well-being although the exact pathways and the biological mechanisms are not yet clear. . . . Psychoneuroimmunology, an emerging and still controversial field of knowledge, may go a long way to explaining a biological pathway linking social and environmental factors with the performance of the immune system and hence the health status of individuals.[17]

As was the case with the discussion of social and physical environments, however, the report failed to consider that mental states are even more important when the immune system is weakened by surgery or disease. And by classifying the issue as one of individual response, the report ignored the importance of social, physical, and psychological environments in creating these responses.

PRODUCTIVITY AND WEALTH

Both secure employment and secure income are important to health. As *Nurturing Health* made clear, the economy establishes the context for health. 'Greater wealth (socio-economic status) is associated with greater health; poorer and middle income people appear to be more vulnerable than wealthy people to a variety of ailments. The type of ailments that disproportionately affect poor people change over time.'[18] Moreover, 'when socio-economic differences are narrowed, population health status improves'[19] for those on every rung of the ladder. The young are particularly at risk. 'The harmful effects of poverty on the physical and mental health of children can be partially offset by public programs. Intervention can reduce the number of Low Birth Weight babies, who are prone to suffer major health problems.'[20]

If prosperity and equity are important to maintaining the health of the overall population, they must also be important to health services. In fact, although differences related to sex, race, and class remain,[21] governments have successfully reduced inequality in access to care through the collective provision of a wide range of services and supports. However, the use of the lessons from the determinants of health research to justify cuts to publicly funded health care has the effect of increasing inequality, with damaging consequences for health status.

HEALTH CARE

'Since the traditional medical care system concentrates on the treatment of ill health and disability, it can only make a limited contribution to the prevention of illness by nurturing overall good health,' stated the 1991 Ontario report.[22] In keeping with other reports of the day, it maintained that 'Research suggests there may be an optimal ceiling for spending on the formal health care system—past a certain point such spending could be a drag on the nation's economy and hence on its health.'[23] Later, the National Forum on Health embraced a similar position, expressing its belief that 'in Canada we spend enough money on health care.'[24]

Few would contest the claim in *Nurturing Health* that 'there is limited scope for effective medical intervention with many of the leading causes of death' or its contention that there must be a limit on health care spending.[25] However, the critique was mostly about health care based on a medical model and its failure to cure biologically defined ills. There was little discussion of how the services could be designed to improve health in ways that apply the knowledge about the determinants of health to the system itself. Moreover, the critique was for the most part based on overall population trends, not on the individuals who have been helped by the system. Whatever has caused our illness or disability, we want to have access to good health care when we are ill or disabled. Too often, the individuals who need care disappear in the emphasis on health determinants.

The Ontario report, like similar ones in other provinces, treated health care as one factor determining health. It did little to explore the links among the other determinants and with the health-care system. Instead, because health care was defined as only one determinant of health, and not a terribly significant one at that, the reports focused primarily on reducing the contributions of government to the health-care system. Rather than linking health care to the other determinants of health, the reports saw care as competing with these determinants.

GOVERNMENT RESPONSIBILITIES

The WHO definition of health makes clear that ensuring health is a government responsibility. It does not see health as simply an individual problem. According to WHO, governments must provide adequate health and social measures not only because citizens have a right to health but also because the promotion of health is critical to the attainment of peace and security. In addition, all governments have an interest in promoting health measures throughout the world because poor health in one country could be a threat to all. AIDS has clearly demonstrated the reason for collective concern and government involvement.

The Canadian government commissions and reports that set the stage for the reforms of the 1990s certainly did not deny the need for government intervention. According to these reports governments must play a leadership role in health, but this role must be fundamentally changed. The British Columbia report, *Closer to Home*, made it clear that the 'traditional focus of our health care system is the curing of illness and not the prevention of disease. . . . It is time to change this focus. Increased spending on hospitals, equipment or health care will not necessarily improve health status. More money should be spent on prevention of illness or injury and on protecting health. The least amount of money possible should be spent on providing the necessary, high quality curative services.'[26] All the reports and commissions of the late 1980s and early 1990s echoed this claim. The emphasis in government action was to shift from treatments and cures to prevention and health promotion.

Governments have for a long time taken responsibility for some aspects of health determinants. They have provided clean water and education, regulated housing and waste, offered inoculations and lunch programs, and provided some protection against unemployment and health hazards at work. Public health services devoted to prevention have been in place for over a century. Yet, although cutbacks are being carried out in health care in the name of new research demonstrating the overriding importance of the determinants of health, governments are at the same time removing the regulations designed to protect health, privatizing those services that promoted health, and reducing the supports available to the unemployed and those without homes. Nowhere are these trends clearer than in the case of water, as the recent tragedies in Walkerton, Ontario, and North Battleford, Saskatchewan, exemplify. At the same time, governments continue to lay off health-care workers and to threaten the security of those who remain.

Although all the provincial reports of the 1990s stressed the need to 'review the efficiency, effectiveness and suitability of our health system',[27] they provided little indication that we need to challenge the assumptions on which 'the high quality, curative services' are based. Effectiveness, efficiency, and suitability were mainly defined in terms of the traditional assumptions of the system and of the 'free' market. They were not considered in relation to how health is determined within the system. Rather, we are to have less of the same provided by the public system and more provided in the private sphere.[28]

To the extent that prevention has become the focus, resources have been shifted from health care itself. A paradoxical effect of this shift has been to reinforce the cuts-and-chemicals approach to care. Squeezed health-care budgets mean shorter hospital stays and home care visits, which in turn mean less attention to issues of health education and social support. For example, in the 1990 report of the Saskatchewan Commission, *Future Directions for Health Care in Saskatchewan*,[29] the concern was expressed that 'Despite sophisticated delivery systems and advanced technology and specialization, there will always be those in society for whom complete treatment and recovery is not possible.' While the report went on to say that those who cannot be treated and cured should be cared for with 'compassion and understanding', the implication was that the same concerns do not apply when dealing with those who can be treated and cured. The determinants of health were listed as an addition to, rather than a fundamental critique of, current practices in the curative system.

Clearly, nutrition, cleanliness, social support, and other aspects of the social and physical environments are often more critical for the recovery of those who are being treated than they are for those who are healthy. And the same factors that determine the health of workers outside the health-care system determine the health of those within it. However, little in the various government reports encouraged governments to reform care within the system in ways that reflect concern about the determinants of health. Instead, the reforms being put into practice frequently serve to emphasize the dominant medical model of health, a model based on assumptions that in many ways counter the determinants of health established in these reports.

To understand how reforms can serve to emphasize some of the worst aspects of the system while ignoring the determinants of health, let us now examine what is meant by the medical model and the assumptions about health that are part of that model.

THE BASIC ASSUMPTIONS OF CANADIAN HEALTH-CARE DELIVERY

The Canadian health care system is centred on, and dominated by, allopathic medicine. Although we have come to think of this approach to health care as the only approach, a system focused on penetration of the body 'physically by surgery and chemically by drugs'[30] is just one of many ways to deal with illness or disability. There are other ways of addressing health problems and constructing a health-care system. Chiropractic, for example, is based on 'locating, correcting and adjusting the interference with nerve transmission and expression in the spinal column and other articulations without the use of drugs or surgery'.[31] Unlike allopathic approaches, chiropractic treatment does not require hospitalization or very expensive technology. Nor, usually, does acupuncture. 'Acupuncture and acupressure both stress how the work of their therapies is to release blockages in the flow and balance of the body after which the body will heal itself.'[32] A system based on acupuncture would also create health-care structures different from those found in Canada today.

Allopathic medicine, or what we often think of as regular or orthodox medicine, is based on a particular set of assumptions. These assumptions are reflected in both the structure and the relations of the health-care system. Yet many of these assumptions are quite different from those identified by the various reports as the determinants of health; they are also different from those found in what we usually call alternative and/or complementary therapies. For our analytical purposes, these assumptions are set out explicitly, simply, and separately in the following section. For many of those who work in the system, however, they are often implicit or even unrecognized. In real life these assumptions typically overlap and interact in a more complicated way than we set out in the following sections.

Before setting out the assumptions underlying allopathic medicine, however, we need to make it clear that we make no claims concerning the efficacy of alternative or complementary therapies. Many lack a scientific basis, in whole or in part, at least as science is conventionally practised. This lack, of course, may stem in part from a reluctance by scientists using an allopathic framework to examine the extent to which these therapies have a scientific basis, if any. This reluctance does now appear to be diminishing.

ASSUMPTION 1. THE DETERMINANTS OF ILLNESS ARE PRIMARILY BIOLOGICAL

As Edward Shorter points out in *Bedside Manners*, diagnosis in modern allopathic medicine stems from 'linking changes observed in the tissues after death to the patient's signs and symptoms during life' and from the 'new science of microbiology' that made it possible to see how germs produce disease.[33] To a large extent, mind and body are defined as separate, with diagnosis of illness or disability focused on discovering a specific injury, germ, or cancerous cell that causes the problem. Psychological problems are reduced to biology and typically treated with drugs. Much less frequently, if more drastically, they are treated with electroshock or surgery. Little attention is paid to the interaction between mind and body, as it is assumed that there are different causes for the problems in each.

Directly related to the assumption of a biological base for health problems is the use of tests designed to identify the cause of symptoms. Given that illness is assumed to be identifiable in tissues, blood, organs, or bones, tests that allow us to 'see' the specific cause are a central part of diagnosis. If test results are negative, problems are often attributed to mental rather than physical causes. All too often, if a physical cause cannot be readily identified, the complaint will be dismissed as 'all in the head'. This is especially the case for women.

This assumption of biological causes also has an impact on doctor-patient relationships. With identifiable biological causes in mind, doctors need only spend a very limited time with patients to determine the specific problem. A prescription can be offered or tests can be ordered immediately. Walk-in clinics, where patients are served quickly by a stranger trained in the diagnosis of these biological ills, become possible when it is assumed that there is a readily identifiable cause that requires little knowledge about the person as an individual. Moreover, patients are usually seen individually in the doctor's office, without the involvement of family or friends, because it is assumed that physiological problems need not be situated within a social context. The assumption means people are treated as isolated individuals.

ASSUMPTION 2. THE ENGINEERING MODEL OF THE BODY

To a large extent, modern medicine assumes that the body works much like any other machine. It is made up of a series of parts that can be fixed. Once the part and the problem are identified, there are recognized procedures to follow and specific locations for treatment. This model allows for specialization in allopathic medicine. Because the body is conceived of as a collection of components, these parts can be separated for the purposes of diagnosis and treatment by experts in particular parts. Sections of hospitals or even whole hospitals can be structured to deal with particular component parts. So, for example, Sunnybrook Medical Centre in Toronto can specialize in what the then president called 'six major "product lines": trauma, cancer, aging, heart and circulation, mental health, and rehabilitation'.[34] Like the hospitals, patients can be classified according to the part with the problem.

This engineering model of the body, combined with the assumption of specific causes, also makes possible a fee-for-service system to determine doctors' pay. Fee-for-service is very similar to piecework payments in manufacturing, where workers are paid for each component made. In our health-care system, most doctors' fees are based on the specific part treated or task done, rather than on the basis of the number of people treated or the amount of time worked. In addition, this model allows hospitals and other institutions to calculate the amount of work time required from other workers on the basis of the specific part being fixed. With an approach that assumes parts to be fixed, work for and with a patient can be divided into discrete tasks that are measured and counted.

ASSUMPTION 3. HEALTH CARE IS PRIMARILY ABOUT CURING ILLNESS OR DISABILITY

Central to modern medicine, especially in North America, is the notion of intervention to bring about cure. The assumption is that most physical and psychological problems are subject to treatment and cure. Furthermore, it is often assumed that it is better to intervene if intervention is possible. Drugs and surgery are used to cure the diagnosed illness or injury. The purpose is to return patients to 'normal'.

This curative approach, combined with the engineering model of the body, provides a basis for establishing acute-care hospitals that focus primarily on fixing a specific part as quickly as possible. On the assumption that a cure is primarily about applying a particular technique, hospitals can put a great deal of energy into shortening patient stays to cover only the minimum period required for the particular treatment. Surgery can be done on an outpatient basis, with people arriving at and leaving from the hospital within hours of surgery or other treatment, because the major concern is getting the procedure done. Psychological support before and after treatment, feeding, bathing, and talking with the patient are defined as non-medical tasks. Increasingly, jobs related to food, cleaning, and laundry are called 'hotel services', reflecting the assumption that these have nothing to do with cure or even health. Similarly, management techniques developed in industry are transferred to health care on the assumption that fixing a care part is not much different from fixing a car part. The care process, like making cars, can be assessed in value-added terms.[35] Anyone who does not fit into the category of 'quickly cured' is assigned to another kind of institution, such as chronic care hospitals, group homes, or nursing homes. These other institutions are much less well funded than acute-care hospitals and their doctors, and thus are typically hard-pressed to provide care, as distinct from treatment, notwithstanding both their mandate to provide care and their widespread practice of imposing user fees to cover some of their costs. The situation is even more severe in the home care sector.

ASSUMPTION 4. MEDICINE IS SCIENTIFIC

Allopathic medicine is scientific medicine. 'Scientific medicine taught that each disease had a single well-defined cause, and that the control of the disease could best be achieved by attacking the causative organism or by correcting the function of the diseased part of the body.'[36] Science determines cause, effect, and cure. It is assumed that the effectiveness of tests, drugs, surgery, and other techniques used in treatment has been scientifically established and agreed upon. This is taken to mean that all procedures have been rigorously examined, following strict, value-free procedures that take all relevant factors into account. In the best, if costly, of circumstances, this means the 'gold standard' of experimentation using double-blind, randomized clinical trials. It is assumed not only that such research has been done, but also that it can be done and that everyone can and should agree on what constitutes scientific evidence. At the same time, it is assumed that any treatment that cannot be examined or explained by such procedures is not effective or useful.

When both physiological cause and scientific 'proof' are taken for granted, it is possible to define medicine as the application of standard techniques. Clinical care pathways, with their message that there is one best way to diagnose and to treat, become more prevalent. It is assumed that all patients with the same problem will display very similar symptoms, will follow basically the same pattern of disease development, and will take very similar times for treatment and recovery. It is therefore possible to develop formulas to determine the times for patient cures and discharge. It is also possible to divide up the tasks into separate parts, many of which can be done by people quickly trained to apply the specific, proven technique.

ASSUMPTION 5. THE DOCTOR AS AUTHORITY AND EXPERT

Throughout most of the past century, doctors' training and position have reflected and reinforced these assumptions. Doctors' education has stressed the biological and physical sciences upon which drug therapy and surgery are based. This lengthy training in scientifically established procedures, applied to largely physiologically determined problems, was assumed to make doctors the objective experts who name the appropriate diagnosis and treatment and apply the necessary cure.

Doctors' authority over both patients and other health care workers is justified in terms of these assumptions. Because only doctors have the training in the full range of scientific evidence and correct procedures, they need to determine what patients do and what is done to them. It is assumed that patients lack the necessary knowledge and often the necessary will to follow appropriate procedures. Similarly, it is assumed that doctors' superior knowledge means that only they can know what procedures can be safely delegated to others who work in the system. Doctors' power over both patients and the system is necessary and desirable because health care is about fixing body parts based on expert knowledge of scientifically established procedures, and only doctors have this knowledge. And it is often assumed that most of the improvements in health care over the past century can be attributed to the curative powers of doctors.

Two current news items from Ontario, both of which stem directly from bilateral agreements between the government and the Ontario Medical Association, illustrate the power exercised by doctors over other health professionals. First, the provincial government has decided to eliminate payment for services performed by rehab therapists and by audiologists unless they work under the supervision of and in the same premises as doctors.[37] Second, the province's pilot Family Health Networks have failed to hire in significant numbers nurse practitioners (NPs), who are trained to perform many of the tasks traditionally performed by family physicians, despite a shortage of family physicians in most parts of the province. These new Networks, the centrepiece of the province's efforts at reforming primary care, include more than 160 family physicians, but only seven NPs, according to a PricewaterhouseCoopers report commissioned by the government.[38]

CHALLENGING THE ASSUMPTIONS

These assumptions are so integral to our health-care system and have been around for so long that they seem to be based on simple common sense. To a large extent, within the system alternatives have become unthinkable. But the health-care system came to be based on these assumptions not simply or even primarily because they were demonstrated to be the most effective means of improving the health of the population. Doctors became dominant mainly as a result of a power struggle, although they have retained much of their strength because many of their techniques have proved effective in restoring health.

CHALLENGE 1. DOCTORS' AUTHORITY AND EXPERTISE

Indeed, allopathic doctors' authority did not begin with their knowledge of scientific evidence. Rather, it preceded the development of the kinds of scientific techniques on which today's medicine is based. As early as the eighteenth century, a group of medical practitioners tried to gain dominance by pressuring the state to give them the exclusive right to practise medicine.[39] Although the struggle between 'regular' and 'irregular' healers lasted for many years, the dominance of allopaths was eventually established.

Their demands for a monopoly, however, were not based on the demonstrated efficacy of their treatments or on biomedical science. And their demands were met largely because of their class, race, and sex rather than because of their treatments and cures. By the mid-nineteenth century, before most discoveries based on biomedical science were made, Colleges of Physicians and Surgeons were incorporated in many jurisdictions to ensure that these practitioners had the right to control who practised and to eliminate other alternatives such as the Thomsonian herbalists, the homeopaths, and the eclectics who 'rejected certain of the theories and practices of the mainstream profession'.[40] As David Naylor makes clear in *Private Practice, Public Payment*, the 'emergence of rival schools such as homeopathy and eclecticism can be taken as evidence that there was no firm scientific consensus concerning most aspects of practice.'[41] One group was successful in using its political connections to win state support and exclude competition. Moreover, in restricting entry to those who attended particular university programs, they ensured dominance by men of particular classes and races.

But they were not as successful in convincing the population that their treatments were better than those of the many others offering their services. Although one group of doctors was legitimated by the state, alternative approaches did not disappear. As Geoffrey Bilson points out in his study of cholera, the brutal, often irrelevant, or even dangerous treatment provided by the licensed doctors encouraged many people 'to abandon the regular medical men and turn to those offering less daunting regimes'.[42]

This was particularly the case with midwifery. In 1865, organized medical men in Ontario were successful in getting the state to grant them the exclusive right to attend childbirths.[43] Because there was a surplus of graduates from medical school, they wanted not only to eliminate competition from the unorganized women who served as midwives but also to use childbirth as a way of becoming family practitioners. But this monopoly was not based on evidence that these allopathic practitioners were safer and more effective in attending birth. In fact, a Saskatchewan medical officer reported in 1919 that 'maternal mortality was much higher in the 50 per cent of confinements attended by medical men.' Although the higher death rate may have partially reflected the more risky cases covered by doctors, the officer went on to explain that 'a very large number of women were confined without either nurse or doctor in attendance, and in these cases, maternal mortality was much lower.' When the officer presented his report to the practitioners with the monopoly, he 'was very strongly taken to task by some of the members for even compiling the figures.'[44]

Not surprisingly, some women continued to resist the medical control over childbirth. A Prairie woman explained that she first called a doctor to attend her child's birth when she was told she had to have a doctor in attendance. 'So we sent for one and they was three hours late and I had everything done, had the baby dressed and myself washed and the afterbirth taken out and put in the heater. And then he came and felt my pulse and said, "Well you're just as nature led you. That's forty-five dollars please."'[45] That was the last time she called the doctor when she was ready to give birth. Indeed, midwifery never entirely disappeared, in spite of doctors' state-backed power, precisely because many women resisted doctors' claims and fees.

However, with the discovery of germs and the gradual acceptance of germ theory, intervention by the licensed practitioners became less risky for patients. With the development of chloroform, surgery became less painful. With practice and with some new knowledge about anatomy and microbiology, allopaths developed more effective and less dangerous techniques. With better sanitation, nutrition, and housing, health improved as well and medicine claimed much of the credit. These developments contributed to doctors' power and legitimacy, but were not the only factors in establishing their authority. Allopaths used their political connections and their collective strength to establish their monopoly on treatment as well as the dominance of their assumptions throughout the health care system.

As state enforcement systems became more rigorous and organized, it became easier to ensure this dominance. Lengthy periods of formal education in prestigious universities helped, too, although it should be noted that many medical doctors have fewer years of formal education than most university professors, and professors are granted significantly less power and authority. Business also played an important role in financing and implementing a report that ensured the 'triumph of the specific aetiology paradigm',[46] the one called scientific medicine. What came to be known as the Flexner Report (1910) was conducted for the Carnegie Foundation by a schoolmaster who had no experience with medicine. He visited 155 medical colleges in the United States and Canada, and claimed he could determine 'in a matter of hours' whether a school met scientific standards. On the basis of a report that did not follow medicine's rules of scientific investigation, alternative schools were closed and the new scientific paradigm was installed as the only approach.[47] In his study of allopaths, John Moskop concludes that Flexner-inspired 'efforts gave organized medicine state-supported and virtually unassailable authority over the growth of the profession and the nature of its work.'[48]

This state support helped doctors control much more than their own work. The allopaths continually fought to restrict the power of others within and outside the system. As a result of their efforts, some practitioners could no longer legally practise, while others, such as pharmacists, were restricted to certain kinds of activities.[49] In part because they gained power first, in part because they were university-educated white men in a society where sex, race, and class meant power, and in part because they were vigilant in their efforts to remain dominant, these allopathic doctors were also able to determine the conditions under which the female nurses, and later the therapists, aides, technicians, housekeepers, dieticians, and clerical workers practised. Although nurses in Ontario, for example, first tried to gain control over certification and registration as early as 1905, they were not successful until the 1950s and they still had doctors taking part in the decisions.[50]

Here, too, physicians' power over others was not based primarily on evidence that such authority was necessary to provide the best care. The hierarchical organization of care, the lesser power of others in the system and the elimination of some practitioners were not the result of scientific evidence demonstrating that this authority and these structures were critical for patients or for the system.

When, in the late 1950s, the Canadian government introduced publicly funded hospital insurance that covered half the costs of specified services, doctors were firmly in charge of these institutions. And these institutions were much safer and more effective than in the past. The introduction of sulpha and antibiotics, combined with some new diagnostic tools and procedures, had significantly enhanced the reputation of doctors, as had the mass media and public education systems.[51] There was little public critique of doctors' methods and assumptions, although alternatives and skepticism had not disappeared. By guaranteeing payment for hospital services as they existed then, governments at various levels were consolidating and reinforcing doctors' power. They were also helping them get better at the job. By the early 1970s, all provinces, with federal participation, had established publicly funded medical insurance, guaranteeing payment for a whole range of procedures based on what individual doctors considered necessary, and thus further reinforcing the dominance of both the doctors and their assumptions about care. Initially at least, taxpayer-funded medicare further ensured 'the protection of solo, fee-for-service practice against alternative modes of organization'.[52]

Although many of the treatments provided by doctors are safe and effective today, it cannot be assumed that this is the case for all treatments. A 1991 report prepared for the federal, provincial, and territorial deputy ministers of health concluded that, among doctors, there 'is a poor awareness of evidence about effectiveness, and there are few good mechanisms to implement changes in practice patterns among practising physicians.'[53] In addition, it found a 'lack of uniform standards of clinical competence for licensure', 'inadequate attention to self-regulation of practice to overlapping "scopes of capability" and the need for continuing competence review', and 'deficiencies in both the amount and quality of basic clinical and management information'. In other words, self-government was not ensuring quality. The gatekeepers to practice were not adequately keeping the gates.[54]

The assumption, then, that doctors' authority is based simply on their knowledge and expertise is incorrect. Their right to a monopoly, to self-government, and to direct the system preceded much of the scientific knowledge on which the claim is based. State support was critical to the establishment and continuation of medical authority, although a number of medical breakthroughs helped considerably in supporting doctors' claims. Certainly doctors continue to be challenged by patients, by alternative therapists, and by other health care workers. And attempts to reduce state expenditures and the dramatic changes taking place within the system are placing some limits on doctors' power. But even though various reports suggest more teamwork or that the physician is no longer 'the only person qualified to decide what treatment or studies are appropriate for a patient',[55] governments have resisted directly taking on the question of doctors' authority or the hierarchical structure of most health care. In Canada, doctors remain both the gatekeepers for other doctors and patients and the most powerful group within the system. Doctors are still in charge of treatment and cure. Indeed, many cutbacks have meant an increasing focus on quick treatment and cure, thus ensuring that doctors are at the centre of acute care.

This is not to argue that doctors should be stripped of all their powers over patients, other doctors, and other workers in health care. Nor is it to argue that doctors have no expertise based on scientific evidence. In many circumstances, doctors' knowledge is critical, as is their right to direct a team quickly and to insist a patient follow treatment. But it is to argue that this is not inevitably or self-evidently the case. Instead of assuming either that doctors must be in control or that they should not have any independent power, we need to retain the tension between skepticism about doctors' power and knowledge and recognition of an expertise in particular fields that requires considerable independence. We need to do so without firmly rejecting or embracing either doctors' authority or their subjugation to others.

In addition, it is clear from the determinants of health that control over, or at least participation in, decision-making is a central factor in health. The question of control, then, has to be considered in terms of all health-care workers, not simply in terms of doctors and patients. Power must be shared in ways that still recognize the particular skills each brings to his or her work and still make health care the central concern. Solutions cannot be sought in creating an alternative hierarchy, for instance by increasing the power of managers who base decisions on bureaucratic and financial criteria rather than on health considerations.

CHALLENGE 2. MEDICINE IS SCIENTIFIC

There are also questions to be raised about the science on which the doctors' authority and expertise are assumed to be based. Considerable evidence suggests that not all drugs, devices, and procedures have been rigorously and systematically tested to ensure their safety and effectiveness. And a great deal of evidence indicates that doctors do not always know or properly apply the scientific information that is available.

In Canada, the testing of drugs is largely left to those developing and manufacturing them for profit. Although the federal government's Health Products and Foods Branch (formerly Health Protection Branch) does examine a summary of the company's test data before issuing the notice of compliance that allows drugs to be marketed in Canada, it does no independent testing of its own. There are two approval stages in this federal process. The first requires testing done on tissue cultures and on small animals to see if the drug has any therapeutic value, to see how it is processed, and to see whether it has any major negative impact on the rest of the body. Tests must be done on at least two mammalian species, one of which is not a rodent, to determine the dosage range.[56] Once the Health Products and Foods Branch has examined the reports on these tests, it can approve the drug for three phases of clinical testing on humans. Healthy volunteers are given the drug to see if there are significant side effects. Then small pilot studies and larger clinical trials on ill people, some of whom are given the drug being tested and others who are given an established drug or a non-drug, are done. A notice of compliance is given after the company submits reports on these trials.

Once approved, drugs do not have to undergo regular reviews, although companies are required to report side effects that have been detected, usually as a result of normal use of the drug. The government also accepts voluntary reports on side effects from other sources, although this is not a very systematic process. The Branch's term for this procedure is the 'spontaneous' reporting of adverse drug reactions (ADRs). Meanwhile, it estimates that:

> over 51% of approved drugs have serious side effects not detected before marketing approval. This may be because the studies conducted did not last long enough for the effects to become manifest or because patients likely to experience problems are not always enrolled in the trials. In addition, in clinical trials often fewer than 3 000 patients are given a new drug, making it likely that an ADR with an incidence of 1 in 10 000 will remain undetected.[57]

The testing of medical devices is also left to the manufacturers. Only those devices that are to be implanted for 30 days or more and menstrual tampons, long-term contact lenses, and test kits for AIDS need a notice of compliance from the government. And these controls were introduced only after considerable protest and evidence-gathering by those who used the devices. There are voluntary guidelines for other products and, in order to register products, firms must submit information on the purpose and directions for use. Moreover, the Bureau of Radiation and Medical Devices that oversees this process can require additional information.[58] But 'new health care technologies become widely disseminated before they are rigorously evaluated.'[59] One of the companies relied on to do its own safety tests is Litton Systems Canada, which used to make cruise missile components but began to produce medical equipment when the defence industry declined.[60]

The testing of medical procedures is not really covered by formal regulation. This helps explain why one prominent advocate for an increased emphasis on quality has estimated that only 15 to 20 per cent of medical procedures have ever been subjected to any clear, scientific examination and that there are no systematic data on how the others have been developed and tested.[61] It may also help explain why a study of the management of menopause found that some 'physicians gave estrogen to all their patients; others were more selective in their prescribing habits. The one common factor was that each physician believed absolutely in the correctness of his or her own particular approach to the menopausal patient.'[62]

There are a number of reasons why the apparently thorough processes to approve drugs and devices do not always ensure that those on the market are safe and effective. First, drugs introduced before this procedure was established in the early 1960s were not subject to these requirements, and many of them remain on the market today. Many devices have never been tested. In *Safety Last*, Nicholas Regush maintained that 'only 5 per cent of medical devices are assessed for safety by federal reviewers.'[63] The Health Protection Branch found that 450 of the 7,000 prescription drugs on the market before the new rules were introduced were worthless or lacked medical benefit.[64] The United States Food and Drug Administration concluded that 40 per cent of the drugs introduced before 1962 that it studied had 'no effective indication'.[65]

Second, the balance of power between the federal government's Health Products and Foods Branch and the drug industry it regulates has been markedly shifted in favour of the industry. The Branch's annual budget was slashed from $237 million in 1993–4 to just $136 million in 1996–7,[66] and all of its in-house labs to test drugs were shut down. This had devastating effects on the numbers of government scientists and on their capacity to assess the data coming from the industry. Some rehiring has since occurred, but this has been overshadowed by several other developments. The drug labs were not reopened, preventing the Branch from independently monitoring what the drug companies tell it about their trials or their production of approved drugs. The Branch also remains unable to undertake its own research on drugs it suspects might have negative side effects. The Branch's management has referred on more than one occasion to the industry as its 'clients', with the public largely relegated to 'stakeholder' or 'beneficiary' status.[67] Under a new cost-recovery program, the industry 'clients' now pay for 70 per cent of the costs of the Branch's drug approval process.[68]

Meanwhile, the Branch undertook a 'Transition' exercise highlighting risk management (weighing commercial and political risks along with safety risks), and proposing the establishment of special operating agencies for drug and medical device approvals, thus removing them from direct ministerial accountability and mandating such agencies to promote trade as well as safety.[69] Under pressure from the industry (and from some disease-specific advocacy organizations) the Branch's Therapeutic Products Program (TPP) 'has managed to decrease new drug submission review times from 1200 to 600 days despite a 50 per cent cut in federal funding since 1995.' Further re-engineering is needed, however, to reach the TPP's 300-day target, a task assigned to its Advisory Panel on Product Licensing Review.[70]

Third, drug companies increasingly control what research is conducted and how it is assessed. As a result, many drugs are approved that, at best, have little or no effect or, at worst, may cause serious damage. As the National

Forum on Health observed, the drug industry has become the predominant source of biomedical research funding, and its 'research efforts and priorities are ultimately driven by the prospects for development of profitable products and favourable marketing environments.' As a result, biomedical research is 'narrowed in focus and skewed in the direction of drug- and product-related research'.[71]

The problem is not uniquely Canadian. To take an important example cited by business columnist David Crane, 'the drug industry wants a high-profit pill to be taken daily, protected by decades of patent protection, rather than a simple shot that might prevent AIDS.' After commenting on how the research agenda is 'distorted by profit-seeking activities', he concluded: 'We need a review of world trade rules on intellectual property to reduce the power of corporations to control fundamental knowledge.'[72] A similar line of reasoning prompted the National Forum on Health to recommend that the drug industry's commitments to increased research funding 'be converted into specific required contributions for health research broadly defined, at full arm's length from the industry, to be administered by the national research granting agencies and allocated through the normal peer-reviewed granting process.'[73]

Instead, university-based researchers now face increased requirements from these national agencies for 'partnerships' with other funders, which in practice usually means the drug companies. The warning from the National Forum that researchers are becoming 'hostage to the political priorities of the industry'[74] has to date not been heeded. When not held hostage, the independent research community is at least being pressured by the industry, as is illustrated by the court case brought by Bristol-Myers Squibb Canada against the non-profit Canadian Co-ordinating Office for Health Technology Assessment (CCOHTA). Bristol-Myers sought to prevent distribution of a CCOHTA report suggesting similar clinical effects for one of its heart disease drugs and for four competing drugs. CCOHTA successfully defended itself against an injunction and subsequent appeal filed by Bristol-Myers, but only after spending 'a demanding six months' in a legal battle to defend the right to publish its scientific opinion.[75]

By setting the research agenda, the drug firms determine which drugs are brought forward for approval. As one executive sympathetic to the industry put it, 'No manufacturer can afford to restrict his production to genuinely significant pharmaceutical innovations.'[76] Thus, just over 8 per cent of the 404 new patented drugs marketed for human use in Canada between 1991 and 1995 were considered by the Patented Medicine Price Review Board to be either 'breakthrough' drugs or substantial improvements over existing drugs.[77] The rest were either 'me-too' drugs that altered slightly the composition of drugs already on the market, or 'line extensions' that altered dosage or format or approved the existing drug as treatment for a different condition. Sometimes research on drugs that could be quite useful is abandoned or not undertaken because the potential profits are low. So, for example, the therapeutic possibilities of garlic are not explored by the drug companies because it is much too accessible to the general population. And some products are developed to treat problems that do not call for intervention. For example, while the best treatment for infectious diarrhea is fluid intake and 'specific drugs are neither available or required', pharmaceutical companies produce a wide range of products to treat diarrhea.[78]

Some of the new drugs and devices are not simply useless. The Dalkon Shield is only the most famous of similar contraceptive devices that had to be removed from the market after a public outcry about the 'alarmingly high rate of pelvic inflammatory disease'.[79] In this case, problems had been reported from the time similar devices were first introduced in 1909.

In addition to the problem of the industry's degree of control over the research agenda, there is also the problem of how the clinical trials are carried out. At the most straightforward level, there is no guarantee that the trials have been conducted as described. Perhaps the best-known example of this is the case of a Canadian doctor who has been found guilty of falsifying research data on breast cancer patients.[80] More significantly, inappropriate comparators on occasion have been selected in trials funded by the pharmaceutical industry. The selection of existing drugs known to be inferior, rather than those known to be superior, can make a new drug appear to be an improvement when it is not.[81]

Fourth, although the approval requirements may seem quite rigorous, many side effects cannot be assessed through the short and limited official process. More in-depth research done long after a drug is on the market can reveal serious consequences. For example, a study published in the *New England Journal of Medicine* found that the drug Indomethacin, used for 20 years to prevent premature labour, could seriously harm very premature infants.[82] Manitoba researchers have found that several commonly used antihistamines promoted the growth of cancer in mice.[83] A seven-year study at six Canadian hospitals indicated that the drug Ritodrine, prescribed to prevent premature birth, did little to reduce the length of pregnancy but did cause chest pain, irregular heart beat, and fluid-filled lungs.[84] The damage that diet drugs can do to heart valves took years to identify.

Moreover, there is no systematic procedure for ensuring that research on long-term effects is performed and acted upon. Only when individual doctors or hospitals happen to notice and report patterns in side effects is there any organized way of collecting these data. Canada often depends on the United States for such data, and then waits to see what is done with the data south of the border. For example, sales of silicone breast implants were suspended in Canada only after many individuals reported complaints to the Federal Drug Administration in the United States. A member of Parliament, herself an implant recipient, claimed that 'We have been after the federal government for well over a year to do some proper research into safety. The minister said he was not interested in anecdotal evidence and was waiting to see what the FDA would do.'[85]

Short-term research can reveal significant information about the impact of drugs or devices, but only if the research is done in ways that recognize differences among various groups. This recognition is often lacking, particularly in terms of age and sex differences. Clinical trials are too often based on the false assumption that what applies to adult males applies equally to adult females and children. Thus, 'even though women's patterns of disease and their responses to treatment are not always the same as men's, most research into conditions that are shared by men and women focuses on male experience as the norm.'[86] Studies examining the role of acetylsalicylic acid (Aspirin) in strokes 'were conducted almost entirely on men. The animal tests of potential drugs for stroke have mostly been done on male rats, too, and young ones at that.'[87] Indeed, even research on breast cancer treatments is often done on male mice.[88] Similarly, 'the effects of drugs in people over the age of 65 years are rarely evaluated' and, 'even though pediatric patients metabolize and excrete drugs differently from adults',[89] children are not often the subjects in trials. Although the populations involved in trials have recently been made more diverse, there is no systematic effort to review the approvals granted before this greater diversity was introduced.

Aside from the approval process another issue for scientific medicine concerns how drugs, devices, and procedures are used. Doctors rely heavily on drug companies for much of their information about what medications to prescribe. As Joel Lexchin makes clear in his survey of the research, the 'more doctors rely on commercial sources for their information, the less rational they are as prescribers: they are more likely to prescribe the wrong drug in the wrong formulation for the wrong reason in an incorrect dosage for an inappropriate length of time.'[90] A comprehensive review of the literature on drug utilization published in 1987 concluded that there continue to be problems in physicians' prescribing practices that relate 'both to over-prescribing of drugs for which there is no evidence of efficacy, as well as under-prescribing of preventative medications like vaccines for immunization of children and adults'. Among the reasons given for these prescribing problems were:

- inadequate training of physicians during medical school years on the day-to-day application of drug knowledge;

- inadequate sources of objective information available to practising physicians about drug properties and indications;

- the limited time available to practising physicians to study and evaluate the therapeutic claims for newly marketed drugs;

- the widespread custom of physicians to continue their drug education by relying mainly on the promotional activities of the drug companies; and

- the exceedingly rapid turnover in the popularity of prescription drugs.[91]

These reasons remain at least as valid today as they were in 1987.

Inappropriate prescribing is clearly evident for two populations that are seldom the focus of drug research: women and the elderly. A Saskatchewan study reported that, for central nervous system prescriptions, 'the discrepancy in rates of prescribing to men and women was particularly large for those 20–29.'[92] It is estimated that 200,000 Canadians have been prescribed the anti-depressant Prozac and that three-quarters of them are women.[93] Although the drug is 'extolled by some enthusiasts as just the thing to help parents cope with their kids or to make chronic loners stop fearing rejection', users may 'experience nausea, nervousness and insomnia and their sex life can suffer'.[94] A Quebec study found that the 'prevalence of questionable high-risk prescribing, especially of psychotropic drugs, is substantial among elderly people' as well.[95] Similarly, a New Brunswick study found significant differences among doctors' prescribing practices for the elderly. High prescribers 'had more practice days, saw more patients per day, performed more services per day, billed more per patient and billed on average 30% more during the study period.'[96]

Inappropriate prescribing does not simply reflect the training of doctors and the education they receive from drug companies. It also reflects doctors' values and specific interests. Women and the elderly, a majority of whom are also women, receive more prescriptions for mood-modifiers than do men, in part because many doctors define women as more emotional and are more likely to see women's problems as 'all in their heads'.[97] It is also much easier for doctors to prescribe pills than to discuss the social conditions that may give rise to the problem treated with mood modifiers. The values of doctors and the interests of the drug companies often combine to create treatments that do not conform to the scientific application of scientifically demonstrated cures.

It is not only the assumption that drugs and devices have been thoroughly tested and proven effective that needs to be challenged. So, too, does the assumption that such research can always be done in traditional scientific ways. For example, it was not study of tissues or reactions of laboratory animals that led a Canadian hospital to use cuddling to a human breast as a treatment for premature babies. Instead, it was experience in a Bogata hospital, where incubators were scarce. The treatment appears effective but scientific trials may not be able to establish the connection. Nor would drug companies, the principal funders of biomedical research, have any interest in supporting research to determine whether cuddling is an effective therapy for premature babies.

Even drugs and devices that have been examined according to the protocols, following all the rules, are still only best guesses in terms of their efficacy (under ideal conditions) and effectiveness (under actual, real-world conditions). Decisions about approving and using drugs are always based on a weighing of risks, not on sure bets. The best science in health care is about probabilities, both because each individual is unique and because treatments interact with a complex, thinking, human being. It is simply not possible to test all the combinations of drugs or combinations of individual circumstances and conditions that may influence the impact of any treatment. Individual variations in patients and practitioners help explain why an Ontario study found significant geographical variations in surgery rates and why simple formulas for procedures based on 'science' would limit the possibilities for taking such factors into account.[98]

As we shall see in the next sections, scientific procedure in medicine excludes the social context and social values that may be at least as important as what happens in the particular tissue that is the focus of concern. And it often excludes the complex interrelationships within the human body and mind. Moreover, a focus on science that stresses overall patterns tends to ignore the fact that each person is an individual who responds in a different way. Although there are rules to follow, both research and the practice of medicine are arts as well as sciences and much of medical practice cannot be entirely transformed into measurable procedures that follow the same rules each time. The techniques used in medicine 'share the features of all human activity in that they are a combination of serendipity, painstaking accumulation of knowledge and inspired guesswork.'[99] They also reflect human values and structural constraints. The devotion to science can be at the expense of the 'inspired hunch', which is the most common means of medical advance.[100] It also may be at the expense of the individual patient and practitioner. While we do need better science, we also need to remain skeptical of all scientific findings (adopting what is itself a scientific attitude) and to remember that no two human beings are the same.

Little has been done to ensure that doctors are trained in how to monitor and report on complications created by drugs and devices, or that the information they receive on drugs from drug companies is balanced by information from other sources. Although there are now guidelines for relationships between doctors and drug companies, there is also tension on the degree of access the industry should have to medical students, and drug companies are playing an even greater role in the continuing education of doctors. Moreover, the guidelines on drug company advertising in medical journals are weak, even though research indicates that such advertisements are often misleading.[101] And the industry is pushing for authorization to advertise specific brand-name prescription drugs directly to consumers, as is allowed in the United States and seeps into Canada through US magazines and television. The effect of such advertising would be to place additional, non-scientific pressure on doctors. All these changes make it less rather than more likely that rigorous, scientific procedures will be followed in those areas where they could be the most useful.

At the same time, the various reports on health care have called for more rigorous, scientific assessments of policies and procedures, leading to 'evidence-based decision-making' that 'must be universally and consistently adopted', according to the National Forum on Health.[102] Alberta's *Rainbow Report*, for example, calls for a 'comprehensive, continuous, and consolidated assessment of technologies. . . . This assessment should include scientific, medical/clinical effectiveness, efficiency, and safety; current necessity and effectiveness, including direct and indirect costs and social/psychological impact including possible legal and ethical dilemmas.' It goes on to say that current assessment is 'a sporadic and spontaneous type of activity . . . the assessment process is largely a matter of writing reports based on published sources in an effort to convince government officials that the sought-after technology is worthwhile, beneficial and probably cost-effective.'[103]

Two points in particular are important to note in light of these recommendations. First, although the various reports suggest the need for independent research, they often fail to discuss the specific problems created by commercial interests. This leaves the door open to the new emphasis on partnership research, which encourages researchers to work with the companies whose major interest is in selling the technologies, not in creating more effective, efficient, and suitable care. Meanwhile, cutbacks have ensured there is less rather than more independent research, less rather than more systematic assessment. A partial exception to this failure is the National Forum on Health, which warned that 'Private industry also has an enormous influence on the dissemination of information and adoption of new interventions . . . aggressively and effectively marketed by private manufacturers.'[104] At the same time, the National Forum was uncritical of the heavy involvement of the private sector in the development of health information systems.

Second, although the reports indicate the need to take into account issues not usually addressed in scientific research, there is little discussion of the problem of applying traditional scientific methods to the task. Methods designed to examine the impact of a single treatment on tissue samples and rats or even on whole people in clinical trials are seldom appropriate in assessing social and psychological responses or ethical and legal issues. As a whole range of social scientists have made clear, survey data or control group procedures are usually poor tools for capturing the responses of individuals. As a former health services researcher explained: 'They only accepted as "evidence" that which could be summarized on one graph. Because complexity was devalued and context denied, our professional skills as health service researchers were no longer seen as useful.'[105] But these reports recommend that quality control be determined by survey data and quantitative techniques. *Future Directions for Health Care in Saskatchewan*, for example, recommends data-gathering systems 'to measure a patient's severity of illness and essential care level'. It is assumed that such a formula will mean 'people will receive exactly the amount and type of service they need at a particular time.'[106] Such an approach means less rather than more investigation of ethical dilemmas, cultural differences, indirect costs, and social/psychological impacts. It also ignores the fact that people, not cars or chocolates, are involved in the process. Quality control in health cannot be based exclusively on scientific data, no matter how well collected, because the data can never capture the particular situation, body, or mind of an individual.

This is not to argue that there is no place for science, that scientific procedures are either useless or ignored, or that no research has contributed to the development of new treatments and cures. Certainly, it is far better to have rigorous procedures, and every effort should be made to ensure that systematic, long-term research is carried out by independent researchers who do not depend for support on the companies making the drugs or devices. However, here, too, we should retain a healthy skepticism. Quantitative, experimental, and survey techniques cannot easily examine ethical and legal questions, many of the social and psychological issues, or even many of the problems with more recognizable biological roots. At issue is not whether to use a scientific approach but rather the recognition that science is limited and cannot produce simple objective truth.

Quantitative measures are seldom free of value judgements. Consider the example provided by Glouberman and Mintzberg:

> A surgeon in a London hospital transplanted the livers of ten patients. Two died, and eight survived. One of the latter was a young woman, whose cancer of five years earlier had returned, while the liver of another was slowly being rejected, necessitating a second transplant. Of the remaining six, only three were able to resume normal working lives. Asked about his success rate, the surgeon claimed eight out of ten. Indeed, he was prepared to claim nine out of eleven after the retransplant (since he counts livers, not people!). An immunologist, who felt the surgeon should not have operated on the young woman, put the rate at seven out of ten, while an administrator put it at six out of ten. The nurses, most aware of the lives of those who could not return to work, put it at three out of ten. And the right answer? Take your pick.[107]

In addition to value judgements, professional, clinical judgements must be taken into account. As the National Forum put it, in what was otherwise overwhelmingly a report celebrating evidence-based decision-making, 'clinical judgement . . . should not be replaced, but rather complemented with good evidence. . . . One cannot exist without the other.'[108]

Also at issue is the question of control, of who decides what research is done, how it is done, what information is provided, and how products are disseminated. These decisions are now more likely to be made with profits, rather than health, in mind.

CHALLENGE 3. MEDICINE AS CURE

The assumption that medicine provides treatment and cure rests on the assumption that science has determined cause and cure. Yet, as the previous section makes clear, many treatments have not been scientifically established and some cannot be established through traditional scientific means, especially randomized clinical trials. Many treatments are irrelevant and some are dangerous.

This is partly the reason why allopathic cures are not the main reason for the improved health and increasing longevity of the Canadian population. In recent years, some drugs have been credited with preventing heart disease, although heart problems are still a major killer in Canada and improvements may be at least as much the result of changes in diet and reduced smoking as they are of changes in cures. While drugs and surgical procedures contribute to longer and better life for some heart attack victims, the more aggressive use of these therapies in the United States than in Canada does not appear to affect survival rates. It may affect somewhat the incidence of subsequent chest pain.[109] Similarly, in spite of recent significant increases in fetal heart monitoring and cancer surgery rates, there has not been any significant improvement in survival rates from childbirth or most cancers.

Although surgery and drugs certainly make some people better, most of those who pass through the health-care system are not cured in the process. Many of those treated in the health-care system have one of two problems that cannot be fixed by current medical means. Some have chronic diseases or disabilities that are not subject to cure through currently available drugs or surgery. Those with chronic diseases may have their pain relieved by drugs or surgery and may improve through physical therapy, but they are seldom cured. This may help explain why one study found that the three most frequently prescribed drugs in Saskatchewan were mood-modifiers.[110] These drugs simply help people survive with their psychosocial and/or economic problems; they do not provide cures. Many others seeking help have viruses or other diseases or conditions, such as hypertension, arthritis, chronic bronchitis, and cardiac disease, that cannot be effectively treated by medical means.[111]

Antibiotics, for example, are not infrequently prescribed for viral infections, which they do not effectively treat. Indeed, such prescription is harmful in that the antibiotic can prompt the development of bacterial 'super bugs' that are resistant to antibiotics. Even though little of what is done in the health-care system results in cure, the system is structured around the assumption that this is mainly what happens. People can certainly be helped by caring professionals but the stress on cure makes it less likely that those who cannot easily be cured will get the assistance they need, assistance based on a different view of what determines health.

With a focus on cure, it is often assumed that people can and should be treated with drugs or surgery, even if there is little possibility or evidence that this intervention will cure the problem, or even improve or continue life. For example, a Montreal study that included 331 newborns in intensive care and 293 other newborns found that just over three-quarters of them received 1–26 different drugs, 'averaging 6.19 drugs per baby'.[112] No research on the usefulness of these drug treatments is reported. Just as is the case with the many drugs given to women defined as infertile,[113] little research has been done on the long-term effects of these interventions.

Similarly, surgery may be done on elderly cancer patients who have very little possibility of being cured, or people may have their breathing done by machines that keep them technically alive but can never restore them to health. Costly or risky tests may be offered to detect problems that cannot be cured. Although magnetic resonance imaging (MRI) technology can help in some cases, in others this costly technology means the production of sophisticated pictures that just confirm diagnoses developed in other ways, often indicating incurable problems. To take another example, amniocentesis involves the insertion of a needle to remove fluid from the sac surrounding the fetus. The procedure, used to detect Down's syndrome, is usually carried out between the sixteenth and twentieth week of pregnancy and the results take as long as three to four weeks to produce. If the tests indicate Down's syndrome, nothing can be done to cure the fetus, although women can decide to have an abortion at this point.[114] About one in 200 women has a miscarriage as a result of the test and Down's syndrome occurs in about one in 600 births. Given that the test is usually offered only to women over 35 years of age (the incidence of Down's syndrome rises with the mother's age), the risk of miscarriage is about equal to the risk of having such a child.[115] But the very presence of the techniques, combined with a curative approach, makes amniocentesis testing the most likely approach.

The new rush to fertility treatment also reflects the emphasis on cure. Increasingly, medicine is intervening to help women get pregnant. Infertility is being defined by doctors as one year of unprotected sexual intercourse not resulting in pregnancy, even though there is plenty of evidence to suggest that conception often takes much longer for healthy people. The treatments can be complex and invasive. They are certainly disruptive and possibly dangerous. Yet it is quite possible that no physiological problem is being addressed. A few weeks on vacation would perhaps be more effective.[116] The emphasis on defining non-pregnancy as a problem to be treated, in understanding it as biological and intervening chemically and surgically, can mean that alternative approaches are not explored, while unnecessary treatment is undertaken.

The presence of drugs, machines, and techniques encourages their use, even if their use has only a remote chance of having any positive effect, causes certain discomfort, and may cause harm. A neo-natal nurse interviewed for Laura Sky's film, *To Hurt and to Heal*, explained that:

> Nature very rarely takes its own way here. We're always intervening. If nature took its own way, a lot of these patients would, that live now, wouldn't live. And the ones that don't live often take too long to die. And that's the nature of the whole environment. It's just machinery. Modern machinery, modern medicine's just gone, just gone high tech.

There is an enormous pressure to try any means available to produce a cure or to get test results, while alternative, non-curative techniques and less invasive approaches with slower and less spectacular effects are much less likely to be applied. Fetal heart monitors, for instance, are routinely attached to pregnant women during labour to identify fetal distress and often replace the professional attendant for long periods of time. Although studies have indicated that the monitor reduces the costs of nursing care, it increases the number of Caesarean sections and does not reduce the number of neonatal deaths.[117] Similarly, a survey of 523 Canadian hospitals found that 46 per cent gave babies liquids other than breast milk, even though this practice may discourage breast-feeding and encourage infections. Only 14 per cent had lactation consultants to advise women on breast-feeding. A quarter of the hospitals regularly gave free formula samples to new mothers and four out of five hospitals had exclusive contracts with a formula company.[118] Technologies, devices, and cures, rather than care and education, were predominant.

While the focus on cure means that some people get treatment they do not need, it also means that others do not receive the help that could provide long-term benefit because they cannot easily be cured. As Joan Eakin puts it in her study of stroke patients, they fall outside the central focus on 'doing something'.[119] When stroke patients are admitted to acute-care hospitals, they initially receive intensive care but are often neglected after that. The reason for the neglect, Eakin maintains, can be found in the focus on 'immediate and intensive treatment'. Staff assumed 'nothing could be done', even though there was much that could be done; 'physical, emotional and social support and rehabilitation were clearly not "nothing".'[120]

For a number of reasons, this problem is not easily solved simply by dividing the curables from the incurables and sending each group to different institutions. First, it is often not possible to determine whether or not people can be restored to their former state of health. Second, the treatments cannot and should not be separated. The 'physical, emotional and social support' Eakin discusses, and the 'compassion and understanding' the Saskatchewan report says are necessary for those who cannot be cured, are critical whatever the diagnosis and treatment. They should not be the last resort when 'nothing can be done'. Third, all the health-care institutions are based, to a large extent, on the same assumptions, so merely dividing up the problems among different types of institution does little to address them, although it may make care cheaper. Too often those defined as incurable receive only the minimum care required. Indeed, the care is often defined as custodial, as if it is simply about maintenance.

For similar reasons, the problems inherent to the curative approach cannot be solved simply by focusing more on prevention and promotion, defined as a way of maintaining health outside the curative system. As is the case with curables and incurables, the line between prevention and cure is not so easily drawn. Diabetes can be treated but not cured. Although we are unsure about ways to prevent it, we do know that diet may reduce the possibilities of additional complications. The diet, exercise, security, housing, cleanliness, and support that are the central features of prevention are also central features of cure. And more stress on advanced technology and specialization, as the Saskatchewan report suggests, begs the question of why we have so much ineffective technology and so few cures.

Yet the solutions offered in most government reports involve a new emphasis on prevention outside the curative system and an allocation of patients both to different institutions and to different practitioners, depending on their curability. More of doctors' work that is not specifically curative would be done by nurses and more of those who cannot be cured would be placed in special facilities or sent home to be maintained. Within the curative system, there is to be greater emphasis not on prevention but on cure measured in terms of outcomes. These outcomes are defined primarily in terms of length of patient stays. Such an approach could only be based on the assumption that patients can be quickly and accurately diagnosed and cured. Yet it is clear that many who enter the curative system do not emerge from it cured, that cure cannot be easily separated from prevention and care, and that the curables cannot be easily separated from the incurables. Nor can health-care work be neatly packaged into those tasks that contribute to treatment and those that do not. For example, even though cleaning in hospitals is often classified as housekeeping, it bears little relation to the kinds of cleaning women do in the home. What is cleaned and how it must be cleaned are very different in both places.

This is not to argue that there are no cures, that treatment is irrelevant, or that everyone should be served by the same type of hospital and by a doctor. There can be no question that the curative system saves many lives and improves many others, and that some specialization in terms of facilities and caregivers is appropriate. Cure and prevention, however, should not be treated as alternative approaches but rather as combined approaches, albeit ones that remain in considerable tension.

It is important to question constantly the need for tests, for intervention, and for drugs, at the same time working to improve the techniques used for cure and for the relief of pain or suffering. Much more eloquently than any scientific report could, the neonatal nurse in the Sky film described the contradictions inherent to modern techniques:

> The wonderful invention called the respirator—the first big machine. That machine, oh God . . . I have a love and hate relationship with that machine. 'Cause that's the machine that just keeps the body going when everything else is gone. What can I say? It's our machine. It's the machine of the ICU. It's the respirator. It's the machine that makes people live, when by all rights they should be dead. And it's the machine that saves lives. And it's the machine that prolongs death.

It is also important to remember that cure and care are integrally related and cannot be separated into assigned institutions or among specific workers. Because cure is not simply a one-shot application of a scientifically proven procedure on an inanimate subject exactly the same as the previous subject, the effectiveness and efficiency of hospitals cannot be measured primarily in terms of how soon people leave.

CHALLENGE 4. THE ENGINEERING MODEL

Similar questions need to be raised about the engineering model of the body. It is even more difficult to separate body parts from each other to determine treatment and cure than it is to separate the curables from the incurables. Chest pain may indicate gall bladder problems and antibiotics for ear infections can encourage yeast infections in the vagina.

This interconnectedness of body parts is one of the reasons there is such a high rate of iatrogenic illnesses—those caused by medical treatment. Treatment for one body part often conflicts with treatment for another part or affects other body parts. In his book *Limits to Medicine*, Ivan Illich maintains that 'one out of every five patients admitted to a typical research hospital acquires an iatrogenic disease, sometimes trivial, sometimes requiring special treatment, and in one case in thirty leading to death.'[121]

The interaction of drugs, intended for specific body parts, is often a cause of illness, especially among the elderly. 'Drug-related illness is the primary reason for 1 per cent to 5 per cent of medical visits, 3 per cent to 23 per cent of hospital admissions and 1 in 1000 deaths.'[122] A Quebec study of elderly people who visited a physician at least once during the year but who lived outside a health care institution found that '13.0 per cent received a questionable high-risk psychotropic drug combination'.[123] Drug-related illnesses are not restricted to the elderly, however. Women in particular suffer from drug interactions and over-treatment.[124]

The engineering model, especially when combined with the curative approach, contributes to the over-prescribing patterns of doctors. A study of prescribing patterns among New Brunswick doctors treating patients over age 65 found that the busiest doctors were the ones prescribing the most drugs.[125] The greater use of drugs was linked to very short visits with the doctor. Such short visits can be explained only by a focus on parts to be fixed by specific cures, with little concern for the links among parts or for the whole person.

The fee-for-service system, which attaches a price to treatment of particular body parts or the use of particular procedures, also contributes to these short visits and the tendency to prescribe more than one drug. A researcher in the New Brunswick study said of the fee-for-service system: 'It's not rewarding the physician who sits down and talks to the patients. It rewards the physician who sits there with his hand cocked like a trigger, ready to write a prescription as soon as you have a complaint out of your mouth.'[126] This may help explain why an Ontario report found that, even after adjusting for price and population increases, there was a 9 per cent increase in fee-for-service payments between 1989–90 and 1991–2. Doctors were doing more things, and more expensive things, to their patients.[127]

The body parts approach not only affects doctors; it also affects the entire organization of work in health care. With this engineering assumption, it is possible to assign the responsibility for different parts to different people and to divide up the work of individual health-care workers into tiny, interchangeable parts. So, for example, a nurse long employed by an organization providing home care has had her full-time job transformed into a part-time one. Although she now works at least as many hours as she did previously, she is no longer assigned to follow particular patients through their illnesses. Instead, she is constantly moved around among patients to ensure, as much as possible, that every minute of her time is devoted to treatment. She is therefore unable to help the same patient over a period of time adjust to such problems as a diagnosis of diabetes or cancer. This fragmentation is even more obvious in hospitals. As one hospital worker interviewed for 'Voices from the Ward' put it: 'We process people just . . . like in a chocolate factory.'[128]

Specialization is also based on the assumption of parts to be fixed and it, too, can be questioned. While clearly there are advantages in having practitioners develop expertise in particular areas, there are also problems with this approach. In treating the part, one specialist may provide treatment that conflicts with, or masks, problems created in another. A dermatologist, for example, may prescribe cream for a skin ailment but the rash may be the result of blood pressure pills prescribed by the heart doctor. Moreover, specialization means patients must travel from doctor to doctor, none of whom is likely to have a full view of the entire patient.

There is considerable evidence that fee-for-service payment promotes quick-fix treatments that may be useless or harmful. There is also plenty of evidence to indicate that the body is a complex, interconnected organism that cannot easily be carved up for service. However, while the various government reports talk about 'people being the focus of the health system',[129] they do little to challenge the engineering model of the body. Instead, in many ways they encourage specialization in services and the allocation of specific parts to different health-care workers. With new monitoring systems care of the patient will be fragmented further, as each patient is classified according to the part to be fixed and each function measured as if it were the same as an oil change on the car. As much as possible, the part to be fixed will be quickly treated in the doctor's office, the outpatient clinic, or the day surgery, with little time for consideration of other, connected body parts, let alone for social and psychological support.[130]

This is not to argue that expertise should be abandoned or that all institutions should respond to all needs. But health care should begin with the assumption that people are the focus and that systems must be designed to make whole people, rather than body parts, the central concern. The tension between specialization and integration must be recognized and maintained, not resolved by simply choosing one alternative.

CHALLENGE 5. HEALTH AS MAINLY BIOLOGICAL

The challenge to the assumption that illness and disability are primarily the result of readily identifiable biological causes is directly linked to the fact that people are not simply or even mainly collections of parts to be fixed.

Our common sense tells us that minds and bodies are inextricably linked. Significant scientific evidence indicates that this is the case. For example, a British study found that 'the attitude of fifty-seven women treated with mastectomy from early-stage breast cancer was related to survival ten years later.'[131] Minds not only influence healing; they also affect the tests on which doctors rely. Research shows, for instance, that blood pressure tests taken in the doctor's office or the hospital may be artificially high simply because the patient is anxious about the test itself.[132] People cannot be separated from their social context. Even genes, the basic biological components, 'are better understood not as directing operations but as participating in complex interaction, subject themselves to influences from their environment and participating in changing that environment.'[133]

The determinants of health identified in the government reports and set out in the earlier sections of this chapter clearly show that the social context is critical to maintaining health. What is much less clear in these reports is that the same factors are critical in both diagnosis and cure. There is a recognition that 'social and physical environments . . . have a major impact on people's health.'[134] But these environments are not discussed in relation to the provision of care, even though the assumptions of allopathic medicine largely ignore them. And although there is a recognition that psychological factors are critical to the body's immune system and the capacity to both resist and recover from disease,[135] there is scant discussion of how this conflicts with current assumptions underlying the organization of health care.

The determinants of health as set out in these reports directly challenge some basic assumptions of allopathic medicine. Biological causes cannot be separated from social contexts, minds cannot be separated from bodies, and body parts cannot be separated from each other. The recognition that bodies must be understood and problems with them must be diagnosed in their social contexts necessarily leads to the conclusion that each individual is unique, given that the social influences on bodies and minds vary from individual to individual.

This is not to suggest that no tests should be done, that no research focused on biological factors should be conducted, or that no doctor should see a patient alone. However, it is necessary to recognize the contradiction between establishing the importance of social and physical environments outside the health-care system and restructuring health care to focus more exclusively on biological causes and the fixing of body parts. We need to integrate this knowledge into the restructuring of care to ensure that care delivery links body part and body part, mind and body, body and social context.

CONCLUSION

There are a number of reasons why Canada developed a health-care system dominated by allopathic doctors and based on a curative approach to the scientifically determined biological changes in body parts. First, a particular group of medical men were able to use their collective strength and political connections to gain an exclusive right to determine the education and licensing of practitioners. Through similar processes, they won the right to determine the conditions under which others provided care in the formal health system. Second, many of their treatments and cures proved effective, helping these doctors to gain considerable prestige and power. Third, state funding allowed for enormous expansion in the system while reinforcing medical dominance. The various levels of government legitimated a health-care system focused on cuts and chemicals both through their funding practices and through the granting of a monopoly to allopathic practitioners. The struggle for medicare was a struggle for access to an existing system, not a struggle over the basic assumptions of the allopathic approach.

The publicly funded health care system certainly made access more equitable and certainly helped many people survive or regain their health.[136] While there is clear evidence that the significant overall improvements in health and in longevity were primarily the result of improvements in sanitation, housing, nutrition, working conditions, and income distribution,[137] many individuals who fell ill or became disabled were helped by the government-supported system. However, the government legitimation of one approach did not mean all others disappeared. Midwives and homeopaths, acupuncturists and massage therapists, continued to practise, albeit often underground. Moreover, most care was still provided at home and communities still offered services that were outside the formal care system.

Through medicare, the various governments supported the assumptions on which the drugs and surgery approach to health was based. But close to 30 years ago, a widely distributed federal government document began to stress prevention.[138] The Lalonde Report did not critique the assumptions of the curative approach in terms of determinants of health. Rather, it set up prevention as an additional and complementary approach. Prevention was primarily defined, and taken up, in terms of individual lifestyle. Personal habits such as drinking, smoking, exercise, and diet were stressed. While later reports also talked about other factors such as income, the emphasis was still mainly on changing individuals and their habits. The Nova Scotia Provincial Health Council, for example, points out that 'Nova Scotia females had the highest rate of death in the country from breast cancer and above the national rates for lung cancer, intestinal cancer, pneumonia, lung disease, and accidental falls.'[139] Although any or all of these may be the result of work environment—including the environment in health-care institutions—the solution is defined in terms of 'the need to re-allocate resources towards prevention and early intervention; and the need for greater communication, education, participation and empowerment related to health'.[140] It is what could be called a yoga and yogurt or carrots and condoms approach to health.

For the state, there is a clear advantage to this emphasis on personal behaviour. First, it is a relatively low-cost strategy that has support from a broad spectrum of publics. Second, although tobacco and alcohol manufacturers have complained, the lifestyle approach leaves corporations relatively free of state interference and creates new markets for selling those low-fat and high-fibre products, and those exercise machines. Third, it creates the appearance of government action on health promotion while placing the responsibility firmly on the individual. Fourth, it promotes an ideology of individual responsibility rather than of collective responsibility.

For the public in general, and for women in particular, there are clear disadvantages. First, women are expected to improve the health practices of not only themselves but also their spouses and children. Second, the lifestyle approach blames the victims of what are often social conditions beyond their control, increasing the stress levels on individuals who do not have the power to change their situation. Third, health promotion and disease prevention defined primarily in terms of lifestyle do little about the major determinants of health. Many of what are defined as personal practices are structured by social and economic circumstance and by working conditions, and are reflected in the inequalities of health status related to class, race, sex, and location.[141]

This is not to suggest that governments have entirely ignored the social and economic conditions that determine health. During the same period in which governments developed medicare, they also put significant effort into improving housing, into providing income for those without employment, into formal education and training for work, into old age pensions and family allowances, into social assistance and social support. But at the same time as government reports are putting a renewed stress on the social and economic determinants of health, governments are cutting back in all these areas and are failing to apply their research on what determines health to the internal workings of the health-care sector. They have moved from a focus on cuts and chemicals to one on carrots and condoms for individuals, but have largely ignored the social determinants of health, whether outside or within the health-care sector.

To be sure, governments have been presented with, and indeed on occasion have implemented, ideas about care delivery based on other assumptions. Perhaps the best example of governments supporting another approach is the licensing of midwives in Ontario and their integration into the public payment scheme. This midwifery scheme is based on assumptions that differ significantly from those in allopathic medicine. Although the midwives have extensive professional training, they are not set up as the sole experts in the field and their relations with patients and other health-care workers are not based on an assumed need for authority. Instead, their patients are encouraged to make informed choices about how and where childbirth will happen. The midwives describe themselves as catching rather than delivering babies. They are assisting, not directing, mothers. Midwives work in teams and families are encouraged to be part of the process. Scientific knowledge is part of the midwives' education but there is a focus on integrating knowledge about the social context and from other sources based on experience, rather than exclusively on traditional scientific procedures. Instead of emphasizing biology, they are woman- and family-centred. Instead of diagnosing parts to be fixed at one point in time, they stress continuity of care by the same team of midwives. The focus is on normal childbirth and health promotion, not disease, treatment, or 'cure', although certainly midwives are prepared to intervene, or to seek intervention by doctors and nurses, if that intervention is necessary.[142]

The midwives provide an example of how health care could integrate different assumptions. Their practice is not built on a separation of promotion and prevention from health care and intervention but rather on an integration of these approaches. However, the presence of a few midwives and their state support does little to alter the assumptions built into the overall system. Midwives remain an alternative to current practice rather than a first step in structuring care with the determinants of health in mind. Similarly, nurse practitioners have demonstrated that they can provide care that is, in many areas, at least equivalent to what physicians can offer in terms of outcomes. And, compared to physicians, they are focused more on both the whole patient and on health promotion.[143] In Ontario, the university program for nurse practitioners was discontinued in 1983 primarily because there was a sufficient supply, or even an oversupply, of doctors. Once again, nurse practitioners are being educated just as the supply of physicians declines. Whether they will primarily fill the hole left by doctors unwilling to practise in remote areas and late at night, or contribute to a new emphasis on promoting health for whole people, remains to be seen.

Both midwives and nurse practitioners provide examples of how health promotion and curative approaches can be combined. So do old-fashioned public health practices, such as dentists, doctors, and nurses visiting schools to provide education and health inspections. Yet these approaches are hardly central to current health reforms.

RECOMMENDED READINGS

David Coburn, Carl D'Arcy, and George M. Torrance, eds, *Health and Canadian Society: Sociological Perspectives*, 3rd edn. Toronto: University of Toronto Press, 1998. While this entire volume will be of interest to those who want to explore specific aspects of health and care in Canada, Part III is most revelant to the issues discussed in this chapter. It focuses on the social factors in health, with several articles devoted to an examination of health issues for particular racial/cultural groups in Canada.

R.G. Evans, M.L. Barer, and T.R. Marmor, eds, *Why Are Some People Healthy and Others Not? The Determinants of Health of Populations*. New York: Aldine de Gruyter, 1994. These authors, mainly economists, present the arguments and evidence for a population health approach. The book has become a classic text in the field of population health.

B. Poland et al., 'Wealth, Equity and Health Care: A Critique of a "Population Health Perspective" on the Determinants of Health', *Social Science and Medicine* 46, 7 (1998): 785–98. Taking a political economy perspective that starts with global forces influencing health, the authors provide a theoretical analysis of the problems inherent in a population health approach.

*acute car[e]
hospitals central
to medical
model*

Who Provides:
The Institutions

∽

These problematic assumptions of the medical model are reflected in the way health-care institutions are organized. Public funding of health institutions and services has primarily served to support and reinforce provisions based on a medical model. In spite of the emphasis on the social determinants of health, recent reforms have been focused on greater efficiency and effectiveness defined primarily in market terms. This application of reform strategies taken from the for-profit production sector is made possible by the medical model, which is then reinforced by these strategies. At best, the reforms have mainly meant less of the same. At worst, they have placed increasing emphasis on the most problematic aspects of the allopathic approach. In the process, they are undermining confidence in public care.

At the same time, the reforms transfer necessary care from the public to the private sphere in at least four ways. First, moving more people out of hospitals and into residential facilities—or more frequently into the home—means more care is provided in for-profit private facilities and by for-profit services. Second, more care is provided through payment by individuals than is shared collectively through the tax system. Third, more services are provided without pay, mainly by women in the home. And finally, more of the care within the public system is provided by for-profit firms or based on for-profit principles. Although justified as both better and cheaper care, these reforms can mean a deterioration in the health of many and an increase in long-term health costs for both governments and individuals.

HOSPITALS: THE CORE OF ALLOPATHIC MEDICINE

ESTABLISHING THE INSTITUTIONAL BASE

Acute-care hospitals—those concerned with treating sharp or severe changes in health—are central to a system based on the medical model. Although governments at various levels have played a significant role in their development, they have certainly not been the only players.

The first hospital in North America was founded in Quebec City, early in the seventeenth century, by three Augustinian nuns and funded by a French noblewoman.[1] In at least three ways, this hospital set the pattern for those to follow. It was a non-profit institution governed by non-government officials, and it was staffed chiefly by women. But in many ways it and other hospitals of the period were different from today's institutions. First, they were not very healthy for the patients. Before the acceptance of germ theory and development in hygiene that limited contagious diseases, hospitals were dangerous places to be. Homes were the preferred and safer places for care, especially since there were very few effective medical treatments. Early hospitals were primarily for the poor who had no alternative place to go. Not surprisingly, as Pryke points out in his study of nineteenth-century Halifax, 'Hospitals and lazarettos had a deservedly low reputation among the poor.'[2]

Second, these were usually all-purpose institutions, providing for those with a wide range of problems. 'A hospital for the indigent' in Halifax 'functioned as a refuge for paupers, an orphanage, a lying-in hospital and a lunatic asylum.'[3] There were few drugs, little equipment, and virtually no tests. Specialization was a factor neither in the organization of the hospital nor in the structuring of the work.

Third, most of the people employed in the hospitals had little formal training. Like the institutions, the women working in them were not specialized in terms of tasks or the area of the hospital in which they worked. The same women did everything from cooking and cleaning to bathing and comforting.[4] Doctors trained in a variety of ways and using a variety of approaches were involved, but they were not the only ones to determine admission, release, or even treatment. Boundaries among care providers were not carefully defined.

Not until the early part of this century did hospitals begin to develop better treatment, better reputations, and more of the characteristics they display today. Improved knowledge of the human body and of hygiene made treatment and care not only less dangerous but also more effective. Increasingly, this new knowledge was systematically offered to those employed in the institutions. Both the implementation of the 1910 Flexner report and the state-supported monopoly of allopaths meant doctors received more consistent and lengthy education in the universities, built on the assumptions of scientific medicine. These factors also meant that doctors' power within hospitals increased enormously. Florence Nightingale's philosophy, nurses' efforts in Canada to improve their conditions, and the doctor's demand for 'more intelligent assistance from the attending nurse in the advanced scientific treatment of his patients'[5] resulted in more formal training for nurses in the hospital setting. The Nightingale philosophy included a strong belief in hygiene, preventive measures, and social support, but it was also based on a military model of organization, with supreme power placed in the hands of the doctor.

Improved knowledge of the human body and of hygiene also made hospitals safer. There was a new emphasis on providing a clean environment and on separating people according to their illnesses to prevent the spread of disease. Anaesthetics and sterile equipment made operations more endurable. Later, antibiotics controlled infection in operations and helped save those with a variety of bacterial diseases. Other drugs also proved effective in treating a wide range of ailments. Techniques such as blood transfusions were developed and diagnostic tools such as x-rays helped doctors identify problems. Not incidentally, these tools were expensive to own and operate, required considerable space, often involved the combined efforts of several people, and usually demanded specific skills. They were therefore mainly located in hospitals.

All of these developments meant that both doctors and nurses offered more of their services in the hospitals, although many nurses still worked in private homes and most doctors made house calls until the 1940s.[6] Hospitals offered significant advantages over private homes. They were easier to keep clean and sterile. Equipment was cheaper to buy and use in a setting where it could be available to a large number of care providers and patients. Trained people could work in teams to consult with and support each other in applying their increasingly sophisticated skills. Services such as food preparation, laundry, and record-keeping could be developed to accommodate both the special needs of those with illnesses and handicaps and the special problems encountered in an institution where waste is often toxic and materials often dangerous. Although the dramatic overall increases in life expectancy and the significant decreases in infant mortality and contagious diseases during the first half of the twentieth century can be attributed primarily to cleaner water, safer food, and better housing,[7] developments in hospital care were responsible for improving the life chances of many individuals. Doctors and researchers could, and did, claim some of the credit for this progress. But nursing, therapy, laboratory work, better record-keeping and nutrition, and cleaner environments also played a central role. In other words, many of the same factors were critical to improvements in health in and out of the hospital.

When World War II ended, hospital care enjoyed a sound reputation and hospitals were used by all classes for a wide range of health problems. By 1945, there were 1,102 hospitals in Canada, three-quarters of which operated on a non-profit basis.[8] There was one hospital bed for every 109 Canadians, although many of the facilities were old and out of date.[9] And most of them had to be paid for by the patient, often at considerable sacrifice. The issue for most Canadians of the time was how to pay for hospital care, rather than how to structure that care.

SHARING THE RISKS

HOSPITAL INSURANCE

In the years before the war, Canadians had suffered through the Great Depression. Returning to peace after years of another kind of sacrifice, Canadians demanded government action to provide them with security and to prevent another depression. 'There was a mood of rebellion against the universal risks of unemployment and sickness, disability and old age, widow-hood and poverty.'[10] One of the risks they demanded be shared was the cost of health care. Canadians wanted equal access to health care without the individual financial risk it entailed. Provinces and municipalities had a variety of methods designed to assist some parts of the population in paying for health care, but coverage was uneven and unequal.

Aware of the rebellious mood and practised at intervention from its experience during the war, the federal government proposed a national health insurance plan. But the British North America Act had made health care largely a provincial matter, although it gave most of the taxing power to the federal government. The provinces resisted incursions into their area of jurisdiction and could not agree on a joint program for social security. The 1946 Federal-Provincial Conference to discuss health insurance fell apart. Soon after, however, the federal government used its financial clout to get the provinces to agree to the national health grants program that helped plan and finance hospital construction.

Announced in 1948, the grants committed the federal government to covering half the cost of approved hospital construction. These hospitals, however, were for the most part to remain in non-government hands. The grants were intended to be, and indeed were, the first step towards a national health insurance scheme.[11] And this step reinforced the growing emphasis on hospital care based on a medical model. Between 1948 and 1955, 270 additional hospitals appeared and more than 40,000 additional beds became available.[12] Tuberculosis hospitals based largely on rest, social support, healthy food, and clean environments gradually disappeared. Other specialized hospitals and specialized units within hospitals that treated patients mainly with surgery and drugs expanded rapidly. There was an increasing emphasis on specific units designed to deal with particular body parts.

By 1955, there were 1,216 hospitals, 90 per cent of which were non-profit.[13] These non-profit hospitals, however, still charged for their services and only 40 per cent of the population had some hospital insurance. In addition, many of those with insurance still had to pay many costs themselves, and those without insurance often risked enormous personal debts.[14] Not surprisingly, those least likely to have insurance were those with the lowest incomes. Yet a survey published by the Dominion Bureau of Statistics showed that those with the lowest incomes also had the greatest need for hospital services.[15] Although those with the highest incomes spent the most on health-care services, the poor spent as much time as the rich in hospital, principally because their living and working conditions led to diseases and disabilities that required hospital care. The research also indicated significant variations from province to province in access to care and in health-care facilities.

The survey helped fuel the increasing demands for a national hospital insurance scheme. So did the fact that many of the poor defaulted on the health-care bills they simply could not pay, leaving provinces and hospitals with mounting debts. The provincial hospital insurance scheme introduced in Saskatchewan in 1947 demonstrated that public coverage was possible without disrupting many of the existing practices.

The various historians who have analyzed the processes leading to the introduction of national health insurance stress the power struggles among insurance companies fearing loss of profits, provincial government officials fearing federal incursion, hospitals fearing loss of religious influence, and doctors fearing loss of control over hospitals.[16] Some mention the unions and women's groups who campaigned for accessible care. But few discuss in any detail the many people who saw their businesses, their families, and their health destroyed by enormous hospital bills.

The Ontario Coalition of Senior Citizens' Organizations has attempted to fill some of this gap by bringing together patients' experiences in *Life Before Medicare*. The book recounts story after story of suffering and death caused by 'No Money, No Care'.[17] One woman wrote about a baby born at home: 'The doctor didn't come to the house when they called because they still hadn't paid the bill from the birth of their first child.' The baby had trouble eating, and the baby's health got steadily worse. When the baby was almost two months old, the family finally had enough money to take the child to the hospital. The initially minor problem with the baby's digestive system was diagnosed, but the treatment was too late. 'The baby was starving to death and not even intravenous fluids could save her at this late stage'.[18] Another told of a woman dying in screaming pain because she did not want her family to become debt-ridden with bills for her cancer care. And lifetime debt was often a problem. When a young man needed surgery to straighten his back after polio, 'One third of the cattle had to be sold to pay for the operation and the hospital'.[19] Patients had a great deal to gain from a collective sharing of risks.

In a sense, all these groups won when the federal government introduced the Hospital Insurance and Diagnostic Services Act in 1957. Under this Act, the provinces continued to direct their own plans but the federal government agreed to cover half the costs of specified services. Included in the insured costs were accommodation and meals on a standard ward, necessary nursing services, laboratory and diagnostic tests, drugs and similar preparations, use of operating rooms and anaesthetic facilities, routine surgical supplies, radiology and physiotherapy, as well as the services of other hospital employees.[20] Some outpatient services could also be covered.[21] The federal government would pay for half the cost of these services only if they were provided to everyone on uniform terms and conditions. Specifically excluded were 'tuberculosis hospitals and sanitoria, hospitals or institutions for the mentally ill, and institutions providing custodial care, such as nursing homes and homes for the aged.'[22]

Eventually, payment by the federal government was conditional on five principles that were primarily about equality in access to health-care services. (1) In order to be eligible, coverage had to be *universal*. Services had to be provided to virtually all insurable residents under uniform terms and conditions, without regard to ability to pay, age, or illness. In addition, the Act specified that providers had to receive reasonable compensation. (2) Services also had to be *accessible*, defined as ensuring 'reasonable access to insured services by insured persons'.[23] (3) And they had to be *comprehensive*, covering all necessary services, and (4) *portable* across the country. (5) As well, hospital and physician insurance plans had to be *non-profit* and administered by a public authority responsible to the provincial government. These criteria meant that Canadians, especially those with few financial resources, were guaranteed hospital care without fear of debt. The risks of illness were to be shared and quality of care was not based on profit. Health care did not become equally available to everyone, but differences in access based on income were significantly reduced.[24]

Gains in accessibility did not mean large losses for those struggling over power within the institutions. For the moment at least, most hospitals remained non-profit. Little change in their power structure was required and local control was largely retained. Insurance companies could still insure additional services such as private rooms, drugs, and dental and physician care. Additional services could still be provided by both profit and non-profit organizations. Doctors could still control admissions and discharges, treatment, and the organization of health-care work. Indeed, the Act strengthened doctors' power considerably because now there were few financial constraints on their decisions about what was to be done to whom and by whom. Doctors decided what was necessary and therefore paid for by the state.

While federal financial support for hospital insurance significantly improved access to hospitals, it also served to reinforce the medical model of health care. Because the federal plan offered to match only those costs incurred within hospitals, 'provincial governments had financial incentive to fund as much in-patient care through hospitals as possible.'[25] It was assumed that a clear distinction could be drawn between necessary and unnecessary care. This distinction could be made because identification of necessary care was based on a scientifically established diagnosis determined by a doctor and provided in a hospital. Care was defined, therefore, primarily in terms of treatment and cure offered in specialized units devoted to the fixing of particular body parts. The medical model was secure, legitimated, and paid for by the state. As Taylor points out in his study of Canadian health insurance policy, the 'services were to be provided by independent parties—the hospitals—for the needs of second parties—the patients, as ordered by still other parties—their physicians.'[26] What really changed was who paid the bills, and with governments guaranteeing payment, much more of the same was possible. However, this emphasis also laid the foundation for new managerial strategies designed to use such distinctions as a means of restricting doctors' power.

Necessary care covered more than tests, drugs, and surgery. It also included meals, accommodation, and the entire range of services provided by hospital employees. Although the focus was on cure, this was understood to involve more than simply what medical practitioners do. Although non-curative facilities were not funded under this federal program, it was understood that treatment included food, a clean environment, and accurate records, as well as social and psychological support. This is important to note because, as we shall see later, such services are increasingly called 'hotel services' and defined out of care.

Moreover, the non-profit basis of the system meant that hospitals could focus more on care than on the bottom line. Patients could remain in the hospital as long as they required skilled care, and care could include back rubs to prevent bed sores and chats to provide comfort, because short-term costs were not the main concern. In addition, their non-profit structure meant they did not have to compete with other hospitals for patients. As a result, there was less pressure to develop spectacular surgery to promote their services, to confine services to particular kinds of illnesses that were more profitable, or to introduce the latest technology as a means of attracting customers. While the combination of non-profit institutions and state funding helped dilute the worst aspects of this medical model, hospitals were limited in their options by the power that rested to a large extent in doctors' hands and, perhaps more importantly, by the assumptions of the medical model.

Public health insurance, then, was not about state medicine but about a government-organized scheme to pay for existing services. By the time it was introduced, hospitals were making an important contribution to the health of individuals, and Canadians wanted access to their services. In spite of dire predictions, hospital insurance did not result in a rush to take advantage of 'free' services. In fact, in the years immediately after hospital insurance was introduced the annual rate of increase in bed use declined slightly.[27] Insurance did, however, make access to care more equitable among individuals and among regions. And it did ensure that doctors, with practices based on the medical model, would be the gatekeepers to the system.

PHYSICIAN INSURANCE

The only major expenditure not covered by hospital insurance was the income of those who controlled most of the institutional costs, the physicians. Although doctors determined who entered and left the hospital and what was done to them while they were there, very few of the physicians and surgeons were actually employed by these institutions. Most doctors were, and are, self-employed in private practices. This partly explains why doctors' services in or out of the hospital were not included in the Act on hospital insurance. However, it was estimated that a mere 38 per cent of the population of the time had some form of purchased insurance to cover physicians' bills and that payments from these plans covered only 30 per cent of payments made to doctors. Yet Canadians continued to spend enormous amounts of money on doctors' services. In 1955, just before state hospital insurance was introduced, the total expenditure on physicians' services was estimated at $206 million. By 1966 it had nearly tripled, to $605 million.[28] At the same time, research clearly indicated major class differences in access to physician services, with low-income groups using physician services the least.[29]

As was the case with hospital insurance, the combination of defaulted payments and the heavy burden on individuals who had to bear physicians' costs contributed to increasing pressure for a state-sponsored health plan to cover doctors' bills. So did the more general support for the notion of shared risks. Many of the same players struggled over whether or not there should be a plan and what form it should take.

However, when it came to state intervention to cover the costs of doctors' services, most of the physicians were united against a universal government plan and were its most visible and vociferous opponents. Although some physicians had been interested in such a plan during the Depression when too many of their patients could not pay their bills, not many were supportive during the prosperous post-war years when fewer patients defaulted. At most, they wanted the state to pay for those without sufficient resources and to allow the physicians to collect privately from the rest. Their preference was a voluntary insurance plan directed by doctors; many such schemes were already in place. The doctors feared both for their incomes and for their independence. They were concerned that self-rule, the right to determine who was ill with what ailments, and their power within the system would be undermined by state intervention.

When the social democratic government in Saskatchewan once again led the way and attempted to introduce a plan to cover doctors' services, the doctors responded by threatening to leave, by striking, and by encouraging their patients to oppose the plan. Patients were warned that their illnesses would become public knowledge, and that their doctors would no longer be available and would no longer be able to diagnose and treat on the basis of their expert knowledge alone. Many patients responded to the threats by supporting the doctors. Even those not currently patients and supportive of a state plan could be frightened into believing they would find themselves suddenly in a life-threatening position with no doctor to provide treatment.

Resistance was not a major problem in other areas, however. Opposition from insurance companies was not as strong as it might have been if the field had been dominated by for-profit organizations that would have more than jobs to lose. And most Canadians who were insured for doctors' services were covered by non-profit medical insurance plans.[30] Moreover, many of the for-profit private plans were in competition with the doctor-sponsored schemes, making co-operation among them more difficult.[31] Major employers were generally in favour of some kind of state plan because unions were becoming increasingly successful in demanding that their contracts cover medical insurance. Health-care costs, after all, can be significant for employers. Without a state health-care plan, private businesses in the United States 'have spent about as much on health care as they earned in after-tax profits.'[32] State plans mean everyone shares the costs and individual employers with strong unions therefore pay much less. Employers not only have an interest in sharing costs; they also have an interest in maintaining a healthy workforce. As the Royal Commission on Health

Services made clear in its 1964 report, 'No enlightened government can ignore that the economic capacities of its citizens to be productive depends upon their health and vigour as much as upon education.'[33]

In spite of strong, organized opposition from doctors in particular, the struggle in Saskatchewan and, later, at the federal level ended with a state scheme to cover physician services. This by no means meant the doctors lost, at least not initially. The price the state paid for compliance by the majority of physicians was a scheme based on fee-for-service, professional autonomy, and private practice. Introduced in 1966, the federal Medical Care Act was 'not designed to change the structure of medical practice or to interfere with the authority of physicians but only to pay for medical care.'[34] As was the case with hospital insurance, little changed in terms of how doctors practised. State intervention primarily meant that the government guaranteed all bills would be paid. The result was much more of the same. It was public payment for private practice.[35]

Like the hospital insurance scheme, the Medical Care Act left responsibility for physician services in provincial hands but put strong pressure on provinces to develop plans by offering to pay for half of specified expenditures. And like hospital insurance, payment would be made only if physician services were provided according to the same five principles—universality, accessibility, comprehensiveness, portability, and non-profitability. In most cases, only allopathic doctors were fully covered, although other kinds of practitioners—naturopaths, chiropractors, dentists, optometrists, nurses, and physiotherapists—had lobbied to be included. Some provinces did pay for limited services by some of these other practitioners. Doctors were allowed to opt out of the scheme entirely, but few did. Few left the country either. A partial explanation of why the doctors failed to follow through on their threats can be found not only in their successful retention of power but also in their new conditions of work. After medicare, doctors' hours of work decreased, as did their house calls and telephone conversations, while their incomes increased.[36] The state guaranteed medical doctors, unlike any other professionals, well-paid employment.

Although insurance companies lost out on most medical coverage, they were still permitted to cover uninsured costs, among them those treatments defined as unnecessary or not covered by the provincial plans, such as cosmetic surgery and many drugs. They also included those practitioners not included in the Act, such as dentists and massage therapists. Drugs prescribed outside the hospital, and some tests and services, were not part of either federal health plan and were thus also available for insurance coverage by non-state enterprises.

Like hospital insurance, medical insurance was chiefly about access. And access certainly improved under the plan, although people did not rush out to get 'free' medical advice. A 1973 study of the plan's impact by Philip Enterline and his colleagues noted 'the increased frequency with which physicians were seen for a series of common and important medical symptoms. This suggests that the removal of economic barriers to medical care may actually improve the general level of health of the population.'[37] At the same time, at least in the short run, there was if anything a decrease in the overall volume of services, suggesting that people did not rush to the doctor simply because the service was 'free'. The 1995 study by the Ontario Coalition of Senior Citizens' Organizations, mentioned above, contrasts experiences before and after medicare in terms of what life without fear of debilitating medical costs meant for Canadians.[38] Combined with the example of the United States today, their stories suggest that when individuals alone bear the costs the results can be devastating.

While there was a significant change in access to health care and undoubtedly in the financial consequences of medical treatment for individuals, there was little change in the kinds of treatment people received. Indeed, the Medical Care Act gave additional strong support to the medical model of care. Individual doctors determined what was defined as necessary care and, within the confines of a negotiated agreement with doctors about what should be covered, the governments paid. This power was based on the notion of the doctor as expert, the objective, knowledgeable person who applies proven diagnosis and techniques. The adoption of the fee-for-service method of payment was based on the assumption of parts to be fixed, with doctors negotiating the price of specified parts or procedures. With a price attached to each part or procedure, there was a built-in focus on tests, treatment, and short visits for care. The restriction of payment to allopathic practitioners also reinforced the emphasis on treatment and cure. Meanwhile, the isolation that accompanied this reinforcement of private practice also encouraged uncertain doctors to guide and protect themselves by ordering as many tests as possible.[39]

EXCEPTIONAL QUEBEC
Although the federal government and most provinces appeared to accept without question the medical model, Quebec set up its own Commission in 1965 to respond to the federal offer to pay half of the doctors' bills and to explore other ways of approaching provision. The Castonguay-Nepveau Commission produced quite a different model for care. Prevention, rather than cure, was to be the focus. Prevention was not to be structured separately from cure but rather made integral to it, and care was to be continuous rather than episodic. The plan was to integrate services under one roof within local community service centres (CLSCs), to establish departments of community health within hospitals, and to encourage practitioners to work in teams rather than in solo practice. The doctor was not seen as the only expert, nor as an expert who diagnosed simply on the basis of scientifically established truth about biologically determined illnesses. Teams could consult about appropriate strategies for care, basing their diagnoses on knowledge about whole people and their social environments. The teams were to include people equipped to deal with economic and social issues, as well as with a variety of other, more traditionally defined medical problems. Not only

whole people but whole families were to be accommodated in clinics located within their communities, and these communities would have a say in how the clinic was organized, staffed, and operated. In keeping with this approach to whole persons in their social context, staff would be paid on salary, not on the basis of parts to be fixed, and professionals would no longer be exclusively self-regulated. Services were to be centrally co-ordinated and rationalized to eliminate duplication and gaps.

Many of the community clinics that were to be the core of the health care system were set up after medicare was introduced in 1971, and a significant number remain today. Some even function as intended. However, a number of factors combined to prevent them and other reforms from fulfilling the promise as set out in the Commission report.[40] The most important factor was resistance from physicians. The doctors responded by refusing to work in the CLSCs, by setting up alternative clinics, by dominating the community boards, and by continuing to make curative hospital care the centre of their approach. In hospitals, outpatient and emergency services competed with the community-based ones. Also important was the state's lack of commitment to a fundamentally different strategy. The government made it clear that the mechanisms for participation 'do not alter the distribution of power prevailing before their introduction. They can be compared to a kind of permanent opinion poll of users.'[41] In the end, fee-for-service payments, the medical model, and allopathic practitioners prevailed. The 'most profitable sectors of medical care were left in private hands, while the state, through public establishments and in particular the CLSCs, took charge of the unprofitable parts: health care for the disadvantaged and in isolated regions, preventative medicine and public health services.'[42] The co-ordination and rationalization of services put more power in the hands of professionals and bureaucrats while increasing dependency on hospitals and doctor-centred care.[43]

CUTTING BACK ON CARE

FEDERAL STRATEGIES

The federal government soon became concerned about the costs of an open-ended scheme that promised to pay for half of services determined as necessary by doctors. Although Canada's health-care costs did not rise more quickly than those of other countries, the federal government argued that matching grants made it impossible to plan and that costs were escalating. Less than a decade after medicare was introduced, the federal government changed the funding arrangements. The 1977 Established Programs Financing (EPF) formula moved away from a matching plan to an allocation based on past expenditures, growth in the overall economy, population, some provincial equalization payments to limit disparities, and a transfer of some taxation rights to the provinces. Basically, the new arrangements meant a cap on cash transfers from the federal government and more financial responsibility to the provinces and territories. It also meant more choice in provincial spending.

There was a new per capita payment to support nursing homes and other residential care, as well as home and ambulatory care. However, a significant proportion of the funding simply represented a transfer from the welfare budget, rather than additional money, and thus did not constitute a dramatic change from previous practice. This approach to funding was designed to encourage provinces to move as many people as possible out of expensive acute-care institutions and into less expensive care in residential facilities and in private homes, where much of the care was provided without pay by female relatives. Rather than challenge the medical model, this move reinforced it by assuming both that a clear line could be drawn between the curable and incurable and that the incurable needed less care and less-skilled care.

The 1984 Canada Health Act clearly set out the five principles of public care, while bringing hospital and medical insurance together into one neat package. However, the federal government had less and less power to ensure that the principles were indeed being respected. Unlike the original legislation, the new funding arrangements were not based on the scrutiny of provincial health-care budgets but rather on populations, economic trends, and past performance. The federal government could thus not easily assess whether services were universally provided, accessible, comprehensive, portable, and administered by a non-profit organization. At the same time, the Act explicitly forbade extra-billing by physicians and threatened to reduce payments to provinces in direct proportion to the number of doctors who were charging patients over and above the rates set in provincial negotiations. It also redefined services to include those that were 'medically necessary for the purpose of maintaining health, preventing disease or diagnosing or treating an injury, illness or disability'.[44] This redefinition was designed to prevent provinces from charging fees to patients defined as temporary chronics, not subject to immediate cure and thus not legitimately housed in acute-care facilities. In addition, the Canada Health Act referred to 'health practitioners' rather than doctors, and thus opened the door to the possibility of provinces allowing other, less expensive health-care workers to be paid directly by the provinces.[45]

Since then, the federal government has continued to withdraw from the health-care field. Direct funding has declined and so has the federal department devoted to health. Responsibility for health is being increasingly transferred to the provinces and the private sector, with less and less pressure from the federal government to follow the five principles of the Canada Health Act.[46]

The February 1995 federal budget announced the merging of the EPF transfers for health and post-secondary education with the Canada Assistance Plan (CAP) transfers for social assistance to create a new Canada Health and Social Transfer (CHST). The budget cut billions of dollars each year from these programs, beginning in 1996–7. Within six or seven years, payments to Quebec, Alberta, British Columbia, and Ontario were scheduled to disappear entirely and payments to the remaining provinces and territories would be gone within a few years thereafter. The 1999 budget restored much of the money cut from health care in 1995, but by then considerable damage had already been done to the public system. Moreover, this new funding did little to restore the federal government's capacity to enforce the five principles of the Canada Health Act or to restore faith in the public system. Indeed, the Social Union Framework Agreement (SUFA) of 1999 between the federal and provincial/territorial governments that was an integral part of the new financing merely required provincial/territorial governments to promise to spend the money on health care and to measure outcomes.

Instead of strengthening the federal government's capacity to enforce the five principles, improve care, and prevent privatization, the SUFA committed the federal government to obtaining agreement from the majority of provinces before introducing any new initiatives.[47] There was no clear means of limiting further erosion of public care. Thus, when the Alberta government introduced legislation allowing for-profit hospitals and when Ontario sent radiation patients to a for-profit concern, the federal government did not reduce funding to either province or even take any effective steps to limit these developments. Meanwhile, the federal government has appointed yet another Commission to look at the future of health care. But there is little reason to believe that this will result in any more effective change than the previous National Forum on Health, a group that recommended national home care and pharmacare programs as well as more public control of pharmaceutical research.[48]

PROVINCIAL STRATEGIES

Partly in response to such changes in federal financing, the provinces have adopted similar strategies. Although the particular practices vary from province to province, the overall pattern is clear. For example, Ontario dramatically reduced global budgets to hospitals and ordered some major ones closed, while Nova Scotia amalgamated four Halifax hospitals into a single complex. In Quebec, regional and social services cut cleaning, laundry, and administration of support services, and in Saskatchewan and Manitoba the regional health authorities created to manage local care received smaller global budgets. Alberta approved private, for-profit eye clinics, while BC reduced hospital staff by 10 per cent and plans more reductions. None of these strategies addresses the problems inherent in the dominant medical model. In fact, they serve to perpetuate these problems and limit the public system, setting the stage for further privatization.[49]

STRATEGIES FOR DOCTORS

A number of strategies have been designed to alter doctors' practices. In response to the Canada Health Act and the accompanying threat of reduced transfers, the provinces moved to prevent extra-billing. Physicians objected strongly, arguing that the prohibition interferes with their independence and their ability to determine what is best for their patients. In Ontario, for instance, physicians responded by striking in 1986 when the Ontario government tried to enforce the Act. But the federal government held firm and the popular interpretation of the struggle as one undertaken by greedy doctors helped make it easier for the province to enforce the ban on extra-billing. Some doctors still managed to charge patients for such services as keeping records and making phone calls.[50] Some did not bill the medical plan directly but instead charged patients and filed a form for reimbursement to the patient. And most continued to charge for the limited number of services not covered by the fee-for-service plan. The number of such services has been increasing in recent years, however, as governments remove some procedures from their billing schedules and fail to include some new ones.[51] By the end of the 1990s, no federal penalties were being applied because of extra-billing, although Nova Scotia is still being penalized for allowing private clinics to charge facility fees for medically necessary services.[52] The lack of penalties is based on the assumption that the legislative prohibition of extra-billing means it is not happening. However, there does not seem to be any systematic means of ensuring that the prohibition is effective in practice.

Some provinces tried to respond to reduced federal contributions by freezing doctors' fees. These freezes had little effect on provincial budgets, however, and in fact spending on physicians' services increased. These seemingly contradictory phenomena are explained both by the doctors' power and by the fee structure. Doctors can control how many patients they see for how long and what they do for them. The variable fee structure means that more complicated diagnoses and treatments pay more than simpler ones, and preventive measures pay little if anything at all. With medicare, there was 'a marked tendency for the number of relatively higher-priced services to increase much more than the lower priced.' Research in Quebec suggests that such increases 'largely reflect changes in physicians' behaviour—their billing practices and the acts they decide to perform.'[53] Data from Ontario demonstrate that physicians' incomes continued to increase, despite freezes on fees, primarily because doctors saw more patients for shorter periods of time. They also diagnosed and treated people for more acute illnesses.[54]

Freezing or even lowering fees in a system based on fee-for-service, where the practitioner largely determines the number of patients seen and how they are diagnosed, not only does little to lower costs, it also increases the focus on curative approaches to particular body parts. The fee structure also encourages quick-fix rather than preventive solutions. Research from the Maritimes indicates that physicians 'seeing a lot of patients in their office in one day are spending less time with each patient and prescribing more drugs.'[55] Moreover, when fees are structured to pay more for more acute illnesses, there is considerable incentive to diagnose and treat the most complicated illnesses.

Some provinces tried placing caps on physicians' incomes, or lowering rates for services after doctors reach a ceiling. This may help control direct costs for physician services but it does little to ensure a more preventive approach based on the whole person understood within the context of the individual's social environment. Doctors may follow their usual practices until the cap is reached and then simply take a vacation or reduce services. There is no incentive in the cap to do less complicated service, to order fewer tests, to practise more preventive medicine, or to spend more time with patients.[56]

There are similar problems with another government strategy—limiting the number of doctors who graduate or who are assigned billing numbers. While fewer doctors likely produce fewer bills, the strategy does little to alter the overall structure of the system or to challenge the way individual doctors practise. And with today's talk of doctor shortages in many areas, such strategies are no longer on the agenda. Indeed, doctors have been winning increases in their fees at the same time as enrolments in medical schools and immigration of physicians have once again been allowed to increase.

Nevertheless, doctors have been facing restraints as a result of reforms in other areas. When the numbers of hospital beds are reduced, for example, doctors are more restricted in their ability to admit or keep patients in the hospital. Moreover, as hospitals are managed more by people and practices taken from the for-profit sector, doctors find their behaviour increasingly influenced by decisions based on non-medical principles. And evidence-based decision-making is similarly designed to direct doctors' practices in ways that take finances into account and limit their power. So, for example, a doctor is expected to send a mother home within 24 hours of birth unless there is clear justification for a longer stay.[57] Doctors have resisted the controls, often claiming a 'brain drain' to the US by doctors seeking greater freedom, better pay, and higher funding for care institutions. However, the data challenge this claim. There was indeed a marked exodus around 1996, during the height of the cuts, but fewer have left in recent years and the number returning increased by about 34 per cent between 1995 and 1999.[58] This is perhaps best explained by the controls from managed care companies that doctors face in the United States and the even greater cutbacks in care funding in many areas.[59]

While governments have made only limited adjustments to doctors' fee schedules in response to federal cutbacks, they have been more cautious about introducing programs to make direct payment to other, less costly practitioners such as nurse practitioners or midwives. These practitioners are cheaper not only because they receive lower individual incomes but also because they incur fewer institutional costs. They are often more focused on preventive measures that keep people out of institutions. Although strong opposition from the allopaths has prevented significant changes, provinces are gradually increasing the range and number of other health-care practitioners who can bill the government and/or can perform some of the procedures previously reserved for doctors.

PRIMARY CARE

These tentative moves are now being bolstered across the country as provinces introduce what is commonly called primary care reform. A current federal/provincial/territorial agreement provides funding for pilot projects intended to test models for altering the way people first gain entry to the health-care system, or for what is usually called primary care. Yet various models have long been in place and have proven their effectiveness, leaving their practitioners asking why we need to test models at all. As the Community Health Co-operative Federation explains, years of experience have taught us that 'everyday health care services can best be delivered through interdisciplinary teams in community health care centres'.[60] The CLSCs in Quebec can make similar claims.

However, the models now being tested tend to be centred more on group physician practices that include a larger role for nurse practitioners and nurses, rather than on broader interdisciplinary teams focused on prevention. Indeed, Quebec's Clair Commission on health-care reform suggests the creation of a network of family physician practices rather than an extension of the successful CLSC model.[61] With entry to other services determined by the family or family physicians in primary care centres, the intent is to reduce the use of specialists and thus reduce costs. Various provider payment schemes are also being tested, with a clear preference in the models for salaries as the dominant form. This is not surprising given the research suggesting that salaries can help control costs while promoting prevention strategies and continuity in care.[62] This emphasis on doctors and a variety of payment schemes is one of the reasons that a significant proportion of doctors are in support of some proposed reforms.

What is new in the models is the promise of 24-hour services open seven days a week. This reform is an attempt to reduce the use of emergency rooms while extending access to care. Hidden behind the emphasis on 24/7 care, salaries, and the nurses' expanded role, however, is a much more fundamental challenge to public care. Many of these models include a plan for payment based on capitation and rostering. Capitation means payment based on the number of people served, rather than on the number of specific services provided or tasks done. Rostering refers to the requirement that patients enrol with a specific group of physicians or a specific clinic, and that the practice and/or the patient would be financially penalized for using other services. Thus, the primary care centre would be paid on the basis of the number of patients signed up for care, regardless of the care provided, and patients would be significantly restricted in where they could go for care.

Capitation and rostering would fundamentally transform both care and payment. It could reduce access without improving care. Under the current system, Canadians can access any service they need and seek a second opinion when they think it is necessary. There is little evidence that Canadians abuse this right, and this choice has been an important factor in the popularity of the Canadian public health-care system. Moreover, evidence indicates that the overwhelming majority of patients return to the same doctor when this is possible and appropriate.[63] Under rostering, they would have this choice only when they enrol and not when they need a service. The unenrolled could be denied care in that centre, or at least denied care unless they pay a fee. And many may find it difficult to enrol because they cannot find an open space in a primary care service or because the service does not want to enrol a high-risk patient. Sicker patients are more expensive patients to serve and thus mean the overall expenses of the primary care groups will rise and income fall. Thus, at the same time as capitation may remove the perverse incentives inherent in fee-for-service to provide excess care, it may promote even more perverse incentives to avoid patients who need expensive services or to deny services that are expensive.[64] Not insignificantly, capitation and rostering are the preferred mechanism of for-profit managed care organizations in the United States precisely because they avoid risky patients and cut costs by denying care or by passing the risk onto the doctors. They are also preferred by these corporations because such payment methods allow finances to play a major role in medical choices, significantly limiting doctors' power through the application of accounting principles based on a medical model for care or transferring the financial risk to doctors.

The CLSCs and Community Health Centres have already demonstrated that it is possible to provide effective multidisciplinary care based on global budgets, with services open to those who need them, and to do so while encouraging continuity. The move to capitation and rostering has far less evidence to support such a dramatic change in the current practices and some evidence to suggest it will significantly reduce access to care. Yet capitation and rostering have not been central to public debates. Indeed, they have been hidden behind promises for services available at all hours to those who sign up. A recent survey explored the issue by asking citizens if they would register with a family physician based on the assurance that they would receive 'necessary medical services day and night and arrange for medical specialists and other health services as needed'.[65] Such questions, even when qualified by asking if people would be willing to do so if there are restrictions on seeing other physicians without referral, hardly constitute full public debate. Indeed, they suggest an attempt to encourage public support rather than informed choice. Yet capitation and rostering set the stage for further privatization because they fit so well with US for-profit models for care, providing another example of transformations in care that happen without public participation in decision-making. Under the free trade agreements now in place, the risk of US firms moving in to take over such groups is always there. Moreover, rostering and capitation constitute a fundamental transformation in the funding of care. We now fund services rather than people, making it more difficult to discriminate against individuals. Under rostering and capitation, we could be funding individuals rather than services, which would make it easier to discriminate against individuals.

Whether or not these reforms challenge the dominance of the medical model will depend in large measure on which models are adopted and on the extent to which they remain physician-directed. If the main model still has doctors paid based on economic incentives and nurses providing care primarily during the hours when physicians are not available, the medical model will remain at the centre of care. Primary care reform would thus effectively mean less of the same. If rostering and capitation are adopted as universal strategies, public health care as we know it will be transformed and the opportunities for US-style care will be increased.

HOSPITAL STRATEGIES

'On October 4, 1998, Calgary's Bow Valley Health Centre, a city hospital, blew up'.[66] Thus begins the Canadian Institute for Health Information's report on *Health in Canada 2000*. While provinces have moved cautiously in relation to expenditures on doctors, they have taken more dramatic steps to reduce the funds that go to hospital care. Initially, most provinces moved to global hospital financing and significant reductions in the hospital's share of the overall health budget. Following the example of the federal government, many provinces developed a formula based largely on past expenditures and population to set the amount that would go to each hospital or group of hospitals, and then left it to the individual hospital or regional hospital authority to figure out how to work within that budget. Some provinces have moved to base payment on the kind and number of cases and have begun to intervene more actively in how hospitals are run. More obviously, hospitals have been closed, amalgamated, transformed into other kinds of care facilities, or simply blown up or demolished, so that by the end of the twentieth century there were fewer than 800 hospitals in Canada (see Table 3.1).

These strategies have helped reduce the rate of increase in hospital expenditures, but they have done little to alter the dominance of the medical model. In fact, in many ways they have served to increase the emphasis on a curative approach to body parts treated by experts who assume mainly biological causes, and have led to further privatization. Alberta, for example, sold a hospital the province closed and then argued it should be opened as a for-profit facility because the services are required. And such strategies may not reduce overall long-term health costs or improve health.

Hospitals have responded to the increased financial pressure in quite similar ways, a not surprising development given the dominance of the medical model and the similarity in systems.

> Over the last decade, the number of hospital beds, the number of admissions and the length of stays have dropped, year after year. Compared with 1984/85, hospitals in 1997/98 had about 25 per cent fewer beds, but visits to hospital emergency rooms and clinics were up 9 per cent. There were also almost three times as many outpatient services in 1997/98 as in 1984/85.[67]

Because labour accounts for most of care costs and services, these changes inevitably meant job loss.[68]

Hospitals have been able to close beds and reduce the number of employees by shortening stays, performing more day surgery, contracting out and standardizing services, and providing more treatment on an outpatient basis. They have also moved people into other services. 'Under the new funding format, provinces shifted a lot of chronic and long-term care out of hospitals into

Table 3.1 Canadian Hospitals, 1998–1999

	PUBLIC HOSPITALS (748)	PRIVATE HOSPITALS (16)	FEDERAL (13)
General	With long-term care: 379 Without long-term care: 280 Total: 659	Without long-term care: 1 Total: 1	With long-term care: 8 Without long-term care: 1 Total: 9
Specialty	Pediatric: 6 Psychiatric (long-term): 25 Psychiatric (short-term): 7 Other specialty: 6 Total: 44	Psychiatric (short-term): 1 Other specialty: 5 Total: 6	Psychiatric (short-term): 3 Total: 3
Rehabilitation	Total: 15	Total: 1	
Extended Care/ Chronic	Total: 30	Total: 8	Total: 1

SOURCE: Canadian Institute for Health Information, Annual Hospital Survey, 1998–9.

special care institutions, a process that was particularly pronounced in the case of psychiatric services.'[69] Those not sent to other facilities were sent home.

There are conflicting claims about the impact of these strategies on patient care. The Manitoba Centre for Health Policy and Evaluation, for example, concludes that 'bed closures have not, in general, had a negative impact on patients' access to hospitals, the quality of care provided, or the health of Winnipeg residents'.[70] This assessment appears to be supported by an Ontario patient satisfaction survey indicating that just over 70 per cent of respondents felt they received excellent care, with men more likely than women to rate care as excellent.[71] In contrast, a study of 40 families undertaken by Ontario's Caledon Institute found deteriorating quality and access to care.[72] And an examination of the literature on nursing care reports that 'increased workloads improve short-term productivity but increase long-term costs, as nurse stress and illness may lead to poor judgement and low productivity that can hurt patients'.[73]

Part of this discrepancy can be explained by the measures and techniques used in the assessments. In the Manitoba study, access to services is defined in terms of the number of people processed by the institution, not in terms of whether the procedures were successful in improving people's health and in reducing overall government expenditures. Efficiency is equated with the number of procedures done and parts fixed or at least treated. Outcomes are recorded by length of stay, not state of health in the longer term. Success is to a large extent reported in terms of doing more operations and other procedures, rather than in terms of reducing the need for such services or making people well. Quality measures were limited to the number of people with one of three conditions dying within 30 days and the number visiting a doctor or hospital within 30 days of release. No data are provided in the Manitoba study on the health of care providers.

Patient satisfaction surveys raise another set of definitional and methodological questions. While it is important to ask patients how they feel about the care they receive, given that patients' feelings about care are important to their health, survey questions provide only limited options in terms of both what is asked and the choice of responses. And with 60 per cent of those surveyed not responding to the Ontario questionnaire, there are issues about who did not respond. Those not returning the questionnaires may be those too ill to answer or those unable to answer because of language or other barriers. Moreover, patients are not always in a position to assess much of the care they receive. As a BC nurse put it, 'people can be very satisfied while they are eating cyanide. I mean they don't know if they've had good or bad care.' She went on to explain that we should be concerned about how patients experience the care, but cautions that 'patient satisfaction . . . is not a thermometer for the health care system.'[74]

The Caledon research team actually interviewed those who received care and tracked them for two years, while the nursing research brought together a host of literature using a variety of means to assess impact. It may well be the case that hospital strategies failed to show negative results in the Manitoba or Ontario research in part because providers have struggled to make up for the inadequacies of the system at the expense of their own health.[75] Moreover, Manitoba might have better after-hospital care, compared to other provinces, that fills in the gaps left by changes in hospital care. Some Ontario hospitals, for example, are showing increasing readmission rates.[76] It is also worth noting that the majority of Ontario patients did not rate either housekeeping or support services such as food in the excellent category. These are precisely the services that have been contracted out to for-profit firms on the grounds that they can be more effectively and efficiently provided by the for-profit sector.[77]

The measures used by the Manitoba Centre for Health Policy and Evaluation fit quite nicely with the dominant medical model, although they contradict what have been established as the determinants of health. The techniques, and the measurement of success, are taken from the industrial sector and applied to people as if these were products to be made or serviced. This is possible only if medical care is understood as a scientifically determined diagnosis of a problem in a particular part of the body that is largely unconnected to the rest. Only if it is assumed that the part can be treated with either cuts or chemicals, without attention to the psychological state of the person or consideration of the social context before and after treatment, can quality be assessed in terms of lengths of hospital stays and numbers of procedures or quality defined as still living and not seeking more doctor and hospital care. One hospital worker explained that, as a consequence, 'we are not giving quality, we are giving quantity.' Indeed, quality is too often defined as quantity, even when quantity may indicate failure to make people well.[78] As one BC nurse put it, the statistics may look good but 'there are some people who go home and struggle for two weeks that the health care system never knows about.'[79] This increasing emphasis on the medical model and this failure to take the other determinants of health into account become evident with a closer examination of each strategy.

1. Shorter Stays

Certainly new technologies have made it possible to shorten the length of time some procedures, and recovery, normally take. Hysterectomies, for example, can now be done without major external incisions and gall stones may be zapped without any incisions at all. As a result, patients have less risk of external infections and require less time to return to their previous state. Moreover, the new philosophy suggests that patients have less risk of blood clots and other complications if they begin moving around as soon as possible after surgery. Furthermore, some equipment has become both more mobile and more affordable, and thus can be more readily used outside the hospital setting. For many people, then, shorter stays may be appropriate.

In addition, the environment in hospitals may mean patients cannot leave soon enough. Cutbacks in cleaning too often leave visible signs of dirt and may increase the risk of infection. Cutbacks in staff mean there is often no one available to answer call bells or questions. And growing reliance on relatives to help patients means there are frequently a number of non-health-care workers crowded in the room, reducing privacy and making rest impossible. Crowding into a room also increases the risk of spreading infection, especially if there are cutbacks in cleaning and other services. Indeed, Canada is now following the US pattern of increasing rates of infection from antibiotic-resistant superbugs.[80] Food is seldom inviting and is increasingly prepackaged in ways that may reduce both nutrition and appeal. Translation services may no longer be available and there may be little time to accommodate cultural differences.[81] As a result, homes may seem better alternatives.

But shorter stays can also be dangerous to the patient and a threat to overall costs. The experiences of a former patient, recorded after he called a telephone number set up by the Ontario Council of Hospital Unions (OCHU) to receive complaints, indicate what shorter stays can mean in terms of both the patient and the hospital.

> I'm an amputee. I am also diabetic and have a heart condition. In February, I had to have an operation on my stump.
>
> On the day they sent me home from the hospital, my blood sugar was very high. It's normally in the 9–10 range but that day it was in the teens. I was still in terrible pain from the operation. The wound was raw with forty something stitches in. The pain was unbelievable, like they were still cutting away at it. I was feeling like I could pass out at any minute. I felt nauseous and weak. I told them I wasn't well enough to be discharged. But they said I was fine and had to go.
>
> It was snowing that day. The driveway at my apartment was in bad condition. All I had was these crutches, and when I went to take a step, I lost my balance and fell hard. If I had been stronger, I could have dealt with this easy and made it into the apartment building. But I was still feeling sick and weak and I just fell, passed out, and when I came to was in horrible pain. I think I must have been in shock. I could feel the inside of the tensor bandage was wet and I knew there was a lot of damage.
>
> I had to get myself up two flights of stairs, which I crawled up. My friend is not well herself and couldn't lift or strain, so she couldn't help me much. I had to mostly get up to the apartment myself. When I got the bandage off, there was not one stitch left in the stump. Every single one was gone. The incisions looked like they'd been split open with an axe.
>
> The ambulance took me back to emergency at the same hospital. I hadn't even had time to take the band off my arm from the last visit. I'd only been gone an hour or so. Anyway, they restitched the wound in the emergency but they didn't do a proper job of it. There's not enough padding over the femur bone. The skin's pulled so tight that I can't use the prosthesis. I can't walk.
>
> So all this means I have to go through surgery again, to have the femur bone shortened to build up the flap of skin. That's going to mean two months more healing, another 4–6 weeks of rehab. And all this time, I've got no money coming in. I feel like this ordeal is never going to end. I'm having to live on my savings. It's taken me my whole life to earn this money and now I'm spending it foolishly. It's not right, you know. They shouldn't be treating people like this, especially not when you're sick and hurting.[82]

The focus for this patient was on the cutting and stitching of the piece that was diagnosed as the problem, as the medical model would suggest. Little consideration was given to what was going on in the rest of his body, to his psychological state, or to the conditions at his home—aspects that are also determinants of health. As a result, he had to be admitted to hospital for a second time and to undergo additional surgery. This not only increased the stress level for the patient—another important determinant of health—but also reduced his income—yet another determinant of health. The health-care system incurred the additional costs of admission to emergency and of a second operation. And with less income, a second operation, and an increased stress level, this may not be the end of the services he requires. However, given that most hospitals treat each admission as a new one, this patient would likely be counted as part of the increase in outpatient services and surgery.

This may be an extreme example of the problems created by shorter hospital stays. Nevertheless, it clearly demonstrates that quality cannot be determined by length of stay alone and that surveys of patient satisfaction may fail to capture significant consequences for care. It also suggests that developing formulas for standard lengths of stay may be inappropriate. Data from a large Ontario hospital[83] demonstrate this in relation to the now common practice of sending newborn babies and their mothers home soon after delivery. Nearly 12 per cent of the babies born without complications who were sent home early were readmitted within a month. Formulas are a problem especially, as more and more patients are admitted to the hospital only when they have severe health problems and more have several complicated problems at the same time.

The problems of short stays for those with complicated conditions were illustrated by an example offered to the Ontario Minister of Health by an organization representing seniors:

> A man of 70, his left side paralysed as the result of a former stroke, is rushed to the hospital to be treated for congestive heart failure and pneumonia. In the course of the treatment that saves his life, he is given a powerful antibiotic.
> Recovering in hospital, the man is too weak to sit up unassisted and finds himself incontinent. He also develops a severe case of diarrhea, a not uncommon reaction to the antibiotic. Still, he is sent home to his apartment, where he lives alone.

According to the standard for treatment, the man had been fixed. All he needed now was custodial work. An elderly neighbour tried to help, but his condition deteriorated. He was refused admission to one hospital but eventually readmitted to another. During his time at home, he was prescribed medication that the pharmacist claimed should be administered only in hospital. Not only that, it cost '$1,000 and would not be covered by medicare because it was given outside the hospital.'[84] While the Manitoba study would pick up this readmission, it would not pick up the 'so much agony' a women who had leg surgery told the Caledon researchers she experienced when she was sent home without instructions and in fear about her ability to avoid or detect infection.[85]

Moreover, while better techniques and more mobile equipment help reduce the length of hospital stays, they have not eliminated the need for skilled care before, during, and after treatment. An increasing number of people are being sent home when they still need a great deal of physical assistance, medical treatment, and psychological support. Those with people at home who are knowledgeable, available, and capable of providing such care and with homes that are uncrowded and clean may want to go home as soon as possible. But many people do not have access to this range of resources. New immigrants, for example, may be living alone and be far from family support. The same is often true for Aboriginal people, who can only find treatment far from home, and for the increasing number of Canadians who are homeless.

Indeed, few households have anyone home with the time, the skills, and the capacity to provide such care. Today, the overwhelming majority of both women and men have, and need, labour force jobs that take them out of the home. Many of those sent home very soon after treatment may find themselves home alone for long periods of time. And being home alone is not only frightening when you are ill. It can also be dangerous. Even if there are friends and relatives available, most of them do not have the skills required to do the kinds of tasks or provide the kinds of support these short-stay patients require. While most care was provided at home in the nineteenth century by women, the care that families were expected to provide was food, shelter, some assistance with other physical needs, and comfort. There were many more people in most households to offer such care and the limits on this care meant that people often died. Moreover, the separation of patients from those who were not sick was a major factor in limiting the spread of disease and in reducing the risk to patients from others. In the early part of the twentieth century, quarantine and the movement of care out of the home were significant factors in protecting the health of both the patient and the rest of the household.[86]

Today, people are sent home with complicated machinery, open wounds, and complex requirements that are not easy to fulfill without training. The practice of shortening patient stays could well risk the health of both the patient and their relatives who are expected to provide the care.[87] When hospitals send patients home soon after treatment, they often teach a household member how to do some specific tasks for the patient. But this assumes that health care can be divided up into fragmented tasks that can be easily learned, and ignores the entire literature on the complex skills involved in providing care and on the determinants of health. Baths, as we have seen, are about much more than applying water to skin, and giving injections is about much more than inserting a needle in an appropriate spot. Without the requisite skills, even the most loving, caring, and dedicated person can provide inappropriate or even dangerous treatment or advice. Even the most conscientious housekeepers may not be able to create an environment at home that is safe for a person whose immune system has been weakened by surgery or disease. These unpaid caregivers can also expose themselves to infection, back injury, or stress-related illnesses. In fact, the entire household could be in danger. More than a decade ago, when hospitals began to reduce the length of stay, a Quebec nurse reported that they regularly had families who said: 'We can't cope. We have no money. We don't want to take him.'[88] Today, many more families are given little choice about taking on the job and women in particular are 'conscripted' into caregiving.[89] One woman recently wrote to us to say she was 'under house arrest', caring for severely disabled parents alone at home. Clearly, this is not about the choice to care.

While shorter stays can harm anyone, they are particularly problematic for women. While this impact is considered in greater detail in the next chapter, it is important to note that most of those whose health is at risk from providing care for those sent home early are women, given that women do most of the paid and unpaid caring work. They also do most of the cleaning, cooking, and organizational work that is essential to the recovery process. And the women who have very short hospital stays are being sent to an environment where they bear the major responsibility for the care of others and for the domestic work. This not only means that they are unlikely to have anyone to care for them; it also means that they immediately enter an environment that places significant demands on them even when they are sick. This is particularly the case if there are young children at home. Such demands can delay, rather than help, recovery.

Certainly hospitals save money immediately by shortening hospital stays.[90] They save money in part because hospitals send people home when they still need care that would otherwise be provided by skilled workers in a safe environment. Home may be more supportive, may provide more care—especially given the cutbacks in hospital staff—and may be what people want. But this is not necessarily the case. When people are sent home too soon after treatment, they may increase costs in the long term by risking the health of both the patients and the other household members. They definitely increase costs for the individual households, in terms of both women's time and direct costs for supplies.

2. Outpatient Services and Day Surgery

Like shorter stays, a shift to more outpatient services and day surgery has to some extent been made possible by new technologies and new procedures. And as is the case with shorter stays, many people prefer to be able to leave the hospital, especially as conditions there deteriorate. However, as is also the case with shorter stays, the consequences may often be negative for patients, for households, and for long-term costs, to a large extent because the strategy is built on a medical model rather than on the determinants of health and on cost-saving to the public purse as a priority.

One case described on the Ontario Council of Hospital Unions hotline illustrates the kinds of issues involved:

> I'm concerned that government cuts are leading to extremely inadequate care, especially for elderly people. Consideration should have been given to admitting my mother to hospital, but wasn't. She paid dearly for this. I was

shocked when I was told she was being sent back to the nursing home. She had fallen out of her wheelchair; had a bad fall two days after she was admitted to a nursing home. She had fallen out of the wheelchair and hit her head on the hard floor.

Approximately six hours later, we arrived at the emergency ward. My mother's right eye was swollen, bruised, cut in the corner and full of blood. She had a bruised cheekbone and was not able to move her right arm. They x-rayed her head and arm. The results confirmed her arm was broken. The doctor said in all probability she would not again have full use of it.

Even though there was no indication of a fracture or breaks in the skull, I thought she should be kept 24 hours for observation. She was 79, clearly had a head injury and a broken arm and was unable to communicate the extent of pain she was feeling. However, she was not admitted. They simply gave her a prescription for pain pills, put her arm in a sling and sent her back to the nursing home in minus 38 degree weather.

Two days later the nursing home called me at midnight to say my mother was blue. She was not responding and they were immediately sending her back to the hospital. For the next nine days, my mother remained unconscious. Matters were so serious that on a number of occasions, the staff made efforts to prepare me for her death. When it became apparent that she was going to make it, several nurses began to refer to her as 'the miracle lady'. None expected her to survive.

Needless to say, my mother went through hell. All of the suffering was unnecessary. It has taken her four months to stand up again, with assistance. In the past year, I have heard so much about the public abusing the health-care system. But with all the cutbacks, I think there is every possibility that the system is abusing the public.[91]

Again, this may be an isolated case, but it, too, demonstrates how numbers on outpatient services tell very little about the quality of care or about efficiency, even if efficiency is defined solely in terms of money. The tests determined no serious head injury was involved, although later developments suggest that the test result told only part of the tale. The pressure to release people as quickly as possible adds to the emphasis on taking a single test as conclusive. And the transitory nature of a visit to outpatient services means that those providing care are usually encountering the patient for the first time and thus know little about his or her customary behaviour.

Some patients regularly visit the outpatient services, but this does not guarantee them quality care either. Each visit, the provider can be different, reducing the possibilities for continuity of care. Moreover, the very structure of outpatient care places the emphasis on treating the part as quickly as possible. A regular dialysis patient, for example, explained that familiarity does not solve the problem in the face of continuing pressure from managers pushed to focus on the bottom line:

I've been on dialysis for three years. I have no kidneys. When you talk about cutbacks in the system, they have every effect on people like me. I can tell you what's happening out there with all these government cuts is really bad news.

On Monday, I went for my usual dialysis treatment. There are three machines but one had broken down. I was hooked up to one of the two operational machines, but it also quit after two hours and 15 minutes. [The time required for dialysis is four hours.]

Anyway, the dialysis nurse was planning to hook me up to the remaining machine after the other patient was finished. The nurse reported his plans to the administrator of the unit. But the administrator disputed the plan because it would involve overtime. I overheard this conversation. The administrator told the nurse to take a blood sample and if the potassium level was low enough, to send me home!

So that's what happened. I got sent home and the next two days were hell. For dialysis patients, the Monday appointment is the most important. Your blood is always heavier and there are toxins in it. So when you don't even get a full treatment on Monday, it's much worse for you. I got very little sleep. Urea was coming out of my pores. Even though I was extremely thirsty, I couldn't drink enough water because they hadn't taken the necessary amount of fluid out. I had trouble walking because my feet ached so bad. My legs were jumping when I would try to sleep. I was exhausted, stressed and found the whole ordeal hard on my nerves. By the time I went for my next dialysis session on Wednesday, it took the rest of the week to get back to anywhere near normal and feel okay. All this because overtime was more important than my health.

It's not like this was an isolated event. Last fall, when the dialysis nurse went on pregnancy leave, they hired a replacement but the replacement quit. The hospital said it would cost too much money to train another replacement and they intended to wait until the original nurse returned from home.

I had to get up at 5 a.m., three times a week, to make an 80-mile round trip. I did this from October to January. I would have had to do it to March but the hospital was forced to back down and finally brought in another nurse.

This is a terrible way to treat people who are sick or who are already taxed. Services and people we need are being cut all over the place. At this point, I'd do anything to get the health-care system straightened out.[92]

In this Ontario example, priority was given to efficiency, and efficiency was defined primarily in market terms. The decisions about treatment were made primarily on the basis of a single test and knowledge about money, not knowledge about health, an assessment of the whole person, or a discussion with the patient about the particular situation. But health care does not operate on the same principles as the production of goods, as this patient makes clear. Patients are variable; risks are different; and a whole, thinking, feeling person, not a mechanical part, is at stake.

Nor are people simply non-responsive objects, like chocolates in a factory. A Newfoundland health-care worker explained that:

We have people coming in for diagnostic workups. Often they're discharged back to their homes two, three, four hours away, with no results. This means that one month later, they have to make the same car ride back to hear the results. In many cases, that's a month of hard waiting.[93]

The wait, especially in the absence of contact from the doctor or hospital, can easily create stress levels that lower the immune system, increasing the likelihood of illness or of deterioration in those already ill. Moreover, while waiting for the diagnosis, the person may be spreading a disease to others and, in the process, not only risking their own health but also adding to the costs in the system. Even when a diagnosis is available, people may be sent away with illnesses that constitute a hazard to others, especially if they alone are responsible for ensuring their own treatment. The increase in outpatient services may well be a factor in the re-emergence of old communicable diseases. People with tuberculosis, for example, may forget to take their medicine. They may not understand the importance of taking their medicine and of avoiding practices that increase the risk to others. Outpatient services offer little opportunity to ensure that patients follow through on advice or to base advice on knowledge of whole people in the context of their particular circumstances.

Similar problems develop with those who have day surgery. Take the case of a woman who had a sinus operation:

> My doctor booked me for day surgery for a sinus operation. It was supposed to be real easy. 'No big procedure, no big problem,' the doctor said. In fact, I was scheduled to return to work the following day.
>
> Anyway, I went to the hospital at 2 p.m. and was given a general. I woke up at five p.m. It was like a minute. I came to; they were trying to push me out. I can tell you, I felt awful; dizzy, feverish, not really alert and sick from the anaesthetic. There was a kind of commotion on the floor. They were trying to get everyone up and dressed and out because it was the end of the day and they were trying to clear the surgery.
>
> I told the nurse I wasn't feeling well. But I was handed my dentures and told to go home and rest. They hadn't taken my blood pressure or temperature or anything, so how did they know I was okay to go? My partner was concerned and asked shouldn't I be checked by a doctor before I left. But he was told there was no doctor there because it was day surgery and we were supposed to be out, never mind our conditions.
>
> On my way home, only about an hour later, I started really feeling ill. I figure I was just beginning to go into shock because my partner said I wasn't making sense. The bandage around my nose was drenched with blood. I was dizzy and felt kind of clumsy. My partner drove me as fast as he could to another hospital. I was in shock by the time I got there from the blood loss, so they admitted me immediately. They had to pull all the packing out and cauterize the right side of the nose.
>
> Being treated like a piece of meat—so brutally when you are so vulnerable— has left my nerves in a terrible state. It has actually scared the hell out of me. You know, it's like you really don't matter. Day surgery has its rules and if you don't heal like you're supposed to, well that's too bad. You're out the door anyway. Never mind if you live or die or get really sick. Never mind. It's the rules.
>
> This has triggered so many bad memories for me, so much stuff from my past. I haven't been able to go back to work. I feel absolutely that they can't treat anyone like this. It's wrong. It's terrible medicine. It's leaving people scarred.[94]

Day surgery means that nurses do not have the time the night before to prepare people for surgery, to tell them what to expect during and after surgery. They do not have the time to get to know the patients and to take their particular concerns and physiology into account. Instead, a number of people are admitted together and are often lined up on an assembly line of gurneys waiting for the move to surgery. In the waiting room outside the day surgery, we could not help but overhear a young woman telling the complete stranger next to her about her fears concerning the approaching surgery. She knew nothing about what to expect, she was afraid of surgery and of its consequences. She had not told her mother about the surgery because she knew her mother was opposed to such interventions. Her only source of information and assurance was another patient she did not know, because there were no staff people in the waiting room. An Ontario clerical worker interviewed for a study of changes in health-care work recounted a similar story, this one about a woman who had just been informed by a doctor and nurse, who then had to rush away, that she had cancer: 'She had just been told and she broke down crying and the housekeeper that was cleaning up went over and she said, "Do you want a hug? Should you . . ." This from a housekeeper. There is no time for compassion.'[95] This may be why 30 per cent of Ontario patients surveyed said they did not have a better understanding of their condition when they left the hospital than when they arrived.[96]

Speed becomes the priority and quality gets defined in terms of how quickly the process is done. In Prince Edward Island, workers report there is an admission form designed to be completed in 10 minutes by the patient alone. While few people want to spend hours waiting for admission or doing paperwork, admission is much more than simply a bureaucratic necessity. People being admitted to hospitals are often frightened and alone. The quick form leaves no time for discussion with the patient or even much human contact. In the frightening aftermath of both cutting and chemicals, patients are left to friends, relatives, or even other patients rather than to skilled personnel for support and treatment. Many still require a great deal of what even within this medical model is defined as necessary care. What was previously provided by paid and trained staff working in the hospital is now left to be provided by unpaid and untrained people in the home. Meanwhile, the stress levels resulting from this strategy can mean additional time lost from work, additional income lost, and additional health problems for the patients and for their families.

Like shorter hospital stays, outpatient services and day surgery have been made possible by new techniques and often reflect patient preferences. While the new techniques allow people to be sent home, they have not eliminated the need for skilled care. Money is saved, in the short term, by transferring the caring work to the home. Although new technologies and patient preferences are factors in these new services, the strategies are primarily driven by demand to reduce costs in individual hospitals, not by new technologies, patient preferences, or knowledge of the determinants of health. Based on a medical model and methods taken from the for-profit sector, too often these strategies leave people without skilled assistance, fail to take individual circumstances, cultural practices, and physiologies into account and, as a result, may in the long term mean higher costs for the system as a whole as well as for individuals. Women in particular bear the burden of these higher costs.

3. Cutting Beds and Cutting Staff

Fewer beds mean there is pressure to avoid or delay admittance except for the most complicated cases and to release people as soon as the specific treatment is done. Indeed, this is the intent. However, it does not necessarily guarantee either that the people who are admitted are the most in need or that they receive appropriate care. The number of beds tells us very little about the quality of care or about the health of the population. The use of beds is related much more to the way doctors practise and managers manage than it is to the existence of the beds. Given that doctors determine who enters and leaves a hospital, it would seem much more appropriate to begin with the way doctors diagnose and treat than with some formula for the adequate number of beds or by simply closing beds based on the need to save money. If there are fewer beds, but these are always filled, and filled by people with the most complicated problems involving the most expensive services, the savings may not even be that great because each patient needs more care and because turnover itself creates additional costs.

At the same time, the cuts can mean that the care for those who do fill the beds is inadequate in the terms defined by the determinants of health. An Ontario worker explained how the bed shortages mean that people are pushed out the door before they are ready to go:

> What complicates the system at times is we still have a patient in the bed, [we're] trying to get them up for discharge and out the door, but [for] some reason, they're not feeling well, or they're elderly, or they're slow. And they're trying to get out of bed. We're having somebody that is ready to get into that bed. So that part can be very stressful at times, because you're always feeling you're rushing the patient. Like hurry up and get out of here because there's somebody getting into your bed. And some patients feel very upset that they're being pushed like this.[97]

Being pushed out the door of a hospital is not like being asked to leave your hotel room after checkout time. Few people want to hang around simply to enjoy the luxury of it all. Those who resist leaving often have a very good health reason for doing so. And the rushing may increase the health risks for the patient. Being pushed out the door may be particularly traumatic for those who have difficulty understanding English or French, are far from home, or have no home to go to or relatives to help when they get there. One Newfoundland health-care worker described how this happens in her hospital:

> When there are no beds left on our unit and we have to admit someone from emergency, we have to send one of our patients to another unit. Often times, the doctor doesn't follow the patient to the new unit and he loses continuity of care. With the pressures to discharge early, he may find himself home alone, very sick.[98]

Another claimed that four-bed wards now have five beds squished in and many private rooms have become semi-private. When relatives are allowed to visit at all hours and are encouraged to provide part of the care, then wards become obstacle courses for patients and for those providing the care. Such crowding not only eliminates privacy for those in pain and for those dealing with traumatic experiences before and after surgery; it also makes the sleep that is essential to recovery difficult if not impossible. Moreover, it increases the risk to patients whose immune systems are already weak. They risk infection from these visitors and from other patients. This is particularly the case if cutbacks in beds mean that people with a variety of illnesses are put in the same room, or in the same hallway as they wait for a room to become available. One man in the Caledon project reported that his father, suffering from a stroke, was first kept in emergency and then moved to the maternity ward.[99]

Decision-makers recognize that it makes more sense to develop overall plans for integrated services among hospitals than it does simply to reduce beds in each hospital. But closing or amalgamating hospitals with this medical model in mind does not necessarily provide the most useful health care. Rationalizing services on the basis of market strategies can simply serve to make the problems more widespread, because health care is not a business like the rest. Too often, the result is less continuity of care, less response to individual differences, less time to take the whole person into account, less support from relatives and friends who cannot travel the distances to specialized facilities. At the same time, it may well mean more emphasis on cuts and chemicals, on tests, on turnover, and on centralized decision-making based on concern with costs, not health. According to Markham and Lomas, no empirical evidence demonstrates economic, quality, or human resource gains with multi-hospital arrangements, and some evidence suggests that costs will increase, flexibility and responsiveness to individual needs will decline, and relationships with employees will deteriorate.[100] Amalgamated hospital networks are nonetheless now the norm.

The combination of more rationalized services and restrictions on admittance necessitated by reductions in hospital beds means that only those cases defined as the most severe are admitted and that care is provided farther from home. Under such conditions, people are most in need of the kind of social and psychological support that relatives can provide: such support is often critical to the immune system and to recovery. Yet the more services are centralized and rationalized into specialized facilities, the more difficult it is for relatives and friends to travel the distances to provide such support.[101] Patients, too, have to travel farther for specialized outpatient services. Doctors also have farther to travel in order to treat their hospital patients. In provinces with very small populations, such as Prince Edward Island, regionalization could mean that some services move out of the province altogether.

And cutbacks in staff too often mean that the health-care workers have no time to offer such support. A member of the nursing staff in Prince Edward Island described the problem as follows:

> I go in and take blood pressure and temps and I have to look through a patient. If the patient wants to ask you a question, or wants [you] to stop and talk to them, you have to say, 'I'm sorry. I'll have to get back to you.' You know though that you won't and you can't.[102]

Speaking from the other side of the bed, a BC nurse reported that 'nobody checked my incision. I never got water', confirming what other nurses experienced as 'you can't do this because they're telling you you've got only five minutes to do this, and this and this'.[103] As another explained, 'You hit that ward at a run, and you're always having to say to people, "I haven't got time to do that" and it's a horrible way to nurse'.[104]

With significant reductions in the number of hospital workers, the remaining staff have to focus on doing the most obvious of the treatment procedures, those defined as necessary in the medical model. Specific, fragmented tasks are more and more of what is counted as care. Too often even the basics cannot be fitted into increasingly tight schedules, although these basics are recognized as critical to recovery and the maintenance of health. There is less time for what are increasingly seen as extras such as chatting, comforting, or even informing and cleaning the floor.

With fewer staff, hospitals rely more on technology to do the work. People who are frightened about their physical state are too often left alone with a machine they are unable to talk with, interpret, or control. Fetal monitors, for example, are used to justify fewer nurses in the maternity ward. As one woman explained in a letter to the *Toronto Star*:

> I would have been grateful for a nurse constantly providing me one-on-one care than to have sat alone strapped to that frightful monitor blinking and spitting out graph paper.
> I needed a caring person to make me feel safe, not a machine.[105]

A BC nurse, a patient herself, found that patient-controlled analgesics meant 'you see the nurse even less to get anything for pain 'cause you're doing your own pain control. . . . It's scary'—even for a nurse who understands when medication is safe.[106]

A caring person is not simply a luxury item, a frill that should be eliminated in a truly efficient system. A caring person, as we know from the determinants of health research, can be critical to recovery. Machines are incapable of providing social support and of taking the whole person into account. They are designed to focus on specific body functions and to provide measurements. They cannot report how a person feels or assess the total combination of responses of an individual patient. Indeed, because the machines can measure only specific kinds of responses, they may provide inadequate or even inaccurate information.

Increasingly, relatives are expected to take up the slack when machines cannot do the work. But not only are fewer relatives available, especially with the majority of women in the labour force and with more regional hospitals serving wider geographical areas, but also these relatives do not have the specialized skills needed to deal with the technology. At best, often all they can do is become advocates for the patient and this possibility may be limited for those who cannot easily communicate in English or French. The consequences may be that those without such advocates receive even less care, especially as cutbacks increase. And more and more, even advocacy does little good. An Ontario woman recovering from a partial hysterectomy reports that, when no one came to help with her promised shower, she decided to take one herself. Her bandages got wet but no one answered the bell to deal with the problem.

> So that's how my husband found me five hours later; sitting there with wet bandages. He couldn't get anyone to help so he removed the bandages himself to see what was going on. And what was going on was I was extremely red, not just around the incision but all up the abdomen, almost to the belly button. Again, he couldn't get anyone's attention. He went looking for the cleaning cart himself. I was getting sicker and I was so disoriented, I couldn't think. I had a massive infection but there was no one who came to help me. They were all too busy.[107]

She was sent home with medication for pain and an antibiotic for infection. When the infection got worse, she was readmitted to the hospital. Her readmission is not simply an additional financial cost but also a health cost for her and her family.

Many of the earliest cuts were made among the non-nursing staff. Dietary aides provide just one example. A Newfoundland hospital worker said they are allotted just 10 minutes to feed patients. 'If the tray comes back untouched because nobody had time to feed the patient, I know we've left them hungry.'[108] Yet food, as is clear from the determinants of health research, is critical to recovery from illness and to resistance to disease. Indeed, patients who do not eat may spend longer in the hospital and thus increase expenses.

Similar problems are reported in terms of bathing, another task that may be defined as non-medical and therefore considered reducible to a quick physical act or eliminated entirely. In Quebec in the early 1980s, the new formula for allocating nursing time assigned 20 minutes for the task of giving a partial bath. While this did not necessarily mean that this was the exact amount of time devoted to the job, it was the formula used to calculate the amount of nursing time needed on each ward. A decade later, the Principal Nursing Officer for Canada explained that some formulas allow only six or seven minutes for a total bath. But, as she went on to explain, the time it takes for a bath varies considerably from person to person:

> But the patient happens to have a heart attack or maybe has had a stroke or maybe has arthritis or something and doesn't move as quickly in and out of bed as you and I might. I have to help the person get him into a chair, hope and pray that nobody else is in the shower at the time and I don't have to wait, get him in, get him washed and dried or whatever, get him dressed, back in the chair, back up to the bed. . . . Well, I suggest that even the Holy Ghost couldn't do it in six minutes unless you lifted the patient out, put him in a chair, hosed him down, let him drip dry and then put him back in.[109]

Baths also involve much more than keeping people presentable. Especially for people who are in bed all or most of the day, often in diapers, baths help prevent infection, bed sores, and other kinds of rashes. As a BC nurse explained, 'when a registered nurse is doing a bed bath, that supposedly menial chore, that nurse is doing a head to toe assessment.'[110] Moreover, baths can allow time to comfort, console, and support. Yet baths are increasingly assigned low priority. Returning to the hospital with an infection resulting from earlier surgery, an Ontario woman claims that:

> Anyway, during this stay in the hospital, they never washed me. They didn't help feed me, even though I couldn't feed myself. My husband had to do all that and provide all the care. And everything was not clean. This used to be a clean hospital. But staffing was cut so bad. There was just not enough people.[111]

According to a member of a Nova Scotia hospital nursing staff, children in particular are victims of bed cutbacks and staff cutbacks combined. Neither strategy necessarily eliminates work. They often simply mean staff members work harder and leave more work undone. As a result, there is enormous stress on patients, staff, and relatives, especially female relatives.

> I can take you right now to an adult floor and show you three kids lying, sick, in an adult ward. Their mother can stay with them. They are given a cot or a lounge chair. And then they can cut back on nursing staff. The mother is there to do it. Especially if the child is really sick. . . . The hospital says to the parent, 'You can come in any time' and the parents have to, because there's such a cutback in staff. . . . Kids can't fight for themselves, and parents want to take care of them. So they're an easy target for bed and staff cutbacks.[112]

An Ontario woman's story of her experience with these cutbacks places the consequences in sharp relief.

> My son had acute lymphatic leukemia. When he was first diagnosed, treatment was good. But over the past two years, there have been many dramatic changes in the way children with cancer are treated, so dramatically different that I'm afraid and I'm angry. It's just too much. I'm not the only mother who feels like this—there are many of us. Government cuts for our kids mean the difference between life and a cemetery plot.
>
> Everything is wrong now, for instance, the ratio of nursing staff to the number of patients means that children in very desperate circumstances can't get the help they need. Once there were six to eight RNs on the floor; now there are two or three. What do you think that means in terms of their ability to respond? I'll tell you. It means, for example, that nurses often can't get the electronic devices that calculate the amount of IV going through. That IV can have chem drugs in it, or blood, or other medication. Since there are too few nurses, our kids are being asked to alert the nurses when the IVs needed to be turned off. As parents, we didn't think that was too safe, so we set up a system to relieve each other. We've had to take up 80 to 90 per cent of the other tasks as well that include feeding, bathing, doing beds, cleaning. One boy's mother worked twelve-hour shifts. . . . How do you think it made her feel to worry about whether her son was being looked after when she wasn't there? And how much pressure in terms of extra workload can a person be expected to bear? Bell lights are often ignored because the RNs just can't get there. And these are real emergencies. There are just not enough RNs, RPNs, housekeeping or anyone else to do the jobs.

There used to be a team in housekeeping. Now there's one per shift. It's just not physically possible for them to push all those beds and clean all those rooms. But it's imperative that rooms are clean. Our kids are like AIDS patients. They have absolutely no resistance, nothing to fight off an infection with. They don't need to be exposed to anything more.

It's bad enough what's happening when my son is in hospital. But it's also an ordeal to get him admitted in the first place. There have been some high penalties paid by children for this new admitting policy. Our kids have to be sicker, even in more acute condition, before they'll get a bed. Often there's an 11- or 12-hour wait in emergency. Parents often give their kids Tylenol so they won't convulse while they're waiting. But Tylenol can also mask symptoms. If the special room for children with cancer is full (it can hold two to three), then we have to wait with the general population in emergency. Can you imagine children waiting for this length of time? And in addition, if they have to wait in the general area, they may be exposed to even more germs. It wasn't like this two years ago.

You'd think the hospital and the government would see what the impact is on our children and would try to rectify the situation. But they seem even more determined to cut back further. Now they're phasing out IV teams on the pediatric ward. The Hickman and Port-Cath devices require sterile technique and a lot of experience. If something goes wrong—and it has—it's fatal. Now they are planning on having already overworked RNs do this procedure. IV teams are our lifeline—they're that important. But they will become a thing of the past.[113]

With no time to handle even the most critical tasks, there can be little time to move away from cure. As one member of the Prince Edward Island nursing staff made clear, 'There's no way you can do the preventative work with patients. You simply have no time to spend with them. We hear all this stuff about prevention and promotion. You have no time to do it.'[114] These concerns were echoed by BC nurses, who said they do not even have time to do the preventative strategies such as washing their hands, that are so obviously critical to prevention.[115]

While bed and staff cutbacks may save money in the short run, they can mean both that patients suffer more and that long-term costs are greater. A comparative study of adequately staffed and understaffed wards indicated that 'patients on the understaffed units had a higher incidence of complications.' They had higher rates of infections, heart conditions, and gastrointestinal disorders. And, 'most importantly, patients on the understaffed unit had longer lengths of stay (LOS) than on the appropriately staffed unit.'[116] Without care, as opposed to simply treatment, people very often get sicker and therefore cost the system more in the long run.

4. Contracting Out

Increasingly, hospitals are contracting out services to private, for-profit companies. A major justification for contracting out is the assumption that the private sector is more efficient and effective. Little evidence supports such claims; indeed, there is strong evidence to suggest that for-profit health care is less efficient and effective. In the United States, where for-profit care is more the norm, hospital administrative costs 'are twice as high as are those in Canada.'[117] At the same time, there is every indication that Canadian standards of care compare quite favourably with those in the United States.

Equally important to contracting out is the notion that some services in health care are exactly like those in the private sector. With the medical model in mind, only those jobs directly related to cuts and chemicals get defined as medical jobs that require special skills related to helping people through treatment and recovery. The rest are classified as non-medical and therefore best suited to the application of market principles. At the same time, market principles are also increasingly being applied to skills defined as medical.

Not surprising, the services most likely to be contracted out are food, laundry, and cleaning, those increasingly described as 'hotel services'. Categorizing these as hotel services simultaneously justifies contracting them out and charging fees for them. Yet we know, from determinants-of-health research, that food and clean environments are critical to health. They are even more critical in a hospital setting where germs are more plentiful and dangerous, where waste is an even greater health hazard, where special diets are not only desirable but essential to recovery and resistance, and where many need to be tempted to eat and cannot feed themselves. Contracting out services can mean that profit is the primary goal and that the determinants of health have low or no priority. Indeed, the cleaning and food firms are likely to apply the same techniques used in hotels and offices, where nutrition and sterile conditions are less critical for survival. As Martin explains in his book, *In The Public Interest? Privatisation and Public Sector Reform*, there is a 'climate in which the ability of firms to cut costs came to be regarded as more important than their suitability to carry out the service'.[118]

What gets eliminated first by such firms is social and psychological support. A dietary worker in Newfoundland, now employed by a firm contracted to provide food in pediatrics, reported that 'We aren't allowed to bring coffee or tea to the families of dying children anymore. [The company] won't allow it.' Similarly, a Saskatchewan employee of a contract firm was reprimanded and threatened with firing for providing coffee to the wife and children of a seriously ill patient.[119] Food, too, may be treated differently. Another Newfoundland worker complained that, with contracting out, 'There's no nutrition in the nutritional night-time snack anymore.'[120]

Contracting out may not only alter the quality of service; it may also serve in the long run to increase costs. Initial bids for services may be low, but once hospitals have eliminated their own means of offering the services they may be at the mercy of the firms providing the contracted-out services. Workers in Ontario, for instance, explained that the laundry had been closed and the contract for diapers given to a firm selling disposables. Once the old cloth diapers and the laundry that cleaned them disappeared, the hospital then had little choice but to pay the higher price now being demanded for disposables. Promises for savings on food have not materialized either. 'Since switching from conventional to cook-chill and shared food production [precooked foods and centalized food production], Toronto Hospital has had its first ever deficit in its dietary budget'.[121]

But the 'hotel services' are not the only ones contracted out. Laboratory services are increasingly handed over to for-profit labs, even though one study revealed that the costs were 34 per cent higher than in the public hospital lab and that the services were less comprehensive and less accessible in terms of hours.[122] Indeed, a number of studies suggest that money could best be saved by having the public sector take over the private labs.[123] The management of hospitals has also been contracted out, again based on the twin assumptions that private, for-profit companies are more efficient and that managing a hospital has little to do with knowledge about what makes people sick or well. This, of course, assumes that hospitals are simply businesses like the rest and that the delivery of care is separable from the management of care. According to the president of one contracting firm, there are 'two main reasons hospitals and other institutions turn to contract management services. . . . They want satisfactory quality of service and they want better value for their dollar.'[124] What this too often means, as one Newfoundland hospital worker put it, is that the 'caring institution is being replaced by the money-making corporation.'[125]

What is considered efficient in the short-term reduction of costs in for-profit companies may not be effective in terms of health or costs over a longer period. For example, a hospital maintenance worker was told to stop changing light bulbs on a rotation basis because this was too expensive. Instead, light bulbs would be changed only when they blew out. As a result, this worker found himself changing a bulb during an operation, risking the patient's well-being, and wasting the time of some very expensive personnel who had to wait for the new bulb. In another hospital, management decided to change from linen to disposable drapes to cover patients in the operating room because this would save laundry costs. But the drapes were so light, they could fly off the patient whenever a door was opened or a draft created in the operating room.[126]

Contracting out services may save money in the short term, but this may also mean poor-quality service and service defined strictly in terms of money. In the long term, hospitals may find themselves with reduced services but higher costs both in terms of what they actually pay for services and in terms of patient health.

5. Standardization

Reflecting the new concern with efficiency and effectiveness defined in management terms is the new stress on formulas and evidence-based decision-making intended to standardize care. There is a growing concern with measuring 'quality' in terms of outcomes and setting out care pathways for providers to follow. And outcomes are often defined in the terms of shorter stays, increased turnover, greater use of outpatient services, and reduced expenditures. To reach these outcomes, there is an increasing interest in developing a formula for a typical length of stay for patients and for what happens during that stay based on the lowest possible time it takes parts to be fixed. There is also increasing pressure for the development of formulas to assess doctors' diagnoses and other treatments.

The Hospital Medical Records Institute (HMRI), for example, 'a non-profit, non-government, federally-chartered company that specializes in the provision of health care information services',[127] uses five broad categories of discharges to establish a 'Case Mix Group' average length of stay. The categories that form the basis of this Case Mix Group are 'typical' patients, deaths, transfers, outliers (basically those falling outside the average), and sign-outs. But the focus is on the typical patient in order to move towards 'homogeneity of length of stay'.[128] Quoting from an article entitled 'The Case for Using Industrial Quality Management Science in Health Care Organizations', HMRI claims that the 'elimination of unnecessary variation in clinical practice may similarly improve the quality of care.'[129] Quality is defined mainly in terms of the extent to which everyone is treated the same. According to HMRI, the 'analysis of variation in health care' is at the top of the agenda.[130] Similarly, the Institute for Clinical Evaluative Sciences has produced 'Practice Atlases' that record significant variations in surgical procedures, office visits, and diagnosis among Ontario doctors.[131] The implication of collecting such data is that variation should be eliminated. As Philip Hassen, then president of St Joseph's Health Centre in London, Ontario, put it, the focus is to be 'quality care based in data'.[132] The aim is to standardize the way all patients are treated.

Certainly it is useful to have such data. They can help hospitals and governments plan for the future. And certainly evidence is essential; it is, after all, the basis on which doctors and others should assess their overall practices. But such data also have severe limitations and run the risk of misuse, especially when the medical model, cost reduction, and market strategies dominate planning.

First, the data are primarily about the overall patterns, not about individuals or contexts.[133] As we noted earlier, overall patterns indicate that the most effective strategy for a healthy population is to focus on promotion and prevention, but individuals still get sick and need health care. Similarly, overall patterns in treatment can help guide planning for populations, but those who are treated within the system are unique individuals. Elimination of variation may be the best strategy when chocolates are being made but this is not the case when individuals are being treated. As we have seen, medicine is an art as well as a science. Single causes and single solutions cannot be scientifically determined for whole people. And people do not come in standard packages with standard responses. Pregnancy or breast cancer, for instance, is not precisely the same from woman to woman. In fact, no two pregnancies or breast cancers even in the same woman are exactly the same. The variation results not only from their individual physiology and the changes in this physiology over time, but also from individual social, environmental, and psychological conditions. Culture, race, gender, and power all play roles. As one woman interviewed for a study of minority women explained: 'I'm a different person, this is a different child, it's a different labour'.[134] And each patient is now more likely to differ from others as hospital admissions are increasingly being restricted to the most complicated cases.

The story told by one Ontario patient illustrates the problem with translating data on 'typical' patients into practices on how long people are allowed to stay in the hospital.

> I had an operation to remove the lower bowel because it had ruptured. After three weeks in the hospital, I was in terrible condition. I was feeling sick. And the pain—it was so severe that I was bringing up from it. I was wishing I could die to get out of it. . . .
> They wanted to discharge me but everything still hurt. I was still weak, weak, weak and there was something wrong. But never mind. They were telling me I was fine and it was time for me to go home. I was so sick on that day that I couldn't hold my head up, couldn't get out of bed or get dressed and I was heaving on and off.

She was sent home but a month later she was taken to emergency with a massive infection resulting from a suture. She had a second operation and a long recovery.

> I still feel terrible and I'm angry. Just because you can't heal as quickly as they think you should doesn't mean that you should be treated like this. They just want you out, out, out. They don't listen to you when you say you're still sick and they won't take you seriously to find out what's the matter because they just want your bed. It doesn't make sense if I had to stay in hospital longer the second time around.[135]

Second, there are problems with the data that are collected. Most commonly, they record how many people are processed, not how well individuals are when they leave and how well they remain after release. The limited data on readmission and recovery, such as those produced by the Manitoba Centre for Health Policy and Evaluation, follow only some patients and does so for only a short period of time. Midas may well have better data on the number of customers who return as a result of unsatisfactory work on their mufflers than hospitals do on how many unsatisfied and unhealthy patients are released.

Moreover, what gets measured during the hospital stay is what can be easily measured. This usually means tasks that are directly defined as medical treatment. The number of surgery hours and the number of chemicals given are much more likely to be counted than are comfort, social support, or lasting relief. These figures are primarily about tasks rather than health and are definitely not about health promotion. Furthermore, there are few long-term follow-up studies in Canada to determine what happens to patients after release. We are only now learning about how well people are after treatment by day surgery, outpatient clinics, or short hospital stays because outcome has been primarily defined in terms of release from the hospital, in terms of immediate hospital costs, or in terms of death or readmission within a short period of time.

Patient satisfaction surveys provide some indication of how patients experience care but they are unlikely to assess the health of patients adequately. The usefulness of the data depends on what questions are asked, how they are asked, what alternative responses are offered, and how the data are assessed, as well as on patients' perception of who will be influenced or harmed by the results. They also depend on the language used, especially in a multilingual country like Canada. Satisfaction studies usually claim to show satisfaction, primarily because of the methodology. The design of the questionnaire and the way data are analyzed may encourage positive results. But because the results are given as numbers and defined as scientific, they are often taken as accurate measures. When satisfaction studies use interviews, the rate of satisfaction often drops considerably.[136]

Third, these facts do not speak for themselves. Much depends not only on the design and analysis but also on what is done with the data. Indeed, different research designs can lead to different results. For example, a Saskatchewan study of home care concluded that patients were often better off without home care, while a BC study found that removing home care 'represents a shortening of the quality of life for a significant proportion of people'.[137] Similarly, shorter hospital stays are not necessarily a demonstration of either improved efficiency or effectiveness. As indicated above, they do not even necessarily indicate cost savings in the long run. Shorter stays could represent inadequate care rather than improved quality; low readmission rates could themselves simply hide greater reliance on other services such as home care. And variability in surgical rates does not necessarily mean that doctors are not applying the appropriate treatment. They may not only reflect variability among patients' bodies and social situations but also the fact that medicine is not and cannot be an exact science.

There is no single, appropriate treatment and cure for most health problems. The attempt to eliminate variability is based on the assumption that these facts do speak for themselves and that medicine is, or at least could be, an exact science that can be managed by numbers. Although the data can contribute to overall planning, translating them into standardized procedures for individuals ignores both the variability among people and the fact that much of medicine is not about the simple application of scientifically demonstrated procedures. At the present time, this is more a risk than a current consequence of new managerial practices combined with an emphasis on evidence-based decision-making, but it is still a risk. In the United States, however, managed care organizations have used such data as the basis for authorizing tests and admissions as well as for retrospective denial of what are determined on this basis to be unnecessary services.[138] Accounting rules take precedence over physicians' assessments of individual needs.

6. Deinstitutionalization
Most hospitals treat acutely ill or injured patients. In hospitals that offer rehabilitation and in long-term psychiatric services or chronic care, similar cost-

cutting strategies are also being used. Beds and staff have been cut, entire facilities closed, and some services contracted out. In addition, governments are seeking to move people out of the institutions into other residential care facilities or into the community.

This deinstitutionalization strategy is, of course, not new. When the move towards deinstitutionalization began in the psychiatric hospitals in the early 1970s, it was justified in a variety of ways.[139] First, new drugs and changing attitudes in the general population allowed people to leave the institutions. Second, the move would allow people to become more independent, to live more dignified lives, and to be better integrated into the community. Third, it was what people wanted. Fourth, it would save money. The same justifications are being used today to further cut back on the number of patients admitted to long-term psychiatric services and to reduce the numbers in extended and rehabilitative care.

Certainly there is a great deal of support for such claims. In large part because care is based on the medical model in these institutions as well, patients have often found the institutions less than satisfactory. Those in extended care, for whom there was no quick treatment or cure, frequently received only the minimum of custodial care and were often given little privacy or social support. With cutbacks, conditions are deteriorating further. Those in psychiatric facilities too often had iatrogenic effects from their aggressive treatments, were offered little independence, and were severely restricted in terms of space and social contacts. It is not surprising, then, that many have indicated that they would prefer to be out of the institution and others would prefer to remain as long as possible in their own homes. Care at home or in the community could mean greater independence, more social support, and improved chances for health promotion and the prevention of illness and injury.

Although it was justified and supported on other grounds, deinstitutionalization was and is mainly about saving money. One psychiatrist explained:

> We began reading Erving Goffman and Ernest Gruenberg from New York State and how hospitals screw people up. So we took tens of thousands of patients and threw them out of the hospital without any support system. We said we were going to follow up, but the fact of the matter is nobody really understood, so the bureaucrats were delighted to get them out of the hospital.[140]

The promised community support system never materialized. Ontario research indicated that many of those released lived in deplorable conditions and many ended up back in the institution because there was no co-ordinated system of support.[141] Similar patterns are evident today. As a result, the potential for better health is not being realized.

In moving people out of institutions, governments acknowledged the complaints about how the institutions worked. While governments and institutions have responded to pressure for some patient rights such as refusal of treatment and informed consent, the reforms do not address the larger, structural problems within the institutions. Instead, deinstitutionalization has primarily meant less of the same or worse. Cutting staff, closing beds, and increasing the emphasis on a particular medical model often intensify the worst aspects of the system. Those in extended care may get more drugs, fewer baths, and less time to be fed; those in psychiatric institutions too often receive more chemicals and have less freedom and less time to discuss their problems. As was the case when deinstitutionalization began in the early seventies, governments are increasingly talking about care as a community and private responsibility.

At the same time, those who want and need hospital care find it more difficult to get admitted. Here, too, the data on overall preferences and patterns are used to justify the reduction in service and to deny admittance to individuals. Yet mothers of schizophrenics may find they cannot get their adult children into the hospital when they fear their children are about to have a violent episode; those caring for the sick elderly find their relatives put on long waiting lists; rehabilitation patients may find themselves at home long before they feel confident on crutches.

As is the case when people are sent home early from acute-care hospitals, seen as outpatients, or treated in day surgery, the need for care does not disappear with release from the institution. Although the process is described as sending people back to the community, this community largely exists in the imagination of those justifying the policy. In most cases, back to the community means shifting responsibility to women who do the unpaid caring work in their own homes or the unpaid caring work as volunteers in the homes of others and in community centres. Women account for two-thirds of volunteers providing care and companionship and of those distributing food or other items.[142] And they constitute three-quarters of those volunteers who prepare and serve food. In their own homes women do almost all this work.[143] But most women are already overburdened with paid jobs and domestic work. Few have the time and even fewer have the skills to provide the kinds of long-term care required by those who are deinstitutionalized. As a result, care may be inadequate or even dangerous.

This is not sending the care back to the community, for such care has never been primarily provided in the community. In the past, most of the elderly who were very ill and most of those with severe disabilities did not survive. Many of those who did were cared for in institutions. Deinstitutionalization mainly means a privatization of care rather than an elimination of the need for care. It shifts the caring work out of the public sector and primarily into the hands of women.

LONG-TERM CARE FACILITIES

When governments talk of releasing people from acute-care facilities, they do not always mean simply sending them home. The number of people in hospitals has also been reduced by shifting patients into residential care facilities or what is increasingly called long-term care.

There have been residential care facilities in Canada since the founding of the nation. They became increasingly specialized over the years, with facilities for those defined as psychiatrically disabled, developmentally delayed, emotionally disturbed, and suffering with drug addictions. Together, such specialized facilities accounted in 1990 for just over half of all residential care facilities in Canada but for only a quarter of all approved beds in residential care. The overwhelming majority of long-term care residents were in homes for the aged and nursing homes.[144] However, the various reform strategies have blurred the distinctions among these facilities. There are fewer specialized facilities so that long-term care has become the more appropriate name for all residential care. Equally important, the distinction between hospital and long-term care has also become increasingly blurred as more of those requiring complex care are sent to such facilities.

Long-term care facilities differ from acute-care hospitals in at least four ways. First, their principal purpose is to provide custodial care rather than treatment. They are primarily intended to maintain people rather than to cure them, although this distinction itself is based on a particular medical model. Second, many more of them are private, for-profit institutions. Third, they are less expensive to operate, which is one of the reasons governments want to shift as much care as possible to them. Fourth, they can charge patients for many services. The shift to long-term care, then, is a form of privatization in two senses: more of the services are provided in private, for-profit facilities and more of them are paid for by the patient. Long-term care facilities are not only cheaper to operate but also cost governments less because patients pay more.

However, the move to the for-profit sector does not mean that governments no longer pay for services. Even if the facility is operated for profit, governments still pay a large share of patient costs. Public, non-profit, and for-profit facilities all use public monies and all can charge for some aspects of their services. Frequently, public payment for private service includes a profit for the organization providing care.

Long-term care is much cheaper than hospital care and only half as expensive as chronic-care services.[145] But the lower costs cannot be attributed to greater efficiency in the profit-making institutions. As an Ontario Conservative Minister of Health explained in 1969, experience with for-profit nursing homes demonstrated 'that they are concerned about one thing only, making as much money as possible and giving as little as possible in return to the patients.' He went on to argue that the 'sooner this is gotten into on a public basis, the sooner we will be able to provide good quality care for this segment of our population'.[146] While little research has been done to compare for-profit and not-for-profit services in this area, some evidence indicates that the for-profit facilities are less efficient and effective than the public and non-profit private ones. In her study of Ontario nursing homes, Tarman concludes that 'the private sector, especially the for-profit, is the least likely to provide services that are equally accessible, fully accountable and of good quality.'[147] More recent and more systematic data are hard to find, however, in part because the for-profit facilities claim that confidentiality is necessary to maintain competition. Nevertheless, more and more care is being provided by for-profit firms.

Costs are lower than in hospitals in large measure because of the assumptions built into long-term care. Those who are defined as subject to quick improvement and cure are mainly admitted to the hospitals, where a wide range of technologies and treatments is applied. And those applying the treatments and tests are defined as highly skilled medical workers. The rest are sent home or, if they cannot survive outside an institution, are admitted to long-term care facilities. Doctors are seldom present, on the assumption that much of the care is custodial. Significantly fewer registered nurses are employed, and more people without formal training provide care. Indeed, Ontario has removed both the requirement that each nursing home patient receive a minimum of 2.5 hours of nursing care a day and that at least one RN be on the premises.[148]

However, reforms now mean that what was previously defined as acute care is increasingly required in these facilities. As one provider explained, patients now have catheters and colonoscopies, oxygen masks and IVs. 'We never used to have any like that. They weren't allowed to bring them in.'[149] Moreover, a growing number have dementia or Alzheimer's, often combined with other more physical problems. A majority require what is defined as heavy care. And in Ontario at least, these ill elderly are mixed in with the younger people released from other institutions and who are suffering from a variety of health problems. The variety of patients creates a volatile mix and increases enormously the demands on providers. A Ministry of Health survey in that province found that three-quarters of the staff did not have adequate time to meet patient needs. In spite of the complex patient needs, the caring work is still provided by those with little or no formal training for the new demands.

The assumptions on which long-term care is based also mean that there are fewer staff per patient and they are paid less than those who work in hospitals. While a number of factors help account for these differences, part of the explanation can be found in the assumption that long-term care work does not require a great deal of skill and training because treatment is not the centre of the work. This assumption not only ignores the fact that people require more, and more complicated, care. It also ignores the determinants of health literature demonstrating that social and psychological support, food, exercise, and a clean environment are all critical to health. Even if the assumption is accepted that little can be done for these people in terms of direct treatment and we ignore the escalating requirements for what was previosuly defined as acute or psychiatric care, it is clear that residents in long-term care facilities need skilled help because of the special health problems they face. Failure to provide skilled help in terms of walking and feeding, bathing and consoling can contribute to additional health problems for these care recipients and can add to the long-term costs as patients require more care.

A decade ago, an Ontario group demonstrated the 'lack of privacy, lack of a stimulating environment, lack of personal power, lack of meaningful communication, and poor medical care' found in nursing homes.[150] Recent cutbacks and restructuring strategies only exaggerate these problems. One worker in a Saskatchewan nursing home explained that:

> One staff person is doing the work of three. Management is not replacing staff who are on sick leave and they're cutting support services. . . . You can imagine what this means for our workload. It feels impossible. The workload has increased and the workforce has decreased.

This extra workload means:

> We have no time to relate to the patient. Management tells us to act as though we are in their own homes when we are doing maintenance and repairs in their rooms. But I can't even stop and talk for a minute. What kind of life is that?
> In nursing, it's so frustrating. You're always rushing. Before you could do your work at a normal pace. Now it's like you're working in a factory. You pull off the sheets, splash water on the residents—they really resent this. There's no time for the important little things. You promise to come back 'if I have time'. But you know there won't be any time. I hate having to treat people like that.[151]

People are defined according to their classified need and the job increasingly gets done as if cars were being made instead of people being cared for in ways that will contribute to their health. Take eating, for example. More and more of the people in nursing homes cannot feed themselves and more of them find it difficult to eat. Food for them is much more than a necessary daily requirement. They need to be tempted to eat and eating can provide one of the few occasions for social interaction. Without food, and without social support, their health will deteriorate. Yet another Saskatchewan worker described mealtime in the nursing home as follows:

> You can be one staff person feeding four or five residents at one time. You start with number one and then number two, three, four and five. It's like an assembly line. It's so degrading.
> You know, with all this terribly impersonal care, the irony is that we're charging them even more money. The residents have to pay a user fee for all the supplies we use with them. Everything from rubber gloves, to powder, creams and medication. They have to buy all this from the pharmacy in the nursing home. I mean, even the rubber gloves we use.[152]

In Ontario, the workers report that baths are no longer given every day, even for those who are bed-ridden and in danger of getting bedsores if they do not have their bath. Increasingly, full baths are given only once a week, and one Ontario resident complained to the Minister of Health that new cutbacks meant that he had missed a number of those weekly baths. Some facilities are also cutting back on the number of times patients are walked, with the result that some patients can no longer get out of bed for a walk.[153] One provider reported that, with only four caregivers looking after 75 residents at night, they have to put catheters on most of the male residents in order to deal with the demand for toilet assistance.[154] This means that 'you're no longer putting your parents or grandparents in a home where they're going to be cared for. Basically, it's a warehouse.'[155]

Certainly, the shift to long-term care can save money in the short run, given current assumptions about the need for care and the skills required in these institutions. But this shift will not keep people in the best state of health possible or even prevent them from deteriorating. And it may not save money in the long run.

HOME CARE

Hospitals are now only for those defined as acutely ill and for relatively short periods of time, while surgery is increasingly done on an outpatient basis. Long-term care facilities are now only for those with severe and long-term disabilities. The rest of care is theoretically provided in the community, sometimes through home care. The demand for home care services has increased enormously over the last decade in the wake of reforms. With those discharged early from hospitals, sent home from day surgery, and deinstitutionalized added to the services traditionally used mainly by the frail elderly, the supply of home care services has failed to fill this growing need.

National health-care strategies began with hospitals and moved on to doctors. Then they basically stopped before explicitly covering the full spectrum of care services seen as necessary for effective and efficient care by both Tommy Douglas, a founding father of medicare,[156] and by Emmett Hall, the head of the Royal Commission on Health Services that established the federal medical program. Both saw home care as a necessary feature of public health, one that would ensure that care was provided in the most effective and efficient manner.[157] Although home care is not specifically included in the Canada Health Act, in 1995 Diane Marleau, then federal Minister of Health, wrote to the provinces and territories stating that the Act was clearly intended to ensure that all Canadians received medically necessary care regardless of venue.[158] This seems to imply that at least care in the home that fits with the medical model should also be provided without fees and in a comprehensive manner. Recognizing that home care has become an increasingly important part of the health-care system and a necessary component of an effective health system, the National Forum on Health recommended it be explicitly made part of public care.[159] However, governments seem to be moving in the opposite direction.

All provinces have publicly funded home care programs that grew slowly and somewhat haphazardly over the years. In 1994, when the cuts to health care described above were just beginning to take effect, it was estimated that 90 per cent of home care services were publicly funded.[160] This public funding paid for the full cost of necessary nursing and therapy services, while support services such as homemaking, personal care, housecleaning, food, and transportation were often provided with user fees attached. The nature and extent of the services vary from province to province, with some also offering supplies and equipment without charge. In the past, most provinces directly hired those providing nursing and other therapies while contracting out other services, primarily to non-profit organizations such as the Victorian Order of Nurses and the Red Cross. Increasingly, however, the entire range of services is being contracted out to whatever organization has the lowest bid.

Manitoba experimented with contracting out its home care services to a for-profit firm. The experiment demonstrated that public care was at least as cost-effective and the province reverted to a system based primarily on home care services delivered directly by public service workers.[161] Ontario did not experiment. It simply assumed competition ensures cheaper care. That province's managed competition model has transferred much of the publicly paid for work to for-profit organizations. Indeed, the specifications for competition virtually ensured that such organizations would win at least some of the contracts for care. Just how much public care is now delivered by such firms is difficult to tell because there are no data readily available on the proportion of care provided by for-profit firms. However, the Canadian Union of Public Employees estimates that 52 per cent of the contracts for nursing services went to for-profit firms.[162] How much of the public money spent on these services went to profit rather than care is not known. We do know that the publicly supported home care programs account for a tiny part of government spending on care and vary considerably across the country. In 1998, they represented only 4 per cent of public health expenditures.[163]

Nor are there readily available data on the extent to which such small budgets mean that individuals, families, and private insurance now pay for care. One reason for this lack of data is the adoption of market strategies. Given that companies are competing against each other for clients, they are unwilling to release such data.[164] Another reason is that expenditures are hidden in individual households rather than documented in public institutions. As a study of BC home care points out, 'it is not yet known whether the burden of costs is simply shifted to the shoulders of clients and their caregivers'.[165] Yet, US government research indicates that 'For every $120 of taxpayer money spent on home care agencies, an estimated $287 worth of unpaid services is provided by the housebound person's family and friends.'[166] And these estimates do not include the costs for supplies, equipment, and special foods. In Canada, numerous studies indicate that women take on most of the unpaid personal care work at great cost to themselves,[167] and provinces and territories are covering many more people without a great deal more money. As a result, priority for paid care goes to those who have immediate acute-care needs and who have no families. The frail elderly receive less support and less money goes to ensuring people are fed, bathed, comforted, and living in clean surroundings. And the paid providers are finding it increasingly difficult to cope under current conditions. In a recent study, 'almost 60 per cent of home care providers reported they lost workers to other areas of health care.'[168]

These strategies undoubtedly save money for governments in the short term. Indeed, cost estimates indicate savings from 'one half to three quarters of the costs for clients in facility care'.[169] However, evidence suggests that this may not be the case for long, especially if the larger health picture is considered and individual suffering is taken into account. According to a study undertaken in British Columbia:

> ignoring the maintenance and preventative aspects of home care may not only lead to increased costs in the overall health system, but may also lead to suffering and emotional distress for a significant proportion of the people who are cut from care. The data also reveal that many of the people who are cut from home care come back into the continuing care system, possibly in worse health than if they had never left. This represents a shortening of the quality of life for a significant portion of the people who are cut from care. These are clearly negative consquences in both human and fiscal terms.[170]

A phone line established by Ontario's Care Watch to examine patients' experiences with home care services found half did not receive enough hours of care, a third had problems with the cost of care, and more than a quarter worried about the competence of their caregivers.[171] Clearly, the shift to care at home is not without costs. And the conclusions of both studies do not take into account the impact on the health of unpaid providers, undoubtedly another long-term cost.

The BC report goes on to say that the cuts in home care services represent a fundamental shift in philosophy—a move away from a universal model, with everyone having the right to care, to a residual model, with governments paying only when people cannot pay.[172] In other words, it is a clear example of privatization, as responsibility is shifted from the collective to the individual.

CONCLUSION

There can be no question that government financial support has made health care more accessible. But public funding, until recently, has done little to alter health-care practice. This is not socialist medicine but private medicine paid for with public funds. This private medicine is primarily based on a medical model, which focuses on the application of what are assumed to be scientifically established treatments to body parts while largely ignoring the other determinants of health.

Public funding supported the expansion of a system centred on acute care. Cutbacks, rather than shifting the focus to prevention and health promotion as various government reports claim is necessary, have mainly meant less of the same. As a result, health care has become less accessible and the focus on the dominant medical model within the system has intensified. There is more treatment but less care, more focus on cuts and chemicals and less on the overall determinants of health. Instead of saving money while improving health, these practices may end up costing more in terms of both the health of Canadians and the public funds necessary to treat the ill and disabled.

Much of the reform has concentrated on getting people out of the institutions, especially out of hospitals that provide acute care, rather than on changing the focus of the institutions. The move is justified on the basis of patient preferences and quality of care. It is assumed that the best source of such determinants of health as social and psychological support, good food, and a clean environment is the home. Yet these determinants require time and, increasingly, skill as more and more of those sent home need a great deal of health care. But there are few people at home to do the work and even fewer who have the necessary skills, even if they have the desire. Particularly at risk are those who are poor and alone, the majority of whom are women. When Toronto newspaper columnist Helen Henderson detailed examples of seniors who found 'themselves sick and alone without proper help', she was 'deluged with letters from readers with similar stories'.[173]

Meanwhile, there is little discussion of the advantages of institutional care. Institutions can provide comprehensive, skilled, diverse, accessible, appropriate, 24-hour care that not only helps people return to health but to stay that way. Laura Sky's film, *Jake's Life*, eloquently demonstrates how institutional care for a severely disabled child can be joyous rather than restrictive, especially when there are skilled providers who have time to care. Current cutbacks, however, are making this less possible and may be making short-term gains at the price of long-term pain.

RECOMMENDED READINGS

Helen Heeney, compiler, *Life Before Medicare: Canadian Experiences*. Toronto: Ontario Coalition of Senior Citizens Organizations, 1995. So much of the literature on health care talks about the problems with the existing system, often blaming these problems on the failure to provide private choice. This book provides stark and personal pictures of what life in Canada was like without a public health-care system. It provides a sharp warning to us all about the hazards a mainly private system entails.

Josephine Rekart, *Public Funds, Private Provision*. Vancouver: University of British Columbia Press, 1993. Rekart provides one of the few analyses of health-care services that extends beyond doctors and hospitals. She offers a way of understanding developments on the fringes of the public system, where for-profit or voluntary providers prevail and where Canadians must increasingly seek care.

Malcolm Taylor, *Health Insurance and Canadian Public Policy*. Montreal and Kingston: McGill-Queen's University Press, 1987. The most thorough and detailed analysis of the development of the Canadian public health-care system, Taylor's book is one everyone interested in our system should own.

CHAPTER

4

Who Provides:
The People

The medical model is not only evident in the way institutions are structured. It is also evident in the organization of work. As Torrance makes clear, 'Medical control of hospitals by the 1870s ensured that the occupations that grew up there would remain subordinate.'[1] The medical men were in charge and their views largely prevailed. These views included more than their assumptions about treatment and cure. Their assumptions about the proper place for the women who provided most of the care were equally important in the structuring of work.

The doctors have not always had everything their own way, however. Two forms of opposition have been at work. First, others working in the system do not entirely share the doctors' commitment to the medical model. These other workers spend much more time than doctors with patients, and this continual contact helps create a different view of what is involved in health care. Moreover, in gaining their monopoly of diagnosis and treatment, allopaths were leaving the necessary caring and preventive work to others. Involved in tasks that went beyond the medical model, these other workers often developed assumptions about care that put them in conflict with the doctors' perspective. These different experiences and views tend to dilute the strength of the medical model. Second, others in the health-care labour force joined with those doing similar work to resist doctors' authority. In some cases, they imitated the strategies used by the medical profession. In others, they formed unions that followed a different means of defending workers' interests. The dramatic growth and increasing specialization in health-care work constituted both a reflection of and a resistance to the dominant medical model.

Today, cutbacks in health care and calls for reform in primary care are placing some new limits on doctors' power. So is the increasing power of managers bent on cost control and committed to market techniques. But these challenges often serve to strengthen, rather than weaken, the dominant medical model. New managerial strategies based on a particular notion of scientific practice allow the application of industrial techniques to the organization of health-care work and to doctors' practices. This approach increases the focus on treatment and cure while making care and prevention more difficult. Consequently, it often threatens the health of both workers and patients. Moreover, like the approach of the medical men, these strategies are based on assumptions about women, who through their work who provide most of the daily care. As a result, the people most affected by such changes are women.

DEVELOPING THE HEALTH-CARE WORKFORCE

SEX MATTERS

Health-care work has traditionally been women's work. Certainly, the doctors who established a monopoly over care in the nineteenth century were men, who used the requirement for a university education as a means of preventing anyone other than white males who could afford higher education from entering the profession.[2] But doctors were, and are, a small minority of those working in the health-care field. Most health care has been and is provided by women. In 1996, nearly 80 per cent of those with paid work in health care were women and 13.5 per cent of employed women worked in health services (see Table 4.1). More detailed survey research shows that women do the nursing, housekeeping, dietary, and clerical work while men do the doctoring, managing, engineering, 'heavy' cleaning, and skilled trades work.[3] Since restrictions on women entering medicine have been lifted, the number of women has steadily increased, and women are now a majority of those in medical schools. Women not only predominate in the paid health-care workforce. They also form the overwhelming majority of those who have provided and continue to provide unpaid health-care services, either in their own homes for relatives or in the community as volunteers.

This division of labour plays a central role in the development of health care, in the dominance of the medical model, and in the current reforms. Just as the emphasis on cure in our modern health-care system can largely be explained in terms of the power of medical men, the invisibility of care can be understood primarily as a reflection of women's position and power as caregivers. This invisibility helps explain why care is not counted as part of the new, efficient, health-care system.

Until well into the twentieth century, it was mainly women who diagnosed, dosed, and treated household members. They were also responsible for keeping family members healthy. Most health care was not yet based on the kinds of scientific principles later developed and taught in universities and practised in hospitals. Women learned the skills they brought to their caring work from other women. 'The typical Ojibwa woman could set a broken leg, stitch a wound, and gather and administer medicinal plants for dozens of ailments.'[4] European women arrived equipped with 'mothers' instructions and prescriptions' to treat everything from convulsions to severed fingers.[5] And, as *The Canadian Home Cook Book*[6] explained, women were 'responsible for the

Table 4.1 Labour Force in Health Industries, Canada, 1996

Industry	% of all Women in the Labour Force	% of all Men in the Labour Force	% of Women in the Industry
Hospitals	6.3	1.3	80.2
Other Institutions	3.0	0.4	84.2
Non-Institutional Health Services	0.9	0.2	76.4
Offices of Physicians, Surgeons, and Dentists in Private Practice	1.9	0.6	73.6
Offices of Other Health Practitioners	0.6	0.1	78.0
Medical and Other Health Laboratories	0.3	0.1	76.5
Health Associations and Agencies*	0.5	0.1	76.5
Totals	13.5	2.9	79.5

*Also includes social services, many of which could be defined as health services.

SOURCE: Statistics Canada, 96 Census: Industry and Class of Worker (Cat. no. 93F0020XCB96004). Available at: <http://www.statcan.ca/english/census96/mar17/occupa/occ.htm>. Accessed 25 Mar. 2001.

health of the household' through the production and preservation of food, the ventilation and heating of rooms, the clothing and supervision of children, and what *The Great Nineteenth Century Medicine Manual* termed 'simple home remedies and good nursing' for the sick.[7]

Health care, then, was the sum and integration of these tasks and skills. But the whole of health care was more than simply individual tasks separately or even collectively provided. Each of the tasks and skills involved an interpersonal component: the provision of biological, social, and emotional support. Such care was difficult to see precisely because it was often part of other tasks and skills. When a mother was feeding a sick child, for example, she was usually comforting and encouraging, offering verbal and non-verbal signals that the child was important and was a participant. She was not only seeking to get the task done but also to provide the kind of support that would make the child want to eat and to feel better. Her caring was usually a critical component in recovery. This caring was difficult to see because it was most often provided by women, without formal training, to household members. It was assumed that such care was a product of emotional attachment to the person and of women's natural instincts, of their unlearned skills and drives that came with the rest of women's biological equipment. Even when care was provided in homes or institutions by paid female workers or by nuns, it was frequently assumed that women had no need to learn the skills for the job.

As medicine and health care developed along scientific lines, it became increasingly evident that more formal training was needed for those who were to promote health and provide care. Germ theory meant new standards of cleanliness were required; new techniques meant that doctors required skilled assistance in their surgery and that patients had complicated care regimes afterward. Even though women were formally trained to do the work, the skills involved were often invisible or undervalued. This invisibility and undervaluing reflected the traditional association with at-home care-givers, the assumption of women's instinctive capacities and women's limited power. As the Ontario Pay Equity Commission made clear in its decision on job evaluation schemes applied to nursing work:

> Many job related skills are not treated as skills by evaluators, but rather as qualities 'intrinsic to being a woman' and therefore not compensable. Many compensation systems have made invisible the skills and responsibility required in women's work. These skills were associated with women's work in the home: patience and effective personal relations in raising and nurturing children, or care giving for ill or aging family members. Gender bias is embedded in conventional skill definitions of job complexity and human capital characteristics. Those skills were invisible in job evaluation and were considered natural attributes of women as opposed to skills required on the job.[8]

The caring, comforting, and nurturing aspects of women's jobs are the most invisible and the least valued in monetary or other measurement terms, even though, as the Commission points out in another decision, 'Caring is a learned skill, which is acquired through the nurse's background and formal education.'[9] And caring is not counted even though a growing body of research indicates that it can increase the likelihood of healthy outcomes, reduce mortality, and boost the immune system.[10] Indeed, the fact that research on the importance of caring is so recent itself both reflects and reinforces the invisibility of the work.

But the undervaluing and invisibility of the skills involved in nursing work do not simply reflect its association with women and homes. They also reflect the power relations between women and men in general, and between doctors and women health-care workers in particular. Doctors were able to impose their model of health care because they had power related to both their class and sex. Women's work in health care was defined in relation to that of doctors and their medical model. Doctors actively worked to ensure that women would be prevented from diagnosing and from providing some kinds of treatments. They restricted women to particular areas of work and made all women's work subject to doctors' orders.[11] Moreover, focused as they were on cure, these doctors seldom investigated the importance of caring to health. Even as women enter doctoring in greater numbers, they often do so at the price of conforming to these past practices.

Of course, women did not simply accept this state of affairs. They struggled to carve out a place for themselves within health-care work. They were limited, however, by a number of factors. First, in late nineteenth- and early twentieth-century Canada, when the medical model became dominant, women had little power and few resources. Second, there was a high turnover among those who worked in health care, primarily because most women left the paid workforce once they married. While many wanted to leave to accommodate their work as wives and mothers, regulations and policies meant they had little choice about keeping their jobs after marriage. Third, women were mainly employed outside institutions, usually in private homes. Both the turnover and the scattered nature of their workplaces meant it was difficult to develop collective strategies, especially when women did not generally have access to the kinds of clubs and other meeting places available to men. Fourth, women themselves disagreed about whether they should stress the caring aspects of their work or imitate the scientific emphasis of the medical men. Women have also disagreed about whether they have special caring skills by virtue of their sex or whether the skills involved in health care were learned and different from those employed in the home.

Over the last hundred years, health-care work for both women and men has become more specialized and increasingly based on formal training, although women still rely heavily on informal learning among women. Indeed, the craft of nursing still has as its foundation the long apprenticeship girls and young women experience in the home.[12] Most men's work is based on the dominant medical model. It is in many ways the most highly valued as well as the most powerful. While women have made significant gains in terms of power and recognition, much of their work remains invisible and undervalued. New management schemes based on the notion that what counts is what can be counted reinforce this invisibility and undervaluing.

NURSES: THE PRIMARY HEALTH-CARE WORKFORCE

Those who do nursing constitute the basic health-care workforce. According to the 1996 census, nearly half a million people worked in nursing, therapy, and related assisting jobs. They accounted for two-thirds of those employed in what were classified as occupations in medicine and health. Ninety per cent of those in the nursing labour force were women.[13]

While most of the caring work in and out of institutions has traditionally been done by women, not until schools of nursing began to appear in the last quarter of the nineteenth century could we talk about nursing as an occupation. Most Canadian schools, in theory at least, were based on the Nightingale tradition, although there was little of the autonomy that Nightingale prescribed.[14] Student nurses provided a large part of the health-care labour force and much of their learning was done on the ward rather than in the lecture hall.[15] Gradually, however, more time was spent on formal learning than on learning through doing. Increasing emphasis on classroom and book learning coincided with the emergence of scientific medicine and reflected its influence.

The first graduates began work in the late nineteenth century. Nursing first appears in the Canadian census as an occupational category in 1901, with 208 student and graduate nurses counted. This compared to just over 5,000 physicians. Nurses were not outnumbered for long, however. By 1931, the census indicated there were more than 30,000 nurses, three times the number of doctors.[16] Certainly most of the work of bathing, feeding, comforting, walking, and toileting those treated by doctors had always been done by women, some of whom were paid, but without formal training they were seldom recognized as nurses. Nursing, then, is in many ways a twentieth-century occupation.

From the time of the first schools until well into the twentieth century, almost all the women who worked in health care were classified as nurses or student nurses. They did all of the work on the wards, combining a wide variety of tasks and skills in what was defined as nursing. Although nurses increasingly outnumbered the men and although they could claim increasingly sophisticated and standardized training, they still remained subordinate to the medical men. The nature of their work, however, was not simply an expression of their lack of power or of the medical model. It was also a reflection of their attempts to gain recognition and to carve out a place for themselves in the health-care system. Perhaps most importantly, it grew out of their experiences of more sustained interaction with patients and their families.

Gorham points out in her summary of nursing history that nurses often asserted their rights 'in a way that accommodated medicine's assumption of primacy and accepted and even capitalized on gender differences'.[17] This meant adopting many of the approaches inherent to the dominant medical model. It often meant stressing hygiene and order.[18] But it also meant retaining much of the caring that implied different assumptions about health. The caring was sometimes defended as an attribute of women and sometimes as a learned skill, but always as necessary to health. Nurses working daily and closely with patients did not need scientific experiments to demonstrate the importance of comfort, support, and assurance to both recovery and resistance to disease. Although, as McPherson puts it, 'For nurses, caring was curing',[19] Gorham notes that 'the medical profession nonetheless assumed caring was subordinate to curing and would be delegated whenever possible to the modern nurse.'[20] While nurses saw caring as central to their work and as critical to health, doctors saw it as secondary to the main job of cure.

This emphasis on caring did not mean that nurses rejected the medical model entirely. Indeed, in many ways they embraced the scientific paradigm and standardized their teaching and practice along medical lines. According to McPherson, nurses then 'could integrate caring and curing in daily tasks'.[21] Such integration was never easy, and it has been a constant source of tension, in large part because caring and curing are based on different assumptions. Perhaps this tension explains why it was not until recently that caring became an explicit, rather than simply an implicit, part of nursing education. '[P]rofessional caring in nursing is operationally different from natural caring',[22] that is, the kind of caring any loving person can provide. According to the College of Nurses of Ontario:

> Nursing is a preventative, educational, restorative, and supportive health-related service, provided in a caring manner, for the purpose of enhancing a person's quality of life or, when life can no longer be sustained, assisting a person to a peaceful and dignified death.[23]

For nurses, caring involves more than a feeling response. It includes 'those assistive, supportive, or facilitative acts directed towards another, in order to improve or to maintain a favorably healthy condition of life'.[24] As the testimony before the Ontario Pay Equity Commission made clear, caring means learned capacities such as the 'communication skills required to deal with seriously ill or infirm patients, those in drug induced states or low functioning clients'; 'patience, caring and listening skills in dealing with patients or grieving families',[25] as well as the skills necessary to 'teach patients how to gain and maintain health', to 'act as a patient advocate', and to build trust.[26] A Quebec RN identified her communication skills as her most important skills and explained that there is 'a lot of dealing with families, with patients who are dying. Heart patients are very stressed patients. They're often very angry. A lot of depression. You have to deal with that. A lot of patients . . . have . . . vascular diseases, which means there are amputations and lots of pain. So you have to be pretty good.'[27]

And caring means developing these skills in relation to the curative and preventive functions they perform. Caring for cancer patients, for example, means knowing how to provide support and comfort in relation to the specific, medical acts that are prescribed. It means not only teaching patients how to do some of the treatment for themselves but also how to cope emotionally with the trauma. It means being able to answer questions about the physical and psychological impact of treatment in relation to themselves and their relatives. It means constantly interacting and reassuring on the basis of technical knowledge and skill, not simply on the basis of caring about the individual. Similarly, bathing a patient involves a complex of skills. A nurse needs to know how patients can and should be moved; she needs to be able to assure them and encourage their co-operation; she helps them handle the physical and the psychological discomfort of the bathing process; and she often has to work co-operatively with others to get the job done. Caring in nursing is not about becoming a close personal friend but about the assumptions and skills of professional practice.

This caring does not always fit neatly with the dominant medical model. Indeed, it is often in opposition to it. As Patricia Yaros, an American nurse, points out:

> the medical model promotes the concept of disease as being separate from the person, excludes the human from the environment, and attempts to reduce all life phenomena to singular causations. As women and as nurses, this is antagonistic and contradictory to our personal and professional experiences.[28]

In contact with patients for often extended periods of time, nurses learn the importance of interaction and reassurance. They cannot help but be aware of the link between how persons are treated as individuals and how they respond to medical treatment. Nurses experience the significance of both the social and physical environment on the ability to resist and recover from disease.

The professional caring component has not always been clearly articulated. Nor has it been frequently investigated according to the scientific paradigm. The invisibility of caring and the uncomfortable accommodation with the medical model have resulted in tensions within nursing and between nurses and others. Some nurses have argued for more emphasis on university education, science, and treatment as a means of gaining power and respect, of acquiring the kinds of prestige enjoyed by doctors.[29] The rapid growth in medical science and in the health-care workforce, combined with new managerial techniques, has encouraged this emphasis.

FRAGMENTATION OF NURSING WORK

The enormous expansion in health care that took place after World War II, the introduction of medicare, and the development of new technology were accompanied by an increasing division of labour in nursing. The emphasis on parts to be treated and the separation of cure from prevention made such divisions possible. With this approach, treatment could be assigned to one set of workers while caring and prevention tasks, such as feeding, bathing, and walking, could be assigned to another.

The growing fragmentation of nursing work was evident in the Canadian census. For 1941, 1951, and 1961, census data indicated just two kinds of workers in the nursing category: graduate nurses and nurses-in-training.[30] By 1971, however, the census had added categories to include nursing assistants, nursing aides and orderlies, therapists, and other assisting occupations.[31] And these categories leave out the many who were hired to do other kinds of work—cleaning, preparing and delivering food, admitting and keeping records on patients—no longer done solely by nursing staff. During the same period the census started to list 'other occupations' in medicine and health, such as dieticians and nutritionists, radiology technologists, and respiratory technicians. All the tasks in each of these categories had previously been done by those simply called nurses. The census data reflect the fact that nursing has become more narrowly defined and more closely linked to a particular medical model.

Division of labour, however, was not simply the inevitable outcome of growing size and new medical developments. It also reflected a variety of pressures, and strategies to respond to pressures. As a result, the overall tendency towards more fragmentation of the work was fraught with contradictory developments. A great deal of pressure came from governments and hospital directors concerned about finances. Some came from nurses themselves.

Those who had been called graduate nurses, but who were now called registered nurses or RNs to distinguish them from other nurses, had become increasingly powerful during this period. They made it clear that they were unwilling to accept the low pay and low status of nursing work. They used their associations and later their unions to demand improvements in pay, working conditions, and power relations.[32] The nursing shortage throughout much of the post-war period not only enhanced women's strength in negotiations; it also made it more likely that nurses stayed in the workforce and worked for change. Moreover, the increasing concentration of nurses in hospitals brought nurses together in ways that allowed them to share their complaints and to develop collective strategies.

Those managing the system responded to the RNs' growing strength and rising pay by encouraging the hiring of workers who could do some of the nursing work with less formal training and for less pay. Many registered nurses were not opposed to these developments, because the new division of labour promised to free them from the more unpleasant and repetitive tasks. Some were concerned that too much time was being spent on clerical and housekeeping tasks,[33] tasks they increasingly defined as outside their medical work. In fact, registered nurses' associations fought for the exclusive right to perform certain medical tasks and for university education as a requirement. In doing so, they were not only imitating the strategies used by doctors to gain power but also reinforcing some aspects of the medical model. At the same time they were ensuring that those doing the work had the necessary skills and, given the focus of much nursing education, were often combining these exclusive rights with a caring model.

Unlike doctors, however, most registered nurses did not end up as specialists. In 1999, nearly three-quarters of them were still classified as staff or community health nurses involved in general duty. This lack of specialization reflects both their limited power and their refusal to accept entirely the medical model. However, the recent increase in the Clinical Nurses Specialist category and the growth in graduate work suggest a move away from this pattern. More also work in the community, although nearly two-thirds were still employed in hospitals at the turn of this century.[34] However, the new division of labour was until recently more evident among others doing nursing work, such as aides and technicians.

Initially, the growth in numbers among these other nurses was most rapid for the registered nursing assistants, now increasingly called licensed practical nurses or registered practical nurses. Between 1971 and 1981, the number of RNAs increased from 27,285 to 40,545.[35] These RNAs had fewer years of formal education than RNs. Their more limited preparation was used as the justification for lower pay and more restricted duties. But these nurses also organized and won rights similar to those of registered nurses, although they continued to be restricted in terms of some medical acts. Like RNs, RNAs became more expensive and difficult to control. At the same time, there was further financial pressure placed on health care by governments—prompting three quite different responses in terms of employment practices for nursing.

One response was to look outside Canada for nurses trained in other countries. Initially, such nurses were recruited from the United States, the United

Kingdom, and Australia. However, nurses were increasingly drawn from Asia, Africa, and the Caribbean. By 1984 one in five immigrant nurses came from these areas, and by 1999 only 40 per cent came from the US or the UK.[36] In his study of state regulation of nursing and teaching, Wotherspoon explains that this strategy to fill shortages by employing nurses trained in other jurisdictions is made possible by the medical model. The characteristics of the worker matter less as technical skills related to body parts matter more. Such skills can be learned anywhere if cultural context and the characteristics of patients no longer matter. Employers are able to employ foreign-trained nurses not only to fill demand but also as a means of fragmenting the workforce. 'With respect to nursing, racism and threats of job reclassification operate under those circumstances to fragment the workforce and undermine possible collective mobilization or job action on the part of nurses while racist and patriarchial practices may serve to reinforce the maintenance of a relatively docile workforce.'[37] At the same time, many of those with foreign credentials are denied recognition of their skills.[38] Such nurses are frequently employed in other health-care occupations where their skills are demanded but not recognized.

A second kind of response also involved using nurses against each other. For some jobs, RNs rather than RNAs were hired. RNs were not much more expensive and, unlike RNAs, they could do the entire range of nursing tasks. So in some intensive care wards, for example, only RNs were employed and they did everything from giving needles and attaching intravenous apparatus to bathing patients and cleaning up vomit. This strategy became less feasible, however, as the nursing shortage meant both that RNs were less available and that they had become more successful at demanding higher wages. Another approach, often called primary care nursing, assigned RNs to specific patients, making them responsible for all the patients' needs. This approach was more appropriate for the caring model, given that it focused on the patient rather than the task. However, the Quebec nurses we interviewed said that this practice far too often meant they were given responsibility but no power to determine patient care or their own allocation of time. Moreover, given that the strategy was designed to cut costs, the number of patients assigned to each nurse was too large to allow for adequate care. As a result, primary care mainly meant that individual nurses, not the system, were blamed for problems.

More recently, the monopoly that doctors, RNs, and RNAs hold on certain kinds of work has been challenged by moves to deregulate the professions.[39] A number of provinces have been reviewing licensing practices with a view to removing restrictions on scope of practice. A range of people would be allowed to perform many of the specific functions now restricted to particular registered practitioners. These efforts mean RNs may be used to replace doctors at more tasks at the same time as more RN tasks may be done by other providers, on down the hierachy. This too may be a deskilling process indicating an emphasis on body parts and the assumption that care can be divided up into easily learned specific tasks based on a curative model. But it is a contradictory process. Some nurses gain not only skills but the recognition of skills at the same time.[40]

While some RNAs were being replaced by RNs because of the scope of practice regulations, nursing attendants were sought in increasing numbers as a means of delegating some of the nurses' work. These attendants had less formal education in health care than RNAs; a significant proportion had no formal training outside the workplace. A significant proportion were also foreign-born. Again, the years of schooling were used as a justification for paying less, as was the more restricted list of required tasks. The census data make this shift in strategy clear. Between 1986 and 1991, the number of RNAs decreased from 37,335 to 30,510 while the number of nursing attendants increased from 74,755 to 89,700.[41] RNAs were still replacing some of the nurses in hospitals and especially in homes for the aged, a process reflected in their increased number between 1991 and 1996. But nursing attendants were also replacing RNAs in many areas, with the number of nurses aides and orderlies increasing to 123,475 by 1996.[42]

At the same time as some tasks have been reassigned to different categories of nurses, other tasks have been defined out of nursing altogether. Although nurses initially did most of the administration, the cleaning, and the food delivery, today these tasks are chiefly done by workers classified as non-nursing support staff. The way the census presents the numbers makes it difficult to determine exactly how rapidly and to what extent these jobs grew, but one indication comes from hospital statistics. By 1990, 37 per cent of the public hospital expenses in Canada were classified as administrative and supportive, compared to the 34 per cent spent on what was classified as nursing.[43]

Those classified as housekeeping, dietary, clerical, and maintenance staff have also organized, forming strong unions to protect not only their right to decent wages and job security but also their right to provide care. As noted in Chapter 3, employers have responded to their growing strength by redefining their work as 'hotel services' rather than as health-care services and by applying the strategies used in hotels to limit the power of these workers. Once these services are defined as outside the health care field, they can also be contracted out to private-sector firms, where lower wages, more limited training, and non-unionized work are the norm.

The number of administrators has also grown significantly over the years and administration is increasingly separated from health care. Between 1981 and 1986, the total number of administrators in medicine and health grew by 67 per cent.[44] In the past, most administrators were people who had come from health-care work and climbed the administrative ladder. Today more and more administrators have been trained as managers rather than as health-care workers. A 1993 survey of health-care managers found that nearly half had no clinical experience and the number has undoubtedly increased since then, although it is difficult to find out by how much.[45] This was particularly true of the men in health care. As those involved in the survey put it, the data reflect the 'increasing interest on the part of the healthcare industry to learn more from the private sector to increase efficiencies. One way of capturing that expertise is to hire individuals from the private sector.'[46] It is increasingly assumed that management skills are technical skills applicable in any organization and that training in health care is unnecessary. Without the kind of experience that comes from directly working with patients, administrators are more likely to see health-care institutions as organizations that operate like car plants, banks, or hotels.

Although cleaning, laundry, and dietary work are now often referred to as 'hotel services', reflecting the assumption that these, too, are jobs that are the same throughout the system, both health-care institutions and the patients within them create and face very different risks from those of tourists staying in hotels. Patients are much more vulnerable and produce much more dangerous germs than guests in hotels. Although both the census and administrators may see those who clean, do laundry, and deliver food as non-health-care workers, that is not the view or experience of the workers themselves. In his study of workers in an Ontario hospital, White found that the women who did the cleaning and dietary work defined themselves as health-care workers and actively participated in providing some kinds of support to patients. One housekeeper explained that she often stopped to talk to patients who were lonely. 'The dears [patients] appreciate it . . . the days are better for them . . . I must say I liked it too.'[47] Other Ontario workers described how they translated, helped patients dial phone numbers and attract the attention of nurses, took them for walks, and picked up objects that had fallen to the floor.

Here, too, workers have been organizing to protect their rights and to ensure their involvement in care. A large proportion of those employed in health-care institutions in cleaning, laundry, dietary, clerical, and maintenance work belong to a union. These unions have fought for, and won, significant improvements in their pay, benefits, job security, and conditions of work. White's study of one Ontario strike clearly shows that employees went out not only because their own conditions of work were deteriorating but because they were concerned about what was happening to patient care and to their possibilities for contributing to that care.[48] And here, too, employers have responded by further dividing the work and by reducing the range of skills defined as necessary. The workers we interviewed in Ontario repeatedly talked about how new work organizations were narrowing the definition of their work and reducing their jobs to a series of quickly learned tasks.

The practice of dividing nursing work into discrete tasks and allocating many of the tasks to workers who are quickly trained and paid low wages is evident among those who are often called generic workers. Although they usually have such titles as personal care providers, these generic workers are being assigned much of the work earlier delegated from RNs to RNAs to nursing attendants. These workers have even less formal training and are increasingly employed to provide the in-home care required by shorter patient stays, day surgery, outpatient clinics, and deinstitutionalization.[49]

Certainly some division of labour improved the way work was done at the same time as it improved the quality of the service. In large hospitals it made sense to have skilled cooks prepare the food, guided by nutritionists who had considerable expertise in the needs of patients. And it made sense to have people trained in new techniques related to germ theory do the cleaning in a variety of areas. It also made sense to have those educated in medical terminology keep many of the records and to have those operating the radiology, laboratory, and respiratory equipment take specialized training in these areas. What is now more narrowly defined as nursing work benefited from some specialization as well.

Consider the case when various nurses work in teams. Such teamwork was possible when the nurses were employed in institutions where those with more formal education could help ensure the quality of service and where additional help was available. Indeed, teamwork was essential to nursing and compensated for the weaknesses in the new division of labour. By combining their skills and their efforts, the various kinds of nurses could ensure that care was integrated rather than fragmented according to specific tasks. So, for example, a number of nurses with various amounts of training would co-operate to change a patient's bed. At least one would have the medical knowledge required to take the patient's particular physical problems into account; all of them would know how to work together to lift in ways that avoided injury to themselves and the patient. And more than one would have the skills necessary to encourage co-operation and to comfort the patient.

But when the division of labour is used to save money by substituting less skilled for more skilled labour, as it has been in many cases, it can reduce the quality of care. When it is used to define nursing work more narrowly and to fragment nursing work into discrete tasks, each of which is to be performed by a person with minimum training, care is undermined. This is particularly the case when care is to be provided by individuals working alone in private homes. Care, as we have seen, depends on the integration of various nursing tasks within a health framework. It is part of bathing, feeding, turning, injecting, teaching, recording, cleaning, bandaging, and examining. It requires a range of specialized skills, understood from a health perspective. The division of nursing into specific separate tasks fits comfortably with a medical model of the body as a collection of separate parts to be fixed. But it does not fit well with a nursing model of care, with current research on health, or with most people's experiences. And new managerial strategies in health care are further emphasizing the division of labour and the medical model on which it is based.

MANAGING NURSING WORK

Those managing the various parts of the health-care system have introduced a range of practices designed to reduce labour costs and increase control over the health-care workers. In many cases, these management techniques were first developed for private-sector goods-production jobs. Health-care managers have adopted these strategies on the assumption that for-profit organizations are more efficient and effective. The dominant medical model, based as it is on the assumption of parts to be fixed, made such adoption possible.

Yet there is no evidence to support the notion that the private sector is necessarily more efficient. Indeed, a great deal of evidence indicates that the American for-profit health-care system is much less efficient and effective than our non-profit one. It serves far fewer people at a much higher per-person cost with no evidence that those who are served are healthier than their Canadian counterparts. The disability-free life expectancy for US males is 67.5 years compared to 70.0 in Canada, and the life expectancy rate for men is two years more in Canada than it is in the United States.[50]

There is even less evidence to suggest that techniques designed to increase the production of goods such as cars or services such as making hamburgers will prove effective in the health-care sector. In fact, there is every reason to believe that techniques must be different when the object is maintaining and improving health or easing dying. Unlike cars and hamburgers, people interact in the health-care process and they are infinitely variable. Furthermore, the consequences of poor services in the health-care sector can be more devastating, given the vulnerable states of those receiving the services.

But lack of evidence demonstrating that private-sector methods will make health-care services more effective and efficient has not stopped health-care managements from introducing schemes to reduce personnel costs. Like the private sector, they have employed more part-time and casual workers. They have moved workers around to meet peak demand and increased the amount of supervision. They have conducted time-budget studies and used these measurements to reduce staff. They have contracted out some work to the private sector and given other aspects of health care entirely to the private sector. And they have adopted what is usually called continuous quality improvement or total quality management (TQM) as a means of reorganizing entire personnel systems. Although some expenses have been reduced by these techniques, there has been little evaluation of these strategies for either human or financial costs over the long term.

Assigning the Fragments: Part-time Work

In 1999, just over half of the registered nurses employed in Canada had only part-time work.[51] The proportion working part-time in nursing homes is even higher, where for-profit delivery is common.[52] Moreover, many of the RNs counted as working full-time did so on an irregular basis[53] and 'an increasing number of RNs have more than one employer'.[54] Although the number with part-time hours has decreased somewhat in the last couple of years with the acknowledged nursing shortage, the number working for more than one employer has steadily increased. This suggests that employers have responded to the shortage not by creating permanent jobs but by hiring nurses for more hours.

By employing people part-time or on a casual basis, employers save money in two ways. First, they often pay fewer benefits and lower wages for these employees. This advantage is limited to some extent in health care by the relatively high unionization rates among part-time employees. But part-time unionized workers are still cheaper than those employed full-time; nonunionized workers are cheaper still. It is particularly important to note that most part-time and casual workers, unionized or not, do not get paid if they stay home sick. Second, employers pay part-time workers only when they work and employers can hire them to work only at peak demand. Moreover, people who are working for short periods of time can work harder than those employed for more hours.

Health-care employers are in a particularly advantaged position in terms of hiring workers part-time because most of their employees are women and women are easier than men to employ part-time. This is the case not only because most women have other work at home but also because they are competing with many other women in this segregated work. Furthermore, the hours of health-care work make it difficult for many women to juggle full-time work and their domestic responsibilities.

But the increase in part-time work in health care cannot simply be explained in terms of women's preference or need for part-time employment. It must also be understood as a management strategy to cut costs and increase control over the work. Many of the women who take part-time or casual employment do so because it is the only work available. According to a 1997 report, such numbers suggest that 'an increasing proportion of part-time working is not voluntary, but rather a consequence of cost-cutting measures in the funding and organization of the health care system'.[55] Moreover, increasing stress and rising workloads in health care mean that a growing number of women find it impossible to function full-time in the job. With absentee and disability rates higher than in other professions, many nurses increasingly find they cannot work full-time under these conditions.[56]

Part-time and casual work fit easily with the notion of applying treatment to a particular part, making it possible to parcel out tasks to any person with the specific training in that task. Such work, however, conflicts with a broader notion of care and of health promotion and prevention, as well as with the understanding of caregiving as highly skilled work.

Those employed part-time cannot easily treat the patient as a whole person because they move around the hospital and stay only a short time in any one place. As one nurse explained, it is difficult even to learn the name of the patient if you are not regularly employed on the ward.[57] Instead of dealing with the whole patient, these part-time and casual workers focus on the task to be done. Familiarity with the patient is not just an extra luxury we cannot afford. It is basic to health and costs. Lack of familiarity can mean the care provider misses important signs of distress or misinterprets signals from the patient. Such interpretation is not a technical skill universally applied, as it would be in the car plant. It is also about understanding the individual variation based on a particular body, a particular combination of health problems, and a particular history. With only occasional or temporary contact, health-care workers may respond in ways that harm the patient and that result in more costs to the system.

Lack of familiarity with patients is not the only problem resulting from the growth in part-time and casual employment. According to the workers we have interviewed, part-time and casual workers often find themselves in new work environments. The equipment and procedures are frequently unfamiliar to them, especially in these times of rapid developments in technology. The workers may not know how to proceed or may proceed in ways that risk the machines and the patients. For example, a Quebec RN was concerned about operating a new intravenous feeding system: 'If you don't know what it is all about, you can cause death within a minute.'[58] Ontario dietary workers were concerned about the quality of the work done by part-time employees. 'There's a temp on nourishment right now and they just don't do a good job. They are students filling in.'[59] In addition to the concern over risk, those employed regularly in a section say they have to spend a great deal of time showing part-time and casual workers how to work in the area and with these patients. The result is time lost for both the regular and part-time or casual employees and time lost for the patient, time that in health care may be critical.

Part-time or casual work also has costs for the workers, and thus indirectly for patients and the system. Not paid when they are sick, part-time health-care workers tell us they go in even when they are ill. This practice not only means that they risk getting sicker but also that they risk making patients sick. Part-time health-care workers in Ontario said they too often prepare food, clean bathrooms, and give patients medications when they themselves are sick because otherwise these workers would not have enough money to eat.

Hours and shifts are irregular, making it difficult for the body and the household to adjust. As one Quebec RN explained:

> Like, one evening I'd be a relief on the floor and two evenings later I'd be relief for the evening supervisor or the night supervisor. . . . My continuing to go to work on this basis was a contributing factor in what I now see as the breakdown of the marriage. . . . The tension at home was increasing. . . . Like, I'd get home and the children would just be leaving for school. I'd try to cram everything into a few minutes. . . . You wouldn't have adequate sleep. . . .
> And, as most people know who work night duty, it changes your body clock entirely. You develop a certain look which is characteristic of people who work at night, unless they've worked it for years and years and their whole bio-chemical adjustment is complete. But when you're shifting around, maybe working evenings one week and night duty the next, your sleeping patterns are constantly changing. When you're off, you're trying to readjust to your family's lifestyle. So you've got all kinds of mucking up with the body's system. And it can be very, very wearing. You get dragged out. Whether you've maintained a good diet, or exercise, or whatever, you still end up feeling haggard and worn out. . . . I found myself with less and less energy to cope with all the demands. And thinking about it when I came home, I recognized that these may be the signs of a sort of burnout.[60]

Another Quebec nurse explained that the combination of irregular hours and heavy workloads means that 'When they [the children] do something, I really get mad. I shout and scream and I can't avoid it.' The problem is not restricted to nurses, and it increases along with the workload and irregular hours. A Montreal woman with a junior administrative job described her relation with her son in terms of her increasing stress: 'Sometimes, if I'm very, very tired and frustrated from my work, and he happens to ask me a question, I become verbally abusive to him. Badly.' She was not only verbally abusive to her son, however. 'I really beat him badly. . . . It's my work.'[61]

Dragged-out, burned-out workers, worried about their partners and children, do not provide the best kind of care at work. Indeed, much of the reported increase in violence towards patients may be attributable to the increasing stress experienced by workers. Moreover, irregular employment also means irregular pay. One nurse put it very simply: 'If I don't work much, I cannot buy the things I need.'[62] The lack of financial security adds further to the pressure on those employed part-time and this stress, too, makes it difficult to provide good care.

While the increasing use of part-time and casual workers may cut costs in the short term, the long-term costs for both workers and patients may be great.

WHAT COUNTS IS WHAT CAN BE COUNTED: MEASURING OUT CARE

The increasing use of part-time and casual labour, as well as the practice of 'floating' workers around the facility depending on demand, has been greatly helped by new computer technology combined with an old management strategy. The old strategy is a variation on the time-motion studies first introduced by F.W. Taylor almost a century ago.[63] The notion of this approach is quite simple. Observe workers at their jobs and time each specific part of the job. The data can also be recorded by workers themselves. The next step is to figure out ways to fragment jobs into these tasks and reduce the time it takes to do each task. Work is then allocated on the assumed time it takes to do each task.[64] Work sampling and patient classification schemes are newer versions of this old strategy, newer ways of measuring the parts of the job. The computer allows the easy recording and calculation of times, as well as the easy allocation of workers according to these times.

Health-care practices based on such studies have been introduced under various acronyms. For nursing work, Quebec introduced the PRN formula; in Ontario there was a system called GRASP. Whatever the name, the studies follow the same principles and are justified on the same terms. The Quebec formula, for example, was first introduced in 1977 into several Quebec hospitals.[65] Those promoting the scheme made it quite clear that the purpose was to quantify care, to reduce care to a numeric formula.

> La Formule d'évaluation du Niveau des Soins Infirmiers Réquis par le bénéficiaire permet de déterminer la quantité de soins réquis par chaque bénéficiaire pendant une période de vingt-quatre (24) heures.[66] (The formula allows the determination of the level of RN required for each patient during a 24-hour period.)

The PRN formula had a list of 154 factors grouped into categories such as respiration, communication, and therapy. Each factor had a value equivalent to minutes, indicating the total amount of personnel minutes required on average to complete the task.[67] This formula could then be used to determine precisely the number and kind of workers needed for each area of the hospital. With such a formula, administrators could begin to talk in terms of half a worker for half a day in a particular ward and the staff complement could be reduced to an absolute minimum.

Again, such a strategy can be introduced only if it is assumed that care can be divided into discrete, measurable tasks of average duration, ignoring the people who are the patients and the people who care for the patients, and instead assuming a set of parts to be fixed by a set of uniform workers. Patients become average patients with average needs based on their diagnosis. The infinite variety of patients' problems and responses disappears in the formula. This approach becomes even more problematic in today's institutions because the people who are admitted or treated are increasingly those with a combination of very complex ills. And the variety among workers' ways of providing care, their response rates, and their skills also disappear in this approach. Moreover, the formulas measure tasks and visible actions with visible outcomes. What disappears from the formula is the care.

A Quebec RN's experience graphically illustrates how care is excluded. Her patient was a woman who had contracted AIDS through a blood transfusion. Because AIDS was a newly diagnosed illness, doctors were warning against contact and the patient was unable to hug her children or her husband. Most friends stayed away out of fear. She cried all day, alone and untreated in her room. The nurse decided to give her a bath and to spend the bath time comforting the woman. This nurse was severely reprimanded for assuming unnecessary care, an act outside the formula. While bathing is counted in the formula, the six or seven minutes allocated allow no time for chat, no time for encouragement—in other words, no time for care. Bathing is reduced to a minimum physical task and not enough time is allowed for even that.

In interviews in Quebec, BC, and Ontario, health-care workers said that they were initially enthusiastic about the system because the promoters assured them it would help increase staff by demonstrating how overworked they were. According to one Ontario RNA, 'They told us that if we do the numbers properly, they could say . . . according to the numbers, you do need an extra half person and you can have it because it says so in the numbers. And so I was actually quite pleased at first. Finally it's going to show what we do in a day.' She reported that the numbers did indeed indicate that, according to the formula, the unit was understaffed, but the solution was to change the formula, not increase the staff. Another Ontario RNA had a similar story. The system 'was showing that we needed an extra full nurse on our floor, which we didn't get. Also, it says we need an extra person for [the] three-to-eleven [shift]. And all of a sudden they were going to revamp the numbers and our numbers were cut in half.' Yet another Ontario RNA told the same story.

The patient classification system showed that they were working at 120 per cent. The response was to change the numbers in ways that said they were only working at 90 per cent. 'So they're going to say, 'You're working fine, you don't need more staff', when in actual fact you do because they just fiddled around those numbers and made them a little bit different. So it now appears that you are working at 80 per cent when in actual, two weeks ago you were doing the same thing and working at 120 per cent. So it could be a good thing if they would leave it.' Moreover, the numbers, she said, are developed by people who 'sit in the office and make decisions'. They decide that 'people don't need their bed done every day. . . . The fact that there are people that are elderly . . . so we're talking about patients who are, if they are incontinent, they drip and drip and all the rest of it . . . so there's reality lacking as far as the kind of care that's needed.'[68] A BC nurse echoed this claim, saying that their documentation task force did not have anyone with experience doing bedside nursing, 'all these people who haven't seen a dirty bottom in their lives or at least for many years'.[69] Although the transformation of care into numbers appears to bring science into work distribution, the practice suggests scientific principles are not the basis of decision-making.

The systems underestimate the time necessary for any task, in part because they do not count care and in part because they leave out much of the variety in patients and workers. Average time is calculated, rather than actual time with any particular patient, and averages can camouflage enormous differences. The systems also underestimate the time necessary because their main purpose is to control workers and reduce the cost of labour by eliminating all time not taken with a specific task and by increasing workloads. The numbers are used to cut staff drastically and, as a result, the staff drastically cuts care.

A Quebec nurse explained that the initial cutbacks in the early 1980s meant she went from looking after three mothers and three babies to five mothers and five babies. Before, 'On avait beaucoup plus de temps de considérer le côté psychologique de la maman, le temps d'arreter et l'aider a nourrir son enfant, de la conseiller. . . . Tout notre nursing est basé sur l'enseignment—de a à z. Quand la maman retourne chez elle, elle sait . . . Elle peut aller d'elle même'.[70] (We had much more time to consider the mother's psychological side, time to stop and help feed her child, to counsel her. . . . All our nursing is based on teaching—from a to z. When the mother goes home, she knows . . . she's able to do it herself.) But with the new workload based on the numbers, there was no longer time to do the counselling and teaching, much of which did not fit with a formula based on observed tasks reduced to their minimum. A nursing aide in an Ontario long-term care facility reports her workload has increased from 5 to 10 patients a day. As a result, 'a lot of people get frustrated with themselves because they're used to leaving at the end of their shift and having everything done. . . . They've worked three times as fast or three times as hard to make sure it's all done.'[71]

In Ontario, the nurses say they now have time only for the most basic tasks, and often the basics such as bathing, walking, turning, and toileting do not get done. More patients are put in diapers because there are not enough staff to take the patients to the toilet. And those who get diapers may not get them changed very often. New formulas have been developed to govern the number of times these diapers are changed, with some institutions limiting patients to four diapers a day. Yet these basic, non-medical acts can mean the difference between recovery and permanent immobility or even death. In her study of nursing homes and homes for the aged, Helmstadter found that the nurses became pill-pushers.

> 'We have no time for the patients', one nurse wrote, 'we just give pills.' There is not time for these nurses to take report or get information from other staff about the residents. Yet it is these nurses whose contacts with the residents frequently consist of simply handing them their pills, who must write out the care plans on which the nursing department's budgets are based.[72]

In the early 1980s, pharmacists were timed to determine that it took less than a minute to prepare a prescription, but Quebec physiotherapy was spared the numbers game. According to one therapist, 'We've always been a department that produced well and provided high-quality physiotherapy. And I think for these reasons the hospital looked rather favourably on physiotherapy and also as far as I'm aware, there were no cutbacks in professional staff. The cuts seem to come in non-professional areas.'[73] Ten years later, the physiotherapists and other professional staff were no longer excluded, in spite of continued high-quality service. In Ontario, physiotherapy sessions per patient were reduced in one hospital from a half-hour to 15 minutes; in another, the number of patients per therapist was significantly increased.

Similar schemes are used throughout health-care facilities. In cleaning, for example, there is a formula for the length of time it takes to clean each area. Such formulas, the workers say, do not seem to have been based on any actual observations within health care. It seems likely that these measurements come from studies in other sectors, especially when health-care managers are increasingly describing cleaning, food, and laundry services as 'hotel services'.

So, for instance, only a few minutes are credited for cleaning a patient's table. However, within the health-care system, there are few standard tables. Often 'a person has spilled pop all over it or there's vomit or pee on it, for all you know. It's not just an empty desk that you wipe off.'[74] The problem is not simply that a partially or quickly cleaned desk will look bad. It can constitute a risk to the health of the patient if it is not properly cleaned by people knowledgeable about the risks. Bathrooms, too, are allocated times that seem to be based on the notion of an empty room that has no special cleaning needs. Sometimes as little as seven minutes is allowed. Yet bathrooms are particularly dangerous places for people who are ill. If improperly cleaned, they can cause dangerous infections, especially given that people who are already ill are using them. Moreover, slips and falls are much more likely in bathrooms that are quickly cleaned or left unclean for long periods.

Work has also been carefully measured in the food and laundry services. An Ontario hospital worker in food services reported that 'Every job we do is timed. We have a time limit on everything . . . the slower you are the more you get behind. . . . They just load extra jobs on top of what you have to do and expect you to do it.'[75] In Quebec, a dietary aide explained that, with the new system, she has to 'throw everything on the tray together . . . then we go, go, go. . . . We had it good one time, girl, I mean we had a lot of people, a lot I mean. . . . You were tired when your shift was over but now you're tired, exhausted, you're everything. When I go home, the first thing I do is go upstairs, throw all my stuff on a hanger and get into bed.'[76] Tired workers make mistakes. Again, food services in health care are different from those in hotels. There are all kinds of special diets required and any errors in fulfilling these special needs could cause serious harm to the patient.

The most immediately obvious result of these measurement systems is that everyone's workload has increased. In Ontario, formulas meant that cleaners were assigned more than twice as much area as they had previously cleaned. For example, in one hospital, there used to be 15 cleaners in one area; now there are seven. Some of the cutbacks in housekeeping have been achieved through a practice called cycle cleaning. Instead of cleaning each area every day, some are cleaned on alternate days and left undone in between. The rest is achieved by either reducing the quality or by each individual working harder and faster. Because cleaners still feel a commitment to health care and because they know the importance of a clean environment to health, many workers still try to provide the old quality at the new pace. The same is true for those employed throughout health care.

This intensification of labour has profound consequences for both health-care workers and patients. Injury and illness rates increase and so does the incidence of violence. Working at higher speeds with less help, employees report higher injury rates on the job. Every week, an average of 8.4 per cent of those providers employed full-time missed work because they were sick or injured.[77] It seems likely that workers who are injuring themselves may be injuring patients at the same time. Data from Ontario indicating rising rates of misadventures suggest this is the case.[78] We do know that patients have become increasingly frustrated with the cutbacks and are becoming more violent. At one Toronto hospital, for example, the number of reported assaults on workers had increased from 26 in 1990 to 118 in 1993. A BC study funded by the Workers' Compensation Board revealed that 'compensation claims resulting from acts of force or violence increased tenfold in the 1990s' and that claims were highest among the care aides who came in direct contact with patients.[79] At the same time, the number of assaults on patients by employees is also increasing, and this, too, is related to overwork for employees and a lack of care for patients.

Injury and violence are not the only products of increased workloads and speed-ups. More and more workers are suffering from work-related stress, with a variety of consequences. Providers' stress and illness may lead to 'poor judgement and low productivity that can hurt patients'.[80] One Ontario RNA echoed the reports of many others. 'What's happening is the stress is making people physically ill.' Before they reach the point of diagnosed physical illness, workers find they 'have no patience for the patients', as one worker put it.[81] They have even less patience when, as is increasingly the case, injured or sick workers are not replaced and those remaining have to take on the extra work. This stress spills over into the home. Asked about what these speed-ups mean for their households, a group of long-term care providers said 'no sex'. Another said 'I fight more with everyone.'[82]

With workloads that are too heavy, employees worry about providing inadequate service and this, too, adds to the stress. Worker after worker we have interviewed found it more difficult to take pride in their work or to feel they are helping people because there is no time to put care into the work or to provide the minimum service. Cleaners said they were ashamed of how dirty the hospital had become; clerical workers feared that records were not properly transcribed; physiotherapists worried that patients were sent home without adequate preparation for survival on their own; dietary workers were concerned that dangerous food was getting to patients and that patients regularly went hungry because there was no food available outside meal hours. These workers said they had health-care jobs because they wanted to help people. However, they increasingly found that not only was it more difficult to help but also, because of the way they had to do the work, there was a growing risk of causing harm. If the job must be done quickly, the errors could cause permanent harm or even death. Without organizational time, workers can make mistakes in planning and implementing care. Without organizational time, it is also more difficult to organize the kind of teams that can both limit the number of errors and reduce injuries for workers.

These systems designed to measure health-care work are presented as objective means of determining the necessary work. They are defended as scientific assessments that are in keeping with medicine's traditions and that can therefore improve the quality of medicine. But such measurements are necessarily based on assumptions about how the body works and about what is necessary for health. They are also based on the notion that all aspects of the work can be measured in this manner. They are possible only if it is assumed that care can be defined as a series of procedures applied to average individuals. And they are open to considerable manipulation.

Only a particular medical model allows care to be divided into a series of discrete parts to be measured. Only a curative approach allows a focus on cuts and chemicals, bandages and IVs, and when combined with a focus on cost-cutting it could become lethal. A care model requires a more integrated approach that means neither individuals nor their treatment can be divided into separate parts. Current measurements leave care out. When their primary purpose is to reduce labour time, they tend to underestimate the time required for even the tasks that are recognized. Moreover, these times tend to be manipulated as a means of increasing workloads and managerial control over workers. The result is often extreme overwork for health-care providers and poor care for patients. Both processes have long-term costs, even if they mean short-term financial savings.

THE 90-SECOND MINUTE: MANAGING SCHEMES IN HEALTH-CARE REFORM

A number of management strategies were brought together under more integrated schemes most frequently called total quality management (TQM) or continuous quality improvement (CQI). Total quality management was first introduced in Japanese production industries. In the United States, some saw it as the reason for the Japanese economic miracle and looked to it as a way of restoring America's primacy. Then hospitals in the United States joined those in manufacturing and other businesses.[83] Finally, Canadian health-care managers sought to imitate our neighbours to the south and started to apply total quality management techniques to our health-care system. According to the Ontario Premier's Council on Health Strategy, the

> health sector can learn a great deal from modern management science—and particularly from the Japanese and American experiences in the total quality management of individuals and organizations. Equally applicable to manufacturing or service operations, continuous quality improvement includes teamwork in everything; customer or patient satisfaction; a total quality approach; employee empowerment; automation; innovation by everybody; management through vision and values; strategic choices; developing core competencies; and focusing on the interdependencies in the organization.[84]

Such strategies were at the core of health-care reform in the 1990s. Currrent managerial strategies follow many of the same practices, albeit under different names.

The techniques were attractive in part because they seemed to take account of the kinds of concerns about caring that many critics of the health-care system had expressed while offering a way to save money. Quoting a consultant from Boston University, the then chief executive officer of a major Canadian hospital claimed that 'total quality management may be more natural to health care than even to industry or business because the practices of the majority of health care professionals are value-based in concepts of service, care, and compassion for the sick and injured.'[85]

Employers in Canadian health care enthusiastically embraced total quality management strategies. Indeed, some administrators and consultants successfully lobbied to make these strategies a condition for hospital accreditation.[86] A former Minister of Health in Ontario, Frances Lankin, previously a union activist, endorsed the book written by the CEO mentioned above, writing that 'Total quality management provides hospitals with effective ways of producing high quality results and low-cost solutions to secure the future of our Canadian health system. Hassen shows how hospitals can achieve results through the active involvement, ownership, and commitment of people in their work.'[87]

To understand the problems created by this seemingly attractive approach, we need to look at its assumptions and how they fit with care. The most frequently referenced author for those extolling the virtues of total quality management in health care is Edward Deming.[88] The 14 points he offers in *Out of the Crisis* provide the basic principles for the theory, although these are translated in various ways for the health-care industry. While each of the points seems to make sense, they are often contradictory. In the following brief outline some of the points are set out. Summaries of the points do not tell the whole story, however. It is often in the explanations of these points and how they are implemented that the contradictions in the theory become clear.

Central to total quality management is the notion of continuous quality improvement. This comes from focusing on processes rather than outcomes and from responding to customer needs. Each process is improved by autonomous employees working in teams, committed to improving both the product and the process because they have pride in their work and have adopted a new philosophy. Training, education, and self-improvement replace inspection, monitoring, slogans, exhortations, and targets, as workers learn to focus on zero defects and innovation and as everybody works together to accomplish the transformation. Fear is driven out of the work relationship, providing a firm basis for the new approach.

But the autonomy that is critical to continuous quality improvement is accomplished by management taking leadership. Management spreads the philosophy and designs the new work organization. In other words, it is top-down rather than bottom-up autonomy. Management is still very much in charge, although some middle managers are supposed to develop innovative ways to eliminate their own jobs as workplace hierarchies are flattened. Workers improve processes so fewer people are required to do the work. Under such circumstances, it is difficult to drive out fear.

And quality is improved through the elimination of variation in processes and outcomes, as well as through innovation. Yet variation itself is often a source of innovation, and uniformity is unlikely to respond to diverse customer needs. Indeed, the elimination of variation is likely to discourage rather than encourage the experimentation with new work processes that may improve quality. The elimination of variation also contradicts the notion of employee empowerment and pride in work. It contradicts, as well, the notion of professional autonomy that is so critical to care.

This contradiction is most evident in the reliance on 'statistical thinking'. As Berwick, Godfrey, and Roessner explain in *Curing Health Care*,[89] 'It is a characteristic of quality management to invest heavily in the design and deployment of measurement. The agenda for measurement is extensive.' A report prepared for the Canadian deputy ministers of health makes as central to its recommendations the notion that 'If you can't measure it, you can't manage it', the slogan of the vice-president of United Health Care Corporation.[90] This measurement of everything is simply a new form of monitoring and control, the very things that are to be eliminated by the new work processes directed by autonomous workers.

Emphasis on measurement also contradicts the emphasis on multi-skilled workers involved in an integrated work process. Measurement based on the transformation of work into numbers necessarily involves at least the conceptual fragmentation of tasks into discrete units that can be counted. It is much more suited to Taylorist approaches to work organization than to theories that argue for multi-skills, an educated workforce, and integrated processes.

Similarly, the statistical assessment of customer satisfaction also undermines the notion of responding to needs defined by customers. To be readily counted, customer response must to be organized into pre-packaged options. The customer ticks off the most appropriate (or least appropriate) box on the survey question, but has no say in determining the question or the range of possible answers. Moreover, this approach to measuring satisfaction fails to take into account power and knowledge differentials among customers. These differentials distort the notion of simply responding to a variety of customer needs and offer few ways of assessing which needs are to be satisfied. Power differentials are particularly important in health care, when few patients feel they have the knowledge necessary to evaluate many aspects of treatment.

Berwick, Godfrey, and Roessner reject earlier quality assurance programs in health care on the grounds that they lack a general theory to provide the basis for change.[91] However, the total quality management theory they and others embrace is fraught with contradictions that bring the entire theory into question. Even more questions arise when we examine the translation of this theory into practice in health care.

According to an annual report of Toronto's Women's College Hospital, a large metropolitan hospital that has prided itself in responding to women's needs, total quality management 'breaks that traditional notion that higher quality is going to cost more'.[92] It sounded particularly attractive to nurses because it builds on their concern for quality, for team co-operation, and for autonomous work. It also built on their past practices, their traditional ways of providing care. In his book on the application of this approach to a major hospital in Canada, Hassen speaks of the need to 'trust people to do their jobs', and to have 'shared decision-making and self-directed teams'. He recognizes that the 'people best qualified to make positive changes are the ones doing the work', that 'learning from each other' is central to developing new skills, and that health-care workers are accustomed both 'to working in multidisciplinary teams' and to peer review.[93]

The total quality scheme seemed to fit nicely with providers' notion of care, combining caring and curing while reducing costs. But instead of reinforcing such approaches to care, the translation of total quality management into practice in hospitals is undermining them. The reasons for the failure can be found in the contradictions within the theory, in the problems with the medical model on which it is based, and in the focus on cuts rather than on care. As it is being implemented in health care, total quality management is increasing fear and making teamwork more difficult while reducing the power of employees and the quality of care.

Let us first look at fear. Deming recognized that fear prevents people from working effectively. Yet total quality management was introduced into Canadian health care as a means of cutting costs—and the greatest costs are labour costs. In industry, and even in the profit-making American health care system, it is possible to argue that continuous improvements in quality and output will attract more customers to the service and thus prevent job loss. However, in the Canadian non-profit system, which is both more universal and more accessible than its American counterpart, hospitals are not competing with each other for more patients. Nor should they be. The argument falls apart, especially when the purpose is to reduce services and the number of patients.

This has already become clear in Canada. Richardson, in a report prepared for the United Nurses of Alberta, offers the example of a major hospital that distributed a paper on new directions and change. It spoke of visions, missions, values, and strategic directions, all from a total quality management approach. 'Embedded in this seductive language was the announcement that 78 registered nurses and 76 licensed practical nurses would be laid off and 74 nursing attendants would be hired to replace them.'[94] Moreover, there was no evidence that 'customer service' improved or that more 'customers' were attracted to the hospital. Such patterns were repeated across Canada, resulting in nearly 6,000 fewer nurses working as nurses in 1999 compared to 1994.[95]

Similarly, Ontario hospital workers have said that the patient classifications systems were used not for continuously improving quality but for reducing the number of workers. As one registered nursing assistant explained, the system 'was showing that we needed an extra full nurse on our floor, which we didn't get. Also, it says we need an extra person from three to eleven. And all of a sudden they're going to revamp the numbers. And a lot of the numbers got cut almost in half. It still showed . . . we need an extra half person, which we seldom get.' Another described how management launched a campaign that would not only save linen but save jobs. 'And we felt really bad because they said . . . in one month, you've already saved a full position. But nobody's job was saved. All those people were laid off.'[96]

As Deming recognized, it is hard to work effectively for the company when you live in fear. But cutbacks and new managerial approaches have left a legacy of fear. Interviewed at the height of cutbacks, an Ontario registered nursing assistant reported that 'nurses are so scared of losing their job now that there's so much tension on the floors now, and you even have . . . the people on the same shifts fighting against each other.'[97] The majority of nurses who left Canada during this period did so because they lost their jobs or downsizing drove them out, a clear indication that the fear was justified.[98] While nurses are now much in demand—in large measure because of these managerial strategies—there is little evidence that the fear generated by such strategies has disappeared.

Fear and new management strategies have often served to undermine tra-ditional teams in health care, even though new management is supposed to build teams. As Richardson points out, teams in these schemes are intended to compete against each other and so are individuals within teams.[99] While women employed in health care have long been accustomed to working in teams, they have used them as a source of support rather than of competition or surveillance and as a spontaneous way of dealing with workloads. The old ways of doing have become less and less possible under new managerial strategies, and the new ways cannot work in practice. One BC nurse explained that when administrators want to send in more patients, 'you're supposed to get together in this little huddle' to discuss how to do this extra work. 'It's wonderful on paper but it's not functional because you're all too busy to get together in this little huddle and have a discussion. And besides, nobody wants another patient. They've all got too many now.'[100]

A survey conducted at one major hospital before total quality management was introduced indicated that 72 per cent of the staff felt teamwork was their greatest source of strength. But total quality management was not satisfied with these old teams. With TQM came a 'Team Meeting package' developed by a hospital-management research team, complete with project worksheets to track activities, anonymous assessments by individual team members, agendas, and other tracking documents.[101] In practice, this means that the innovation, support, and trust are gone. A clerical worker in an Ontario hospital explained:

> Before, where somebody would finish the work and say 'Okay, what have you got to do? And, I'll help you with that', they won't now. They don't want to get involved. Besides not having the time, if they did have the time, they won't [offer to help] in any case because it's their job and they can't afford to take any more on. But in case something gets to be theirs, they don't want to take it on. And it's turning co-workers against each other. Whereas before they worked as a unit, now they're turning against each other.[102]

The increasing use of part-time staff also undermines the traditional teams. Those working together on a shift may not know each other and therefore have not developed a method for sharing knowledge and the workload. Instead, new part-time workers are often seen as a burden because they do not know the routine and because they require the already overburdened, more permanent staff to take on a teaching job. Cutbacks in the number of staff have further reduced the possibilities for teamwork. In nursing work, 'It takes a nursing assistant, it takes a registered nursing assistant, and it takes the regis-tered nurse to work as a team.'[103] But staff reductions implemented under new management schemes often mean these people are no longer together on a shift. With team members required to take up the slack when workers are sick, there is enormous pressure on workers to come in even when they are ill.

The new teams are less effective than the old, in part because of fear and in part because they have been organized primarily as a way of controlling work-ers rather than as a way of co-operating to get the work done. The undermin-ing of traditional teams and the increasing fear also undermine the possibility of workers gaining more power. Many of those who work in the health-care field were attracted to the stress on empowerment because they have a tradition of discussing health-care practices and patients as part of the decision-making process. They also have a tradition of taking initiative in dealing with patients, families, or other workers. However, new management schemes often served to limit these traditional forms of worker autonomy and power in health care. Flattened hierarchies, initially attractive, have come under increasing criticism. BC nurses reported to us that the loss of their nurse managers frequently meant the loss of their advocate who served as a buffer with administration and the loss of someone who can take overall responsibility for the unit.

In both *Curing Health Care* and *Rx for Hospitals*,[104] the authors make it clear that management designs and implements the new work organization, although physicians are to be enticed into the process. In the hospital described by Hassen in *Rx for Hospitals*, the Quality Council included the chief executive officer, five vice-presidents, the chair of the medical advisory committee, and the director of total quality management. Others were occasionally consulted. The Quality of Worklife Steering Committee is described by Hassen as a model of the collaboration that is central to total quality management. A significant number of employees and union executive members served on this Committee, along with the Director of Personnel and the Director of Total Quality Management. However, what they got to discuss was such issues as employees' charitable contributions, long-term service recognition awards, a child-care program, a discount booklet, an employee handbook that includes the TQM perspective, a staff development fund, and a '"new ideas" initiative'.[105] Involvement in these areas hardly constitutes worker empowerment, even under old management practices.

Richardson reports that in Alberta some hospitals invited nurses to participate in 'shared governance structures'.[106] This sharing was often offered when layoffs or closures were anticipated. Nurses were invited to help when the decision was about who goes or how new patients are to be covered with existing resources, rather than about how to govern or about how to treat patients. In his study on TQM, Anderson describes one Ontario hospital where 'workers were faced with the choice of having the employees make cuts through TQM or having the management decide on who was to go.'[107]

At the same time as new committees are established to involve employees, often in minor or lose-lose decisions, old union structures are being gradually undermined. As Hassen makes clear, in order for TQM to work, 'traditional concepts of labour relations would have to be challenged and significantly altered.'[108] The stress on individuals and on commitment to the workplace is in direct opposition to union practices. The union, as Anderson points out, is in danger of being treated as:

> one of many interest groups or stakeholders which have to be accommodated. For example, in a hospital there are doctors, professionals, patients, volunteers, the community, and finally general employees and nurses, even though the latter groups form the vast majority of the workforce.

> Committees are struck with all or many of these groups. The union input in the so-called 'collective' decision-making process is then minimal.[109]

But this emphasis on the individuals, as opposed to their unions, has not necessarily meant that individuals have more power. Indeed, the new management systems have also frequently meant that individuals have even less discretion, fewer choices, and less say.

Increasingly, established licensing protections are also being challenged. Licensing regulations were introduced to give workers some power, and some new regulations are seen as a means of expanding the power of various nurses' groups by allowing them to undertake practices previously reserved for others. However, they may also mean a loss of more integrated approaches to care.

Multi-skilling, another basic component of new management, is directly linked to these efforts to change who does what in health care. According to the theory, continuous quality improvement will result from multi-skilling, shared knowledge, and on-the-job training. Multi-skilling, by definition, depends on extensive training to ensure that many workers have a broad range of skills. There are assumed to be three advantages to this strategy. First, with a very broad range of skills, employees can move quickly among a wide variety of jobs. No time will be lost waiting for another worker or switching from job to job. Second, job satisfaction will increase for workers because they will be able to participate in a number of different tasks and learn more skills. Third, this shared knowledge and range of skills will encourage innovation from workers with an overview of the job.

Here, too, the traditions in health-care work should fit right in with this approach. Women in this field have long taught each other necessary skills and helped each other out by working in teams. The teams pooled their skills to get the job done. Reports, for example, were often done by those with a variety of shared knowledge, as were lifting, bathing, walking, and comforting. The teams often improvised to get the job done, and felt considerable satisfaction from the use of their skills.

But those interviewed in Ontario maintained that the stress on reducing labour time left little time for traditional ways of knowing or for traditional teamwork. Combined with the increasing use of part-time employees and the constant redeployment of workers throughout the hospital, the new work organization has meant workers do not have time to train or be trained. This is particularly problematic in health care, where so many specialized skills are required in every area and where new technology and procedures are introduced on a daily basis. A registered practical nurse sent to emergency said that:

> at times, during breaks and stuff, I'm alone there. I have maybe three patients on the monitor. I can tell you I can't read it. I can't run a strip off and say this is exactly what's wrong with this patient, his heart. A doctor came in that day and said, 'What can you tell me about this patient?' I said, 'The only thing I can tell you is that every time he stands up, his heart rate goes up to 128. The nurse has gone to lunch and I'm the only person here right now.'[110]

Long-term care workers report that they are increasingly expected to provide acute care or look after people with severe mental health problems, although little training has been provided to help them do this new work.[111] The focus is more often on assigning more tasks to already overworked employees than on increasing their education and training. It is more on multi-tasking than on multi-skilling. Assigning tasks to those not educated for the job increases the risk levels for both workers and patients. And the stress levels and fear of job loss mean that workers are less able or willing to teach others.

Multi-skilling is also often about removing the hard-won restrictions on scope of practice. Under existing legislation, there are clear rules about such things as who can give certain kinds of medications or insert a catheter. While some of these restrictions were primarily about maintaining power, many of them reflected and reinforced a particular approach to care. The restrictions were based on the assumption of integrated and necessary skills, on the notion that giving a needle was more than a technical task and that giving medication to an ill person was about more than just reading a label. With multi-skilling, these 'artificial' restrictions are under attack.

The removal of restrictions on scope of practice prepares the way for the lowest-cost care provider (LCCP). This LCCP is frequently defined as a person who has been given the minimum amount of training to acquire a particular technical skill. The strategy can be used to replace doctors with RNs and RNs and RNAs with health-care aides or with the new personal service worker. This kind of multi-skilling, especially without education that encompasses the overall issues in health care, reduces the job to tasks that may be done inadequately; inadequate care can mean injury or even death. Moreover, multi-skilling can mean that workers are focused on the tasks rather than on health care or the person, further emphasizing the separation of the person into body parts to be fixed, with little attention to the person who inhabits the parts.

The multi-skilling strategy can also be used as a means of devaluing work and the workers and of reducing their power. RNs and RNAs laid off during the cutbacks were pressured to take on jobs classified as requiring different and more limited skills, of becoming those lowest-cost care providers. In some cases, they were required to take short courses before they could undertake the work in spite of their training. However, if they maintain their licences as RNs or RNAs, they still have the same responsibilities and can be charged by their colleges if they fail to act as licensed nurses. Thus, employers get skilled workers at lower costs. The effect is to further disempower workers, a development contrary to the announced theory, if not the practice, of TQM.

The purpose of employee multi-skilling in the total quality management system is the elimination of waste and variation. Waste can too often be defined as the care components, as those actions that do not have an immediate, obvious result. It is certainly defined as the elimination of any breathing time between tasks and of any time taken to do any tasks not specified in the patient care plan. The elimination of both kinds of waste means a greater emphasis on cuts and chemicals, rather than prevention and care.

The focus is on value-added care. What is defined as adding value are those procedures 'for which the customer can be charged, e.g. the pill, the IV, the dressings. Non-value added work is all the work that cannot easily be directly charged to the patient, e.g. walking time, pouring meds, transporting patients, etc.'[112] Quality is measured primarily in terms of outcomes that can be easily counted. Outcomes are not measured in terms of how well patients are but rather in terms of how quickly they are processed and how quickly they leave, dead or alive. So, for example, Hassen uses as a primary indication of improved quality the speedier processing of admissions, not how healthy people are weeks after leaving or even how effective their treatment was during their stay.[113]

The elimination of waste is also about eliminating those aspects of services not defined as part of care. Food services, for example, have been increasingly cut back, too often without regard to the actual needs of the patients and without recognition of the role of food in health. One Ontario health-care worker explained that 'Nourishments have been cut way back. If you have somebody that's nauseated, not eating, would like a ginger ale, you have to go back to the desk, fill out a form with so and so's name and room number. One can of ginger ale, please. Sign it. Proceed to wait until the kitchen picks up the slip . . . and this person hasn't eaten for days or anything else.' Another gave the example of 'a cancer patient [who] is living on ice cream and ginger ale or milkshakes. You can't get one after seven o'clock at night because there is nobody there'. Yet another explained that 'We don't make the toast and the coffee any more and the patients' biggest complaint is coffee and toast. Coffee is made too far in advance and so is the toast. [It's] like rubber.'[114] While coffee and toast may seem like luxuries, for diabetics or people who have been without food or have little appetite, the way food is served and when it is served can make a significant difference in health.

Similar strategies to eliminate waste are evident in the housekeeping services. Increasingly, the kinds of practices used in hotels are used in hospitals. According to one group of Ontario workers, 'The bathroom vents are filthy. They need to be vacuumed probably every second day minimum I would think, same as the curtains. We had a patient with asthma, and I was closing the curtains and I looked up and all this stuff is just hanging on the curtains, just at the top, okay, because it has come out of the vent system and it's hit the curtains.' As this RNA went on to point out, such 'stuff' on the curtain constitutes a significant danger to the patient with asthma.[115]

Directly linked to the elimination of waste is the elimination of variation in what is done for each patient and how long it is done. The intent is to develop formulas for everything from treatments to length of stay. Even averages based on past practices are to be reduced. As *When Less Is Better: Using Canada's Hospitals Efficiently* puts it, 'Using average length of stay as a benchmark thwarts the management exercise because averages do not provide targets which are sufficiently exacting.'[116] The report also provides an example of clinical practice guidelines:

> Computer software of clinical algorithms based on guidelines for use as a pre-surgery screening tool. Prior to the bookings for elective surgery the booking official is directed by the software to ask the patient a series of questions. Based on the answers to the questions, the projected procedure is validated or otherwise. Examples of such software are those developed by Value Health Sciences and Health Resources Management.[117]

These measures do not account for variations among patients in terms of their ability to report and assess their problems, their emotional state, their culturally related perceptions, and their social relations. Indeed, the purpose of these measures is to eliminate as much variation as possible both among patients and, as a consequence, among providers. Such formulas almost necessarily leave out personal interaction, social support, and patients' anxiety about the process. In other words, some of the most important care components are outside the formulas. They thus also leave out the discretion of the providers. The utilization report seems to suggest that these formulas can be applied by someone untrained in health care, a 'booking official' who simply fills in the blanks.

Central to the elimination of both waste and variation is the reliance on 'statistical thinking' and the measurement of everything. As we have seen, in health care the medical model that divides the body up into parts to be treated allows the kind of measurement necessary to continuous quality improvement theory and practice. At the same time, the emphasis on data reinforces the stress on doing things to people rather than on the provision of care to the whole person. The focus is on cuts and chemicals, on procedures that can be counted, timed, and costed. This emphasis has profound consequences for care providers.

In the Ontario study, worker after worker in the hospitals said that continuous quality improvement meant more control over the worker, an intensification of labour, more time spent filling out charts, and less time providing quality health care. A physiotherapy assistant explained that her workday is divided into 15-minute segments and she has to account in writing for her work in each of these segments. More importantly, she has to provide considerable justification for any variations within this 15-minute formula. But this breakdown of physiotherapy into equal, short segments is happening precisely when she has to treat patients who have a much greater variety of ailments and who require much more complex treatments than in the past. The process means she takes more time to report and has less discretion to treat individual patients. Yet physiotherapy is obviously part of the health promotion that is supposed to be our new priority. The calculation of patient times eliminates the variation but allows little time for the real differences among people, especially among those who are ill with complex problems, and allows no time for care.

Continuous 'improvement' means a continuous reduction in time. Healthcare workers say they are already working well beyond the quality limit, unable to provide more than the basics. Rooms are cleaned less thoroughly, beds and diapers are changed less often, patients are walked and turned less frequently. It is very difficult to automate many of the tasks in health care. Further reducing times for procedures means that workers must work faster, that more essential tasks are left undone, and that little care is provided. It also means an increasing focus on drugs and surgical or other intervention rather than on health promotion. The timing of tasks is first used to develop formulas and then the formulas are used to reduce the time for each task and the number of people doing the tasks. What was initially counted as taking five minutes then becomes counted as taking four. This is often done without any change in the process or in the number of patients. Indeed, with the new limits on admissions and stays, those patients who are in institutions require more care. Even though fewer staff will be looking after the same number of people, the data will show quality improvement because the statistical formula has been changed. And the institutions with the lowest numbers and the least time become the norm to which others strive.

Such recording and measurement mean both less discretion for the workers and more time spent recording. They do not necessarily mean better quality or even more accurate data. The Ontario workers often called their report sheets, the ones that were supposed to be the quality control, the 'lie' sheets because they could not possibly do all the tasks listed but they had to check off the forms. One worker summed up the process as follows: 'Quality is about filling in sheets about standards you cannot meet.' Linens and diapers are carefully counted; formulas are developed for eliminating waste and variation. Diapers are to be changed only four times a day and nursing staff no longer have the power to use their own judgement about patient needs. As one registered nursing assistant in Ontario put it, 'You can't look at a patient and tell whether their bed needs to be changed or not? I mean, what happened to our judgement along the way? That's what I feel. . . . They're picking us to death.' And 'it was such a rush job, you don't feel good about it.'[118]

The pride Deming thought was critical to the TQM approach is impossible when the workers no longer have time to do even a minimum job, let alone a good one, and no longer have any discretion in their work. This is particularly problematic in health care, where women have long been committed to the work and have been willing to forgo other rewards because they felt they were helping the sick. This has been the case for the cleaners, the clerical workers, and the dietary aides, as well as for the nursing staff.

The statistical method of both assessing and improving quality does not do much to improve patient power either, even though the theory claims to be centred on customer satisfaction. As we have seen, formulas are developed to ensure that patients stay the shortest possible time in the hospital. The formulas are based on averages developed from surveys of patient populations. Even though patients differ both in their recovery rates and in their options for care outside the institution, patients are increasingly treated as if they all fit the formula because total quality management strives to reduce variation.

Shorter patient stays also mean, as one Ontario worker explained, 'They're not here long enough to complain.'[119] Patient input is often limited to surveys, which are in turn defined as accountability.[120] As Aronson makes clear, on the basis of her study of consultations in health care reform, patient input is 'analogous to seeking data on customer preferences for use in product development'.[121] Like those designed to indicate preferences between kinds of soap, these surveys decide what the alternatives are and simply ask patients to select one of these alternatives. When patients are offered choices, they are seldom provided with the knowledge necessary to make informed selection and seldom offered a range of alternatives that would help make such choices meaningful. Fewer choices for the providers necessarily mean fewer choices for the patients.

While patients are being surveyed about satisfaction, they are offered less in terms of care. The formulas for treatment allow for both less variation and less care. The increasingly rushed health-care workers often have no time for care, comfort, or explanation. According to more than one Ontario nurse, 'Patients are scared and they are demanding more because they are scared.' 'And what happens is when a patient comes in, they say, 'Why don't we get this anymore? And why are you not here?' Well, we don't get it anymore, we cannot supply that anymore.'[122] Time for responding to questions and answering call bells is gone in many institutions.[123] Rather than power, patients have fewer choices about how much care they receive where; rather than satisfaction, they have more limited care.

In sum, as the proponents of TQM claim, the health-care system should be ideally suited to such approaches. Health-care systems already have a labour force dedicated to and proud of the work, accustomed to working in teams and teaching each other, concerned about the quality of their work and satisfying their 'customers', and interested in sharing decision-making and willing to offer suggestions for improvements. This is particularly true of the women who form the majority of those who work in the health-care system. But TQM moved health-care workers farther away from their traditional practices, intensifying their labour, fragmenting their work, separating them from each other, and making it more difficult to work in teams, to innovate, to respond to patient needs, or to take pride in their work. As a result, it undermined care and, all too often, the health of both patients and workers.

Part of the problem with TQM can be found in the contradictory nature of the theory itself. Part can be found in the way it is implemented, with most of the stress placed on reducing costs, eliminating variation, and downsizing the workforce rather than on eliminating fear, empowering workers, and improving the quality of service. But much of it can be attributed to the very purpose of the approach and the medical model on which it is based, which are at odds with the provision of care. Health care has many characteristics that make it an ideal candidate for TQM, yet it also has many qualities that make it inappropriate for a system primarily designed for the production of goods and the processing of parts. The emphasis on statistical thinking necessarily reduces workers' discretion, focuses on discrete tasks done to the body parts of individuals rather than on providing care for the whole person, and makes it less possible to provide quality care that takes individual needs and preferences into account.

PATIENT-FOCUSED CARE: RE-ENGINEERING CARE

Directly related to and growing out of total quality management approaches is patient-focused care (PFC). Like TQM, this scheme also talks about empowerment, multi-skilling, quality, vision, statistical thinking, eliminating variation, value-added work, and process. But patient-focused care also talks about re-engineering the entire system. Unlike TQM, PCF is not so much concerned with building on past skills and commitment as it is in breaking with the past and beginning again.

Here, too, the terminology may sound attractive, especially to those critical of past practices in health care that did not structure work around patients and their needs. Indeed, it seems to respond to many of the critiques raised in this book. However, in spite of the promise, patient-focused care, like TQM, helps move health care further away from satisfying overall patient needs, further restricts institutional services to specific treatments, and further limits care providers' power. It does so both because it is based on an engineering model of the body and because it is primarily aimed at reducing costs and controlling workers rather than at improving care.

Patient-focused care differs from TQM in two fundamental ways. First, it is introduced explicitly from the top. An emphasis on top-down decision-making is seen as necessary for the total restructuring that is defined as required. Second, the most important restructuring has to do with an entire reorganization of services that are fragmented and compartmentalized among job classification and work units.

A re-engineering of work organization is at the heart of the strategy. Departments such as x-ray, laboratory, housekeeping, and admitting are described as silos or chimneys that must be eliminated in favour of integrated units that combine all the services required by a patient. Instead of moving patients around to various departments, all the services except the most expensive ones will be found in units based on their care requirements. These care requirements do not correspond with old units such as maternity and geriatrics but instead reflect what have been determined as care requirements. Work, too, would be integrated, with divisions among care providers eliminated. In place of old job classifications would come new multi-skilled workers. Each of these workers, united in teams, could take up any task in the new multi-service units.

At first blush, this appears to be a good way to reintegrate services and bring back care. The patient, rather than the part to be fixed, could be at the centre. Care would no longer be divided up mainly in relation to body parts or special skills. Care providers could have a range of skills that would bring together caring and curing. Feeding, walking, talking, listening, comforting could become part of the curative procedures. Teams of highly skilled providers could work together to design and implement care. Time spent waiting in hallways for x-rays and lab work could disappear. In fact, some of these benefits may be apparent when the plans are first introduced, given that many of the old skills and methods will still be used by those employed in the new work organizations.

But this is unlikely to be the case in the long run, primarily because of the assumptions behind and the purposes of the scheme. Like TQM, the basis of change is still the medical model and statistical thinking. Patient care plans become even more dependent on formulas, on standardized methods of treatment, and on filling in the blanks. The eventual purpose is still the elimination of waste through the elimination of variation among patient treatments and among care providers. Any time not spent on value-added work, especially idle time used to share information, consult, comfort, or just plain rest, is to be wiped out. Teams become at least as much about surveillance and the elimination of union protections and old loyalties as they are about shared decision-making or collective work practices. The system is also intended to create a new generic worker who has the lowest, rather than the highest, level of skills required for the job. As Richardson concludes on the basis of her research on *Patient-Focused Care* in the United States:

> There is no question that the advent of the generic health care workers ushers in an era of lesser-skilled, inadequately-trained, inexperienced and less-qualified health care providers. This entire process of throwing workers into a boiling pot, melting them down and recasting them into multi-skilled health care practitioners who are unlicensed and whose work is unregulated, means tens of millions of dollars in health care savings and an equivalent reduction in the quality and safety of patient care.[124]

Eventually, the scheme is intended to significantly reduce staff along with the pay and benefits of those who remain. It seems unlikely that these reductions will mean that quality is improved. Rather, it is much more likely that exhausted and disgruntled staff, inadequately prepared for the work, will be providing inferior care.

There is certainly room to improve work organization in health care. The need for improvement and for cost-cutting has been recognized by most who work in the system. Both total quality management and re-engineering strategies have been attractive precisely because they promised to make health care more effective in terms of how work gets done and how care is provided. And some better methods have been introduced. But, for the most part, the new management processes in health are making it increasingly difficult to provide care. And as managers embrace one new theory after another, the system increasingly lacks the kind of stability necessary for employee satisfaction and confidence in patient care.

COMMUNITY CARE

Reforms in health care have two main themes. First, there are strategies to keep people out of institutions as much as possible and to reduce the length of stay in institutions to the shortest possible time. In justifying the first strategy, proponents usually cite advances in drugs and technology. But they also express concerns over the risks of institutional care and extol the virtues of home care or community care. According to *When Less Is Better*:

> The risk of nosocomial [hospital-generated] infections and adverse effects of hospitalization are well documented. Complications, such as respiratory infections, falls and adverse drug reactions have been reported to occur in up to 70 per cent of elderly admissions. The elderly are especially vulnerable to functional decline due to aspects of hospital care such as forced bed rest, immobilizing procedures and devices (e.g. intravenous lines, catheters, oxygen), restraint use and lack of encouragement of independence in self care. The environmental change may result in confusion and exacerbate the loss of autonomy that comes with admission. There is also very real concern about the growing number of interventions involving the frail elderly for whom the expectation of benefit may be too small to justify intervention.
>   The adverse effects of hospitalization on pediatric and psychiatric patients are also well documented.[125]

Instead of suggesting ways to prevent hospital infections, to ensure patients are walked and encouraged towards independence, the report promotes dehospitalization and ignores the problems that remain for the many who must enter institutions. Although the report does note evidence indicating that 'patients discharged too early are discharged in medically unstable states',[126] it nevertheless claims that 'The patient returns to a more familiar environment, which usually has psychosocial benefits, there is a decreased risk of acquired hospital infection and prompt hospital discharge engenders a positive feeling among clinicians and patients.'[127] There is no discussion of the risks patients may face at home or of the variations in homes.

In keeping with a wide variety of provincial documents, the most important solution offered for both high hospital costs and poor hospital care is to send people home. There, most expenses for the physical environment and many of those for necessary equipment are covered by the patient. Moreover, homes are seen as havens from a heartless institutional world, the place where treatment and care can be combined in a safe setting that offers comfort, independence, and choice. Care in the home or 'community' is assumed to be better for virtually everyone and to be preferred by virtually everyone.

The second strategy is directly related to the dehospitalization strategy. It involves shifting as much work as possible to the lowest-cost care provider. This can mean shifting more of the doctor's work to the RN and more of the RN's work to the RNA and on down the line. But increasingly, this LCCP is someone with little or no training who works outside an institution. These providers are often low-cost because unions are much more difficult to organize or maintain when workers are scattered throughout small organizations or employed in private homes. But these home care and community care workers do not form the majority of the lowest-cost care providers. The very lowest-cost care provider is the woman who does the work for no pay in the home or as a volunteer in the community. Study after study has demonstrated that care by family members and community is really another way of saying care by women. Women are the overwhelming majority of caregivers and they provide the overwhelming majority of care.[128]

The strategies designed to send people closer to home assume that a woman is available to take on the additional work and that she has the necessary skills or at least can be quickly taught to do the tasks. When reports such as the Ontario Ministry of Health's *Building Partnerships in Long-Term Care* talk about supporting 'consumers who choose to remain as long as possible in the familiar surroundings of their homes or with family', the impression is left that most people have a large group of people of both sexes around to provide good caring work. Only a little support and pressure from the government are necessary.[129] However, a great deal of evidence challenges these assumptions.

WOMEN AT HOME: THE OTHER WORKFORCE

As is the case with institutional care, care outside institutions is mainly women's work. What care women provide depends on a range and mix of factors, but most of the care is done by women unpaid and untrained for the job.

Government policies obviously play a critical role. As care moves outside the medically necessary doctor and hospital care explicitly covered by the Canada Health Act, there is no national standard for formal, public care. This is one reason why the National Forum on Health recommended national home care and pharmacare programs.[130] As a result, there are significant variations in the supports available to informal caregivers and those who need care.

Provinces and territories provide professional home care services such as nursing and physiotherapy without charge. But many charge user fees for homemaking, personal care, housecleaning, or transportation. Some provide supplies and equipment without cost while others charge; some cover required medications while others do not. Some have extensive provisions for respite care that offers unpaid providers some relief while others provide very limited access. There is also considerable variation in eligibility rules and in the limits placed on services, creating even greater differences in supports available.[131]

Ontario, for example, has established maximums of '80 hours of homemaking services per month for the first month; and 60 hours thereafter' and 4 nursing visits per day as maximums regardless of need,[132] and has introduced user fees for drugs purchased under the public plans for the elderly, the disabled, and those on welfare. All others must make their own arrangements for drugs required at home. By contrast, BC's policy is to make community nursing 'available 7 days a week, 24 hours a day', and home support services have a maximum of 120 hours per month, although more can be provided if a supervisor approves the additional hours.[133] Moreover, because BC has a universal pharmacare program and no or low user fees for particular groups, those receiving home care in that province have many of the drugs covered by the provincial plan.[134] Access to institutional facilities also differs somewhat across provinces. While only 1 per cent of Canadians live in such facilities,[135] the eligibility requirements, the location, the number of beds available, the nature of the services provided, and the fees charged vary in ways that limit options for those caregivers and care recipients who need such services.

Government policies on direct and indirect financial support also influence the care provided. Direct financial support for care providers is quite limited and equally varied. For the decade between 1984 and 1994, Nova Scotia provided compensation to caregivers, most of whom were young females in rural areas. This means-tested program paid considerably less than minimum wage for quite heavy workloads and primarily served to reinforce caregiving as undervalued women's work.[136] Quebec now provides up to $600 to caregivers to purchase respite care, again based on a means-tested system.

Most provincial financial support, however, comes indirectly through the tax system for deductions related to medical expenses, attendant allowances, and disability. Since 1998, the federal government has offered the Caregiver Tax Credit. This allows those who live with and care for an elderly relative to claim up to $400 if the claimant's annual income is less than $13,853.[137] These deductions and credits mean little to the many low-income women who provide care, given that they have little income from which to deduct the taxes and that they may have 'to absorb the cost of additional caregiving services before being eligible for reimbursements'.[138] There is, however, little research on the impact of direct financial compensation programs on caregivers or recipients.[139]

Access to formal services and other government financial supports for caregivers are clearly important to both care providers and care recipients. Yet, contrary to much popular discussion, the availability of formal care does not automatically mean less informal care is provided. Indeed, study after study demonstrates that between 85 per cent and 90 per cent of care is provided informally.[140] Even these figures may understate the amount of informal care provided, given that 'it is probably also the case that a lot more help is exchanged in families than is ever reported in surveys because people do not consciously think about what they are doing in providing help.'[141] This is particularly the case for women who may see their caregiving work as a simple extension of usual practices. As various researchers explain, for women, caring about someone very often is equated with caring for them, and the work as well as the skill of care become invisible in the process.[142]

Informal and formal care are complementary rather than alternative forms of support.[143] Instead of replacing informal caregivers, formal services are more likely to fill in when there are no informal caregivers or to provide some services that are supplemental to informal care.[144] As a study conducted for Statistics Canada concludes, 'the informal network operates in concert with the formal delivery system'[145] and the availability of formal services does not mean families and friends shirk their responsibilities. Nor does access to formal services mean people rush to use them. The overwhelming majority of health problems are managed through self-care. And 'most people who consult a physician have tried treating themselves before seeking medical advice'.[146] This is especially the case for women.

In addition to providing formal services, governments also influence the care provided through employment regulations. No jurisdiction requires employers to provide 'caregiver leave'. However, some employment or labour standards legislation allows short-term and unpaid leave.[147] While most collective agreements simply reflect the statutory emphasis on parental, sick, and bereavement leave, some include additional leave provisions for those with disabilities and for personal reasons. The Public Service Alliance of Canada, for example, has negotiated leave with pay for family-related responsibilities. In this case, family is broadly defined to include not only spouses and common-law partners but also any dependent children. Parents as well as step-parents or foster parents are considered family and so are any relatives permanently residing in the employee's household or with whom the employee resides. The paid leave is only for a maximum of five days, although leave without pay is allowed for long-term care of a parent for up to five years.[148]

Physical location also influences what care is provided, in part because formal services vary within provinces. Urban populations often have better access to care supports than do rural ones. 'Poor quality housing and insufficient health and social services characterize many rural communities. Distance makes access to services more difficult and adversely affects rural women's ability to provide care.'[149] Declining employment opportunities in rural areas, combined with health-care reforms, mean fewer resources for increasing needs. This, in turn, means greater disparities in ability to cope.[150] Native communities in particular frequently lack formal, community-based services.[151]

Similarly, those living in large urban centres are more likely to find services that respond to their particular cultural or religious practices. For example, concentrated populations mean urban Japanese Canadians can access some culturally sensitive programs. Such access can affect whether or not they use formal services at all, regardless of need, and may matter as much as quality and location in seeking care.[152]

Physical location also matters in terms of informal caregiving. The further away friends, relatives, and volunteers are, the more difficult it is to provide direct personal care. Children move away for education or employment; people immigrate, leaving their relatives behind. Nevertheless, many people provide care at a distance, especially care of the management sort.[153] Or they move themselves or others in order to give care. In 1996, nearly half a million Canadians moved to give or receive care. The majority of those who moved were married; more than a third had children under the age of 15 and had paid work. Those who move, then, have a range of caregiving responsibilities. While daughters are the most likely to make such moves, a significant proportion are friends (18 per cent) or other relatives.[154] Living arrangements do not play a central role in emotional support, and may be provided in person or by telephone, e-mail, or letter from anywhere. But living with someone may be the major determinant of help with activities of daily living and can be even more important than a marital or blood relationship.[155]

Social location matters at least as much as physical location in terms of what care is provided. Being a mother or a daughter is critical, because daughters and mothers are the most common primary caregivers, followed by spouses, friends, and volunteers.[156] We have little Canadian information on caregiving among same-sex couples or singles, but we do know that the gay and lesbian communities have formed support organizations and care services, especially for those suffering from HIV/AIDS.[157]

Gender and income also have a profound influence on what care is provided. According to a recent study, 'Women family members were expected to supplement home care services without pay and at great personal expense in terms of their own health, incomes, benefits, career development and pension accumulation, while men were not under as much pressure to do so.'[158] Financial costs were picked up by recipients and families; those without money do without and those who are poor or isolated fare worst of all. Deinstitutionalization, early discharge, day surgery, and cutbacks in public health services all shift more care work and care costs onto individuals and families, and especially onto women. The more care is privatized, the more poor people cannot afford care. Those without homes or relatives are particularly at risk of not receiving care.[159]

Finally, the needs of the person receiving care are a critical component in what care is provided. Those who are expected to recover after day surgery or early discharge from a hospital place high, immediate demands on caregivers for assistance in the full range of caregiving activities. Patients recovering from cardiac surgery, for example, require monitoring for their heart rate, for infection, and for wound healing; they need reassurance and comfort, as well as help in eating, bathing, going to the toilet, keeping the house in order, and managing their diet and exercise program.[160] However, these demands are expected to diminish over time until eventually care is no longer required. The situation is quite different for someone suffering from Alzheimer's or multiple sclerosis. Care needs can only increase with time and last until death.

Care varies as well with the stage of an illness. Initially, cancer care may mainly involve management and emotional support. During and after treatment it may require the full range of care forms. If the cancer is successfully treated, the need for all but emotional and social support may disappear. But if the treatment fails, then care needs gradually, or perhaps quite quickly, increase, ending over a relatively short term in death.

Chronic diseases, too, have stages that create varying needs for care. Multiple sclerosis, for instance, may go into remission, allowing a person to live relatively independently for long periods. Arthritis and rheumatism may mean that only heavy housework and house maintenance are a problem for a long time, with more needs appearing over time. Stroke patients may fully recover after temporary severe disability, or they may become quite dependent for the rest of their lives.[161]

Some chronic diseases and disabilities, however, exist from birth and mean that life is only possible with the provision of the full range of care or with one form of care throughout life.[162] Others may become paraplegic suddenly as a result of an accident. Care throughout life, or for most of it, is not uncommon. Of the 53 women interviewed for a study of rural caregivers, five had been caregiving for more than 20 years and one had been doing so for 35 years. Such caregivers provide care 'all the time', often with little support from the formal system.[163]

Care needs also increase with age, although often not as much as current media reports and policy discussions suggest. According to a recent study based on Statistics Canada data, 'when it comes to receiving assistance from others, similar proportions of seniors and non-seniors received assistance. And across age groups, only a minority reported that they received no assistance.'[164] Another Statistics Canada report describes seniors as a diverse group that is aging well.[165] More than nine out of 10 seniors live in a private household, and although over half say they get some help with household chores and personal tasks, half also say that they provide care to others.[166] In other words, care is for many seniors an exchange of services. Nevertheless, a significant number of seniors do need care. Of the 30 per cent who required health-related personal assistance, three out of four needed assistance with daily living activities and a quarter required extensive personal care. Women were not only more likely to need care but also more likely to have those needs go unmet. The lower the income and education, the greater the unmet need. And living alone also meant that the necessary care was less likely to be provided.[167]

In short, what unpaid care is provided depends on government policies and on the health issue, as well as on physical and social location. Formal care does not substitute for informal care. Rather, most care is informal or self-care and formal services supplement this care rather than the other way around. And it is mainly women who provide this care, often at considerable cost to their own well-being.

As daughters, mothers, partners, friends, or volunteers, women comprise the overwhelming majority of unpaid primary caregivers and spend more time than men in providing care. Women are much more likely than men to provide personal care and offer emotional support. Men's contributions are more likely to be concentrated in care management, household maintenance, shopping, and transportation.[168] In other words, women are more likely to provide the care that is daily and inflexible while men provide care that can be more easily planned and organized around paid work.[169] And men are more likely than women to get formal help when they do provide care, on the assumptions that they must have paid jobs and that they lack the skills necessary to provide care.[170] Yet the majority of women are now in the labour force, most have paid work because they need the income, and few have the kind of skills required to provide the care now expected to be delivered at home.[171] However, women provide personal care even when they have paid jobs, although higher-income women may be able to become more care managers than care providers.[172]

The little research that has been done about differences among women caregivers suggests that income and education matter at least as much as culture in terms of the kinds and amounts of care provided.[173] While most women want to provide various kinds of informal care, they do not want to be 'conscripted' into this relationship.[174] And the poorer women are, regardless of their culture, the more likely they are to have little choice about providing care.[175]

Some men have, and continue, to provide the full range of care. Like women, they care for their spouses. However, fewer men are called on for such care because their wives usually outlive them, given women's greater longevity and the pattern of men marrying women younger than themselves. Men care for their parents, too, providing up to a quarter of the care.[176] Men also care for their same-sex partners and serve as volunteers who manage care, provide transport and support, deliver meals, and do household chores.[177] And like women, men may provide care to siblings, in-laws, or other relatives.[178]

Friends also provide considerable caregiving, although we know less about them than we do about the spouses, mothers, and children who are caregivers. A Statistics Canada study found that nearly one in five of those who had moved in order to provide care were friends, rather than relatives, suggesting that friends do much more than offer the occasional visit.[179]

We know even less about differences among caregivers related to culture. The existing research does not indicate major differences in the provision of care but some in the stated commitment to care. For example, Japanese Canadians express a high commitment to filial obligation. This is reflected in the provision of emotional support but not in support through financial or other services.[180] Some cultural groups are also much more likely than others to live in households that hold several generations, suggesting cross-generational caregiving. But this is not necessarily the case. While East Indian immigrants, for example, tend to live in multi-generational households, it is important not to assume that this, like the lower use of formal services, simply indicates cultural choices. This pattern may be as much about immigration regulations requiring support for sponsored relatives and limited economic resources as it is about preference.[181] That Chinese, Greek, and Italian elderly are less likely to live alone than are other Canadians may reflect low incomes, lack of pensions, and immigration rules as much as cultural values.[182] Similarly, the fact that Aboriginal seniors are much more likely to live with relatives than are other Canadians may reflect poverty as much as choice or values.[183]

A rapidly growing literature examines the consequences of this care work for the unpaid providers. Not surprisingly, caregiver burden is a common theme. There are many, and varied, aspects to this burden. Many feel inadequate and unprepared for the task. Rural women who provide care describe their frustration, especially with the repetitiveness of the tasks, and the problem of dealing with the unhappiness of the care recipient.[184] They have to convince their husbands to allow them to bathe them and, like others who care for younger adults with severe physical disabilities, describe the 'difficult and potentially hazardous situations resulting from a combination of the weight of the person being bathed and the lack of strength of both parties'.[185] Lack of training for what is highly skilled caregiving creates additional stress on relationships. For many caregivers, the most emotionally upsetting activities are those related to bladder and bowel management, in part because they are such intimate tasks. Male caregivers found bathing their wives disturbing for similar reasons.[186] Rural caregivers feel ineffective in dealing with mood swings of the care recipient and with their own guilt—guilt about being healthy, about not understanding the illness, and about not making the right choices for the care recipient.[187] Such guilt is widely shared among caregivers, especially by the women who provide most of the care. This guilt may be compounded by their role as sole confidante and decision-maker and by cultural pressures.[188] Caregivers who move to provide care, like those who live in or close by, report changes in their sleep patterns, a decline in overall health, depression, a reduction in their social activities and holidays, and extra expenses.[189] A study of caregivers for those with Parkinson's suggests that the strain is greater the closer the caregiver is to the recipient.[190] In other words, loving the recipient may make it harder to care.

Stress of all sorts is a recurring theme, as is family conflict over who provides care and what kind of care is required. Conflicts may also arise between informal and formal caregivers, over what care should be provided and how it should be provided. Moreover, shifting care to homes means that formal services invade the household and 'boundaries separating these domains' are continually crossed, creating greater strain on the entire household.[191] New policy initiatives urge partnerships between families and paid providers, but this may well be more an exploitative relationship than a partnership, especially if the primary purpose is the reduction of public expenditure. In the partnership, 'most family caregivers were left socially isolated without adequate resources to provide care. Intentionally or not, holding family caregivers accountable for the provision of care without adequate resources is completely unacceptable.'[192] Indeed, these researchers, on nurse/family relationships, warn that 'failure to provide resources to help family members provide care could risk even further increases in health costs, as injuries or illness' result for caregivers. Moreover, 'failure to provide resources to help family members provide care could risk even further increases in health care costs, as injuries or illnesses of the elder and/or family caregiver ensue.'[193] Privacy is reduced for the entire household and for their relationships. Even before the most recent cutbacks in services, research indicated that caregivers have higher rates of affective and anxiety disorders than non-caregivers and use mental health services twice as much.[194] Caregivers for people with dementia are particularly at risk, and among those, people whose first language is neither English nor French are especially fragile.[195] Immigrants may feel particularly isolated and limited in their access to services that meet their needs.[196] This may contribute to depression, with those who have no outside help suffering the most.[197]

Caregiving can mean career interruption, time lost from work, financial loss and, especially for women, even job loss.[198] One in four employees provides care, and a large proportion of care providers are employed.[199] Not surprisingly, those with both elder- and child-care responsibilities, most of whom are women, are the most likely to lose time at work as a result of caregiving.[200] Indeed, women feel much greater tension than men between their caregiving and their paid work and between their caregiving and other family responsibilities. This is not surprising, given that women do more of the personal care and domestic work.[201] The limited leave allowed for such care, combined with few protections from being fired when caregiver stress leads to missed time at paid jobs, means that caregivers are very vulnerable at work. Those who care for people unrelated by blood or marriage may be particularly at risk. For both women and men, the consequences of such interruptions can be felt far into the future in terms of low pensions and benefits in their own old age.

Although friends and volunteers provide considerable caregiving, virtually all of the research on the burden of caregiving has dealt with relatives, especially the mothers, wives, and daughters who do the majority of the care. This lack of research may not simply reflect a failure to recognize the contribution of friends and volunteers. It may also reflect the fact that friends and volunteers have more choice about where and when they provide care, as well as about what care they provide. There is also a lack of research on same-sex partners, but there is little reason to believe the burden would be lighter for them.

There is considerable discussion in the literature about subjective factors, such as negative attitudes and cultural values towards caregiving that influence the impact on the caregiver. However, 'a belief one is ill-equipped to meet the demands of caregiving may not be unrealistic. Economic factors, a lack of instrumental support or caregiver illness may greatly impede one's ability to cope and may thus be a realistic, objective perception.'[202] In other words, caregivers may perceive a burden because there is one. This is especially the case for those who must provide long-term and constant care.[203]

It should be emphasized, however, that caregiving also has rewards. Caregivers experience warmth and satisfaction; they get joy from helping others and often feel rewarded through the personal interaction and the very real support they often receive in return.[204] Yet, like most human relationships, caregivers' experiences are contradictory.[205] Resentment, stress, frustration, and ill health too often occur along with the good parts, and these negative factors are most likely to occur in the absence of support, relief, and choice. The strain is too often manifested as abuse,[206] not only of the elderly but also of the disabled, whatever their age. Older people with intellectual disabilities may be doubly disadvantaged by prejudice against both the elderly and the disabled. Support groups, while often offered as an inexpensive way to relieve the burden of caregiving, have little impact, especially in the absence of other, more material supports.[207]

What about the burden on care recipients? We know less about this burden or about their views on the relationship. What we do know suggests that they, too, have burdens in addition to those caused by their physical or mental problems or both, especially when their low incomes and cutbacks in services eliminate choices about care. Care receivers may be placed in a position of 'compulsory acquiescence', not primarily by their informal care providers but by the public system's failure to offer them choices.[208] Elderly women experience conflicts between their need for support and the expectation of self-sufficiency, as well as between the media panic over the costs of an aging population and the system's failure to recognize the specificity of their individual needs.[209] Seeking to maintain reciprocity and their pride, these women feel the strain of limiting their demands and the strain within their relationships.[210] Like caregivers, they experience guilt and frustration.[211] On the other hand, having a partner can make a significant difference, even in ill health. Indeed, 'married seniors in poor health enjoy a high level of emotional support and are just as socially engaged as those in good health.'[212] It seems likely this is the case with couples or others who are not married but who have enjoyed a long life together.

As is the case with caregivers, there appear to be significant differences in the burdens felt by women and men. 'Female respondents described feeling guilty when their husbands did laundry and prepared meals if they had never been involved in these tasks before.' At the same time, those women with osteoarthritis or osteoporosis defined help from spouses with mobility, at home or in the community, as simply part of the relationship. Men, on the other hand, did not usually see help from a spouse with such household tasks or with personal care as dependence.[213] In short, like caregivers, care recipients experience contradictory feelings about care and often face increasing burdens as more care is sent home to be provided by untrained and unpaid family or friends.

Certainly many people would like to avoid institutions as much as possible, especially when lean and mean management practices have resulted in an increasing focus on cuts and chemicals while care and prevention components are being eliminated. And certainly many women want to help care for their family members. Indeed, most care is already in the hands of these lowest-cost providers and many of those they care for are more than satisfied with the support. But women already carry heavy household workloads, most are in the labour force, and they are there because their incomes are critical to family survival. Moreover, the kind of care now being sent home requires complex skills that put both the caregiver and the care recipient at risk. Home care, at least in its present form, serves more to reinforce women's responsibility for the caring work than to provide any significant alternative. The social, physical, and financial costs to women are enormous and may cost the health-care system much more in the long run.

Here, too, the issue is not about deciding whether communities and homes are better than institutions or about whether care by mother or daughter is better than care by a professional. It is about managing the tensions between the two in ways that integrate prevention and treatment, caring and curing, while respecting the needs of both groups. As a report prepared by the ARA Consulting Group for the Ontario Ministry of Citizenship explained, in the case of the elderly the 'challenge that society faces is how to provide high quality service *for* and directed *by* dependent seniors, while maintaining equity and choice for women and other care givers, while still achieving an affordable system.'[214] High-quality services for everyone must balance not only these tensions but also those between the different kinds of caregivers and different approaches to care.

COMMUNITY CARE: THE VOLUNTEERS

The various governments are not only talking about sending care to the home. They are also talking about sending care to the community. Although community is seldom defined, the impression is left that little is being done by communities now and that communities are both preferred and better than state-provided institutional care. Moreover, community is often represented as a universal category, involving everyone equally and serving everyone equally. As is the case with care in the home, the impressions left are not supported by the facts. A brief examination of each impression in turn should make this clear.

First, the notion that care has been removed from communities can be challenged. The term 'community' is often used to refer to those groups and organizations that are separate from the state, located throughout the country, close to home. Such groups can often trace at least their origins to voluntary participation. As is the case with care in the home, these kinds of communities are already providing a great deal of care. Organizations such as the Salvation Army and the Victorian Order of Nurses have been providing care since the last century and, in Ontario at least, the Children's Aid Society was formed at the beginning of the twentieth century. Indeed, medicare mainly involved the public funding of existing organizations, and many of these organizations could be classified as community organizations. A great deal of care is already done in the community, where many organizations are already overburdened with work. In British Columbia, for example, family support services, child-care services, and residential services for children in care have always been contracted out by the government to community agencies.[215]

Second, the suggestion that community organizations are different from state organizations needs a great deal of qualification. Embedded in the idea of community is the notion that communities are more democratic and participatory, more responsive to local needs, more innovative, and more involved in advocacy and prevention. Certainly some community organizations fit this description and even more once did. However, many are also large bureaucratic organizations that offer little flexibility. Many are bound to religious beliefs that prevent them from being open to new ideas or participatory in terms of decision-making. Moreover, membership is often restricted to those who meet particular criteria, criteria that limit access.

Third, these communities seldom involve everyone equally. They often depend on voluntary, female labour. A division of labour similar to that in the home appears among the volunteers who form much of the community.

Among those over age 55, women are twice as likely as men to do volunteer work.[216] Younger women are also more likely than men to do volunteer work. According to a Statistics Canada survey, 57 per cent of all 1989 volunteers were women. And women accounted for two-thirds of those providing care or companionship and collecting or distributing food or other items. They also constituted three-quarters of those preparing and serving food. Indeed, well over half of the women who do volunteer work prepare and serve food or provide personal care, while half of the men volunteers promote ideas and do research. The data for the 1990s show very little change in these patterns, and women predominate even among the young volunteers.[217]

The only areas where men form the majority of volunteers is in professional consulting, sitting as a board member, repairing, maintaining, and building facilities, firefighting, search and rescue, and protecting the environment.[218] Such jobs are unlikely to increase much when people are sent home for care in their communities. Heller found that many women, in addition to providing full-time care for those who live with them, 'also provide part-time care to aged friends and relatives elsewhere'.[219] This work will increase with deinstitutionalization, given that women already account for more than three-quarters of those who do volunteer work in the health sector.[220] And as is the case for women's home care work, volunteer work becomes more and more difficult for women who are already carrying double workloads.

At the same time as governments are turning even more to community care, they are developing strategies that limit the most desirable aspects of community care. Much of the innovation, participation, and responsiveness of communities reflects their variety, independence, and separation. The result, as a number of provincial governments point out, is an unco-ordinated and scattered arrangement of services. Ontario, for example, integrated these services into community care access centres (CCACs) that provide one-stop shopping for those seeking care. While there are clear advantages to co-ordination, the single entry point based on a single set of criteria means that those who do not fit these criteria have little or no alternative. They cannot shop around as they did in the past. Community agencies are pressured to shape their services to fit these criteria, especially under conditions of competitive bidding with for-profit firms, thus reducing the opportunities for flexibility and variety.

The need to bid on government contracts also encourages conformity. Increasingly, as Rekart's interviews with executive directors of community agencies in British Columbia suggest, services have 'developed their grantsmanship to the point at which they became familiar with the culture, language and procedures of government'.[221] Because, as one director explained, 'non-profit agencies worry about whether they will still be in business should someone underbid them', they may shape their services to fit government priorities more than those of their constituencies.[222] Having to conform to the more stringent government criteria for clients, they had less flexibility in terms of services and client selection.[223] Dependent on government criteria for funding and swamped with the workload, agencies may also lose their advocacy role.[224] This is particularly the case if they must bid against for-profit agencies for the money because they will have to act like businesses in order to compete. And businesses are seldom more democratic than governments and rarely get involved in advocacy for their clients.

There is, then, no guarantee that communities will be any more responsive, participatory, innovative, and caring than institutional and government-run services. In fact, many of what are called community services are as bureaucratic as government agencies, and new strategies are encouraging more of them to act like the bureaucracies they are supposed to replace. As we shall see in the next chapter, they are largely dependent on government funding. The nature of this funding reduces their possibilities for providing alternative kinds of care. And the nature of the care they are being asked to provide makes them act more like government-run health institutions. Communities have always been active in providing care and many of them have been actively engaged in promoting health. As governments deinstitutionalize, these communities, like households, may well be forced to focus more on treatment and tasks rather than on prevention and health promotion.

Our argument is not intended to reject one particular option, in this case community care. Rather, it is to reject the notion that we must turn from institutions to communities because they necessarily provide better care. Both have much to offer and they are often in conflict in terms of what they offer. The tension between them need not be eliminated, but it must be recognized and accommodated to allow the kinds of participation, responsiveness, and flexibility that the various government documents support.

CONCLUSION

The medical model structures the organization of work in health care. It is a model that fits well with the new rationalization of health care and with the continuation of inequality, especially between women and men. Efficiency and effectiveness are central. And efficiency and effectiveness are defined in strictly short-range economic terms. All that counts is the bottom line and that which can be counted. Quantitative measures of processes and outcomes necessarily focus on body parts and on scientific criteria, and thus leave caring out of the picture.

The result is a pervasive privatization of health care, a process that takes at least four forms. First, there is the application to the health-care system of practices developed in the for-profit and goods-production sectors. We have total quality management, re-engineering, or some new management scheme, just as in the Japanese car plants. Second, there is the selling of services or parts of services to for-profit agencies—services formerly provided on a non-profit basis and integrated into health care. Now we have 'hotel services' within and outside institutions that do the laundry, food, and cleaning as if these had no role to play in health. Third, we have a privatization of payments, with more and more individuals carrying the burden of costs. Deinstitutionalization too often means that care is shifted from the non-profit institutions to the for-profit ones. And, finally, we have the privatization of care itself, as more of the caring work is sent home to the private household where women are expected to do the work without pay.

The costs of this privatization, discussed more fully in the following chapter, are enormous both for the care providers and for those needing care. Work in the institutions has intensified, has become less collegial and less satisfying, and is more dangerous as the focus on cuts and chemicals increases. The same thing has happened to caring work in the home. The ill and disabled too often get more treatment but less care and the results are too often dangerous to their health.

RECOMMENDED READINGS

Pat Armstrong et al., *'Heal Thyself': Managing Health Care Reform*. Aurora, Ont.: Garamond, 2000. Based on interviews with registered nurses, this book explores the impact of managerial reforms from the perspectives of those who struggle to provide care under dramatically changing conditions.

Canadian Institute for Health Information, *Canada's Health Care Providers*. Ottawa: CIHI, 2001. The detailed data on a range of health-care providers are presented with commentary that provides the most comprehensive picture of the health-care labour force available today. It includes a discussion of both education and working environments, offering an important starting point for anyone interested in analyzing work in this sector.

Miriam Edelson, *My Journey with Jake*. Toronto: Between the Lines, 2000. In this personal account of her severely disabled son's life, Edelson makes the search for care visible. She details the struggle to find public support and her success in obtaining institutional care that is sensitive and appropriate. It is a story about the need for good institutional care in a world that increasingly looks to households for such services.

CHAPTER
5

Who Pays

～

In the 1943 *Report on Social Security for Canada*, Leonard Marsh made it clear that the social safety net was about 'the collective pooling of risks'. As he put it:

> In modern economic life there are certain hazards and contingencies, which have to be met, some of them completely unpredictable, some of them uncertain as to time but in other ways reasonably to be anticipated. They may be met in hit-or-miss fashion by individual families or they may never strike any individuals or families; but we know from experience that, collectively speaking, these problems or needs are always present at some place in the community or among the population.[1]

Marsh, and the rest of the generation that had survived the Depression and fought a war, knew that everyone was at risk, even though not everyone would suffer. They also knew that very few had the kinds of income that could provide the financial protection necessary if ill health or unemployment hit. As Marsh explained, 'It is impossible to establish a wage that will allow every worker and his family to meet the heavy disabilities of serious illness, prolonged unemployment, accident and premature death. These are budget-shattering contingencies that strike most unevenly.'[2] Therefore, it is necessary for states to ensure that risks are shared.

Medicare was based on this knowledge, this recognition of shared vulnerability and collective responsibility. It was designed to ensure both that the bills were paid and that no particular individual would suffer economic ruin as a result of illness. As Malcolm Taylor points out about hospital insurance, the 'program achieved its primary objectives of meeting hospitals' operating costs and protecting individuals and families from financially crippling hospital bills.'[3] In the case of Saskatchewan and later of the national scheme, medicare eliminated 'the commercial insurance concepts of deductibles, noninsurable conditions, limitations with respect to age, employment, or membership in groups and experience rating—all designed to protect insurance funds but frequently at the expenses of individual hardship'.[4] These restrictions were eliminated by the conditions for funding set by the federal government. It was willing to contribute to paying for those necessary services that were provided on a uniform basis, that were universally available, that were comprehensive, that could be available across the country, and that were administered by non-profit agencies.

Under medicare, it was mainly the various levels of government that paid for all 'medically necessary' health services. Everyone paid for the costs of the system, largely through general taxes. Everyone gained access to the system without being billed at the point of service. This primarily single-payer system was adopted over a mixed public-private system, not only because it was more equitable but also because it was cheaper. It was cheaper mainly because it reduced administrative costs and produced some economies of scale. It was more equitable because it reduced differences based on ability to pay among provinces as well as among individuals and families.

But what the provinces were willing to pay for was based on a medical model, with doctors primarily responsible for determining necessary care. The fee-for-service payments to doctors were essentially for parts that could be fixed, or at least diagnosed. The payments to institutions were made after itemized lists of specific services were submitted. Funding was chiefly for treatment and cure, and much of it was provided in a hospital setting.

Provincial reports on health-care reform from the late 1980s and early 1990s criticized this funding emphasis and accepted the assumption that costs must be cut. In the words of a 1992 report by the Nova Scotia Provincial Health Council, 'Spending more money has not led to major improvements in health.'[5] Instead of continued investment in these traditional areas, the provincial reports promoted a 'return' to community care and an emphasis on health promotion. Although couched in terms of quality care, the primary purpose of and context for the reports was the need to cut costs immediately. These reports left unchallenged the cuts to federal transfer payments and 'instead recommended a number of initiatives that would enhance cost controls, funding and revenues, efficiencies, and cost effectiveness'.[6] Less would not only be cheaper but better.

Certainly the resulting reforms in public funding shifted the focus away from institutions, especially from acute-care hospitals. However, these reforms often did so by changing funding practices in ways that further emphasized the medical model within institutions and that transferred costs to individuals and families. At the same time, more public money went to private, for-profit organizations and industries. Fewer risks were pooled and more access was determined by ability to pay. While public funds were saved in the short run, the long-term costs for both provinces and individuals increased. And inequalities among provinces, families, and individuals grew.

Following provincial cuts to health spending in the early 1990s came the severe federal cuts in transfer payments to the provinces announced in the 1995 federal budget, the one that introduced the Canada Health and Social Transfer (CHST). The intense criticism of this unilateral announcement from the provinces, from health-care providers, and from the general public prompted the federal government to back off from its plan to eliminate gradually all its transfer payments to the provinces for health, post-secondary education, and social assistance. It also helped spark a reconsideration of the claim that less health-care spending is better, but it would take until 1998 for public spending on health care to return to its 1992 level in real, per capita terms.[7] Meanwhile, much damage was done to the system.

THE HISTORICAL CONTEXT

As the quotation from Marsh makes clear, health care was part of an overall post-war strategy for state intervention to provide social security for Canadians. Those components of the strategy that were defined as health care addressed only some of the determinants of health, although they certainly included 'public responsibility for environmental services', more commonly described as public health.[8] Immunization, well-baby clinics, regulation of food and drugs, sanitation services, and health education were critical components in publicly funded health care. But at the same time, governments at the federal and provincial levels introduced a wide range of programs intended to deal with the other determinants of health. State intervention to promote full employment was at the centre of these initiatives, which included housing and nutrition projects, recreation and education programs, unemployment insurance, and old age pensions. Collectively, they were intended to provide the kind of security and income that all the later provincial reports told us are critical to good health.

A national health-care system was part of the federal-provincial negotiations during the last years of World War II, and negotiations continued long after the war was over. The British North America Act had given the control of most health care to the provinces but left most taxing powers with the federal government. The problems in reaching agreement had more to do with jurisdictional fights than they did with whether or not there should be a state-funded program for health care. Most provinces recognized that the state would have to expand its role in health care, although there was little consensus on how this should be done.

There were a number of reasons for this provincial support. The provinces were under considerable pressure from unions and community groups to develop health-care services. Those who had fought the war demanded a better life. They were not prepared to return to the pre-war 'free-market' system that had bankrupted many and deprived many more. Studies conducted before medicare was introduced demonstrated that about 30 per cent of the population did not have any insurance; many more were in danger of losing theirs when they reached old age or developed illnesses that made them poor risks.[9] The technology and drugs developed during the war made medical care more effective but also made it more expensive. As Marsh had explained, individual employers could not afford the kinds of wages required to cover the costs of care, and individual workers could not put aside the resources necessary to pay unexpected health costs. Both groups pressured the state to intervene to ensure that costs were shared.

Moreover, the recruitment process during the war had made it clear that a significant proportion of Canadians were not in good health. Post-war industries needed healthy workers as much as the war effort required healthy recruits. Health care was recognized as an investment, one in which both employers and employees shared. Provinces were already spending a significant portion of their budgets on health and, given the federal taxing powers, they had few ways of raising additional monies.[10] In addition, research indicated significant differences among provinces in terms of the care provided. Only a federal plan could create greater equality among the provinces.

The funding of health care and other programs was intended to prevent a new economic depression and to forestall the kind of protests that had followed World War I. It was not simply an expenditure in good times. It was part of those good times. It not only helped save lives and return workers to health. It also stimulated economic growth through the jobs created directly and indirectly as a result of investment in health care.

FUNDING CARE

Money has been central to the development of the Canadian public health-care system. Before World War II, federal, provincial, and municipal governments had all invested some funds in various health programs. But Canadians did not gain universal coverage to portable, comprehensive, and accessible services under uniform terms and conditions and under public, non-profit administration until the federal government used its taxing powers to entice provinces to develop programs that conformed to these five principles.

According to the Hospital Insurance and Diagnostic Services Act introduced in 1957, provinces designed and operated their own health-care services. But the federal government agreed to pay for half of specified services as long as provinces conformed to federal standards. These specified services covered all aspects of hospital care, from food and housekeeping to nursing and testing. The list of insured costs made it clear that health care was not restricted to medical procedures. As we have seen, it included accommodation and meals on a standard ward, necessary nursing services, laboratory and other diagnostic tests, drug and similar preparations, use of operating rooms and anaesthetic facilities, routine surgical supplies, radiology and physiotherapy, as well as the services of other hospital employees. Physicians were not part of this insurance scheme but provinces could choose to insure a broad range of outpatient services.[11]

Although health care within hospitals was broadly defined, the definition did not cover homes for the aged, nursing homes, and other institutions that provided what was defined as mainly custodial care. Some of these costs, however, were included under welfare. Mental health centres were not covered either. But not surprisingly, all jurisdictions took up the federal government offer and developed hospital insurance.

When the Medical Care Act was introduced in 1966 it reflected the same strategy. The federal government would cover half the cost of medically required physician services, of dental surgery done in hospitals, and of a limited number of services provided by other professionals.[12] In this case, medicine was very narrowly defined. Optometrists, most dentists, nurses, midwives, chiropractors, and naturopaths were not part of most provincial schemes.[13] Again, within a few years the provinces all introduced plans designed to take advantage of the federal offer.

The offer ensured that provinces developed public health-care systems, and the line-by-line assessment of bills ensured that services conformed to the agreement. But by 1977 the federal government, complaining that its commitment to paying half the costs of medicare was too high and prevented it from being able to plan its spending, unilaterally introduced a new and complex funding formula. As well as cash, it introduced the transfer of some 'tax points' to the provinces, enabling them to occupy 'room' in the personal and corporate income tax fields from which the federal government was partially retreating.

The new formula put a limit on federal funding but continued to allow for growth and to equalize payments among provinces. It also expanded the definition of health services to include other kinds of care. No new services were specifically addressed, however. The Canada Health Act, introduced in 1984, opened the door for the funding of other professionals but provinces did not take up this offer. They did respond, however, to the federal threat to reduce payments if provinces allowed extra-billing for doctors' services or charged user fees for necessary services in hospitals. Extra-billing was disallowed as a result, although the issue of user fees has not disappeared.

The formula introduced to control expenditures in the mid-1970s set the stage for further cutbacks. Although federal contributions continued to grow along with the economy, the government argued that, given the government deficit, this extent of the expenditure growth was unacceptable. In 1986 it limited the level of transfers to economic growth minus two percentage points. This became three percentage points in 1989, followed by a total freeze in 1990 that continued into 1995.[14] These cutbacks increased the economic pressure on provinces and territories as well as on municipalities. All responded with cutbacks of their own.

Then came the budget of February 1995, which announced the establishment of the CHST, along with a further cut of $7 billion from health and social spending in 1996–7 and another $4.5 billion in 1997–8.[15] Although these planned cuts were later rescinded in the face of strenuous opposition, and indeed modest increases were promised instead, the CHST remains in place, making it next to impossible for Canadians to hold either the federal government or the provincial and territorial governments accountable for their levels of health spending. Within the CHST, cash transfers for health care continue to be combined with those for post-secondary education and social assistance, and the federal government continues to link its cash transfers to its estimate of the value of the tax point transfers it provided back in 1977. In February 1999, the federal and nine provincial governments (excluding Quebec) agreed to a Social Union framework, which among other provisions committed all signatories to the support of the five principles of the Canada Health Act and to majority agreement from the provinces before the federal government introduced new initiatives.[16] In the absence of negative sanctions, however, it is far from clear whether these commitments are being or will be respected.

Since the introduction of medicare, the primary funding for core health-care services has come from general tax revenues. Two provinces (British Columbia and Alberta) collect premiums that cover a part of the costs.[17] Four provinces (Ontario, Quebec, Manitoba, and Newfoundland) levy payroll taxes 'earmarked' for health care.[18] The payment of premiums and payroll taxes accounts for a small and diminishing share of provincial health spending, however, and bears no relation to the entitlement to health-care services.

As the Canada Health Act made clear when it brought together the Hospital Insurance and Diagnostic Act and the Medical Care Act, Canadians must have reasonable access to health services without facing financial or other barriers. Under the Act, user fees for necessary services are not allowed, although fees may be charged for extras such as private rooms. Direct charges may also be made for services not deemed medically necessary. In addition, the Act allows for what are called co-payments to cover room and board in chronic-care hospitals. Nursing homes and homes for the aged can charge fees and, although the private share of their funding is gradually increasing, governments still pick up most of the tab.[19] Despite policy changes to move care out of hospitals and thus out from the protections of the Canada Health Act, most health care remains free in the sense that there is no charge at the point of service for medically necessary services. Instead, we all contribute through taxes. In 1998, public payments accounted for 70.1 per cent of all expenditures on health care.[20]

THE IMPACT ON CARE

The funding arrangements that were the basis for both hospital and medical services have had a profound impact on the nature and availability of health services. As a 1991 British Columbia report makes clear, public funding has 'a powerful effect on who is cared for, and how they are cared for'.[21] Many people and organizations benefited from the way public funds were provided in health care, although there were also some negative consequences for the structure of care. In order to assess the impact of current changes in funding, it is necessary first to examine the effect of past practices.

The most important consequence of public funding was the increase in access to health care. The federal funding formula helped equalize services among provinces and territories with quite different access to resources and commitment to the provision of care. Across the country, facilities expanded rapidly, especially in areas that had been underserviced.[22] By 1997–8, the four Atlantic provinces had the highest percentages experiencing hospitalization and among the highest percentages contacting a doctor within the previous 12 months.[23]

At the same time, the accessibility requirement ensured that individual Canadians could receive necessary care without risking financial ruin. It also meant that those with limited resources could use the system when symptoms first developed rather than having to wait until the signs became so severe that they could no longer avoid the financial outlay. Because people could seek aid earlier, less expensive procedures were often possible and lives were often saved. A sickness survey conducted before medicare was introduced revealed 'an inverse relationship between income and sickness and a direct relationship between income and volume of care received'.[24] In other words, the poor were more often ill but the rich got more care. Medicare had an impact on this unequal and inappropriate distribution. As we pointed out in an earlier chapter, a study undertaken in Quebec after medicare was introduced found an 'increased frequency with which physicians were seen for a series of common and important medical symptoms. This suggests that the removal of economic barriers to medical care may actually improve the general level of health of the population.'[25] Patients were still able to choose their own doctor and hospital but they could do so on the basis of quality and need rather than on the basis of fees and personal resources. In 1997–8, low-income Canadians were just as likely as anyone else to contact a doctor. They were also 'more likely than those with higher incomes to be heavy users of physician services, to visit emergency departments, to be admitted to hospital, to take multiple medications, and to require home care services'.[26] They were more likely to suffer ill health, but medicare meant that most of them did not face unreasonable barriers to access to hospitals and physicians.[27]

It was not only the patients relieved of heavy costs who benefited. Doctors and hospitals benefited as well. Both were now guaranteed payment by the government. No longer would they have to make up for bad debts. And the single-payer system meant their administrative costs went down because they had only one place to bill. Hospitals' operating costs were met by governments.[28] Doctors' incomes went up and their hours of work went down, as did their number of home visits.[29] At the same time, the fee-for-service payment system meant that the overwhelming majority of doctors were individual entrepreneurs who had complete control over their own practices. This contrasts sharply with the US system, which, according to one estimate, employs 42 per cent more administrative staff relative to population than does the Canadian system.[30] Meanwhile, an estimated 60 per cent of the female doctors and 40 per cent of the male doctors under age 35 in the United States were on salaries by 1988.[31]

The benefits within the Canadian system were not restricted to patients, doctors, and hospitals, although they did have the most obvious gains. With stable funding and equalization across the country, health-care services expanded rapidly and so did employment in health care. Jobs were created for a wide range of employees, mainly within institutions. Brought together in relatively stable employment situations, these employees were able to form organizations to seek benefits. Before medicare, wages in hospitals were 'below what the Economic Council of Canada set as the poverty line',[32] and this did not count the many women who provided free labour while they underwent their nursing training. Wages have improved considerably with medicare, although in many cases they still remain below average for the women and immigrant men who make up much of the health-care labour force. Public funding meant employers were in a better position to respond to legitimate demands and that employees had more collective strength. These employees also demanded better conditions of work that would not only protect their interests but also those of the patients.[33] Work in health care improved enormously and patients gained better care in the process.

Corporations and other employers facing unions or employee associations of various kinds also benefited from the public funding of health care.[34] Instead of covering the costs of their employees' health care, employers could rely mainly on the general tax system to cover most costs of care. This is the case even in provinces where there are payroll taxes because these taxes are not equivalent to the kinds of costs borne by employers in the US, where there is no similar public system. Indeed, the *World Competitiveness Report* rated Canada as on the top in only two areas: energy costs and health-care costs. In fact, the publicly funded health-care system was a major factor in Canada's rating as fifth overall in terms of competitiveness.[35] It has certainly aided the auto industry, the driving force in the economy of Ontario, Canada's largest province. In 1988, Chrysler calculated that it paid US $700 on health benefits for its current and former workers for every car it produced in the United States, but only US $233 a car in Canada.[36] By 2000, it was anticipated that Ontario would soon produce more vehicles than Michigan, in large part due to an estimated $1,200–$1,500 saving per vehicle on health-care costs.[37]

Moreover, money spent on health care largely remained in Canada and thus stimulated economic growth. The increasing number of people employed in providing services were spending money here. The money to construct facilities, although usually paid to for-profit construction companies, also created jobs in Canada. Similarly, the legislation that allowed the production of generic drugs encouraged pharmaceutical manufacturing in this country and meant more of the profits stayed here than is the case with foreign-owned manufacturers.

Because health is determined by such a complex array of factors, it is not possible to measure the direct contribution of medicare to overall population health. But we do know that mortality rates have declined for all age groups and that life expectancy has increased significantly since medicare was introduced. Infant mortality rates have dropped sharply 'from 38 per 1,000 live births in 1951 to 7 per 1,000 in 1991'[38] and are significantly lower than those in the United States.[39] The declines have been largely attributable to the reduction in death among infants from parasitic diseases, influenza, bronchitis, and pneumonia, and among adults from cardiovascular diseases.[40] Between 1959 and 1974, the annual number of infant deaths from bronchitis and pneumonia decreased from 406 to 96 and from diarrhea and enteritis from 129 to 26 per year.[41] While other factors have played a role in these reductions, it seems clear that health-care services were important in achieving these results. Similarly, it is reasonable to assume that public health services help explain why it is estimated that in 1989 the rate of years of potential life lost to females with diseases of the circulatory system was two-thirds higher in the US than in Canada.[42] Without the same access to care we may see an increase in death from these diseases, given that they have not been eliminated. They have only been controlled.

These measures of the contribution of health care tell us little about whether or not daily life and the ability to perform regularly and well at work have improved with public health care. We do know that more Canadians today define themselves as healthy compared to the 1950–1 sickness survey that helped establish the need for medicare.[43] But whether or not the Canadian population has better health as a result of medicare has recently been brought into question in the public debates. Interviewed by the *Toronto Star* about her report on health-care spending, Judith Maxwell claimed that 'There's no evidence to suggest that people were any sicker in the 1980s. We can't say we got any extra value for that extra money.'[44] But the study[45] she referred to provides no evidence for the reverse assumption that people would be just as well without the development of the health-care system. Many of the gains we have made since medicare was introduced may well turn to losses if the expenditures are cut. We have already seen an increase in the incidence of tuberculosis, a disease we had assumed was under control. Longevity could decline and infant mortality increase without the current system, especially if we do not support the other determinants of health. Moreover, contrary to Maxwell's claim, there does seem to be an increase in the incidence of breast cancer and of sickness related to AIDS, to name just two examples. Both these illnesses require expensive health care that can mean the difference between life and death. In terms of the evidence, then, the most critics can claim in terms of overall health and health care is that we do not have the evidence to demonstrate the clear link. There is certainly evidence to show some improvement in the health of specific individuals.

Although there have been significant benefits from the public funding of care, there have also been some negative consequences. Insurance companies lost revenues and potential revenues when medicare was introduced. Medicare made coverage by private companies for areas covered by public services illegal. As a result, between 1968 and 1969, the number of people enrolled in non-profit medical insurance plans dropped from over eight million to under two million and the drop would have been higher if for-profit plans had been included.[46] The insurance companies were still able to cover additional services such as ambulances, eyeglasses, dental work, private rooms, some kinds of care for travellers, and other aspects of care not defined as necessary in particular jurisdictions. But they were prevented from making profit in a wide range of areas open to profit-making in the United States—and they have never given up the struggle to move into more profit-making areas.

Ironically, one opportunity for private insurers and for privatization more generally is provided by workers' compensation schemes, plausibly the oldest of Canada's welfare state programs.[47] Acting on their financial incentive to get injured workers back on the job as quickly as possible, the managers of these provincial schemes sometimes try to pay to have their clients jump the queue and get rehab services in particular before other patients in greater need. They thus violate, with public funds, the accessibility principle of the Canada Health Act. Fuelled in part by workers' compensation payments, private, for-profit rehab clinics have expanded appreciably in recent years, and at least one US-based insurance company, Liberty Health, purchased a string of rehab clinics and is actively promoting an enlarged role for the private sector in all aspects of workers' compensation.

The nature of federal funding also increased the focus on care by physicians and on institutional care, especially hospital care. Both expanded considerably after the federal government made its offer. Certainly, there was a need for an increase in hospital services to accommodate the new medical possibilities. Indeed, expenditures on hospitals increased not only in Canada but also throughout much of Europe and the United States.[48] However, when the federal government agreed to pay half the costs of hospital care, it encouraged provincial governments to invest in hospitals rather than in other areas of health care, such as clinics and other community services. Between 1960 and 1980, the proportion of health-care money going to institutional care increased from 45 per cent to 54 per cent of total health expenditures.[49] With the financing scheme, 'Provincial governments had financial incentives to fund as much in-patient care through hospitals as possible.'[50]

Similarly, in the wake of medical insurance, the number of physicians grew significantly. In 1968 there was one doctor for every 756 Canadians. By 1983 there was one for every 529 Canadians. Since then, the ratio has remained quite stable, although physicians as a group are now aging.[51] Every graduate from medical school was guaranteed not only employment but also high income. In 1990, the average income for physicians and surgeons employed full-time was $102,370; for male physicians, it was $111,261. This compares to $76,966 for lawyers, $56,073 for chemical engineers, and $62,064 for university professors.[52] This medical doctor income came out of government coffers and accounted for a significant share of health-care costs.

The open-ended funding, combined with fee-for-service doctor payments and the right of doctors to define what is necessary care, virtually gave doctors and institutions blank cheques.[53] Doctors were paid for each and every service they provided and claimed was necessary. Thus, the more people they saw and the more things they did to people, the more income they received. It was a piecework system, based on the medical model, that encouraged doctors to process as many pieces as possible. Moreover, doctors were paid more for some pieces than for others. At best, this meant that doctors were not discouraged from providing the highly rewarded, more complex services. Furthermore, there was no financial disincentive from ordering as many tests and as many hospital services as possible. Under this scheme, there was little financial reward for preventive work. It was treatment the government paid for, not health. And the financing system meant more of the same, not a new means of approaching health.

Canadians were unquestionably better off in terms of health-care services after the public schemes were introduced. More people had access, no one was financially crippled by health-care debts, fewer babies died, and more people lived longer and better lives. While disparity among users did not disappear it did decrease, and access no longer depended primarily on ability to pay.[54] Many of those who worked in the system were better off as well. This was particularly the case for doctors. Employers also benefited from the socialization of care and so did the economy in general, given that health care gave Canada a competitive edge and that money spent on health care remained largely in Canada. But there was a down side to the way health care was funded. The payment method for doctors not only encouraged them to intervene as often and in as complicated a way as possible, it also encouraged the use of institutional facilities, to the neglect of other forms of care. In addition, the public system meant that fewer corporations were able to make a profit out of health care. While this may have been bad for the companies, it was good for the taxpayer because, as we shall see in the next section, Canadian health care costs much less than in the for-profit system south of the border.

THE COSTS OF CARE

The 1995 federal budget cut health-care funding significantly and transferred more financial responsibility to the provinces. Discussions around the budget suggested that, at 10 per cent of gross domestic product (GDP), Canadian health-care expenditures are out of control. 'Citing the European experience, Chrétien has suggested that he would like to get the figure down to 8 or 9 per cent [of GDP], which would bring it in line with countries such as France and Germany.'[55] This kind of argument is made in a number of provincial and federal reports, many of them declaring that Canada is second only to the United States in terms of health-care expenditures. But an analysis of the data indicates that costs are not out of control. Moreover, strategies developed in the name of cost-saving are mainly taken from the US, the most expensive system in the world. Health economist Robert Evans has argued that it is the kind of partial, multiple-source coverage found in the US, 'rather than universal public funding', that 'leads to uncontrollable cost escalation'.[56]

When Prime Minister Chrétien and others talk about the proportion of GDP spent on health care, they are not talking about government expenditures. They are not talking simply about medicare costs. The figures cover all expenditures on health care, both private and public. Even when we look at the combined public and private expenditures, however, it is clear that health-care costs are under control. By 1997, Canada was devoting 9.3 per cent of its GDP to total health-care spending, both public and private. Our share was lower than that of either Germany or France, and had been since 1995, the year Chrétien made his ill-informed suggestion.[57] Moreover, the public share of health-care spending was higher in 19 of the other 26 countries of the OECD, the club of industrialized countries to which Canada belongs.[58] The public share declined in Canada each year from 1992 to 1997. Per capita public spending in real terms (after the effects of inflation are eliminated) actually declined each year from 1993 to 1996.[59] Evans has clearly demonstrated that 'the period of the most rapid escalation *ended* with the establishment of universal coverage' paid for from public funds.[60]

What grew was private spending, as more and more Canadians found themselves paying directly and individually for health-care services or for health insurance. In contrast to public expenditures, real per capita private expenditures grew each year in the 1990–8 period, from between 1.0 and 5.4 per cent a year. Thus, while private spending made up 25.4 per cent of the total in 1990, it increased to 29.9 per cent in 1998.[61]

Much of the focus in provincial government reports has been on the cost and overuse of hospital services, especially acute-care services. Yet hospitals account for a decreasing share of health expenditures. While 44.7 per cent of health spending went to hospitals in 1975, only an estimated 31.8 per cent of health expenditures went to hospitals in 2000.[62] Along with the decline in share going to hospitals has come a decline in admission rates. Indeed, in 1989 Canadian admission rates to acute-care hospitals at 13.8 per cent of the population were significantly lower than the French rate of 20.6 and the German rate of 18.7.[63] Nor were overall hospital admission rates higher than in other countries. In 1989, 14.1 per cent of the Canadian population was admitted to in-patient institutions, compared to 23.3 per cent in France and 21.5 per cent in Germany.[64] These figures do not suggest that Canada has an undue emphasis on hospital care or an overuse of their services when compared to other countries. Once admitted, patients are also averaging shorter stays in acute hospitals. In Winnipeg, for example, the average length of stay dropped from 8.4 days in 1990 to 6.7 days in 1995.[65] As a result of these combined trends, the annual number of acute hospital patient days per 1000 population has been dramatically declining in each province. In 1992–3, at 751, Ontario had far and away the lowest number in the country. The rest ranged from 931 to 1,480.[66] By 1995–6, the Ontario number was down to 607, and the goal of the government agency in charge of closing and merging hospitals, the Health Services Restructuring Commission, was 430.[67]

Notwithstanding the redefinition of hospitals as sites for treating only the most acute of patients and their consequent discharge 'quicker and sicker', the decline in the share of expenditures allocated to hospitals is not accounted for by a shift in public costs to other kinds of institutions. In 1975, these other institutions took 9.2 per cent of the health-care dollar. In 2000, this increased to only an estimated 9.4 per cent. The share going to physicians has declined slightly (from 15.1 to 13.5 per cent), while that going to other health professionals has increased somewhat (from 9 to 11.8 per cent).[68]

Much the most striking change has been the sharp increase in the share spent on drugs, which soared from 8.8 per cent in 1975 to an estimated 15.5 per cent in 2000. By 1997, spending on drugs had overtaken spending on physicians.[69] And these figures do not include the money spent on drugs within hospitals, which account for another 1 per cent of total spending.[70] Using 1998 dollars to eliminate the effects of inflation, Canadians spent $198.50 per capita on drugs in 1985, $276.89 in 1990, $347.73 in 1995, and $409.46 in 1998, for an increase of 106 per cent in the last 13 years for which firm data are available. By comparison, in real per capita terms during these same 13 years, *total* health spending on items other than non-hospital drugs increased by 25 per cent (from $1,887.19 to $2,366.10), while *public* health spending on items other than non-hospital drugs increased by 20 per cent (from $1,517.60 to $1,817.96).[71]

The shift in the allocation of health-care resources becomes particularly apparent when we look at per capita expenditures expressed in 1986 constant dollars—that is, if we take inflation into account. Between 1991 and 1993, per capita hospital expenditures decreased by $17.08 while per capita drug expenditures increased by $20.96.[72] Indeed, between 1980 and 1990, Canada's pharmaceutical-specific inflation rate was by far the highest among all OECD countries. The pharmaceutical-specific inflation rate calculates the excess of pharmaceutical price increases over those of all other goods and services. For Canada, the 1980–90 increase was 4.4. The next highest were the US at 3.8 and then Germany at 2.2. There was a decline for all European countries combined and the overall pharmaceutical inflation rate for OECD countries was 0.[73] If expenditures on drugs had been cut like those on hospitals or even if prices had remained constant, we would have moved a long way towards the Prime Minister's goal. Instead, Canada's pharmaceutical inflation rate has continued to soar. The growth in per capita spending on drugs consistently exceeded the inflation rate throughout the 1990s, with the sole exception of 1996. In 1997, the gap was 8.2 per cent and in 1998 (the latest year for which firm data are available) it was 9.2 per cent.[74]

In sum, Canadian public spending on health care is not significantly out of line with that of other countries, not out of control, and not disproportionately concentrated in acute-care facilities. What is growing disproportionately is the amount of money going to drugs, partly as a result of the 'government's extension of drug patent protection to bring drug prices in line with the highest in the world'.[75] What is also growing is the amount spent privately, by individual Canadians, in a process that is undermining the public system. In his article on health spending, William Tholl maintains that 'those categories of health spending that are under direct government control are now growing only apace with Canada's gross domestic product (GDP). Costs in sectors that are unregulated and largely privately financed, however, continue to grow in both real and relative terms.' Tholl also argues that the 'Canadian health system is undergoing a process of privatization by default.'[76] But recently, signs indicate that the move towards privatization is much more actively and consciously planned than his default argument would suggest.

CUTTING COSTS: WHO PAYS AND WHO PROFITS

The Prime Minister's statement on health-care spending focused exclusively on expenditure reduction. Many of the government documents as well as those coming from academics and practitioners, however, maintain that reform is not simply about cutting costs: it is also about improving health care. The argument is evident in the titles. A paper prepared for the deputy ministers of health is called *When Less Is Better: Using Canada's Hospitals Efficiently.*[77] *Spending Smarter and Spending Less*[78] was written by a medical doctor who is also a policy analyst and by an academic in the health policy field. *Sustainable Health Care for Canada*, a project begun by the Economic Council of Canada, maintains that 'Significant cost savings are feasible, with no reduction in health status.'[79]

All of these studies assume that cost savings can be made by applying techniques developed in the private sector to the public provision of health care. Although the various studies question the effectiveness of health care in general and of medical practice in particular, the application of private-sector practices is necessarily based on the medical model and serves to reinforce it. Partly as a result of this process, new strategies mainly shift services to the private sector and costs to individuals. While this may save the state money in the short term, it may cost governments more in the future. This shifting of costs and mortgaging of the future becomes evident when we examine in more detail the strategies currently being applied or offered as new alternatives.

DOCTORS

In 1993, 15.1 per cent of all health money was spent directly on physicians.[80] However, it has been estimated that doctors account for as much as 80 per cent of health spending through their orders for drugs and tests, surgery, and institutionalization. Yet government reform has done little to tackle directly the fee-for-service system that not only reflects and reinforces the medical model but also encourages health-care use. Instead, reforms have sought to control doctors indirectly in ways that do little to challenge the medical model or transform care.

One of the first strategies used to limit spending was to reduce doctors' fees. 'From 1972 to 1984, the provinces cut fees by 18 per cent in real terms, but by an amazing coincidence, doctors' total billing claims rose by 17 per cent. Similarly, when Quebec froze doctors' fees in the early 1970s, and their real dollar value dropped 9 per cent from 1972 to 1976, doctors increased their billings by almost the same amount, 8.3 per cent.'[81] In other words, the strategy did not work because doctors responded by seeing more patients and offering more complicated services. This method not only failed to reduce costs; it intensified the focus on intervention and cure.

A more current approach is a form of global budgeting applied to doctors' billing. This can involve a cap placed on individual doctors' earnings, that may allow doctors to bill above that amount but payment is reduced for each billable act. Or it may involve an overall cap on physician billing within the province or territory, leaving the doctors to sort out how this is done. In Ontario, the overall cap and the individual cap were combined with an agreement to allow the doctors to incorporate as private businesses. This incorporation, which after some delay seems to be proceeding, means great tax savings for doctors and compromises any savings in health expenditures if lost government revenues are taken into account. Although any of these approaches can help control the amount paid directly to doctors, they do little about the overall costs doctors incur and nothing about the quality of care or the medical model. Doctors may simply decide to work fewer days or hours while practising the rest of the time in their old manner.

Another approach is to limit the number of doctors who are trained and licensed to practise in Canada or who have billing rights in the jurisdiction. This, too, could help control costs by reducing the numbers with the right to charge the government for services and to order services. But it does nothing to address the basis on which the remaining doctors practise. Efforts by the BC government to distribute doctors geographically in a more equitable and efficient way by discounting the fees going to new doctors setting up their practices in large cities have been thwarted by the courts.[82] Some attention is being paid to the way doctors are trained, and this may help expand their notion of care. Ironically, however, this change is happening just as cutbacks in health-care budgets are making it more difficult to consider both care and cure.

Yet another approach is to transfer some of the doctor's work to other, salaried providers such as nurse practitioners and midwives. This may help move away from the medical model in that nurses and midwives are more focused than doctors on care and health promotion. It also helps reduce costs because these other providers are cheaper than doctors for several reasons. They have lower pay, they have few rights to order services that mean additional costs, and they do less intervention. But in carving out some areas for other providers, the reforms often leave doctors even more devoted to the medical model and do little to change their ways of practising. And if the current Ontario pilot projects aimed at reforming primary care are any guide, doctors have little interest in sharing the work with nurse practitioners. In a study commissioned by the provincial government, PricewaterhouseCoopers found that 170 doctors, but only seven nurse practitioners, are working in the 13 pilot projects, which are controlled by the Ontario Medical Association.[83]

One approach does address the way doctors themselves practise. This involves the collection of data on physician practices. *Patterns of Health Care in Ontario*, for example, offers data on variations in surgical services and in hospital utilization.[84] Certainly, such data can offer useful guidelines for doctors and can help the government identify doctors with practices significantly out of line with those of other practitioners. However, there is a real risk that these guidelines will become formulas for practice based on the assumption that scientific knowledge can predetermine the number of Caesareans and heart transplants necessary in each region or even each practice. Quality can become defined in numerical terms.

This has already happened to some extent in hospitals, where it is increasingly assumed that science can establish a formula for length of patient stay based on measurable characteristics. And the formulas are based primarily on the assumption that health care is mainly about treating standard parts that need fixing.

> Our health care system is deteriorating. It is too late for my husband—he died because he did not receive adequate care in the hospital.
>
> My husband went into hospital last January with viral pneumonia. He had many things wrong and it wasn't lack of specialists looking at him. Rather than looking at the whole person, they just focused on the parts. And they missed the most important part, his pneumonia. His kidneys had stopped up and he had a poor heart condition since his angioplasty a year earlier.
>
> We wanted him in the intensive care unit because of his heart and kidney problems. Three years previously, at another hospital, he had been in ICU [the intensive care unit] with a serious bout of pneumonia. My husband had been a doctor there so we knew the staff and we got the care he needed and he recovered. It seems to me that you have to know someone to get adequate care. Unfortunately, we did not know people at the hospital where he died.
>
> The hospital told me that he did not qualify for intensive care according to their new classification system. They have some new tri-level treatment scheme where level 1 patients receive intensive care. My husband was assessed as 'level 2' and placed on a general medical ward. These new standards seem like a way to justify cuts. He was judged not sick enough even though he had a history of heart problems and the kidney specialists were considering dialysis. They told me that my husband did not need intensive care because they had enough staff on the wards. Yet, I saw how understaffed they were. On the night my husband died there were only three nurses for 37 patients, which was not enough.
>
> Over the last two days of his life, his pneumonia worsened. He was really panting for breath. I knew this would strain his heart so I asked if he could not be considered for intensive care and they said no because he didn't 'qualify'. There was only two ICUs with the kind of life support he needed—one was for cardiac arrest and one was for surgical patients.
>
> They focused on treating his kidney; but all the while he was panting for breath. The kidney specialists wanted to start my husband on dialysis but the doctor in charge told me that it would be difficult to gain access to dialysis once my husband came home. However, we agreed to that treatment feeling that we would meet the problem of scarcity of dialysis on an outpatient basis when it arrived. He did receive dialysis on the last day of his life.
>
> On the fifth day in the hospital my husband was really in distress, hallucinating for most of the afternoon. That night, the nurses' chart reported that my husband was crying out for help and he had pulled off his oxygen mask.

They did not monitor him closely. My husband had a cardiac arrest in the middle of the night. When the nurses found him they put out a code blue to get him on resuscitation and life support. Another code blue had been called at the same time and my husband lost the draw. It seems that the hospital could only handle one code blue at a time. I thought that a cardiac arrest victim would have a greater chance of survival in a hospital—not my husband. By the time he was finally placed on life support he was clinically brain dead.

Wouldn't you know it. Now that my husband was clinically brain dead he 'qualified' for the expensive intensive care unit. It wouldn't do him any good but he was in intensive care. It is a really sad commentary on the state of the health care system that a live patient like my husband in desperate need of life support systems is refused entry into ICU. But once he had the cardiac arrest, even though officially recorded as brain dead and beyond the need of further help, he was readily admitted to ICU. A nurse told me that they had beds available in the surgical intensive care unit in the week leading up to his death but my husband didn't qualify.

My husband was a doctor. We trusted the doctors and administration and I believe our trust was very much misplaced. The two-tiered health care system is here already. Since my husband's death, I've heard about other people hiring private-duty nurses to watch over people in the hospital because they are so understaffed. Had I received some straight information about my husband's condition I would gladly have paid for a private-duty nurse or had my family come in to sit with him in shifts because there was not enough staff and he was not monitored closely enough.

After my husband's death we were told by the staff that in five years they will have a multi-systems intensive care unit and then people like my husband would be able to receive the proper care (i.e., all the extra monitoring and life support systems) that he was denied. This was little consolation.

I think they wrote my husband off because he had a number of health problems. With adequate care he beat those problems with his previous illness. This time he simply wasn't given the chance. He died at 68.[85]

The same sort of rationing and rationalizing of medical attention occurs in the United States, where a consulting firm has set formulas that determine, for example, that 'you can't have a cataract removed in more than one eye unless you are fairly young and need both eyes for work; . . . that you can't see a neurologist for epileptic seizures unless anticonvulsant drugs fail . . . you can't have a tonsillectomy unless you have suspected cancer, or six documented cases in a year despite antibiotics, or breathing blockage during sleep.'[86] Rather than challenge the medical model, such formulas simply reinforce it. And rather than improve quality, they may reduce doctors' capacity to base their assessment on the whole person and the complexity of the individual's health or illness.

Evidence suggests that a particular strategy can both save money and change the way doctors practise. The salaried physicians who work in public community clinics tend to order fewer tests, prescribe fewer drugs, recommend less surgery, and spend more time on health prevention and promotion.[87] Although government report after government report has recommended the expansion of such community centres, few have been developed outside Quebec. The limited expansion is not the result of scientific evidence indicating their inadequacies in terms of delivering quality care but rather of organized and unorganized resistance from doctors.[88] Physicians have used a wide range of strategies to prevent the development of such clinics, employing both their political connections and their considerable collective strength to resist change in this direction.

At the same time, private, walk-in clinics have been growing. Instead of saving the system money, however, these clinics tend to increase expenses because patients often visit their own doctor at a later date for the same symptoms.[89] This second visit is not surprising, given that the physician at the walk-in clinic usually sees the patient once only and therefore may have difficulty assessing the problem and may not have the trust of the patient. As we have seen, these clinics are very much reflective of the medical model, assuming as they do that the doctors are simply examining a part that walks in to be fixed. Very little preventive work is possible and it seems likely that drugs would offer a quick fix. Moreover, although the doctors are paid by the government, many are actually working in for-profit clinics. Some of these are foreign-owned, so a portion of Canadian tax dollars for health is leaving the country. And the current Ontario government has promised to open the door further for such clinics by allowing 'US companies to provide health care in private clinics' and 'to waive the tendering process to set up a health clinic'.[90]

Instead of salaries, some provinces have been experimenting with capitation funding of physician services. In Ontario, for example, Health Service Organizations (HSOs) are paid a fixed monthly fee for each person named as a member served by the organization. This fixed fee could work to discourage over-treatment and to encourage health promotion, because physicians' income would not depend on the number of times they see patients or what they do to them. However, the capitation rate is set on the basis of past practices in the existing fee-for-service system and thus can serve to perpetuate current cost structures in other ways. Moreover, the HSO can off-load costs to other providers and may receive more money than it needs if the population is particularly healthy, given that the formula takes 'no explicit account of the needs of the population, other than through adjustment for gender and age'.[91]

Although doctors are central both in determining costs and in billing the system, the reforms have not been primarily aimed at them. When doctors have been the focus, the strategy too often serves to increase the emphasis on the medical model rather than to initiate genuine reform. The changes may reduce doctors' power to assess complex, individual cases while leaving the overall problems with care intact. What are necessary are strategies that help make doctors more accountable for costs and help them arrive at better decisions based on assessments of whole people without removing the kind of independence that is critical to good practice.

HOSPITALS
Although hospital expenditures are declining in terms of both their overall share of costs and expenditures per capita, they still accounted for 32 per cent

of all health-care expenditures in 2000.[92] The majority of hospital funding comes from governments, even though most hospitals are not government-owned. Hospitals are still far and away the single largest item in public health expenditures and it is therefore not surprising that the cost-reduction strategies have focused here. Even though the declining share of health dollars going to hospitals clearly indicates that costs are under control, new cuts would necessarily follow in the wake of additional reductions in transfers from the federal government. While some of the cost-saving measures have improved care or reflected advances in medical practice, others are based on business practices inappropriate to good health care. This becomes more obvious when the strategies are examined in relationship to each other.

As is the case with doctors, government approaches began with limits on funds through global budgets based mainly on the number of patients served. By establishing how much each hospital received, the government could shift some of the responsibility for controlling costs to the individual hospitals. However, according to Michael Rachlis and Carol Kushner, this method of cost control contained 'rather perverse economic incentives' that encouraged hospitals to keep patients longer than necessary.[93] Hospitals saved money this way because the patients who stayed longer were cheaper to care for as they approached recovery.

Alberta and several Ontario hospitals have experimented with another form of funding usually called case-mix funding.[94] The Hospital Medical Records Institute (now part of the Canadian Institute for Health Information) developed a method for classifying case-mix groups that is very similar to the diagnosis-related groups (DRG) approach used in the United States. The DRG system classifies people into about 600 groups in order to establish a formula for payment determined by the diagnosis for the patients treated. 'The DRG system is based on the average cost of treating a patient within the same age range, diagnosed with the same or similar condition, and needing the same type of treatment.'[95] A predetermined amount is then allowed for each patient. 'Outliers' who do not fit the formula can be identified, but the amount paid for their extra days is reduced and hospitals lose money on these patients.[96]

Research on the system in the United States suggests that the approach did save money but it also often resulted in patients being discharged before they were stabilized, a practice that could result in death or greater costs to the system in the long run.[97] It also meant significant cutbacks in nursing staff as a way of meeting the formulas for care, and these cutbacks resulted in a reduction in the quality of care.[98] Because DRGs are based on diagnosis rather than severity of illness, they can classify people unfairly and significantly understate the need for care.[99] The problem is particularly evident in teaching hospitals, which treat the sickest patients who cost more than the averages set out in the formulas.[100] Alternatively, with a process known as 'gaming', the classification scheme can be manipulated to claim for more serious diseases and thus more funds than warranted by the patient's actual conditions. The formulas are based on a medical model that assumed standard sickness and standard people, leaving little allowance for variations among people or for care as well as treatment. And they did not make all the necessary allowances for the kinds of combined and complex problems faced by those entering hospitals today. Yet, as more and more care is provided outside the hospital, admission is increasingly restricted to those who are very ill, making severity of illness a particularly important factor in cost calculations. The DRG system was an approach that 'quickly went sour'[101] in the US, especially among the for-profit hospitals that found they could not survive on these prices even though they claimed greater efficiency than the non-profit ones.[102] Nonetheless, a variation on this theme has been introduced in Canada.

Both because they were faced with reduced resources and because they often saw the private system as more efficient, many hospitals looked to the private sector for management models that would save money. In his book outlining the virtues of total quality management practices in hospitals, Phillip Hassen begins by setting out 'Motorola, Xerox and Federal Express' as models to emulate.[103] According to this former chief executive officer of a major Ontario hospital, the approach can continuously improve patient care and administrative approaches while significantly reducing costs. Manitoba has adopted private-sector practices such as TQM and has even hired an American private-sector consulting firm at a cost of $4 million to cut costs in the system. Like Hassen's strategy, this approach was to improve quality at the same time as it reduced costs.

In the end, the consultant saved far less money than promised, admitting 'that the Canadian system is really very different from that in the United States and therefore the promised savings were really out of reach'.[104] One difference is that our administration costs are already lower. Another big difference between the systems is in for-profit practices that are designed to lure 'customers' away from the competition and reject those who are too expensive. But in our system all customers must be served. Yet another difference relates to the way care differs from delivering mail or making photocopies. The intent of these practices is to eliminate waste and waste is what does not contribute directly to output, defined in terms of leaving the hospital. Waste is usually defined in terms of a medical model, the easily measured aspects of care. Thus, too often, private management strategies see treatment as productive and care as waste. And they tend to see only the narrowly defined treatment as health care and the rest as hotel services not related to health.

These private-sector practices can help speed up some procedures, such as flow through the parking lot and admissions, where the processes are more like those in Xerox. However, they tend to focus on eliminating or controlling employees as the main way to save money. This is not surprising, given that health care is labour-intensive work and that private-sector strategies have usually been about reducing the labour component in production. Nearly half a million people are employed in hospitals and almost two-thirds of them are employed full-time.[105]

Within hospitals, labour is the major expense. In 1991–2, just over 70 per cent of hospital money was spent on wages, salaries, and benefits for non-medical staff. Although many doctors do work in hospitals and although doctors mainly determine what is done to patients as well as who enters and leaves, most are in private practice and therefore are not employees of hospitals. Consequently, the medical staff accounts for only 2.6 per cent of public hospital budgets[106] and little attention has been paid to changing their work. On the other hand, 80 per cent of those employed in hospitals are women and hospitals are a major employer of women, accounting for 7.1 per cent of all employed women in 1991.[107] The largest single group of employees are registered nurses. In 2000, there were about 148,000 registered nurses employed in Canadian public hospitals.[108]

As a result of women's efforts, wages have increased considerably and so have their rights to control over their paid work. This, combined with the view that women do not really need paid employment, helps explain why female health-care workers are bearing the brunt of cost reduction. In Manitoba, the main savings were achieved through layoffs of registered nurses, the highest paid among the predominately female workers. 'While the objective was to ensure nurses would focus more on patients and less on paperwork, the plan also meant a sharp reduction in nursing staff.'[109] The layoffs were followed by such strong opposition framed in terms of concerns over quality of care that the Minister of Health ordered a freeze on cuts and layoffs, promising that henceforth 'decisions related to health care reform would be made to ensure the system is better, rather than merely to save money.'[110] Nursing layoffs have become a prominent political issue in virtually every province, with nurses enjoying widespread public support even when on strike.

But it is not only hospitals with foreign consultants or TQM schemes that are using staff cutbacks as a means of reducing costs. The data on hospital personnel indicate significant reductions in recent years. Across the board, hospitals decreased the total number of registered nurses they employed from about 165,000 in 1991[111] to the 148,000 figure in 2000 while increasing the part-time share from about one-third to about 48 per cent.[112] The reductions in the licensed or practical nurse category were relatively greater up to 1994,[113] and probably greater since then.

This greater reduction in the licensed or practical nurse category may seem odd, given that the average salary for a registered nurse is higher. Although RNs are more expensive, professional regulations have made it necessary to employ them to do certain kinds of work, and the increasing emphasis on high-technology medical intervention has made it difficult for hospitals to substitute other workers for RNs. However, a number of provinces are reconsidering these regulations and some hospitals are breaking down the nursing work into tasks, some of which can be performed by other workers. In the process, the whole person disappears. As a result, registered nurses on occasion experience significant job losses. For example, in the London Health Centre, which introduced TQM, there were 122 layoffs mostly of RNs in 1994, but some were offered jobs in 'lesser-skilled and lesser-paid positions called Primary Care Partners'.[114] And according to the *California Nurse*, the consulting firm hired in Manitoba encouraged hospitals 'to decrease the use of nurses and cross-train lower-paid, lesser-trained employees to perform functions now performed by RNs and other, more professionally skilled caregivers . . . invariably at the expense of RNs and patients'.[115]

Although some of these reductions may be justified by bed closures and better work procedures, most simply mean less care for the patient and more work for those who remain. This is particularly the case since each of the remaining patients requires more care. And the increasing use of part-time workers can save money in terms of both hours worked and benefits, but it may also mean more work for the full-time staff who must train them and poorer quality care by those unfamiliar with the patients or the area of the hospital. Floating nurses around to work in high-demand areas has similar consequences. So does the hiring of temporary workers through agencies. Indeed, agency employees not only move from ward to ward but from hospital to hospital. Some of the tax money used to pay for them goes to profit rather than to care, and many of these workers are without union protection.[116]

In another strategy that copies the private sector, the nurses are replaced by technology. Some, like the monitors that allow nurses to watch patients from a central location, could improve quality as long as they do not substitute for human contact or judgment. But if cost-cutting is the main purpose, this substitution may well be the case. With fetal monitors, for example, too often women are left alone with a machine that may not be able to assess developments accurately and that certainly cannot provide a comforting word. And there is no guarantee that such machines will save money in the long run. Indeed, according to a report from Health and Welfare Canada, it seems to be the case that 'health technology is almost universally cost-expanding rather than cost-reducing.'[117] What is clear is that the strategy of using technology to provide care means public money goes to the companies that produce the machines—often outside the country—rather than to the women who now do the work. It is also clear that such strategies perpetuate the medical model, assuming as they do that there is a scientific diagnosis that can be based on measurable, and de-contextualized, responses.

Reducing nursing staff means that more people are processed by fewer people for less money. However, there has been little research on the health costs to patients and workers or on the long-term financial costs to the system. Indications suggest that these costs may be significant. An American nurse warned those in Manitoba that, as a result of the consultant's work, 'nurses are very uncomfortable; their case loads are higher, and they are in tears when they go home because they don't feel like they have provided the care that their clients required.'[118] In the Canadian hospital offered as a model for TQM, time lost due to worker illness has increased notably.[119] A study of the application of new management techniques to Japanese car plants found that the company increased output significantly without hiring new staff but they 'accomplished this by running the assembly line at a frenzied pace'.[120] Running hospitals at a frenzied pace, however, could be even more problematic, given that the output is not cars, but the health of people who are ill.

The cutbacks in nursing care are pressuring people to bring relatives and friends with them to the hospital or even to hire help to come to the hospital. But many relatives or friends cannot afford to take time from paid work, a necessary strategy especially if the hospital is a significant distance from their place of employment. And with hospital closures, that distance is necessarily lengthening for some patients and their families. Between 1996 and 2001, 275 Canadian hospitals were closed, merged, or converted to other types of care facility.[121] Even more patients cannot afford paid help. The result is a two-tier system that means those with money get more and better care. Moreover, the decline in services increases the pressure for alternative services provided on a payment basis.

At the same time as nursing staff are being cut, employment in other therapeutic areas is not keeping up with the patient workload. As a result, more people must resort to private services to meet their health-care needs. Occupational therapy provides just one example. Between 1988 and 1993, the proportion of occupational therapists employed in general or teaching hospitals declined by 1 per cent. At the same time, the proportion in private practice more than doubled. Private practice went from the eleventh most important job category for occupational therapists to the fifth most important in just five years.[122] Increasingly, these therapists are employed in private, for-profit clinics. According to the business section of the *Toronto Star*, the 'lure of a huge potential market has new companies scrambling into rehabilitation . . . the companies see a wide open field as the province continues to cut its health bill, leaving more services and treatments up to private care.'[123] Many of these new rehabilitation clinics are American, for-profit companies that import American practices and export Canadian profits.

Instead of reducing services, some hospitals are handing over the services to private, for-profit companies. An increasing number of hospitals purchase their laundry, cleaning, and food services from commercial companies. In 1991–2, for example, 44 per cent of reporting hospitals sent their laundry out.[124] Some of this laundry is done by centralized, non-profit services organized by the hospitals. The process has reduced costs considerably while maintaining wages of a unionized workforce because centralized services can take advantage of expensive, labour-saving equipment and high-volume procedures. Sending laundry to for-profit services also seems to save money, both because more technology is used and because wages are often lower in the private sector.

But the use of for-profit services could increase costs in the long run because hospitals that have either closed laundries or failed to build them will have little choice but to purchase the services elsewhere. Moreover, contracting out can incur hidden costs in terms of administration, supervision, and other parts of the infrastructure that are paid for out of the hospital budget.

Indeed, an assessment of such hidden costs led at least one consulting firm to conclude that, unless there is at least a 20 per cent cost saving, 'there is no payoff for the effort, contract development, supervision and risks associated with contracting out'.[125] And the use of services without expertise in health care could risk poor nutrition for patients and inadequately cleaned hospitals. In Calgary, for example, a contracted company assigned one person to clean every 30,000 feet of floor, compared to the one cleaner for every 10,000 feet that the hospital had previously assigned.[126] This, too, could mean greater costs in the long term, especially if the services function as they would in a hotel without taking the special requirements of health care into account.

Staff cutbacks and service purchases have gone hand in hand with alterations in provision for patients designed both to cut costs and to improve care. Public hospitals and beds in public hospitals have disappeared. The bed cuts have been most aggressively pursued in Ontario, the province that already had much the lowest patient days to population ratio in the country when the cuts began in earnest.[127] Between 1990 and 2000 the province's population grew by 9 per cent and its average age increased by a year and a half, but during this time its acute-care beds were cut by 38 per cent and its chronic-care beds by 32 per cent. Meanwhile, the number of long-term care beds remained virtually static, although about 7,000 (or 12 per cent) have been added since early 2000 and another 13,000 are planned.[128] While reducing beds can reduce some costs, it is not clear what the consequences are for care or for long-term costs, given that little research has been done on the issue. The most likely result is less of the same rather than an improvement in quality of care. In Ontario 'the number of patients treated actually increased'[129] as the number of beds declined, which suggests that the process may be simply shifting costs while increasing the focus on treatment and on a medical model of care.

What is clear is that cuts in hospitals and beds have been accomplished in part by increasing the emphasis on the treatment of the parts to be fixed. Bed cutbacks have been combined with a massive shift to outpatient services, to shorter patient stays, and to day surgery. In addition, hospitals are sending patients who cannot readily be cured to other institutions defined as mainly custodial. The shift means that care in hospitals is even more strictly limited to intervention. This may cost the hospital more in the long run if discharged patients have to return with complications. Here, too, we know little about the costs because there is a paucity of research examining the overall impact of these strategies on health expenditures.

We do know that only some costs to hospitals are reduced by these strategies. Others are simply shifted to the individuals and their households. For example, drug costs are covered during hospital stays, as are the costs of other medical supplies. But when most patients go home after day surgery, early discharge, or outpatient visits, they have to cover the costs themselves. In fact, the drugs that make it possible to send people home are increasingly paid for by the individual.[130] Similarly, laboratories now charge for visits to homes to collect specimens but no charge is allowed for specimen collection in hospitals.[131] These patients also cover their own costs for food, laundry, electricity, and cleaning. These costs not only increase for the sick; they also change in kind. Sick people require cleaner environments and different food, for example, and create more mess. And most patients still need care, even though they are not in the hospital. Much of this care must either be provided for free by friends and relatives or be paid for by them. The process of shifting the costs and the care from hospitals can serve to increase long-term costs for the system. As a report from the National Advisory Council on Aging points out, 'overburdened caregivers who don't have community services, such as respite provided by day-care programs, withdraw from caregiving, leaving no recourse but to place the elderly person in an institution.'[132]

Hospitals are not only closing beds and sending people home early. They are also cancelling services. Some of this cancellation may be a useful way to avoid duplication. Not every hospital needs an emergency or obstetrics department, for example. However, some of it may be a way of simply shedding services that are mainly about care rather than cure and that are expensive to maintain. In Toronto, for instance, the District Health Council refused to endorse the 1995–6 operating plans from the Hospital for Sick Children because it was closing the day program for psychotic children, as well as plans of three other metro hospitals because they were closing chronic-care beds.[133] Cutbacks to hospitals, just like competition among hospitals, can mean that each hospital seeks to focus on the most lucrative and highly technical, interventionist treatment, leaving some care in scarce supply. And this scarce supply encourages the entrance of for-profit services to fill the gap. It also encourages people to demand such for-profit possibilities when the publicly funded hospitals withdraw.

In addition to cutting back, hospitals have sought ways to increase their income. One way is to raise the price of services such as parking. Another way is to sell services such as laundry and food preparation to others. In 1991–3, hospitals reported doing 25,183,577 kilograms of laundry and 2,326,404 meal days for others.[134] An increasingly popular third way is to form partnerships with the private sector. Sunnybrook Hospital in Metro Toronto, for example, has joined with Dynacare Laboratories to form SDL laboratories. They proposed to unite in providing laboratory services for hospitals. According to the hospital's CEO, 'It'll be a whole new revenue system for us. We have zero per cent increase from the government and we're looking for new revenues.' The hospital hoped the partnership with a private company would bring in business not only from other Ontario hospitals but also from the United States.[135] Sunnybrook is not alone in seeking such partnerships. Nor has it confined the strategy to labs. Quoting the vice-president of research at Sunnybrook Health Centre, the business section in the *Toronto Star* points out that 'Government spending cuts are driving medical researchers into closer links with business.'[136] The article goes on to describe similar arrangements in other Ontario hospitals. Late in 2001, Ontario went so far as to announce that new hospital buildings in Brampton and Ottawa would be constructed by private developers and leased back to the hospitals.[137] This will ease the short-term pressure on the province's budget, but the long-term cost will almost certainly be higher, whatever the immediate conclusion reached by the government.

Such partnerships may raise money and employ more sophisticated technology that speeds production but they also incur costs. One cost is jobs. Sunnybrook expected that, at least in the short term, 125 full-time and 15 part-time laboratory employees would lose their jobs.[138] Some may have been rehired if the company succeeded in attracting business away from other hospitals, which in turn were expected to lay off people when they closed their labs. Another potential cost is distortion. As the Sunnybrook research vice-president makes clear, 'Working directly with business requires a big change in the culture of the organization.'[139] The new culture could put a stress on profits over people and care, as we have seen is the case in the drug industry. The vice-president acknowledges a danger that outsiders may want to set the agenda but, in his experience, this has not happened yet. Even if the private partners do not set the agenda, there is a risk that the hospitals themselves will begin to set priorities in market, rather than health, terms as they become more involved in profit-seeking enterprises. Such partnerships may open the door to more aspects of the system becoming privatized and beyond public control.

Finally, these partnerships may even cost more in the short term. Ontario's Provincial Auditor has recently calculated that the for-profit cancer clinic set up to deliver after-hours radiation care at Sunnybrook actually costs $500 more per patient than does its public-sector counterpart, notwithstanding a $4 million start-up donation from the government to the for-profit firm. The Health Minister disputes the Provincial Auditor's estimate, but does so by claiming, 'It's a maximum of $100 [more].' It must be added that, at a cost of $3,500 per patient, the after-hours clinic is much cheaper than the $18,000 it was costing to send breast and prostate cancer patients to the US for treatment.[140]

It is clear from the data that Canadian hospitals have costs well under control. The problem is more that their funding has been cut too much. Between 1992 and 1998, the total real per capita spending on Canadian hospitals fell by 10.45 per cent.[141] It is also clear that these publicly funded and publicly responsible hospitals are cheaper and more effective in delivering care than are their American, for-profit counterparts. At the Toronto Hospital, for example, 2.9 per cent of patients died within 30 days of coronary artery bypass surgery, compared to a 3.4 per cent national death rate in US hospitals for the same procedure. The stroke rate following such surgery was 1.1 compared to 2.3.[142] Similarly, the treatment for the same person for the same problem—a suspected heart attack—resulted in a bill for $12,590.34 in a US hospital while the estimated cost in the Canadian hospital was just $3,500.[143] Yet these hospitals are importing American practices, American consultants, and American companies as a means of further cutting back, and in the name of improving care. Many of these practices are increasing the emphasis on the medical model that is often the target of their critiques. And many of the practices are not so much reducing costs as shifting them to individuals while transferring more care to private, for-profit companies.

PROVINCES AND TERRITORIES

Cuts in federal funding put pressure on provinces and territories to reduce the funding to hospitals, which in turn encourages them to introduce strategies that lead not only to cost savings but also to a shift to private care. But the provincial and territorial governments have done much more than simply limit hospital funding. They have taken other steps to promote further the move to private provision and for-profit care. In the process, quality too often declines, inequality increases, and the medical model dominates.

The most obvious strategy is one of delisting services and drugs or failing to fund new treatment. In 1992–3 several provinces reduced coverage for those travelling out of the country and for the number of drugs covered under their plans. Manitoba and Quebec eliminated their children's dental programs. A number of provinces eliminated eye examinations while BC reduced the frequency allowance for such examinations.[144] In some cases people may be better off without the drugs and services. It makes sense to pay for less expensive products that have the same effect as more expensive ones or to refuse to pay for services not demonstrated to do more good than harm. And it seems obvious that refusing to pay for services and drugs will save money.

But it should be noted that some of the services cut, such as eye examinations and dental work, are preventive measures that may save money in the long run. They certainly do not suggest the move towards health promotion used to justify many provincial funding reductions. Moreover, delisting transfers the cost to both the individual and employers while opening further the door to the for-profit provision of services. This, too, seems to contradict a government concern—that employer expenditure on benefits scares off investment. For example, Sedgewick Noble Lowndes, in conjunction with Seaboard Life Insurance Company, has developed 'replacement coverage' that 'is an ideal bridge to carry employees and their dependents over the gaps created by the cutbacks'.[145] Without coverage through general taxation, employees will seek such coverage through their employers and private plans will move in to fill the gap. Other, private services also move in to offer the services for a fee. *Maclean's* on occasion has run several pages of advertisement, sponsored by a for-profit firm, that offer various medical services not covered by provincial plans.[146] While some of these, like plastic surgery for a tummy tuck, are quite justifiably outside the public system, others, such as laser treatment for prostate disease, more reasonably belong in a public plan.

A less obvious strategy is one of shifting care to services allowed to charge user fees. When people are moved from hospitals to other care facilities, such as nursing homes, the embargo on user fees no longer applies. User fees are also creeping up in other ways. The Canada Health Act promised to penalize governments that allowed user fees for most physician and hospital services.

Yet fees are appearing in areas that previously had none. Doctors are increasingly charging patients a fee for such services as keeping or transferring files and ordering prescriptions by telephone. While some provinces are working to limit these practices, at least one province is actively promoting them. Alberta supports the idea of charging fees for services not deemed medically necessary and has allowed private clinics to charge facility fees. Indeed, Alberta has gone one step further in allowing a private eye clinic to bill the provincial system but charge additional fees for services otherwise provided in hospitals without fees. While the federal government seems to have successfully challenged this practice, the victory may well be temporary. It has not yet challenged the controversial Alberta legislation (Bill 11) allowing for the creation of private, for-profit hospitals that will receive public funds to perform selected surgical procedures requiring overnight stays.

User fees are continually promoted as a means of both raising funds and avoiding abuse of the 'free' system while improving care through the more rational distribution of services.[147] As is the case with the other strategies, the assumptions grow out of economic theories of how markets in the private sector operate. But study after study has shown such assumptions are false. The entire range of arguments supporting fees has been most thoroughly investigated in a series of documents produced by the Ontario Premier's Council on Health, Well-Being and Social Justice.[148]

These documents make it clear that the assumption of abuse cannot be supported in fact. Few costs are patient-initiated. The doctors directly accessible to patients account for only 10–14 per cent of money spent on physicians. 'If nearly ninety percent of medicare expenditures are thus a consequence of an explicit physician admission or referral, and some undetermined portion of the rest are initiated by the practitioner, this does not leave a lot of scope for savings by reducing *patient-initiated* "frivolous" demands.'[149] When costs are patient-initiated, the patient usually has just cause even if the diagnosis concludes that the problem is either not serious or not treatable. What may be labelled unnecessary use is much more likely to be initiated by the doctors who charge the fees rather than by the patients who pay them. This is mainly why 'all the evidence indicates that in-patient use is insensitive to patient charges.'[150] And, in any case, the assumption that necessary care can be easily separated from unnecessary care by either patient or physician is not supported in practice.

Not surprisingly, then, fees do not reduce unnecessary use or more rationally distribute care. As one of these reports points out, the assumption that user fees deter unnecessary use is based on economic theories about market purchases. But 'health care isn't like other products and the "market" for health care cannot be analyzed the same way as the market for shoes or VCRs . . . people do not often have sufficient notice in advance to make correct judgements about necessity. This is precisely why they consult their physicians.'[151]

An American study found that coinsurance charges 'reduced the demand for care in situations where care was likely to be highly effective as much as it did in situations where care was deemed to be only rarely effective.'[152] In Canada, a Saskatchewan study concluded that user fees do not lead to more rational distribution of services. Rather, their effect 'is simply to transfer costs from public to private budgets with the burden of such transfers falling disproportionately on the sicker members of the population.'[153] The burden also falls disproportionately on the poor, given that they tend to be sicker and that they can least afford the fee.

Fees do little, if anything, to change the use patterns of the rich. And even if user charges ensured more appropriate use, they would still constitute a tax on the 'really' sick. As another of these documents demonstrates, 'the substitution of user fees for tax finance not only transfers money from the less to the more healthy and wealthy, but if one is wealthy enough, one can be an above average user of care and still come out ahead.'[154] It goes on to explain that 'Increased reliance on user charges, relative to tax finance, improves the access of those more willing/able to pay as well as reducing their share of the total.'[155] In short, user fees do not make the rich pay or result in the more rational and effective use of care. Those with money can continue past practices and those without go without.

Clearly, user fees do generate revenue, although not as much as might be assumed once the costs of administration and defaults on fees are calculated into the revenues. But user fees will do little to change the way health care is delivered or to control costs. Instead, they will change the system from one that assumes everyone has a right to care based on need to one that assumes people should take individual responsibility for their care. Individual responsibility in these terms largely means payment because many health determinants are beyond individual control.

As soon as people start to pay such fees regularly, they will start to demand differential treatment based on ability to pay. This is especially the case when, as is now happening, other services cut back with a resulting increase in waiting time and decline in the quality of service. This combination can lead to a two-tiered system that differs in both access and quality, as those with money increasingly demand special treatment in return for their fee. This has already begun to happen in Alberta, where those with enough money can go to the special eye clinic. Even though they pay only a fraction of the actual cost, they assume their fee gives them the right to special service. At the same time, those who can pay no longer have a vested interest in maintaining quality in the fee-less system. In such two-tiered systems, however, most costs are still covered by the taxpayers and so those able to pay fees get a greater return on their money. Moreover, once fees are introduced, governments are likely to find raising fees is the easiest way to cover costs[156] and thus avoid more basic reforms that could improve care.

In addition, user fees 'provide greater opportunities for (some) providers of care to raise their fees or wages, thus leading to a redistribution of income between providers and payers, or from some providers to others.'[157] The providers who are most likely to benefit are the physicians and others in private practice who can charge fees. With more money going to these providers, there is likely to be less money for the providers, mostly female, who are employees and who are not as likely to operate strictly on the basis of the medical model. The owners of private, fee-charging clinics are also likely to profit, and at the expense of the taxpayer and other services. Those offering private insurance coverage stand to benefit as well from user charges as they move in to cover the additional fees. But in France and the United States, the countries with significant user fees, the result 'is not cost control, but cost expansion through the creation of additional private incomes in the financial services sector.'[158] And many of these private incomes go to those living outside Canada, given that many of the insurance companies are foreign-owned.

The evidence on user fees is clear. User charges influence who gets care, not what care they get. Who gets care are those who can afford it, not necessarily those who need it. User fees do nothing to ensure that those who get care necessarily get what they need. User fees also put more money in the hands of providers and for-profit companies, while doing nothing about overall health-care costs.

In addition to delisting services and allowing user fees, provinces are also promoting a move out of institutions and into the community. Like user fees, this is not a new strategy but rather one than has been more universally applied in recent years. Almost three decades ago most provinces began to move people out of psychiatric hospitals. For some people, the move was made possible by new and better drugs. For some, the move led to greater independence and better lives. But for many, there were no family or friends to provide support, no drugs that helped, and no community services. This in part reflected the fact that the main purpose was cost reduction, even though the strategy was justified in terms of better care and patient preference. In his book on Ontario mental health policy, Harvey Simmons describes the deinstitutionalization that began in 1965 as 'a deliberate policy of reducing the long-stay population of the large mental hospitals regardless of what happened to the patients afterward'.[159] According to one medical superintendent it was based on 'pretty explicit messages that were associated with budget cuts'.[160] One result of the policy was that readmission rates were 'reaching 35 and 50 per cent within a few months of leaving hospital'.[161] In spite of this return rate, expenditures on mental health hospitals declined. But little research was done on the overall costs to governments and individuals of deinstitutionalization. However, a 1982 report concluded that the many problems resulting from or remaining after this strategy could only be addressed by spending more money on both institutional and community care.[162]

The current strategy of dehospitalization and deinstitutionalization is being undertaken for similar reasons, with similar justifications, with a similar lack of investment in community services and with a similar paucity of research on overall costs. It is assumed both that community care is available and that it is cheaper. However, one 1992 study found that, even if only medical expenses are included, home care for some can be more expensive than institutional care. 'The average cost per patient per day of the 10 patients in the study was $370. The average cost per patient per day at St Peter's hospital is $240.'[163] And these costs provide only limited hours of care in the community, compared to 24-hour care in the institution. These costs do not take into account other services such as Meals on Wheels or additional support needed by family caregivers who take up the slack.[164] Even if we ignore the additional costs to individuals, there are real questions about whether or not home care is cheaper. Subsequent studies have not reached agreement on this score, in large part because of the complexity concerning which costs to include and which to exclude. The point here is that the chief motivation for deinstitutionalization seems to be to cut public spending.

The money saved by government is saved mainly because the costs are transferred to others, not because the costs have disappeared. Although there are differences among provinces in the provision of community services, none entirely cover all the required hours of care. Individuals and families must make up the difference either by hiring home care services, usually from the private sector, or by doing all the care themselves.

The move out of institutions means a shift in costs to the individual and a shift of public funds to the private for-profit sector. Some home care is provided by non-profit agencies but an increasing share is done by private, for-profit firms. Their expansion is encouraged by managed competition approaches such as request-for-proposal (RFP) mechanisms. They have the financial resources to 'lowball' their initial bids in order to gain a market foothold, and they can often cross-subsidize their home care and long-term care operations. The non-profit organizations face the dilemma of either having to behave more like the for-profits (for instance, by eliminating the 'extras' they have long provided or by employing more lowest-cost care providers on a part-time and casual basis) or being forced out of operation. The century-old Victorian Order of Nurses, for example, has recently had to pull out of several Ontario communities, largely because maintaining its standards of patient care and provider remuneration meant incurring financial losses a charitable organization could not sustain. In the words of Ambrose Hearn, the chief executive officer of the VON:

> We're prepared to compete, we're not prepared to compromise the care we provide. There ought to be a reasonably level playing field; that is to say, you get some recognition for the added value you bring to the effort. . . . [T]his is about competition in the fullest sense of the word.[165]

While governments are busy cutting back the money that goes to the public provision of care, they are spending money on health-sector industries. On the one hand, we have the federal and most provincial governments preaching and practising severe restaint in their health-care spending, in part on the basis of claims that health care does not make people healthy. On the other hand, we have an Ontario government report maintaining that:

Health care is one of the fastest-growing economic sectors in the world. . . . Other jurisdictions are working hard to bolster their health industries to take advantage of the outstanding opportunity presented by the global boom in health products. . . . That is why we should target the health industries as a growth opportunity for Ontario.'[166]

Although some investment in such companies may help the Ontario economy, it is clear that most of these industries produce products and services that both reflect and reinforce the medical model. As described in the Ontario report, the industries to be promoted have four parts: 'medical devices, pharmaceuticals, biotechnology, and private sector health services'.[167] We have already seen how the industries manufacturing drugs, medical devices, and biotechnology promote the use of their products, regardless of their effectiveness, and emphasize the use of technology or drugs over the provision of care. And it is not clear why tax dollars should be spent on promoting health-care services based on profit. Moreover, the promotion of these industries will require them to use our existing health services to demonstrate the usefulness of their products, and these industries often rely on public investment infrastructure. This could have a distorting effect on even the non-profit services that remain. It will certainly do little to encourage a new approach to health that stresses whole people and health promotion.

In sum, the strategies presented as improving the system while cutting costs are likely to increase the focus on the medical model, which has been under attack for ignoring the determinants of health. In terms of public, non-profit care, these strategies are likely simply to mean less of the same. Moreover, instead of producing the overall limits on health costs that the Prime Minister called for, these strategies are likely to increase costs for individuals and employers while increasing profits for often foreign-owned companies. Such processes are much more likely to redistribute care from those who cannot pay to those who can than they are to make care distribution more effective. The poorest, and the sickest, will get less of the same. The problem is further exacerbated by cutbacks in other social programs and in the regulations that help keep us healthy.

CONCLUSION

'All health care systems in the real world are predominately collectively funded, through various forms of *de facto* taxation.'[168] What mainly differentiates our system from the system in the United States is who pays and who profits. For about the same proportion of government spending, we cover everyone for a wide range of high-quality, basic services while they cover only the military, the poorest, the most severely disabled, and the oldest. One reason for this is that more of the public money in the United States goes to private profit. Another reason is that our non-profit system is more efficient and effective, however these are measured. Both reasons help explain why American expenditures on health care continue to rise while ours remain relatively constant.

Yet in the name of cost-cutting, efficiency, and effectiveness, Canadian governments and institutions are adopting American for-profit practices in the public sector as a means of both improving care and reducing costs. They are also shifting more of the responsibility for provision and payment to for-profit companies and to individuals. This is a more dangerous experiment than it might appear because, according to the North American Free Trade Agreement (NAFTA), once services have been privatized it would be extremely difficult and expensive to return them to the public sector. It will only become more dangerous to the extent that the current round of negotiations for the General Agreement on Trade in Services (GATS) proceeds.[169] A giant American public relations firm has described our public health-care system as 'one of the largest unopened oysters in the Canadian economy',[170] an opportunity to turn public services into private profits.

Of course, Canada's health-care system is already primarily based on private provision. Most hospitals and other institutions are owned by a wide variety of organizations, not by the state. Most doctors are in private practice and most services such as home care are purchased by the government from other organizations. However, although some of the government money currently goes to for-profit institutions, most tax dollars go to non-profit providers, and the current principles of the Canada Health Act, combined with the funding formula, have ensured this is the case. But new strategies are opening the oyster to for-profit provision.

While for-profit organization may make sense in some aspects of government operation, it poses significant dangers and offers no improvement in health care for a number of reasons. First, it is inefficient. Research clearly demonstrates that the Canadian single-payer system 'lends itself to effective supply management and cost control.'[171] The evidence does not support the notion that the kind of private contract management promoted in some provinces is more efficient either. Research in the United States has concluded that for-profit 'contract management does not appear to improve hospitals' productive efficiency'[172] and that 'for-profit management firms emphasize debt financing as an important management tool' without reducing costs.[173] Moreover, as a report on privatization for Health and Welfare Canada pointed out, there is no reason to assume that the public sector is incapable of adopting previously unexplored management techniques that have proven useful in the private sector.[174]

Second, privatization is ineffective, especially at reducing overall health expenditures. The basis of the for-profit system is selling more. This is the main way profit grows. Thus, it is in the interests of for-profit companies to have Canadians spend more, not less, on health care. Another way for-profit organizations increase the return on their investment is to reduce reliance on labour and to cut wages. In health care, this means an even greater emphasis on treatments through drugs and technology and a declining emphasis on care of the whole person. It also means the increasing use of the least skilled provider and the fragmentation of tasks, a process that further emphasizes the medical model.

Third, privatization leads to inaccessibility and inequality. In a for-profit system, more of the money comes from individuals and employers. As a result, the costs for both employers and individual Canadians increase. Those employers who provide health care pay more for labour than those who do not. And individuals with the ability to pay have greater access than those who do not. But both the employers who do not pay and the individuals who do will still benefit from the public funding of care. Access is based more on money but this does not eliminate public funding. Equally important, private payment does nothing to control costs or increase efficiency and effectiveness. It may simply give more of the same to some and less of the same to others.

Fourth, the shift to private provision places heavy burdens on women and families. As we have seen, women provide most of the care in the community and the home. When services focus more on the medical model, they increasingly assign the caring work to women who are expected to do the job without pay at home. And households must carry more of the costs for services and products purchased from the for-profit sector. Clearly, some households will be much better equipped to provide these services than others. The result will be increasing inequality in care and more work for women.

Back in 1985, a survey of the research by Health and Welfare Canada concluded that 'With the exception of a positive contribution to public expenditure control—which becomes a negative contribution if total expenditure control is considered—the benefits of privatization are either absent, or unknown and in some cases questionable.'[175] When more recent evidence is considered the impact of privatization seems even less benign. In short, it is unhealthy to privatize because it is more likely to emphasize the worst aspects of the system and to increase inequality than it is to lead to improved ways of providing care. Equally important, it is also likely to change fundamentally who decides about the distribution and quality of care.

RECOMMENDED READINGS

Colleen Fuller, *Caring for Profit*. Ottawa: Canadian Centre for Policy Alternatives, 1998. Fuller examines in detail the economic pressures within and outside Canada that have a strong influence on current health-care reforms.

David Himmelstein and Steffie Woolhandler, with Ida Hellander, *Bleeding the Patient: The Consequences of Corporate Health Care*. Philadelphia: Common Courage Press, 2001. These American doctors regularly bring together a variety of data sources to demonstrate how effective and efficient it is to have a public health-care system. The book includes comparative data on Canada and the United States, as well as important evidence on the failures of the mainly private US system.

Robert G. Evans, 'Health Care Reform: The Issue from Hell', *Policy Options* (July–Aug. 1993): 35–41. In a few short pages, one of Canada's most prominent health-care economists sets out the major issues in the financing of public services. Although the article was written almost a decade ago, the analysis remains relevant today.

6

Who Decides

Reforms to health care have been implemented not only in the name of cost-cutting, efficiency, and effectiveness but also in the name of greater choice and participation in decision-making. In the early 1990s, the Nova Scotia Provincial Health Council set out to 'involve Nova Scotians in decisions affecting health'.[1] A Commission promised that 'Albertans will enjoy the privilege of choice.'[2] The British Columbia provincial ministry claimed that 'Increased participation is an essential part of a responsive and flexible health system.'[3] Setting out these goals seemed to suggest that the existing public health care left Canadians with little choice.

Yet, contrary to predictions of many opponents to a public health-care system, medicare expanded choices enormously. Doctors could see any patient that called and order any services thought necessary without considering the cost or worrying about payment. Similarly, patients could decide, on the basis of need rather than expense, when to visit the doctor and which doctor to see, which hospital to enter, and which tests to take. A whole range of health-care providers could negotiate better conditions of work in large part because the public system offered stable employment in the field. As a result, health care workers had more choices about their jobs and how they did them. Indeed, a public system meant all citizens, through the political process, had a say in medicare. The importance of this is evident in electoral campaigns. All politicians understand that a promise to protect the system is a condition for election.

Moreover, this expansion in choice did not send health-care costs out of control, especially relative to those in a for-profit system. Comparisons between the US mainly for-profit system and the Canadian public system make it clear that 'partial, multiple source funding, rather than universal, public funding, leads to uncontrollable cost escalation.'[4] Canada was better able to control costs in part because many decisions were collectively made on the basis of need rather than profit.

This universal system did mean that some choices were eliminated and others prevailed. Obviously, there must be some limits on choice if costs are to be controlled and decisions are to be made about the kinds of care that deserve public support. As critics of the health-care system repeatedly point out, 'Health care will spend all it can get.'[5] Even in the most democratic society not all choices can be funded or allowed. There are always tensions between the freedom of the individual and the rights of the collectivity, and among various demands for funding.

Some of the choices governments, providers, and patients have made have not always been healthy. In large part because the funding was based on the dominant medical model with fee-for-service physicians as the central gate-keepers, the public system has remained focused on cuts and chemicals while offering less choice about alternative or additional components of care. In addition, this model stressed the authority of the physician not only in relation to the patient but also in relation to other workers and the system as a whole. This, too, has restricted choices for patients and other providers of care. Equally important, this model fit with new managerial practices that reduced workers' control and increased the authority of those making decisions on the basis of finances rather than health.

There is, then, room for greater participation and more choice, especially for choices that go beyond the medical model. New methods for participation would recognize the tensions between the knowledge of the care provider and the preferences of the care recipient; between the need for community choices and national standards; between the call for equity and the recognition of difference; between demands for every kind of service and those that are the most appropriate; and between the care model and the cost model.

Patients, many health-care providers, and some government agencies have been working towards these goals for years and have enjoyed some successes. However, strategies introduced in the name of greater participation are too often eliminating choices. More private-sector participation frequently means more choices are made on the basis of profit and ability to pay rather than on the basis of need and appropriateness. More provincial control can mean fewer national standards designed to ensure equity in choices about services. More regionalization often means more centralization of services and more decisions made on the basis of formulas that significantly reduce individual choice. More emphasis on cost and the managerial methods of the for-profit sector means less choice for doctors, patients, and other health-care workers. And too often this means basing choice on individual, rather than collective, ability to pay. This reduction in choice is evident in an opinion poll taken at the turn of this century, a decade after promises of more choice, indicating that 70 per cent of Canadians are dissatisfied with how accountable governments are to the public.[6]

PUBLIC DECISIONS

All governments play an important decision-making role in health care. Through legislation, regulation, and funding, or through a refusal to do any of these things, governments make important decisions about who gets what kind of care from whom. In democratic countries, governments are made accountable through the election process. This process does not simply mean that every person gets one vote at election times. It also means that decision-making is more open to public scrutiny and public pressure through a variety of means, among them lobbying, public forums, and demonstrating.

Certainly those who are elected often do not carry out their promises and frequently take actions contrary to those indicated by a vote. Certainly decisions are often made in the bureaucracy by non-elected people, or take place behind closed doors, far from the electorate's view. Certainly choices in health care especially are frequently so complex and are presented in such technical language that the number who feel competent to participate are limited. And certainly governments are more open to pressure from some groups than from others. Moreover, the democratic process is often messy and inefficient. But at least the possibility for scrutiny and control, as well as for decisions that favour equity and participation, exists.

Health care provides a clear example of how democratic decision-making works, warts and all. Public medical care in Canada was a direct result of pressure from the majority of the population, expressed in a wide variety of ways. It has been maintained over the years precisely because of its popularity and its very existence has contributed to that popularity. In terms of saving the system and increasing public participation, change has been justified precisely because Canadian citizens have so clearly indicated that their choice is a public, accountable system.

The system that emerged as a result of this democratic process is complex and far from uniform; it reflects compromises and failed promises. Canada has not developed a universal health system primarily through state provision, with governments directly controlling and operating services. Rather, health care in Canada remains mainly in private hands and governments have used other ways to influence the delivery of care. At the federal level, government has few constitutionally granted rights in the health-care field. The federal government has therefore employed its funding power as a means to enforce national standards of care and ensure universal access. Provinces could decide how best to meet these standards, but they had to meet them if they were to get paid. The federal government has also used its right to regulate as a means of controlling such things as drug prices and quality. At the provincial level, governments have established ministries and legislation setting out conditions for funding that can influence everything from who participates in decisions about care to where care is provided. For example, Ontario dramatically reduced global budgets for hospitals and ordered some major ones closed, while Nova Scotia amalgamated four Halifax hospitals into a single complex. In Quebec, regional and social services cut cleaning, laundry, and administration of support services, and in Saskatchewan and Manitoba the regional health authorities created to manage local care received smaller global budgets. Alberta approved private, for-profit eye clinics while BC reduced hospital staff by 10 per cent. Within their own areas of power, local governments have also used funding and regulations as ways of shaping health care.

Initially, as mainly public payment for private provision, the introduction of hospital and medical insurance did little to change formal power relations and the structure of decision-making within the system. With public payment based on the right to universal, accessible, and comprehensive care, however, the individual Canadian's decision about when to seek care and whose care to seek could be made on the basis of need and access, not ability to pay. Although there were still limitations related to region, race, cultural group, age, and class, the distribution of care was much less unequal than in a user-pay system. In funding mainly non-profit care, government intervention also meant that decisions within the system would be made on the basis of health needs, not on the basis of return on financial investment, competition with other providers, or ways to increase demand. Non-profit provisions also meant no argument could be made about the need for confidentiality based on the need for competition.

Concern over rising expenditures and pressure from various groups working in or using the system have led governments over the years to seek ways of altering decision-making and power relations. Governments have been using their capacity to legislate, regulate, and fund to change how health-care decisions are made. Some of these strategies increase the choices and power of individuals receiving and providing care; others reduce alternatives.

Most recently, the federal government has justified the move away from directly funding care provision that met its standards by claiming greater choice for provinces, even though the provinces already have a great deal of choice about services. By transferring tax points rather than cash, the federal government says that provinces will have more opportunity to develop alternative forms of care. However, severing the link between funding and standards means not only that national standards related to access, comprehensiveness, and non-profit administration are no longer monitored, but also that provinces can use their new tax points to fund rinks for professional hockey rather than health care. In addition, given the very different capacities of provinces to raise taxes, the move increases inequality among provinces. Inequality in access necessarily reduces choices within the system and increases the opportunities for for-profit care. The same could be said of provincial efforts to shift responsibility to municipalities.

While cutting back on directly funding health care, the federal government is encouraging more charitable donations from corporations by offering tax benefits for those who give money to non-profit organizations. Shifting from taxing to tax credits also changes who decides. The corporations that give money can decide who gets it and for what purposes. They decide directly where tax money forgone is allocated. As a consequence, health-care organizations try to shape their decisions in ways that encourage such donations. Often, what attracts donors are spectacular new technologies promising spectacular cures, not less visible preventive work.

Partly in response to changes in federal funding and partly in response to various groups' demands for greater say, provinces have been introducing a variety of reforms in the name of increasing participation.

PRIVATE PROVISION

The institutions and organizations that provide care fall into two basic groups: non-profit and for-profit. There is also some direct provision by various levels of governments. While the federal legislation that introduced hospital insurance would only offer funds to provinces with non-profit administrations, governments do pay for-profit organizations such as long-term care facilities, homecare, and laboratories to provide health-care services. Other regulations and funding practices also influence the for-profit sector. Government policies therefore have a significant impact on health-care decisions regardless of who provides. Some of these policies apply in quite similar ways to both for-profit and non-profit organizations, while others are specific to each sector. It is useful, then, to examine decision-making in these two different kinds of organizations separately.

NON-PROFIT CARE

A complex array of organizations offer non-profit health-care services. Many of them, such as hospitals, are so closely tied to the state that we think of them as public and they are difficult to distinguish from those owned directly by governments. These organizations vary in size, services, composition, and decision-making processes. Some, like the Catholic Church, which operates a significant number of hospitals, do not set democratic processes as their goal, while others, such as a hospice run for AIDS patients, attempt consensus decision-making.

The variety of non-profit organizations is both their strength and their weakness. On the one hand, the range of organizations offers people a choice in workplace and services. If one organization does not provide the kinds of services people require they can go to another. On the other hand, variety limits co-ordination and often results in duplication, not only of services but also of administrative structures. In addition, some non-profit organizations have quite closed decision-making structures. While government attempts to rationalize the delivery of services, cut costs, and increase participation have brought more uniformity to the system, they have also helped eliminate much of the variation offering people and organizations more choices.

Some government interventions have been directly designed to alter decision-making structures. Although there is no one single strategy, all provinces have moved to make decision-making within hospitals and some other institutions more accountable to government and the public. Some have required institutions to open their financial statements to public scrutiny; some have legislated the right to appoint members to the governing boards; still others have required some members to be elected or selected on the basis of their membership in particular groups.

Quebec provides just one example. In 1971, legislation was introduced to require the inclusion of four citizens on the boards of directors in hospitals, nursing homes, social work agencies, and rehabilitation centres. Two of these were to be elected from among those using the facilities and two were to be appointed by the government to represent 'socio-economic groups'. The proportion of seats going to these citizen representatives ranged from four out of 13 to four out of 17.[7]

These citizen representatives did have an influence in some areas. On occasion, they were able to limit cuts and layoffs, to alter professional practices, and to reject or encourage abortion services. 'More importantly, perhaps, the presence of citizens created a kind of "symbolic cut" with the past, introducing slowly but surely into the public mind that everyone could have a say in the operation of the system, and not just the élites as before the reform.'[8]

While these were important developments, they did not signal a fundamental change in the way decisions were made. In her examination of Quebec hospitals, Eakin concluded that 'new representative boards were generally unable to participate meaningfully in hospital decision-making . . . and the remaining élite board members retained considerable authority and control.'[9] In addition to the traditional problems of the links between representatives and their constituencies and the highly technical discussions that dominated the decision-making process, Eakin found that administrators and traditional élites responded to the increased participation of user representatives by shifting decision-making out of the board room.[10] Another investigation concluded that the 'role of users and representatives of socio-economic groups consists more in managing the agencies than in defending the community interests.'[11]

In short, because the strategy consisted mainly of adding a small number of members to a board that continued to follow old practices and to include those traditionally in power, little change was made. Doctors and administrators remained the most powerful forces and they continued to operate on the basis of a medical model that stressed the scientific basis of and need for physicians' authority and stressed efficiency defined primarily in monetary terms.

Much is still done in secret. Indeed, the introduction of competitive bidding has increased the demand for confidentiality. Companies entering the process maintain that secrecy is necessary in order to remain competitive and that the information belongs to them. Even when decision-making is public, the knowledge of medical professionals, technical experts, and the business élite is privileged over the knowledge of users. This tendency is reinforced by resistance from governments and institutions to demands for the inclusion of other health-care providers in governance.

Governments are also increasingly deciding what services non-profit institutions can provide and even whether or not they can continue to exist. More and more provincial governments, for example, decide where such technology as magnetic resonating images (MRIs) are located, who can offer dialysis, or whether or not there will be an emergency service. This planning can mean that technology and services are more effectively distributed, although it can also mean less choice because fewer services will be offered in particular areas.[12] Some provinces are introducing agencies to serve as gatekeepers for a wide range of community organizations and have established formulas for services in them. Most provinces have set up mechanisms to examine hospital services, with a view to co-ordinating services and eliminating overlaps. In a growing number of cases, co-ordination means closing entire institutions and the creation of giant ones that may be less responsive to democratic processes. This can mean less choice or even exclusion. For example, a group appointed by the Ontario government closed a civic hospital in Pembroke, leaving only a Catholic hospital to serve a diverse community that often holds beliefs contrary to those of the Catholic Church.[13]

Moves to co-ordinate decision-making and rationalize services have been carried out under terms such as regionalization, decentralization, and devolution. The idea of establishing an integrated, regional system for health care is not new. It was recommended in a 1969 federal task force on costs[14] and some provinces began moving in this direction shortly afterwards. In the 1990s, however, the strategy gained new popularity. A report prepared for the Ontario Premier's Council on Health, Well-Being and Social Justice defines devolution as 'the transfer of greater control and decision-making for some or all of the planning, funding, management, revenue generation and delivery functions'.[15] The report recognizes that there are degrees of devolution and that the process can involve any or all of these dimensions. Its rationale for such strategies is 'cost containment, improved consumer participation in decision-making (with respect to both the allocation of health and health care resources and the delivery of services), improved integration and coordination of health services, and greater responsiveness to local needs'.[16] However, a background paper for the report concluded that there 'is a paucity of empirical measurement or evaluation criteria to determine whether the expected outcomes of devolution or decentralization, as identified in stated rationales, have been achieved.'[17]

In spite of the lack of evidence demonstrating the strategy's effectiveness in the ways the rationale describes,[18] all provinces except Ontario have introduced some form of devolved, regional structures. In Alberta, for example, 17 Regional Health Authorities replaced some 200 local boards. Initially appointed, with promises for elected membership, these Authorities were given responsibility for determining priorities and allocating resources. More than five years later, there is still little empirical evidence to indicate that regionalization improved co-ordination of care, increased citizen participation or made the system more responsive to local needs. Nor are there elected boards. Rather, a study of process concluded that citizens feel more disenfranchised and that 'a fragmented system, with considerable duplication and health care issues, has developed through regionalization'.[19] Costs rose, with much of the increase going to reorganization instead of care. Neither quality nor access seemed to improve. Rural women who participated in focus group

research reported that their access to care was reduced with the new regional structure, and regional allocation to long-term care meant many people
were sent far away from their families. 'This situation potentially creates
tremendous family unheaval and imposes increased stress upon family members who are encouraged to provide support to long-term care residents.'[20]
More responsibility for individuals with little choice about care did not seem
to have better quality as compensation. The provincial agency asssessing
health outcomes stopped reporting administrative and clinical data when 'it
received negative publicity for some bad numbers' that suggested a deterioration in care.[21]

These outcomes are not surprising, given the emphasis on cost-cutting
combined with centralized overall funding decisions that are shaped by market strategies. As is the case with the participation under TQM, regional
boards may mainly be left with choices about whom to cut. The criteria for
reduction in services and for admissions are often centrally designed to
reduce variation. Such criteria, as we have seen, tend not only to ignore individual characteristics of the whole person but also to reduce the decision-
making scope of care providers. When these criteria become the sole or even
main source of determining service delivery, then patients necessarily participate less in decision-making about their care. What has been called one-stop
shopping may be more efficient in some ways but it also means that you cannot shop around and that your alternatives are limited to a single brand. And
that brand is usually based on the dominant medical model and increasingly
on market kinds of choices.

Although much of the decision-making is centralized and local alternatives
are limited to what to cut, the Regional Authorities in Alberta do have some
choices in terms of who supplies care. Under the Regional Health Authorities
Act, either the Minister of Health or the regional board can contract out the
delivery of care with no restrictions on whether the provider is for-profit or
not. Indeed, the framework of legislation and funding encourages such contracting out as well as fees for many services.[22] This results in considerable
variation within the province in terms of providers and more public tax dollars
going to profit. It may also mean less control for ordinary Canadians and their
governments over who provides care and how tax dollars are spent. Once the
decision to contract out is made at the local level, trade agreements could
mean that foreign investors can operate throughout the country in ways that
significantly reduce local and even federal democratic decision-making.[23]

Research in both Norway and Quebec suggests that in decentralized
power structures the primary actors 'are professionals rather than the local
citizens. These evaluations suggest that "concentrated interests" are more
likely to participate than are "diffuse interests"; providers remain more likely to participate than consumers, and special interest groups more likely than
the general public.'[24] Effectively, one hierarchy is replaced with another. Or
as the Rochon Commission concluded, the democratic process becomes
hostage to corporate interests.[25] Regional or more local boards may be easily

swayed by pressure from such interests, especially in the face of inadequate funding. Moreover, local interests can reflect particular cultures that are too frequently intolerant of the diversity that is critical to equity. In Quebec, the Local Community Service Centres (CLSCs) were intended to provide integrated health care[26] through small centres initiated and controlled by the community they serviced. Staffed by an interdisciplinary team 'offering all preventative, curative, and readaptive nonspecialized health and social services',[27] they had the potential to provide both a service based on a care model and local participation in decision-making. Initially, the strategy encouraged public participation and gave local groups money to establish programs. 'The institutions had full autonomy in their choice of personnel and in the relations they chose to have with other establishments in the network.'[28] A study of a number of CLSCs concluded that there was genuine citizen control over the projects.[29] However, the CLSCs faced strong resistance to participation from traditionally powerful groups, especially from the medical specialists. In the end, these groups were able to limit both public participation and the spread of CLSCs, restricting them to disadvantaged areas. In CLSCs, as in other experiments, there was tension between the tendency for the staff to assume control and the demand for public participation, between the authority of the professionals and the concerns of the public, and between the need for universal standards and for local control. Today, with greater centralization, more rules on how money can be spent and less money to spend, the participation process tends to 'strengthen the technocracy while weakening democracy, political institutions and the power of citizens'.[30] And for-profit organizations are increasingly entering the game at the local level, often supported by the technocratic rules.

The lesson from the CLSCs is neither that local decision-making is impossible nor that local citizens should make all the decisions. In fact, the citizens in Quebec were not always on the side of reform, sometimes demanding more curative services over preventive ones.[31] Rather, the CLSCs indicate that genuine participation requires much more far-reaching reform than simply structuring in representation. It requires new processes and resources, not just new people, if care is to be transformed to respond to needs in appropriate ways that go beyond the medical model, less of the same, and more privatized care. It requires not only a recognition of the tensions but also a method of building them into the structures and processes, instead of favouring one side in these tensions. Providers of all sorts must be included in the decision-making process, along with patients and citizens from our diverse populations. It requires as well that the provincial/territorial regulations promote both universality and diversity, both public health and public participation.

Regionalization, then, does not seem to have increased participation and it has certainly limited choices. Patients have fewer services to choose from and fewer people to provide care when they do gain access to services. Many patients have to travel much farther for care, leaving their social support groups behind. The elimination of variation in everything from meals to bed changes also necessarily means the patients have less say. Elimination in variation also means that those whose race or culture is not the dominant one have more difficulty finding care that fits their needs. Similarly, providers' choices have been curtailed by staff reductions, by the centralization of decision-making done in the name of decentralization, and by moves to eliminate variation. According to one manager, 'They feel they are being abused now.'[32] In addition, hospitals themselves have lost significant decision-making powers to the new regional authorities. As well, there is little evidence that the regionalization process means greater community control or increased responsiveness to local needs or the needs of diverse groups. Instead, regionalization seems to have centralized power while decentralizing responsibility, but without increasing participation and choices for users of the health-care system.

In addition to regionalization, governments have been increasingly using the notions of accountability and evidence to alter decision-making in health care. Both are presented as means of increasing responsibility to citizens or, more frequently, to taxpayers, a much more narrowly defined group reflecting the emphasis on payment over a stress on citizenship rights. Under global budgeting, institutions could make their own decisions about internal allocations, although their budgets were based on government assumptions about what qualified for reimbursement. Even with global budgeting, however, decisions at the ministerial level were increasingly made by professional managers, planners, and economists rather than mainly by health professionals, as they had been in the past.[33] Business principles rather than health principles dominate, with institutions encouraged to do the same. Business plans have become at least as important as care plans in government funding, with health organizations pushed to act like financially competitive enterprises.[34]

In keeping with this trend, global budgets have given way to much more detailed budget criteria. Reporting and bidding requirements are just two of the ways that governments have sought to transform information systems, as well as managerial practices, to fit the emphasis on business practices rather than on health. By establishing the eligible categories for expenditure and means of measuring outcomes that qualify for funding, governments are structuring decision-making within organizations in ways that are very difficult for citizens to see or understand.

Rekart's research on the British Columbia voluntary sector revealed that, in the view of executive directors in these organizations, 'government appeared to be more interested in balancing budgets than in ensuring voluntary agencies provided quality service.'[35] Contracting processes meant that these directors 'developed their grantsmanship to the point at which they became familiar with the culture, language and procedures of government'.[36] In other words, the way to get money was to act like the government planners and economists, not like health-care providers. Cutbacks in funding further reduced the alternatives open to the institutions. In Quebec, the responsibilities offloaded to community organizations have increased enormously at the same time as these organizations have become more and more subject to government control through the funding process. Relations between the government and the voluntary organizations 'are more often than not hierarchical, even if words like "partnership", "concerted action", and "dialogue" are promoted'.[37] Moreover, non-profit organizations are increasingly encouraged to partner with for-profit ones, blurring the distinctions in practice and often making it more difficult for the public to get information because such information is defined as necessarily secret to allow competition.

At all levels of government there is a new emphasis on evidence-based decision-making as a means of ensuring both appropriate expenditures and accountability. The National Forum on Health quoted with approval a BC government document arguing that 'those who provide services and manage the health system should be able to demonstrate that services and programs have improved health beyond that which would have been achieved by doing something else with the same resources'.[38] The Forum heard from citizens that they wanted more say in how decisions are made in health care, and concludes that this can best be done by making 'information widely available in a format that educates and informs the public and provides an incentive to be more active in the administration of care'.[39] While it is clearly the case that citizens need access to information in order to participate, it should also be clear that how useful such information is in terms of participation depends on what counts as appropriate information. Another BC document specifies that health outcomes 'must be defined, measurable, subject to analysis and be able to be independently evaluated'.[40] This emphasis on quantitative measures that can be used to educate the public fits well with the dominant medical model, assuming we can determine what works and what does not for particular populations in some quite accurate way. However, it also embodies all the problems with that model and with quantitative measures themselves. Moreover, the implication in the Forum's report is that people will be better able to look after themselves when they receive such information, but there is no discussion about how this will allow them to participate more generally in policy decisions. The emphasis on educating and informing in particular ways can simply be another means of privatizing the responsibility for health rather than a means of extending collective decision-making, especially when there is no provision for participation in determining what should be counted, how it should be counted, and what should be done with what we find. As Kushner and Rachlis point out in their discussion of evidence, citizens can bring a great deal to the decision-making process, including unique information. And they can also bring 'balance and fresh perspectives'.[41] Participation must mean more than access to evidence collected in particular ways. It must be an exchange that involves genuine power and alternatives, based on the recognition that health care is about much more than technocratic decisions made by experts who have the right evidence. Much of the decision-making in health care is about values, rather than simply about better evidence, and in democracies it should be the citizens who decide which values prevail.

Decision-making is thus also related to policies and practices in research. Governments play a critical role in determining how, where, and what research is done in non-government institutions, as well as in what is done with what is found. Governments have used their funding power to expand choices. An example of this is the five Centres of Excellence for Women's Health. At the same time, however, governments have been limiting the research choices of non-profit concerns by promoting partnerships with the private sector and saleable research. Such priorities can limit choices for both researchers and institutions without significantly improving care or moving away from the medical model.

Perhaps most importantly, dramatic cutbacks in funding—handed down from the federal government to the provinces and from the provinces to regions and municipalities—have significantly reduced choices. With less money and little power, local governments have had fewer choices to make. Many turned to the for-profit sector, with encouragement from their governments. Although some of the money governments cut has now been returned, faith in the public system has been undermined by the cuts. In the process, alternatives have become increasingly framed as more privatization or less care.

While this is not an exhaustive list of the ways governments have shaped decision-making in the non-profit sector, it does indicate how governments have influenced participation and choice in these organizations. Governments have made some organizations more accountable in terms of having to give account and being held to account.[42] But budget cuts, regionalization, and requirements for different representation on boards have often served more to promote the dominant medical model and business practices than to alter decision-making in ways that allow users and providers real choice about health care. Moreover, strategies are usually presented as dichotomous choices between mutually exclusive alternatives, failing to recognize that inevitable, and often desirable, tensions need to be both acknowledged and accommodated—or more insidiously, are presented as the inevitable consequence of evidence. As John Ralston Saul has so eloquently put it, a patient-centred approach 'requires transparency, public involvement, debate. Under a corporatist technocracy the disease-based approach is preferred because it is much more controllable'.[43]

For-Profit Care

The variety of government strategies, such as delisting, contracting out, and cutbacks in services, and institutional practices, such as day surgery, outpatient services, and shorter patient stays, that are shifting responsibility for health-care provision to the for-profit sector or to for-profit practices have already been described. Regulatory changes are also enhancing the scope of for-profit concerns. What have not been considered are the consequences of this shift for participation and decision-making, as well as for equity and access.

These consequences are important to examine, in part, because these transfers have been justified not only in terms of increasing efficiency and reducing cost but also in terms of greater consumer choice and control. The greater efficiency assumed to result from the focus on reducing costs in order to increase profits is supposed to lead to more money for other health-care needs and thus to more choice. Yet, there is no evidence that for-profit services are more efficient or that they ensure money will be there for other care. Indeed, the World Bank has indicated that it is questionable whether or not the for-profit market can provide cost-effective health care.[44] What is clear is that for-profit hospitals 'distort service delivery patterns. They siphon off high revenue patients and vigorously avoid providing care to patient populations who are a financial risk.'[45] By situating hospitals in particular areas and by refusing to provide emergency rooms, they ensure they serve only particular kinds of patients.[46] In other words, one way they reduce costs is to avoid expensive patients and focus on those who can bring the biggest return on investment. This strategy is obvious in the pharmaceutical industry, where research and production stress those drugs that promise to have the highest sales and return the greatest profits.[47] Decisions based on profit rather than care mean that there are fewer alternatives available to patients and that the location of services is less subject to democratic decision-making.

Equally important in terms of democratic-decision-making, for–profit concerns are also focused on increasing demand. For-profit enterprises are not only interested in paying less for workers and other resources to reduce costs; they are also interested in selling more of what they produce to raise profits. This means more and, especially, more high-cost care because such care produces the greatest profits. So, instead of producing less health care and focusing on prevention that would reduce demand, as various government reports recommend, the privatization of care is likely to lead, as it has in the US, to more care and more expensive care. Much of this may be unnecessary or even dangerous. In any case, this emphasis on increasing demand provides some of the explanation for what is frequently described as rising consumer expectations in health care. And these rising expectations are in turn used to justify reductions in public care, even though the privatization offered as a solution is at least part of the problem.

Moreover, for-profit care is likely to lead to a greater emphasis on cuts and chemicals over carrots and condoms, because the former are much more lucrative. In Quebec, the pharmaceutical companies supported the doctors' resistance to CLSCs, promoting instead private clinics based on a curative approach.[48] Glazer's research concluded that, in the United States, the attractive investments 'led to higher national expenditures on health care'[49] and an increasing emphasis on the medical model.[50] This necessarily means a loss of control for citizens because spending more on particular kinds of health care means both patients and governments have fewer choices about alternative ways to allocate their money.

Those promoting for-profit methods claim that competition offers individuals more choices, while keeping costs as low as possible and keeping quality high as a means of attracting customers. However, competition often takes the form of advertising, as it does in the pharmaceutical industry. As various investigations into the drug industry have demonstrated, such advertising seldom provides clear, concise information that fully informs the reader. It is designed mainly to sell goods and services, not to educate and warn of risks.[51] Research in the United States indicates the same emphasis on advertising in the American for-profit hospital system.[52] Moreover, many 'consumers' in health care do not have the necessary knowledge to make informed choices among various products and services. Selecting major surgery is not like choosing a shampoo. The risks are qualitatively different and so is the information required, although people may still be swayed by false advertising claims.[53] People cannot plan on if and when to have a heart attack and are seldom in a position to choose among providers. When they do have a choice, it should be based on information provided by those without a vested interest in greater use.

Furthermore, the existence of various for-profit firms in the same field does not guarantee that there will be competition or that this competition will lead to either quality or choice. Again, this is clearly evident in the drug industry. The Commission that initiated health care in Quebec highlighted the 'abusive prices of drugs' that are 'largely due to the non-competitive nature of the market'. This in turn was largely the result, it appears, of both foreign control in the industry and 'a form of collusion in price setting'.[54] In the American health-care system, it is clear that in the long run competition among hospitals did not lead to improved quality and choice. Rather, it encouraged the development of monopolies and forced non-profit hospitals to act like for-profit ones. Corporate chains expanded across the nation, eliminating many smaller options and increasingly providing just one choice of service. Moreover, there was a move towards 'vertical integration, or the assembling, within one corporation and under one management, of all the various components of a health-care system, from doctors' offices to hospitals, to insurance operations and nursing homes'.[55]

Quality care is certainly not guaranteed by competition either. In *The Great White Lie*, Bogdanich documents the use of unqualified caregivers, unsafe drugs, and unsafe practices, as well as long and sometimes life-threatening waits for service in American for-profit hospitals.[56] Another study found nurses working as many as 80 hours a week without breaks and corners cut on necessary supplies in ways that endangered lives.[57] Patients and workers lost not only their choice in hospitals but their choice in a whole range of other services as well. More and more communities had only one hospital, one choice of clinic for those with insurance, and one kind of service based on a medical model. Furthermore, in contrast to Canadian research, US research shows a clear relationship between income and problems experienced with hospital care. In the US, the poor have more complaints about the care they receive while there is no consistent relationship between income and complaints among Canadians.[58]

Within these giant corporations, the right to decide about life and death 'is shifting away from physicians and community leaders into the hands of corporate bureaucrats and medical industry entrepreneurs—most of whom have never seen the inside of a medical school.'[59] Increasingly, there are formulas for care based on a combination of cost concerns and the dominant medical model. And there are formulas for care that eliminate hospitals and jobs, while transforming much of what remains into part-time, insecure work.[60] And the power of these entrepreneurs does not stop here. As a result of their growing economic strength, these entrepreneurs also have a significant say in the larger policy issues related to the overall structure of health care and the distribution of societal resources at the same time as they limit public access to information on their operations, claiming their ownership of this same information.[61]

Giant American corporations are well placed to move into the Canadian system. They have the capital and the experience to quickly undermine any competition from smaller Canadian for-profit or not-for-profit operations. According to American consumer advocate Ralph Nader, these corporations are anxious 'to subvert if not destroy both the compulsory pricing system for drugs and elements of the universal health insurance system'.[62]

Governments are encouraging the move of American companies into the health-care field in at least three ways. First, by abandoning some services and by sending people to non-hospital institutions or home for care, they are opening the door to private provision. Moreover, by reducing access to public care and by reducing the quality of that care, governments are increasing the demand for alternative care offered on a pay basis. There becomes less and less point to defending public care. Second, under the North American Free Trade Agreement,[63] once these services are open for profit they cannot easily be assumed again under government services, and American companies are welcome to fill the gap. Third, by deregulating some areas and offering additional protection for drug companies, governments are actively promoting private investment in the health-care field. In opening the door to foreign investment in Canadian health care, governments are significantly reducing Canadians' right to decide. More and more decisions about what care to provide and how to provide it will be made on the basis of profit and American concerns.

For-profit health services, then, hold little promise for increased democratic choices, more patient control, or better-quality care. The tendency towards concentration and centralization of for-profit firms, the concern with the bottom line, and the efforts to increase demand for the most expensive products rather than to reform care or promote prevention all contribute to a shift in decision-making towards corporate élites, many of whom live outside Canada and most of whom see profits in cures, not health promotion. The growth of for-profit services, combined with cutbacks in government funding, have pushed more non-profit services in similar directions.[64] However, non-profit companies are still not driven by the same search for profit and all of their resources can be devoted to providing care. Moreover, non-profit organizations have more opportunity to remain small and thus to provide alternative choices and to innovate in ways that promote a care model. And governments have more ways to exercise democratic control over the non-profit companies that are primarily Canadian. But governments have been moving in ways that increase the space for private companies and that increase the government money going to them; at the same time they are reducing the space and the funds for non-profit care and regulating it more vigorously.

WORKER CONTROL

DOCTORS

Public funding for health care initially served to give enormous power to doctors. After they graduated from an expensive education program largely paid for by taxpayers, doctors had guaranteed jobs and guaranteed incomes. For the most part, they determined their own hours of work, their location, and their patient load. Governments paid doctors for almost everything the doctors said was necessary care and allowed doctors to determine who entered and left institutions and what was done to patients by whom when they were there. Governments also protected doctors from competition, granting them monopolies over a wide range of practices and allowing them to govern themselves. Doctors advised governments on policy and often were central to decision-making in the health-care field. Their medical model prevailed throughout the health-care system.

Although doctors remain very powerful within the system, there were signs of encroachment on their dominance from the earliest days of medicare. Some of this pressure came from governments responding to concerns about costs, quality, and democratic control. The Quebec Commission that established medicare in that province was the first to formally and consistently challenge doctors' power, setting out options that have been gradually taken up in other jurisdictions. In promoting group practice and redefining monopoly powers by delegating some acts to other providers, by stressing prevention by a team that included a wide range of practitioners, and by emphasizing general practice, the Commission was clearly suggesting limitations on both doctors' power and the centrality of the medical model.[65] In the CLSCs, boards were to have a say over how doctors practised and were paid. The Commission also recommended doctors be salaried. Arguing that 'the law governing professions was more an expression of the professional groups' strength than a transcription of social and political needs into law',[66] the Commission set out recommendations designed to circumscribe their power. No longer would doctors be able to claim that they could defend both their own interests and those of the public through their governing body. These governing bodies would now include representatives of the community and of the government. At the same time, doctors would become subject to a new Code of the Professions that set uniform standards, and the government would have a direct say in academic standards and admissions.[67] Quebec was also the first jurisdiction to take concrete steps to ensure that doctors serviced the entire province, thus limiting their right to decide on their location.

Not surprisingly, doctors individually, and collectively through their professional organizations, resisted these recommendations and not all of them were implemented. But in the intervening years, governments in all jurisdictions have been gradually moving in these directions.[68] The provincial and territorial ministers of health agreed to limit enrolments in medical schools, although there is now a move to increase the numbers. Various provinces have required the inclusion of citizen representatives on governing bodies and required a more open decision-making process. Professional codes have been redesigned both to limit doctors' powers and to allow more delegation to other practitioners of what were exclusively physician practices. Midwives and nurse practitioners are being licensed to practise in areas formerly reserved for doctors. Restrictions have been placed on fees, and services have been delisted. Some primary-care models promote salaries for doctors and promote teamwork as well as disease prevention. In addition, governments have worked with some teaching hospitals to allow them to employ particular doctors on a salaried basis. There is also more surveillance of billing and prescription practices, a process made easier by electronic technology. Health planners, economists, and others concerned primarily with management rather than medicine are increasingly replacing doctors in policy-making circles. All these developments restrict doctors' choices. Nevertheless, both the structures that favour the dominant medical model and the ideology that supports doctors' claims, along with organized resistance from doctors, have limited the impact on doctors' power.[69] Meanwhile, what is increasingly defined as a doctor shortage is strengthening their position after several years of decline, and this strength is reflected in the fee raises happening across the country.

Government has not been the only source of restrictions on doctors' right to decide on health-care issues. Various groups have been encroaching on doctors' power, often with the support of governments. Hospital administrators, professional organizations and unions, women's groups and other patients' rights organizations have all demanded participation in ways that limit doctors' position as the sole decision-makers in health. The efforts of other health-care providers and of patients' groups will be discussed in subsequent sections but the case of administrators is more appropriately included here.

Government cutbacks have encouraged an emphasis on money and business practice. As a result of both this growing pressure and increasing hospital size, administrators without medical training have been replacing doctors as the chief executive officers. These administrators have developed new managerial practices that limit doctors' choices to some extent. Although day surgery, shorter patient stays, and outpatient services have all been introduced with the collaboration of doctors, these strategies serve to reduce the alternatives open to doctors who previously were the only judges of how long patients stayed. Managerial practices designed to eliminate other health-care workers, reduce the costs of supplies, and turn some services into profit-making enterprises also have an impact on what doctors can do, even if they, too, have been introduced after consultation with the doctors and indeed have been promoted by some in medicine. While doctors still make major decisions about admission and release, increasingly they must justify their orders in relation to formulas for care.

Similarly, governments have been supporting research by organizations such as the Institute for Clinical Evaluative Sciences (ICES), which provides data on practice patterns across Ontario, and the Manitoba Centre for Health Policy and Evaluation, which assesses performance in a wide range of areas directly related to physician practices.[70] Such studies are increasingly being promoted as a means of establishing guidelines for doctors. In the hands of administrators, these guidelines could serve to become formulas for doctors' practices. This has already happened in the United States, where utilization management has had a negative impact on relationships between physicians and the companies that use the formulas to prescribe practice.[71] In recommending utilization management for Canada, *When Less Is Better* describes it as 'the deliberate action by payers or hospital administrators to influence providers of hospital services to increase efficiency and effectiveness with which services are provided'.[72] While guidelines can provide useful references and an important check on doctors' practices, it is important to remember that they are based on past medical practices and privilege certain kinds of information. Thus, they may chiefly serve to perpetuate inappropriate care, albeit in a more uniform and limited fashion that depends on administrators' as well as doctors' decisions. Or they may become the basis for denying care, as they have in the United States.

Partly in response to the growing restrictions on their considerable powers, more than one doctor has threatened to leave for the United States.[73] But they are unlikely to find better conditions there. Indeed, many have returned from the US in recent years.[74] Unlike Canada, the US guarantees neither employment nor income to doctors. As a result, some doctors have much lower income, some are unemployed, and more doctors have fewer choices about employment. Moreover, many more doctors in the US are on salary than is the case in Canada and they are tied to clinics that structure their decision-making much more than in Canada. Furthermore, 'many decisions are made by insurance companies, with varying input by physicians and patients.'[75] And this tends to be the case wherever doctors practise south of the border.

Although doctors remain the most powerful actors in the health-care field, their power is increasingly being circumscribed. Some loss of doctors' power has meant gains for patients and other workers. And some of this loss has helped shift the emphasis to health promotion from intervention. But in many ways, planners and administrators not trained in medicine have gained power at the expense of doctors. Yet these non-medically trained people usually still operate on the basis of the dominant medical model, and too often they emphasize its most problematic aspects as they apply formulas for cost savings and quality improvement to care. While we obviously need some limits on doctors' right to decide—both to shift the emphasis away from this model and to promote the rights of others in making choices about their health—we also want to ensure that doctors retain enough autonomy to base their decisions on their knowledge and assessment of needs. Some of the new initiatives limit their decision-making power without improving care.

OTHER PROVIDERS

In the years since hospital and medical insurance were introduced, other workers in the health-care sector have joined together to make gains in terms of choices. The overwhelming majority of these other workers are women. Largely because of their gender, it was assumed both that they worked for love and that they should be subordinate, especially to doctors. There were similar attitudes about people of colour and immigrants. Their pay, and power, reflected both these assumptions; conditions in health care helped ensure that this was the case. But women, and minority groups, did not passively accept these restrictions.

The growth in demand for women's labour that accompanied the expansion in health-care services helped women resist these assumptions. Responding to this demand and to their need for income,[76] women entered the labour force in large numbers. Many became part of the emerging women's movement and even more organized in the workplace.[77] Some had begun by imitating the men in forming professional organizations. Although they won some exclusive rights to practise in particular areas, they never achieved the kind of control granted to physicians.[78] The overwhelming majority eventually became members of unions. By 1986, 72 per cent of the women employed in public services year-round were unionized[79] and rates were higher within parts of the health-care sector. Health-care workers have used these organizations to fight for improved conditions of work and more say in the decisions that affect their lives.

Wages, pensions, vacations, shifts, and hours of work have all improved significantly as a result of workers' efforts. Health and safety committees had worker representation and gave workers choices about acceptable working conditions. In a number of jurisdictions, health-care workers have also won the right to strike as a means of backing their demands and all unionized workers had the right to grieve against practices that contravened their collective agreements. In Quebec, health-care workers won a form of employment security that gave them rights to other jobs when their own disappeared. Indeed, the very existence of unions often helps protect jobs. When we asked a Quebec health-care worker if the union would act on her behalf, she replied 'absolutely. I saw it acting on behalf of this woman whose job might have been taken away.' With decent wages and conditions of work, all those employed in the system have more choices about their work.

Equally important, health-care providers have gained significantly in terms of control over their jobs. They now have much more say in who does what to them, what work they do, and when and where they work. Job classifications defined what work was to be done and what workers could be asked to do. Seniority rules regulated promotions and other kinds of selections, helping to ensure that the personal preferences of managers did not always prevail. Although registered nurses who were more often accepted as care providers were the most likely to be included, the majority of health-care workers won the right to be consulted on a whole range of issues and to have access to information on decisions that affected their work and the provision of care. More recently, unions have sought to educate both their members and their managers about racism, homophobia, and sexual harassment. And they have sought to develop ways of addressing grievances related to these issues.

Most of these gains were for all health-care workers, regardless of sex, race, or culture. But some were mainly or exclusively victories for women. Women successfully fought for the right to stay in the job after marriage and pregnancy. They also won the right to say no to a range of orders from others in the health system and to sexual harassment. More recently, the successful fight in most jurisdictions for pay equity legislation not only helped guarantee women decent wages but also served to change the more general undervaluing of women's work and old classification schemes based on such assumptions.[80] Similarly, employment equity legislation has helped improve representation from all groups of care providers.

These gains for workers necessarily restricted the choices for institutions and for doctors, although they sometimes increased choices for patients by allowing other providers some say in care and by improving the state of the facility. As one Quebec health-care worker we interviewed explained, 'Hospital workers are fighting for their working conditions and also for the conditions of the people who use the hospital.' Moreover, the recognition of the contribution made by these other providers, as well as certain guarantees for their work, also helped dilute the medical model. With regulated hours of work and breaks, nurses were in better condition to respond to the needs of patients in ways that went beyond intervention. With guaranteed jobs and agreed-upon job descriptions, housekeeping staff were better able to ensure that the institutions were clean in ways that reduced risks and promoted health.

These gains, however, were one of the reasons that governments and administrators sought alternative ways to assert their control. New ways of organizing work, such as total quality management, were introduced in the name of releasing 'the untapped imagination and potential of the health care workforce'.[81] They are said to be designed to cut costs while increasing quality by involving workers in decisions and by encouraging them to work in teams. But too often they undermine traditional teamwork and are used as a means of speeding up work, increasing surveillance, and eliminating care. They are also frequently a way of going around unions and establishing alternative structures that reduce union input. The promised sharing of decision-making, tapping of workers' knowledge, and promoting of teamwork could improve care, but they are unlikely to do so when they are based, as has been the case, on a medical model and a desire to increase control from the top.

Directly related to the new work organizations are the new generic workers, the new job classifications, and the new regulations for professions. Several jurisdictions are reassessing the powers of a whole range of professions with a view to standardizing the regulations that apply to them, opening their practices to more public scrutiny, and limiting their monopoly over particular practices. Old monopolies did help to ensure that the person providing care had been trained for the job. Nevertheless, as is the case with doctors, these reassessments can increase democratic control and can help encourage a move away from a strictly medical model, allowing other providers to enter areas previously forbidden to them. Similarly, various institutions are pressuring unions to reduce significantly the number of job classifications and to broaden job descriptions. Here, too, the changes may serve to eliminate old rigidities that limited flexibility and reduced the range of tasks a particular worker is permitted to do. Broader definitions could mean more choices for health-care workers and greater variety in their work, as well as provide more time for more integrated care.

But this kind of deregulation in both professions and job classifications also opens the door to fewer choices for some workers and to the introduction of generic workers to replace others. One Ontario health-care aide reported that the 'employers are making us into glorified labourers. We're making beds and washing toilets. We used to care for people. Now we're janitors.'[82] A respiratory therapist, like the health care aide interviewed for Laura Sky's study of generic workers, explained that 'The more we give up, the more nervous we become. We're giving up high-volume, low-skill tasks to generic workers. We'll be left with the high skills but the low-volume tasks. Then there will be fewer and fewer of us.'[83]

As a result, more work is done by those without special training. The formal requirements for the job of Patient Care Partner, one title used for generic workers, are grade 12 and 'experience working in a health care environment'.[84] Such workers have few specifically taught skills and few limits on what they are required to do. With fewer regulations, these generic workers can now be asked to perform a range of tasks formerly the exclusive terrain of people in specific professions and job classifications. As a result, the employer can allocate them quickly from one task to another in ways that not only intensify their labour but also reduce their choices about the work and limit their protection from arbitrary orders. Moreover, the increased flexibility can make it easier for work assignment based on tasks defined in terms of a medical model rather than a care model. This, too, means fewer choices for providers and patients.

Health-care workers' choices are being further threatened by state cutbacks and by privatization. Focused on spending cuts, governments are abandoning promises under pay equity legislation, cutting back on the enforcement of health and safety and other regulations, and questioning employment equity legislation. Given that health care is labour-intensive work and that the majority of the money still goes to care, the severe cutbacks set out in the 1995 federal budget necessarily meant fewer jobs. Many provinces significantly reduced employment through regionalization and cuts in global budgets; others reduced wages. Recent increases do not make up for these losses.

In the case of British Columbia, a Health Accord signed by the provincial government, the key unions, and the employer associations promised employment security and set up an agency to supervise the adjustment of workers to the new health-care structures. Relocation, training for new kinds of health-care work, and early retirements planned to fit with employment needs all were part of the package worked out by a panel composed of labour and employer representatives. With employment security and a real say in how decisions about adjustments are made, health-care workers were more prepared to participate in a restructuring of the system that is intended to do more than provide less of the same.[85] However, in most jurisdictions, plans for change are done in secret by groups that seldom include labour as equal partners, and BC, too, has now abandoned the promise of job security and retraining. Under such conditions, workers live in fear for their jobs and have little to gain from encouraging change.

When the cutbacks are accompanied by privatization of services, health-care workers have even less to gain. Workers in the for-profit sector of health care are less likely to be unionized or to have other kinds of protections found in unionized workplaces. This is especially the case when the care is provided in private homes. Much of home care work is done for minimum wages by immigrant women and visible minority women who are paid only for the actual time spent doing a task. While working in a private home may reduce the possibilities for surveillance by the employer, strict time limits placed on carefully defined tasks allow workers little leeway. Meanwhile, home care workers have less control over the environment in which they work than is the case in an institutional setting, given that they are working in someone else's place and have no colleagues to provide support. At the same time, formulas for care make it difficult for them to exercise judgement and respond to unanticipated problems.[86] Moreover, patients have fewer guarantees about the skills of their providers as more of the standards are left to the employers.

Both privatization and cutbacks have stimulated a democratic response. They have encouraged unions to work together and with other groups to influence the changes that are underway. Health care has been characterized by an enormous number of unions and professional organizations, each of which has sought individually to protect its rights. Faced with staggering losses, many of them have come together to respond to government initiatives. They have also formed alliances with organizations such as those that represent seniors and the mentally handicapped in order to protect health care. Such co-operation is not always easy, given old antagonisms and sometimes conflicting interests. But this co-operation does foster new solutions and new compromises in an effort to ensure that high-quality care remains accessible and comprehensive.

In sum, a wide range of health-care workers have used their collective strength to improve significantly their right to decide and to control their conditions of work. While some of their gains were also gains for a caring approach to health, some of their strategies resulted in rigidities that reinforced the medical model and limited the possibilities for innovation along other lines. Responses from institutions and from governments have been carried out in the name of greater participation. Some of these responses have indeed allowed for more democratic control. However, many of them are restricting or even eliminating workers' right to decide while reinforcing a task-oriented approach to care. Instead, they need to balance the workers' need for protection and choice with the system's need for flexibility and innovation.

PATIENTS' RIGHTS

Like the majority of health-care providers, patients had few rights before the advent of publicly funded health care. The most important right they gained with medicare was the right to accessible, universal, comprehensive care under non-profit administration. But the struggle for good care did not end there. Since medicare was introduced, patients have been fighting individually and collectively to increase their say in how the medical model is used and to change that model.

Among the most vocal and visible of the groups fighting for patient rights have been women's groups. This is not surprising, given that, as Sherwin clearly demonstrates in *No Longer Patient*, 'the institution of medicine has been designed in ways that reinforce sexism, and the effects of medical practice are often bad for women'.[87] Much of their early protest centred on issues related to fertility and birth. A Montreal group that later became the Women's Health Press began in the late 1960s to challenge the legal restrictions on the distribution of information on birth control by publishing a booklet offering advice on contraceptives. Along with other groups, they were successful in changing the laws that prevented not only the sharing of information but also the distribution of contraceptive devices. Similarly, the abortion caravan that began in Vancouver and ended in Ottawa in the spring of 1970 was one of the strategies that eventually gave women the right to an abortion without first having to gain a doctor's approval or without proving that a life was at risk.

Women also objected to the medical management of birth that involved increasingly complicated interventions by the doctor in charge. One intervention led to another, as pain relief procedures had to be countered by other drugs that induced more pain and inhibited women's responses in ways that limited their capacity to push during childbirth. And this often led to a forceps delivery.[88] Treatments to induce labour, shaves, enemas, the strapping of women to delivery tables in rooms where admittance was restricted to medical personnel, anaesthetics, and episiotomies were frequently done for the convenience of the medical practitioners rather than for the health of the patient. Some of these practices had no benefit for the patient and some were harmful.[89] All these procedures could be understood more as a means of ensuring doctors were in charge than as a reflection of scientific evidence. Interviewed by Hunsburger for her study of pregnancy and childbirth, one woman explained that when she refused an episiotomy, the doctor asked, 'Who's delivering that baby?' In responding 'I am',[90] the woman was expressing the views of a growing number of women who demanded some control and choice over the birth process.

As a result of various strategies women won the right to decide about a whole range of issues related to pregnancy and birth. Increasingly, women can choose what kind of birth they want to have and who can share in the birth experience. More and more women can decide to have their baby in a birthing room or at home, to have a midwife 'catch' the baby rather than a doctor 'deliver' it, and whether or not to have drugs.

Women did not restrict their challenges to 'female complaints'. Like many other groups, they criticized the excessive use of drugs and the overall emphasis on the medical model. They demanded greater access to information and more education about procedures. They objected to the authoritarian relationships between patient and doctor and established a range of self-help groups that offered a direct challenge to doctors' authority and power. They did research to expose the inadequacy of both the medical model and medical practice.

As Blishen explains in his study of the medical profession, growing suspicion of any authority, combined with increasing educational levels, contributed to these demands.[91] A host of patient groups emerged alongside the women's groups. Their growth reflected not only these developments but also the diffusion of evidence that countered doctors' claims and questioned the value of the medical model. The Internet gave many wide access to alternative sources. Self-help groups proliferated. Some, such as those supporting cancer patients, defined themselves as complementary to the system. Others, such as Alcoholics Anonymous, saw themselves as outside the system, avoiding either critiques or compliment. Still others, however, such those formed to aid 'survivors' of treatments for the mentally ill, were highly critical of medical care. So were those who were concerned about the racism in the system, or at least about the failure of the system to take cultural differences into account.

Together, these efforts led to new regulations and new rights. Patients now have the right to informed choice. They must be told, in a language they understand, about the options available and the risks involved. Patients also have the right to see their own files. They can refuse or request some kinds of treatment, either directly or through means such as a card that says they are willing to donate organs or unwilling to accept blood transfusions. Some provinces have gone even further. The Ontario government's Advocacy Act, for example, is intended 'to contribute to the empowerment of vulnerable persons and to promote respect for their rights, freedoms, autonomy and dignity'.[92] Under this Act, well people can appoint an advocate who can represent them if decisions are required but the patient is no longer capable of making that decision. Ontario also has a project that allows people with disabilities living outside institutions not only to select but also to train their care providers. In addition, patients are increasingly being consulted on health-care reform and institutional structures. Some have even been included on decision-making bodies.

However, at the same time as legislated individual rights have been expanded, collective rights are diminishing, as are actual individual rights. Cutbacks in public care usually mean people have fewer choices in terms of access and quality, especially if the cutbacks result chiefly in less of the same. Shorter patient stays, day surgery, and outpatient services that follow a formula for care necessarily restrict the choices of those who do not fit the formula. The experience of one person who phoned the Ontario Council of Hospital Union's Hotline graphically illustrates the lack of choice:

> I had the unfortunate circumstance of going to hospital. The emergency department is under-staffed terribly. I was sent home from emergency twice in the week prior to finally being admitted. Even though I kept telling them about the terrible cough I had, they never checked my chest, just treated me for the excruciating headache. As it turned out, I had viral pneumonia and had to spend almost a week in hospital.
>
> I wanted help, I felt so sick. After they sent me home the second time from emergency, I was up all the next night coughing and choking. I was so weak by the next day I couldn't even get off the couch and it was getting to the point where I was starting to hallucinate. My mom was calling every half hour to see how I was. When my husband got home at 4:30, he took one look at me, saw I was gasping for breath, and said, 'That's it. You're going back to emergency.'
>
> I got to emergency where they measured the oxygen levels and that's when I heard the nurse say 'My God, get the doctor right away!' My oxygen level had dropped to 40 per cent. Finally, things started to happen. I had a whole raft of doctors and people looking after me. But, even though I was supposed to be admitted, there were no beds available. So they put me in a room the nurses call 'the pit' and I had to stay there for two days because they wouldn't open any beds upstairs.
>
> The pit was a horrible experience. They were treating patients right beside me who were coming in off the street. There was no privacy, no peace. It was a very alarming place to be sick in. People are in and out all night. You can't sleep. There's only one bathroom and it's there for everyone in emergency so you have to wait because it's always occupied. When emergency gets busy they pull the nurses out to the front so there's no help. You put the buzzer on and no one comes and that's pretty scary because my blood oxygen level was low enough to go into cardiac arrest. On one night, that room went for more than two hours without a nurse! But it's not the nurses' fault. These girls ran their asses off and you didn't hear them complain. But they're not machines and they can't be in two or three places at one time giving their 100 per cent. The condition of the place was terrible. The lack of care, the noise, commotion, no sleep, it was horrible. If you're at all sick—and people in emergency are really sick—you shouldn't be in that place. But that's what's happening.
>
> Anyway, I was there on a little stretcher for 48 hours. I had so much pain in my shoulder and back from that stretcher that it took me a month to heal. . . .

After two days, I was moved up to the respiratory floor where I stayed for four days. You could see the cutbacks up there as well. One night my IV backed up and it took over 10 minutes for a nurse to get there. If you wanted something basic like water you had to get it yourself. They brought a glass in the morning and a glass at supper. If you wanted more, it was down the hall in the next wing. I had to take my oxygen mask off and go down to get it. And there was real pressure for beds. I had to stay on discharge day because they had to do more testing. But they couldn't wait to get me out and acted like I was already discharged. They disconnected my phone, threw my clothes on a pile on the chair. They moved in a dozen bouquets for the next person at noon and I wasn't supposed to be leaving until 4 p.m.[93]

Like those in day surgery, women are increasingly being sent home immediately after birth, even if they have little support and a great deal of pressure there. While this may be the preference of healthy, middle-class women who have had easy births and who can afford support at home, it may not be the choice of a woman who has a crowded home and no useful support.

The more general transfer of people out of institutions into the home also reduces choices. Not everyone has a safe and healthy environment at home. Especially for the elderly, homes are too often risky places to be. 'A national survey of seniors living outside of institutions concluded that at least 4 per cent were being mistreated. . . . Other studies estimate the rate of abuse from 3.2 to 10 per cent.'[94] Many who have safe homes have no desire to be dependent on their close relatives for care. Furthermore, as we have seen, the transfer of work to the home reduces the choices of the women who must provide care. A study conducted by the VON in Ontario found that two-thirds of the caregivers provide up to half of all care required by those they look after; almost half this care is medical, as narrowly defined in the medical model. These caregivers get little help or choice. 'While almost all care givers believe that other care givers would benefit from some help, assistance, relief or training, a third indicated that they themselves could benefit from respite care.'[95] The switch to the home is mainly justified in terms of patient preference, but most are home whether they want to be there or not. In Ontario, the average age of admission to homes for the aged is now the mid-eighties. Most of those under this age must stay in someone's home, whatever their preference.

Although the new rules require that patients be allowed informed choice, the information offered is almost always framed in terms of the medical model and the actual options are almost always limited. Moreover, the information can be structured in ways that encourage the medical choice, as it is in drug advertising. Furthermore, consultation too often simply means that patients are allowed to express their views and have little if any impact on policy and practices. They may not be much more effective in changing decision-making than a suggestion box. Similarly, surveys of patients that structure questions in ways that encourage approval and discourage anything but yes-no answers or a ranking of services do little to alter decision-making. And patients' advocates may end up providing much more care than they ever planned. At a public meeting held in Ontario in 1995, a long-time seniors' spokesperson reported that the elderly are increasingly being refused transportation by police to health facilities on the grounds that this is the job of advocates.[96]

There are two lessons to be learned from these developments. First, while patients have made some important gains in terms of choices, many of these gains were not very effective in practice or have been undermined by cutback strategies. Second, as is the case with doctors and other health-care professionals, there is a tension between the rights of patients and those of others. When patients have the right to restrict information on their medications, their unpaid caregivers may suffer. For example, schizophrenics may not be taking their medications. However, the mothers who care for them may not know when the medication is to be taken and thus may not be able to ensure the appropriate treatment is followed. As a result, the mothers may be at physical risk from those for whom they are providing care. When patients have the right to hire and train their providers, the caregiver may have few rights of the sort guaranteed in other kinds of employment. And when patients have the right to choose treatments, they may find the choices more stressful than helpful, given their frequent lack of knowledge about health and medical care.

Here, as elsewhere, it must be recognized that health care is not a service like the rest and that the tensions between patients and others must be acknowledged and accommodated, not eliminated by making a choice for one over the other.

CONCLUSION

In many ways, medicare has meant that all Canadians can decide about health care, because as citizens they have a say in the public system and as patients they both choose their doctor(s) and accept or refuse services. In other ways, doctors still make most of the decisions, even if other health-care workers and patients have won some rights in the period since medicare was introduced.

However, governments at all levels have been fundamentally altering the opportunities to decide. The agreements on free trade, combined with severe cutbacks done in the name of fighting the deficit, have significantly reduced people's choices, and the recent infusion of money has not made up for the loss. Administrators and economists are increasingly making the decisions, and they are making their decisions by applying business practices to a medical model of care. The result is frequently less power for doctors, other health-care workers, and patients. Some government efforts to restrict the powers of practitioners do serve to make the system more flexible and responsive to patients. But many more simply alter who decides without recognizing and accommodating the kinds of tensions between skills and rights that are central to good care. Moreover, many of these decisions are altering health-care provision in ways that leave people little reason to support a public system and little alternative other than to seek for-profit, individually purchased care.

RECOMMENDED READINGS

Pat Armstrong et al. (collaborators), *Exposing Privatization: Women and Health Care Reform in Canada*. Aurora, Ont.: Garamond, 2001. This anthology provides a coast to coast assessment of both what is happening in health-care reform and what we know about the consequences for the women who make up the majority of providers and patients. The frame for the analysis is a broad definition of privatization, understood to encompass the shift in costs and care, as well as the shift to for-profit providers and techniques.

John Dorland and S. Mathwin Davis, eds, *How Many Roads . . . ? Regionalization and Decentralization in Health Care*. Kingston: Queen's University, 1996. Regionalization and decentralization are common features in Canadian health-care reform, strategies undertaken in the name of greater local control. This collection is one of the few examinations of what these strategies mean for public care and democratic accountability.

Daniel Drache and Terry Sullivan, eds, *Health Reform: Public Success, Private Failure*. London: Routledge, 1999. This collection covers a broad spectrum of issues related to the marketization of health care in Canada. Trade agreements, downsizing, decentralization, cost containment, and the transformation of health care into a business are all explored in theoretical and empirical detail.

CHAPTER
7

Who Wins and Who Loses

On the one hand, the argument presented in this book is quite simple. In the name of prevention, health promotion, evidence-based decision-making, and the determinants of health, governments reformed health care in ways that frequently reinforce the dominant medical model and transfer more responsibility for care to individuals and to the private, for-profit sector. Meanwhile, opportunities to remain healthy and to receive useful care are declining. In other words, governments' practices contradict their own research and rationale. Reforms too often mean less of the same provided collectively through state funding and more of the same provided by the private, for-profit sector or following their practices, while individuals take more responsibility for care provision and care payment.

On the other hand, the argument is quite complex. It is complex because it is necessary to understand this medical model, the determinants of health, the political economy, the nature of for-profit services, and the tensions integral to health care in order to understand the problems with the reforms made in the name of improving health care and expanding choices.

Health is much more than an absence of illness. Health is understood to mean the well-being of the whole person that comes from secure employment and decent incomes, from safe physical and social environments, and from social and psychological support—in other words, from food, clothing, shelter, jobs, and joy. Health, then, is fundamentally related to the distribution of power and resources as well as to social relations; in short, it is related to the political economy.

Health also comes from the care provided for those who become ill or disabled. While care is related to a special set of health concerns, it is not separable from the determinants of health. Indeed, security, safety, nutrition, and cleanliness, as well as social and psychological support, are even more important to those who are ill or disabled. Moreover, the working conditions and employment security of those who provide care are critical to health, given that poor work environments for providers necessarily mean poor environments for care.

Instead of building a health-care system around these determinants of health, however, we have built a system based on a particular medical model of care. In this model, people are understood as a series of parts suffering from discrete biological problems that can be fixed by a doctor on the basis of scientifically established procedures. Unquestionably, this approach has saved some lives and improved others. Unquestionably, we still need expert knowledge and we still need to base much of that knowledge on evidence that follows the rigours of scientific inquiry and investigates biological causes. And we still need cuts and chemicals to deal with a whole range of ills.

But our research on the determinants of health tells us that the medical model has severe limits, primarily because it does not address the determinants of health. We need to reform the provision of care in ways that integrate our knowledge about what determines health with our medical knowledge and practice. However, most reforms see the determinants of health as what happens outside health care and these determinants are used as an justification for reducing the funding for care. Prevention is promoted over cure; carrots and condoms over cuts and chemicals.

At the same time, health-care institutions are being reformed mainly by applying practices taken from the for-profit, goods-production sector to medical care. This can work only if it is assumed that body parts are like car parts and if it is assumed that the determinants of health do not apply either to health care or to those providing the care. As a consequence, the care that remains is based even more completely on this medical model. Parts are processed as quickly as possible with as little labour time as possible. Care disappears, in part because it is less visible and not as easy to measure, in part because it is mainly done by women, and in part because it is assumed out of the model. Meanwhile, work for providers becomes more intensive, less satisfying, and less secure. Similarly, evidence-based decision-making rests on the assumption that it is possible to determine what is the right thing to be done at the right time by the right person. This assumption, too, requires a particular view of both people and care that does not fit easily with the care models suggested here.

The context for these changes has been shaped by trade agreements that reflect and reinforce (and even impose) an emphasis on efficiency and effectiveness defined in for-profit terms and delivered by for-profit concerns, often paid for individually. The application of market principles means that an increasing amount of necessary care is no longer provided by the state-funded, not-for-profit sector. Released from health-care facilities quicker and sicker, Canadians must rely more and more either on the unpaid care of relatives and friends, most of whom are women, or, increasingly, on care provided by the for-profit sector and usually with fees attached.

The result is growing inequality, fewer choices, and less-skilled care. These developments may also mean greater costs in the long run, in terms of both health and the direct expenses involved in treating those suffering from being processed too quickly and inappropriately through the system.

Furthermore, for-profit provision has not only proved to be less effective and efficient at delivering quality care; it has also been focused on increasing sales and expanding markets. It could thus lead, as it has in the United States, to more expenditures on health-care services rather than fewer.

The move towards privatization and downsizing necessarily decreases the choices of all Canadians. Less and less care is available on the basis of citizenship; less is open to public scrutiny and choice. Instead of democratic rights and choices, we have accountability. And accountability is defined increasingly in market terms as consumer choice based on numerical evaluation of care. More and more care is based on ability to pay and advertised cures. Moreover, the foreign and conglomerate ownership of private, for-profit providers means fewer decisions are made in Canada for Canadians.

Much of the reform has been set out as a choice between alternatives. Health prevention and the determinants of health should take precedence over health care; institutions are seen as bad while communities are good; centralization is defined as undemocratic and decentralization as providing community control; doctors' authoritarian powers or other workers' rigidities are pitted against patients' rights; a medical primary-care model based on rostering and capitation is contrasted only with solo, limited practices. In each case, the dichotomies are presented as alternatives, one of which needs to be either eliminated or given precedence over the other. In each case, the alternative is described as a means of improving the quality of care while reducing costs and increasing choices. Yet health care in a democratic society will always involve tensions between such dichotomies and, as we know from the determinants of health, would suffer from the elimination of either side in each dichotomy. And it will always involve values, not simply evidence-based technocratic decisions.

We do not provide a blueprint for an alternative solution. Indeed, we do not think there is, or should be, a single solution offered by experts. Instead, we suggest that reform must begin by applying the determinants of health to the provision of services in ways that move towards care models rather than the dominant medical model. This can only be done in a public system that recognizes that care parts are different from car parts and that health is a democratic right of all citizens.

Of course, we are not alone in calling for reforms based on a different model of care. The kinds of people who struggled for a public health-care system in Canada as well as for patient and provider rights are still actively defending the public right to care while critically evaluating the care based on this medical model. They do not always agree on specific strategies, but they are together in defending Canada's best-loved social program. They recognize that we all face the risk of illness and disability and that we have a collective responsibility to share that risk.

Web Sources

Canadian Centre for Policy Alternatives (CCPA): <www.policyalternatives.ca>. Designed as a place to develop critical research and policy analysis, the CCPA often explores health issues in ways that contest the dominant perspectives on care.

Canadian Health Coalition (CHC): <www.healthcoalition.ca>. Bringing together community groups, seniors, and unions, the CHC focuses on protecting and improving public health care and thus produces a wide variety of documents on health care.

Canadian Institute for Health Information (CIHI): <www.cihi.ca>. This organization is now the main source of government data on health care.

Canadian Policy Research Networks (CPRN): <www.cprn.org>. This research organization regularly produces discussion papers on issues related to health and care.

Canadian Women's Health Network (CWHN): <www.cwhn.ca>. The CWHN is a source of a broad range of research on women's health and on health care from a gender perspective. The site links into the four Centres of Excellence for Women's Health and to the Co-ordinating Group on Health Care Reform and Women.

Commission on the Future of Health Care in Canada (Romanow Commission): <www.healthcarecommission.ca/policy.htm>. Appointed by the Prime Minister, the Commission is currently collecting research on health care and is expected to issue a report in late 2002. The Web site offers information on how to access critical centres of research on health care in Canada.

Notes

CHAPTER 1

1. National Forum on Health, *Canada Health Action: Building on the Legacy*, vol. 2, *Synthesis Reports and Issues Papers*, 'Values Working Group Synthesis Report' (Ottawa, 1997), 5.

2. Working Group on Health Services Utilization, 'When Less Is Better: Using Canada's Hospitals Efficiently', paper for the Conference of Federal/Provincial/Territorial Deputy Ministers of Health, June 1994.

3. National Forum on Health, *Canada Health Action*, vol. 2, 5.

4. See, for example, the series on health care produced by the Ontario Premier's Council on Health Strategy in 1991 or the British Columbia Royal Commission on Health Care and Costs, *Closer to Home: A Summary Report* (Victoria, 1991).

5. See, for example, Pat Armstrong et al., *'Heal Thyself': Managing Health Care Reform* (Toronto: Garamond Press, 2000), esp. ch. 4; Robert J. Blendon et al., 'Physicians' Views on Quality of Care: A Five-Country Comparison', *Health Affairs* (May–June 2001): 233–43; Linda H. Aiken et al., 'Nurses' Report on Hospital Care in Five Countries', *Health Affairs* (May–June 2001): 43–53.

6. See, for example, *Toronto Star*, 7 July 2001, K6. In Ontario, restructuring cost one hospital $16.8 million 'without adding a bandage to care. Standardizing differing wage rates blew another $24 million.' And the government will spend $52 million less on ambulance services in 2002 than it did in the previous year.

7. Michael Rachlis et al., *Revitalizing Medicare: Shared Problems, Public Solutions* (Vancouver: Tommy Douglas Research Institute, Jan. 2001).

8. Gerard Anderson and Peter Sotir Hussey, 'Comparing Health System Performance in OECD Countries', *Health Affairs* (May–June 2001): 219–32.

9. See Nancy Hamilton, 'Aging and Health Care Reform', *Health Policy Research Bulletin* (Mar. 2001): 3–4.

10. Morris L. Barer, Robert Evans, and Clyde Hertzman, 'Avalanche or Glacier? Health Care and the Demographic Rhetoric', *Canadian Journal on Aging* 14, 2 (1995): 218.

11. For example, Roy Romanow, head of the Commission on the Future of Health Care, describes the health-care system as 'straining to meet increased demands and rising expectations'. 'Romanow Outlines Mandate for Commission', press release, 1 June 2001, 1.

12. Meri Koivusalo and Eeva Ollila, *Making a Healthy World* (London: Zed Books, 1997), 3.

13. Important exceptions were Torrance's Ph.D. and MA theses, which examined hospitals as health factories. See George Torrance, 'Hospitals as Health Factories', in David Coburn et al., eds, *Health and Canadian Society*, 3rd edn (Toronto: University of Toronto Press, 1998), 438–55.

14. For a discussion of the political economy tradition, see Daniel Drache and Wallace Clement, eds, *The New Practical Guide to Canadian Political Economy* (Toronto: James Lorimer, 1985).

15. Ian Gough, *The Political Economy of the Welfare State* (London: Macmillan, 1979), 34–5.

16. James O'Connor, *The Fiscal Crisis of the State* (New York: St Martin's Press, 1973), 9.

17. Brendan Martin, *In the Public Interest?: Privatisation and Public Sector Reform* (London: Zed Books, 1993), ch. 1.

18. H. Mimoto and P. Cross, 'The Growth of The Federal Debt', *Canadian Economic Observer*, 3 June 1991, 1.

19. Martin, *In the Public Interest?*, 9.

20. O'Connor, *Fiscal Crisis of State*, 243–6.

21. Martin, *In the Public Interest?*, 11.

22. Pat Armstrong and Hugh Armstrong, 'Limited Possibilities and Possible Limits for Pay Equity: Within and Beyond the Ontario Legislation', in Judy Fudge and Patricia McDermott, eds, *Just Wages* (Toronto: University of Toronto Press, 1991), 110–21.

23. Marilyn Waring, *If Women Counted: A New Feminist Economics* (San Francisco: HarperCollins, 1988).

24. Jacqueline Bridges and M. Judith Lynam, 'Informal Carers: A Marxist Analysis of Social, Political, and Economic Forces Underpinning the Role', *Advances in Nursing Science* 15, 3 (1993): 35.

25. See Sharmila L. Mhatre and Raisa B. Deber, 'From Equal Access to Health Care to Equitable Access to Health: A Review of Canadian Provincial Health Commissions and Reports', *International Journal of Health Services* 22, 4 (1992): 656.

CHAPTER 2

1. World Health Organization (WHO), *Ottawa Charter for Health Promotion* (Ottawa: Canadian Public Health Association, 1986).

2. Irving Rootman and John Raeburn, 'The Concept of Health', in Ann Pederson, Michel O'Neill, and Irving Rootman, eds, *Health Promotion in Canada* (Toronto: W.B. Saunders, 1994), 56–71.

3. National Forum on Health, *Canada Health Action: Building on the Legacy*, vol. 1, *Final Report* (Ottawa: Minister of Public Works and Government Services, 1997), 15. Also see Sharmila L. Mhatre and Raisa B. Deber, 'From Equal Access to Health Care to Equitable Access to Health: A Review of Canadian Provincial Health Commissions and Reports', *International Journal of Health Services* 22, 4 (1992): 656.

4. Ontario Premier's Council on Health Strategy, *Nurturing Health: A Framework on the Determinants of Health* (Toronto, 1991).

5. Ibid., 8.

6. James House, Karl Landis, and Debra Umberson, 'Social Relationships and Health', in House, Landis, and Umberson, *The Sociology of Health and Illness: Critical Perspectives* (New York: St Martin's Press, 1990), 85–94.

7. See Carol Baines, Patricia Evans, and Sheila Neysmith, eds, *Women's Caring*, 2nd edn (Toronto: Oxford University Press, 1998).

8. Carol Green-Hernandez, 'Professional Nurse Caring', in Ruth Neil and Robin Watts, eds, *Caring and Nursing: Explorations in Feminist Perspectives* (New York: National League for Nursing, 1991), 89.

9. Kathryn McPherson, 'Looking at Caring and Nursing Through a Feminist Lens', in Neil and Watts, *Caring and Nursing*, 26.

10. Nancy Waxler-Morrison, Joan Anderson, and Elizabeth Morrison, eds, *Cross-Cultural Caring* (Vancouver: University of British Columbia Press, 1990); M. Judith Lynam, 'Towards the Goal of Providing Culturally Sensitive Care: Principles Upon Which To Build Nursing Curricula', *Journal of Advanced Nursing* 17 (1992): 149–57.

11. National Forum on Health, *Canada Health Action: Building on the Legacy*, vol. 2, *Synthesis Reports and Issues Papers* (Ottawa: Minister of Public Works and Government Services, 1997), 'Determinants of Health Working Group Synthesis Report', 51 (emphasis in original). See also Robert L. Jin, Chandrakant P. Shah, and Tomislav J. Svoboda, 'The Impact of Unemployment on Health: A Review of the Evidence', *Canadian Medical Association Journal* 153, 5 (1 Sept. 1995): 529–40.

12. William R. Avison, 'The Health Consequences of Unemployment', in National Forum on Health, *Determinants of Health: Adults and Seniors* (Ste-Foy, Qué.: Éditions MultiMontes, 1998), 22.

13. Ontario Premier's Council, *Nurturing Health*, 7. See also Michael Marmot and Richard G. Wilkinson, eds, *Social Determinants of Health* (Oxford: Oxford University Press, 1999), chs 5–6.

14. See Benjamin H. Gottlieb, 'Protecting and Promoting the Well-Being of Family Caregivers', in National Forum on Health, *Determinants of Health: Settings and Issues* (Editions MultiMondes, 1998), 133–78.

15. See, for example, Heather MacDougall, *Activists and Advocates* (Toronto: Dundurn Press, 1990).

16. Ontario Premier's Council, *Nurturing Health*, 10.

17. Ibid., 12.

18. Ibid., 14.

19. Ibid., 15. See also Richard G. Wilkinson, *Unequal Societies: The Afflictions of Inequality* (New York: Routledge, 1996).

20. Ontario Premier's Council, *Nurturing Health*, 9.

21. B. Singh Bolaria and Rosemary Bolaria, eds, *Racial Minorities in Medicine and Health* (Halifax: Fernwood, 1994). On sex differences, see Statistics Canada, 'How Healthy Are Canadians? 2001 Annual Report: The Health Divide—How the Sexes Differ', *Health Reports* 12, 3 (Apr. 2001).

22. Ontario Premier's Council, *Nurturing Health*, 6.

23. Ibid., 17.

24. National Forum on Health, *Final Report*, 12.

25. Ontario Premier's Council, *Nurturing Health*, 6.

26. British Columbia, Royal Commission on Health Care and Costs, *Closer to Home* (Victoria, 1991), 12–13.

27. The Premier's Commission on Future Health Care for Albertans, *The Rainbow Report: Our Vision for Health* (Edmonton, 1989), 38.

28. The Canadian Institute for Health Information (CIHI) annually publishes data on the public and private shares of health-care spending. The data series goes back to 1975, when the public share was 76.4 per cent. The latest figure was an estimated 71.1 per cent in 2000. Calculated from CIHI, *National Health Expenditure Trends, 1975–1998* (Ottawa: CIHI, 1998), Table A.2.1; CIHI and Health Canada, *Health Care in Canada, 2001* (Ottawa: CIHI, 2001), 72, 73. For further discussion, see Chapter 5.

29. Saskatchewan Commission on Directions in Health Care, *Future Directions for Health Care in Saskatchewan* (Regina, 1990), 19.

30. Evan Willis, *Medical Dominance* (Sydney: George Allen and Unwin, 1983), 2.

31. Quoted in Bernard Blishen, *Doctors in Canada* (Toronto: University of Toronto Press, 1991), 113.

32. Rosalind Coward, *The Whole Truth: The Myth of Alternative Therapies* (London: Faber and Faber, 1989), 49.

33. Edward Shorter, *Bedside Manners: A Troubled History of Doctors and Patients* (New York: Simon and Shuster, 1985), 75–6.

34. Daniel Stoffman, 'Losing Patience: Are Hospital Costs Killing the Taxpayer?', *Canadian Business* (Nov. 1988): 72. With its subsequent government-imposed takeover of Women's College Hospital and the Orthopaedic and Arthritic Hospital to form the Sunnybrook and Women's College Health Sciences Centre, presumably obstetrics and gynecology, along with orthopaedics, have been added to the list.

35. Sara Dimers, 'Total Quality Management—A Strategy for Success', *Housecall* (Women's College Hospital) (1992): 10–11.

36. Joel Lexchin, *The Real Pushers: A Critical Analysis of the Canadian Drug Industry* (Vancouver: New Star, 1984), 209–10.

37. Theresa Boyle, 'New rules cause chaos for audiologists', *Toronto Star*, 7 July 2001, A27.

38. Richard Mackie, 'Project not helping to ease MD shortage', *Globe and Mail*, 9 July 2001, A7.

39. Blishen, *Doctors in Canada*, 9; C. David Naylor, *Private Practice, Public Payment* (Montreal and Kingston: McGill-Queen's University Press, 1986), 16–17.

40. Naylor, *Private Practice*, 18.

41. Ibid.

42. Geoffrey Bilson, 'Canadian Doctors and the Cholera', in S.E.D. Shortt, ed., *Medicine in Canadian Society* (Montreal and Kingston: McGill-Queen's Press, 1981), 118.

43. David Cayley, *Doctoring the Family* (Montreal: CBC, 1985), 7.

44. Ibid., 44.

45. Linda Rasmussen, Lorna Rasmussen, Candace Savage, and Anne Wheeler, *A Harvest Yet to Reap* (Toronto: Women's Press, 1976), 76.

46. Lexchin, *The Real Pushers*, 209.

47. Jeanne Achterberg, *Woman As Healer* (Boston: Shambhala, 1991), 174–5.

48. John C. Moskop, 'The Nature and Limits of Physician Authority', in M.S. Straum and D.E. Larsen, eds, *Doctors, Patients and Society* (Waterloo, Ont.: Wilfrid Laurier University Press, 1981), 34.

49. G.R. Paterson, 'Canadian Pharmacy in Pre-Confederation Medical Legislation', *Journal of the American Medical Association* 200, 10, (1967): 849–52.

50. Jo Ann Whittaker, 'The Search for Legitimacy: Nurses' Registration in British Columbia, 1913–1935', in Barbara Latham and Roberta Pazdro, eds, *Not Just Pin Money* (Victoria: Camosun College, 1984), 315.

51. George Torrance, 'Socio-Historical Overview: The Development of the Canadian Health System', in David Coburn et al., eds, *Health and Canadian Society*, 3rd edn (Toronto: University of Toronto Press, 1998), 17.

52. Moskop, 'The Nature and Limits', 34.

53. Morris L. Barer and Greg Stoddart, 'Toward Integrated Medical Research Policies for Canada', report prepared for the Federal/Provincial/Territorial Conference of Deputy Ministers of Health, June 1991, 13.

54. Since the early 1990s most provincial Colleges of Physicians and Surgeons have taken some steps to review doctors' practices, and the Royal College of Physicians and Surgeons and the College of Family Physicians of Canada have increased continuing medical education requirements from specialists and family doctors, respectively.

55. British Columbia, Royal Commission on Health Care and Costs, *Closer to Home*, 8.

56. Nicholas Regush, *Safety Last: The Failure of the Consumer Health Protection System in Canada* (Toronto: Key Porter Books, 1993), 12. See also James McRae and Francis Tapon, 'Prices, Patents, and R&D Location in the Canadian Pharmaceutical Industry', in Ake Blomqvist and David M. Brown, eds, *Limits To Care* (Montreal: C.D. Howe Institute, 1994), 380.

57. Health Canada, Therapeutic Products Program, 'Recent news about drug risks: application to Canadians', *Canadian Adverse Drug Reaction Newsletter* 8, 4 (Oct. 1998): 1, citing T. Moore et al., 'Time to act on drug safety', *Journal of the American Medical Association* 279, 19 (1998), on serious side effects after approval, and 'General policy topics—adverse drug reaction monitoring', *WHO Drug Info* 11, 1 (1997): 1–4.

58. See Regush, *Safety Last*, 37–8.

59. David Feeny, 'Introduction: Health Care Technlogy', in Feeny, Gordon Guyatt, and Peter Tugwell, eds, *Health Care Technology: Effectiveness, Efficiency and Public Policy* (Montreal: Institute on Public Policy, 1986), 2.

60. Oliver Bertin, 'Health Care Good Medicine for Ailing Firms', *Globe and Mail*, 15 Mar. 1994, B2.

61. Philip Hassen, *Rx for Hospitals: New Hope for Medicare in the Nineties* (Toronto: Stoddart, 1993), 80.

62. Patricia Kaufert and Penny Gilbert, 'Medicalization and Menopause', in David Coburn et al., eds, *Health and Canadian Society*, 2nd edn (Markham, Ont.: Fitzhenry & Whiteside, 1987), 180–1.

63. Regush, *Safety Last*, 36.

64. Ibid., 16.

65. Andrew Chetley, *A Healthy Business: World Health and the Pharmaceutical Industry* (London: Zed Books, 1990), 48.

66. Mark Kennedy, 'Fears raised over cuts to health protection', *Montreal Gazette*, 15 Sept. 1997.

67. Dann Michols, Director General, Drugs Directorate, Health Protection Branch, 'Drugs and Medical Devices Programme: Quality Initiative Bulletin 2. Questions and Answers: Who is our client?' (Feb. 1997 memo). See also Senator Spivak, Standing Senate Committee on Agriculture and Forestry, Evidence, 29 Oct. 1998, concerning the message from Dr Lachance, Director of Veterinary Drugs at the Branch, that industry makes up the clients and that 'if scientists did not cooperate, they could be sent to another department and never heard from again.'

68. Ian Shuggart, Visiting Assistant Deputy Minister, Health Protection Branch Transition, testimony before the Standing Senate Committee, 29 Oct. 1998.

69. For a cogent critique of the Transition initiative, see Canadian Health Coalition, 'Transition = abdication: A citizens' guide to the Health Protection Branch consultation (HPB Transition)' (Ottawa, 1998). By this time, the Branch's food safety scientists had already been transferred to another special operating agency, the Canadian Food Inspection Agency, reporting to two ministers and given conflicting safety and trade promotion mandates.

70. Dann Michols, Director General, Therapeutic Products Programme, 'Can the Therapeutic Products Programme keep up?', *Health Policy Forum* (Summer 2000): 11.

71. National Forum on Health, *Canada Health Action: Building on the Legacy*, vol. 2, *Synthesis Reports and Issues Papers*, 'Directions for a Pharmaceutical Policy in Canada', 7.

72. David Crane, 'Beware profit motive in food, drug research', *Toronto Star*, 20 July 1999, C2.

73. 'Directions for a Pharmaceutical Policy in Canada', 18.

74. Ibid., 7.

75. CCOHTA, 'Spotlight . . . BMS vs CCOHTA', *Connections* (CCOHTA newsletter) 1 (1998): 2.

76. Quoted in Joel Lexchin, 'Profits First: The Pharmaceutical Industry in Canada', in B.S. Bolaria and H.D. Dickinson, eds, *Health, Illness, and Health Care in Canada* (Toronto: Harcourt Brace, 1994), 708.

77. Joel Lexchin, 'Pharmaceuticals: Politics and Policy', in Pat Armstrong, Hugh Armstrong, and David Coburn, eds, *Unhealthy Times: Political Economy Perspectives on Health and Care in Canada* (Toronto: Oxford University Press, 2001), 39.

78. Quoted in Chetley, *A Healthy Business*, 45. See also Joel Lexchin, 'Agents against pediatric diarrhea: assessing the information companies supply to Canadian physicians', *Canadian Family Physician* 40 (1994): 2082–7.

79. Ann Pappert, 'The Rise and Fall of the IUD', in Kathleen McDonnell, ed., *Adverse Effects: Women and the Pharmaceutical Industry* (Toronto: Women's Press, 1986), 168.

80. Canadian Press and Reuters, 'Breast Cancer Researcher Falsified Data in Major Study', *Globe and Mail*, 14 Mar. 1994, A2.

81. Benjamin Djulbegovic et al., 'The uncertainty principle and industry-sponsored research', *Lancet* (2000): 635–8.

82. Reuters, 'Drug That Delays Labour May Harm Fetus, Study Finds', *Globe and Mail*, 25 Nov. 1993, A4.

83. Medical Tribune News Service, 'Allergy Drugs Cancer Suspects', *Toronto Star*, 18 May 1994, A18.

84. Lisa Priest, 'Labour-Halting Drug Called Ineffective and Risk to Health', *Toronto Star*, 31 July 1992, C1.

85. Quoted in Paul Taylor and Rod Mickleburgh, 'Breast Implant Sales Suspended', *Globe and Mail*, 8 Jan. 1992, A4.

86. Susan Sherwin, *No Longer Patient: Feminist Ethics and Health Care* (Philadelphia: Temple University Press, 1992), 166.

87. *The Economist*, 'Smelling a Rat in Medical Research', *Globe and Mail*, 22 Mar. 1993, A7.

88. Ibid., A11.

89. Warren McIsaac, David Naylor, Geoffrey Anderson, and Bernie O'Brien, 'Reflections on a Month in the Life of the Ontario Drug Benefit Plan', *Canadian Medical Association Journal* 150, 4 (1994): 473.

90. Lexchin, 'Profits First', 710.

91. G. Carruthers, T. Goldberg, H. Segal, and E. Sellers, *Drug Utilization: A Comprehensive Review* (Toronto: University of Toronto Faculty of Medicine, 1987), 243–4.

92. Jim Harding, 'Mood-Modifiers and Elderly Women in Canada: The Medicalization of Poverty', in McDonnell, ed, *Adverse Effects*, 61.

93. Lynda Hurst, 'The Lure of Instant Therapy', *Toronto Star*, 27 Mar. 1994, F3.

94. Mark Nichols, 'Questioning Prozac', *Maclean's* (23 May 1994): 36.

95. R.M. Tamblyn et al., 'Questionable Prescribing for Elderly Patients in Quebec', *Canadian Medical Association Journal* 150, 11 (1994): 1801.

96. Warren Davidson, William Molloy, George Somers, and Michel Bedard, 'Relation between Physician Characteristics and Prescribing for Elderly People in New Brunswick', *Canadian Medical Association Journal* 150, 6 (1994): 917.

97. See Harding, 'Mood Modifiers'; Dorothy Smith, and Sara David, eds, *Women Look at Psychiatry* (Vancouver: Press Gang Publishers, 1975); Deborah Findlay and Leslie Miller, 'Through Medical Eyes: The Medicalization of Women's Bodies and Women's Lives', in Bolaria and Dickinson, eds, *Health, Illness and Health Care in Canada*, 276–306.

98. C. David Naylor, Geoffrey M. Anderson, and Vivek Goel, eds, *Patterns of Health Care in Ontario*, vol. 1 (Toronto: Institute for Clinical Evaluative Sciences in Ontario, 1994).

99. Grant Gillett, *Reasonable Care* (Bristol: Bristol Press, 1989), 12.

100. Ibid., 13.

101. Joel Lexchin, 'Canadian marketing codes: how well are they controlling pharmaceutical promotion?', *International Journal of Health Sciences* 24 (1994): 91–104. See also McIsaac et al., 'Reflections on a Month', 476.

102. National Forum on Health, *Canada Health Action: Building on the Legacy*, vol. 2, *Synthesis Reports and Issues Papers*, 'Creating a Culture of Evidence-Based Decision-Making in Health', 12.

103. Premier's Commission on Future Health Care for Albertans, *The Rainbow Report*, 132–3.

104. 'Creating a Culture of Evidence-Based Decision-Making', 16.

105. Roy Carr-Hill, 'Welcome? The Brave New World of Evidence-Based Medicine', *Social Science and Medicine* 41, 11 (1995): 1468.

106. Saskatchewan Commission on Directions in Health Care, *Future Directions*, 90–1, 80.

107. Sholom Glouberman and Henry Mintzberg, 'Managing the Care of Health and the Cure of Disease. Part I: Differentiation', mimeo (Jan. 1999), 11–12.

108. 'Creating a Culture of Evidence-Based Decision-Making', 17.

109. Jean L. Rouleau et al., 'A Comparison of Management Patterns After Acute Myocardial Infarction in Canada and the United States', *New England Journal of Medicine* 328, 11 (18 Mar. 1993): 779–84; Louise Pilote, Normand Racine, and Mark A. Hlatky, 'Differences in the Treatment of Myocardial Infarction in the United States and Canada: Comparison of Two Hospitals', *Archives of Internal Medicine* 154, 10 (23 May 1994): 1090–7.

110. In Harding, 'Mood Modifiers', 52.

111. There is even an evolving uncertainty as to what constitutes a disease. See Larissa Temple et al., 'Defining Disease in the Genomics Era', *Science* 293 (3 Aug. 2001).

112. In Carruthers et al., *Drug Utilization*, 199.

113. World Health Organization, *Summary Report: Consultation on the Place of In Vitro Fertilization on Infertility Care* (Copenhagen, 1990).

114. Abby Lippman, 'Worrying—and Worrying About the Geneticization of Reproduction and Health', in Gwynne Basen, Margrit Eichler, and Lippman, eds, *Misconceptions* (Hull, Que.: Voyageur Publishing, 1993), 42.

115. Charlene Laino, 'Blood Test Could Eliminate Need for Amniocentesis, Doctors Say', *Toronto Star*, 16 May 1994, D3.

116. See Basen, Eichler, and Lippman, eds, *Misconceptions*; Christine Overall, ed., *The Future of Human Reproduction* (Toronto: Women's Press, 1989); Jan Rehner, *Old Myths, New Meanings* (Toronto: Second Story Press, 1989).

117. See Judith Kunisch, 'Electronic Fetal Monitors: Marketing Forces and the Resulting Controversy', in Kathryn Strother Ratcliff, ed., *Healing Technology: Feminist Perspectives* (Ann Arbor: University of Michigan Press, 1992), 56–7.

118. Marlene Habib, 'Giving Up On Breastfeeding', *Toronto Star*, 16 June 1994, B7.

119. Joan M. Eakin, 'Stroke Patients in a Canadian Hospital' in Coburn et al., eds, *Health and Canadian Society*, 2nd edn, 535.

120. Ibid.

121. Ivan Illich, *Limits to Medicine* (London: Penguin, 1976), 32.

122. Tamblyn et al., 'Questionable Prescribing', 1802.

123. Ibid., 1801.

124. H.G. Colt and A.P. Shapiro, 'Drug-induced Illnesses as a Cause of Admission to a Community Hospital', *Journal of the American Geriatric Society* 37 (1989): 323–6.

125. Paul Taylor, 'Busiest MDs Prescribe the Most Drugs', *Globe and Mail*, 15 Mar. 1994, A1.

126. Quoted ibid., A2.

127. Naylor, Anderson, and Goel, eds, *Patterns of Health Care*, 28.

128. Pat Armstrong, Jacqueline Choiniere, Gina Feldberg, and Jerry White, 'Voices from the Ward', in Pat and Hugh Armstrong, Jacqueline Choiniere, Gina Feldberg, and Jerry White, *Take Care: Warning Signals for Canada's Health System* (Toronto: Garamond, 1994), 57. Hereafter cited as 'Voices from the Ward', these extensive interviews were conducted under the aegis of the Ontario Council of Hospital Unions.

129. Premier's Commission on Future Health Care for Albertans, *The Rainbow Report*, vol. 2, 43.

130. Alternatives to fee-for-service remuneration are being considered in the primary care reform initiatives that several provinces are tentatively exploring. These initiatives are discussed in Chapter 3.

131. Joan Borysenko, *Minding the Body, Mending the Mind* (Don Mills, Ont.: Addison-Wesley, 1985), 11.

132. In Nicholas Regush, *Condition Critical* (Toronto: Macmillan, 1987), 217.

133. Lynda Birke, *Women, Feminism and Biology* (Brighton: Harvester, 1986), 58.

134. Ontario Premier's Council, *Nurturing Health*.

135. Ibid.

136. Philip Enterline, Allison McDonald, J. Corbett McDonald, and Nicholas Steinmetz, 'The Distribution of Medical Services Before and After "Free" Medical Care', *Medical Care* 11, 4 (July–Aug. 1973): 269–86.

137. Thomas McKeown, 'Medical Technology and Health Care', in Straum and Larsen, eds, *Doctors, Patients and Society*, 261.

138. Marc Lalonde, *A New Perspective on the Health of Canadians* (Ottawa: Information Canada, 1974). See also Jake Epp, *Achieving Health For All: A Framework for Health Promotion* (Ottawa: Supply and Services Canada, 1986).

139. Nova Scotia Provincial Health Council, *Toward Achieving Nova Scotia's Health Goals: An Initial Plan of Action for Health Care Reform Report* (Halifax, 1992), 58.

140. Ibid. There is no mention, for example, of the pollution produced by the Sydney, Nova Scotia, steel plant and coke ovens. It is now known that at least nine toxic chemicals have spread in unsafe quantities to soil at least 20 kilometres from the tar ponds in which they were deposited. Tera Camus, 'High level of toxins found outside Sydney', *Toronto Star*, 7 Aug. 2001, A2.

141. See, for example, Bolaria and Bolaria, *Racial Minorities*. The imposition of a cash economy on Aboriginal peoples has been particularly harmful to their health status. The resulting incidence of diabetes has been termed a pandemic in National Forum on Health, *Canada Health Action: Building on the Legacy*, vol. 2, *Synthesis Reports and Issues Papers*, 'The Need for an Aboriginal Health Institute in Canada', 6.

142. Transitional Council of the College of Midwives, Policy Documents (Toronto, 1993).

143. Ontario Ministry of Health, 'Utilization of Nurse Practitioners in Ontario', executive summary of discussion paper, McMaster University School of Nursing, Hamilton, Ont., Sept. 1993, 1.

CHAPTER 3

1. Judi Coburn, '"I See and Am Silent": A Short History of Nursing in Ontario, 1850–1930', in David Coburn, Carl D'Arcy, George M. Torrance, and Peter New, eds, *Health and Canadian Society*, 2nd edn (Markham, Ont.: Fitzhenry & Whiteside, 1987), 442.

2. Kenneth G. Pryke, 'Poor Relief and Health Care in Halifax, 1827–1849', in Wendy Mitchinson and Janice Dickin McGinnis, eds, *Essays in the History of Canadian Medicine*, (Toronto: McClelland & Stewart, 1988), 41.

3. Ibid., 43.

4. See Coburn, '"I See and Am Silent"'.

5. National Council of Women of Canada, *Women of Canada: Their Life and Work* (Ottawa: NCWC, 1975), 77.

6. Alice Baumgart, 'The Nursing Workforce in Canada', in Baumgart and Jenniece Larsen, eds, *Canadian Nursing Faces the Future: Development and Change* (Toronto: C.V. Mosby, 1988), 42.

7. Thomas McKeown, 'Medical Technology and Health Care', in M.S. Straum and D.E. Larsen, eds, *Doctors, Patients and Society* (Waterloo, Ont.: Wilfrid Laurier University Press, 1981); Thomas McKeown, *The Role of Medicine: Dream, Mirage or Nemesis* (Princeton, NJ: Princeton University Press, 1979).

8. Statistics Canada, *Historical Statistics of Canada*, 2nd edn (Ottawa: Minister of Supply and Services Canada, 1983), Tables B93–140.

9. Calculated from ibid., Tables B141–88 and A1. There were 12,072,000 Canadians and a bed capacity of 110,754.

10. Malcolm Taylor, *Health Insurance and Canadian Public Policy* (Montreal and Kingston: McGill-Queen's University Press, 1987), 2.

11. Ibid., ch. 4.

12. Statistics Canada, *Historical Statistics of Canada*, 2nd edn, Tables B141–88 and B189–286.

13. Dominion Bureau of Statistics, *Canada 1957* (Ottawa: Queen's Printer, 1957), 267.

14. Ibid., 268.

15. In Taylor, *Health Insurance*, 175.

16. See, for example, Terry Boychuk, *The Making and Meaning of Hospital Policy in the United States and Canada* (Ann Arbor: University of Michigan Press, 1999).

17. Helen Heeney, *Life Before Medicare: Canadian Experiences* (Toronto: Ontario Coalition of Senior Citizens' Organizations, 1995), 76.

18. Ibid., 78.

19. Ibid., 84.

20. Lee Soderstrom, *The Canadian Health System* (London: Croom Helm, 1978), 129.

21. For more complete discussion of this Act, see Pat Armstrong and Hugh Armstrong, with Claudia Fegan, *Universal Health Care: What the United States Can Learn from the Canadian Experience* (New York: New Press, 1998).

22. John H. Babson and Paul Brackstone, 'The Canadian Health Care System: Its History, Current Status and Similarities with the U.S. Health Care System', *Journal of Comparative Sociology* 1, 3 (1973): 24.

23. In Soderstrom, *Canadian Health System*, 133.

24. B. Singh Bolaria and Rosemary Bolaria, eds, *Racial Minorities in Medicine and Health* (Halifax: Fernwood, 1994).

25. Malcolm Brown, *Health Economics and Policy* (Toronto: McClelland & Stewart, 1991), 34.

26. Taylor, *Health Insurance*, 162.

27. Ibid., 234.

28. Task Force Report on the Cost of Health Services in Canada, *Health Services* (Ottawa: Queen's Printer, 1970), Table C–18.

29. John Porter, *The Vertical Mosaic* (Toronto: University of Toronto Press, 1965).

30. Statistics Canada, *Historical Statistics of Canada*, 2nd edn, B514–16.

31. Taylor, *Health Insurance*, 337–8.

32. 'Health Care Dollars', *Consumer Reports* (July 1992): 436.

33. Canada, Royal Commission on Health Services, *Report*, vol. 1 (Ottawa: Queen's Printer, 1964), 6.

34. John C. Moskop, 'The Nature and Limits of Physician Authority', in Straum and Larson, eds, *Doctors, Patients and Society*, 35.

35. David Naylor, *Private Practice, Public Payment* (Montreal and Kingston: McGill-Queen's University Press, 1986).

36. Philip E. Enterline, J. Corbett McDonald, Allison D. McDonald, Lise Davignon, and Vera Salter, 'Effects of "Free" Medical Care on Medical Practice: The Quebec Experience', *New England Journal of Medicine* 288, 2 (1973).

37. Philip Enterline, Allison McDonald, J. Corbett McDonald, Nicholas Steinmetz, 'The Distribution of Medical Services Before and After "Free" Medical Care', *Medical Care* 11, 4 (July–Aug. 1973): 285.

38. Heeney, *Life Before Medicare*.

39. *Consumer Reports* (July 1992): 440.

40. Marc Renaud, 'Reform or Illusion? An Analysis of the Quebec State Intervention in Health', in Coburn et al., *Health and Canadian Society*, 2nd edn, 590–614.

41. Quoted in Frederic Lesemann, *Services and Circuses* (Montreal: Black Rose Books, 1984), 244.

42. Ibid., 250.

43. Renaud, 'Reform or Illusion?', 600.

44. Quoted in Monique Bégin, *Medicare, Canada's Right to Health* (Ottawa: Optimum, 1987), 174.

45. See Geoffrey York, *The High Price of Health* (Toronto: Lorimer, 1987), 92.

46. While it is difficult to determine exactly what share of funding is provided by the federal government, provinces claim that the federal share of total spending in 2001 is 14 per cent, compared to 18 per cent in 1994–5. *Health Edition* (Merck Frosst Canada) 5, 25 (22 June 2001): 1.

47. Government of Canada, A Framework to Improve the Social Union for Canadians. An agreement between the Government of Canada and the Governments of the Provinces and the Territories, 4 Feb. 1999.

48. Commission on the Future of Health Care in Canada, Commissioner Roy Romanow appointed in 2001.

49. For a summary of various provincial strategies, see Pat Armstrong et al., eds, *Exposing Privatization* (Toronto: Garamond, 2001).

50. Kelly Toughill, 'Doctors Charging Extra Fees Up Front', *Toronto Star*, 28 May 1992, A2.

51. Paul Leduc Browne, *Unsafe Practices: Restructuring and Privatization in Ontario Health Care* (Ottawa: Canadian Centre for Policy Alternatives, 2000), 68–70.

52. Health Canada, *Canada Health Act 1999–2000* (Ottawa: Minister of Public Works and Government Services Canada, 2000), 14–15.

53. CSN, *Choisir* (Montreal: mimeo, n.d.), 43, 47.

54. Graph prepared by the Ontario Ministry of Health and distributed to members of the Research Steering Committee of the Ontario Premier's Council on Health, Well-Being and Social Justice, 1992.

55. Quoted in Theresa Boyle, 'Busy MDs Prescribe Drugs More Study Says', *Toronto Star*, 16 March 1994, A3.

56. Calculated from Statistics Canada, *Historical Statistics of Canada*, 2nd edn, B504–13.

57. Denise L. Spitzer, '"They Don't Listen to Your Body": Minority Women, Nurses and Childbirth under Health Reform', in Diana L. Gustafson, ed., *Care and Consequences: The Impact of Health Care Reform* (Halifax: Fernwood, 2000), 85–106.

58. Canadian Health Services Research Foundation, 'Myth: Canadian Doctors Are Leaving for the United States in Droves', *Mythbusters* (July 2001).

59. See, for example, Michael E. Makover, *Mismanaged Care: How Corporate Medicine Jeopardizes Your Health* (New York: Prometheus, 1998), for a physician's view of US reforms.

60. Community Health Co-operative Federation Limited, *Community Health Centres: A Model for Primary Care Reform*. A Brief to the Fyke Commission on Medicare (Regina, Nov. 2001), 2.

61. Québec Commission d'étude sur les Services de Santé et les Services Sociaux (Clair Commission), *Les Solutions Émergentes* (Québec: Ministère de la Santé et les Services Sociaux, 2000).

62. See Michael Rachlis, Robert G. Evans, Patrick Lewis, and Morris L. Barer, *Revitalizing Medicare: Shared Problems, Public Solutions* (Vancouver: Tommy Douglas Research Institute, Jan. 2001); Michael Rachlis, *Modernizing Medicare for the Twenty-First Century* (Victoria: Ministry of Health and Ministry Responsible for Seniors, 2000). Also Brian Hutchinson, Julia Abelson, and John Lavis. 'Primary Care in Canada: So Much Innovation, So Little Change', *Health Affairs* 20, 3 (2001): 116–31.

63. Walter Rosser and Ian Kasperski, 'Organizing Primary Care for an Integrated System', *Healthcare Papers* 1, 1 (Winter 2000): 9.

64. For a further discussion of these issues, see Pat Armstrong and Hugh Armstrong, *Primary Health Care Reform: What Are the Issues and Why Should We Care?* (Ottawa: Canadian Health Coalition, 2000); Rachlis et al., *Revitalizing Medicare*; Rachlis, *Modernizing Medicare*.

65. 'Public Support for Rostering High', *Quid Nova*, Newsletter of the Canadian Health Services Research Foundation 3, 1 (Spring 2000): 5.

66. Canadian Institute for Health Information (CIHI), *Health in Canada 2000: A First Report* (Ottawa, 2000), 1.

67. Ibid., 8.

68. Ontario, Ministry of Health, *Annual Report 1992–93* (Toronto: Ministry of Health, 1994), 4.

69. Brown, *Health Economics and Policy*, 29.

70. Manitoba Centre for Health Policy and Evaluation, *Winnipeg Hospital Bed Closures: Problem or Progress?* (Winnipeg, Feb. 1999), 1.

71. CIHI, *Hospital Report 2001: Acute Care* (Toronto, 2001), 16.

72. Kate Bezanson and Louise Noce, with the assistance of the Speaking Out Team, *Costs, Closures and Confusion: People in Ontario Talk About Health Care* (Toronto: Caledon, May 1999).

73. Andrea Bauman et al., *Commitment and Care: The Benefits of a Healthy Workplace for Nurses, Their Patients and the System* (Ottawa: Canadian Health Services Research Foundation, July 2001), 3.

74. See Pat Armstrong et al., *'Heal Thyself': Managing Health Care Reform* (Toronto: Garamond, 2000).

75. Ibid.

76. CIHI, *Hospital Report 2001*, 41–2.

77. Ibid., 23–4.

78. 'Voices from the Ward'.

79. Armstrong et al., '*Heal Thyself*'.

80. Andrew E. Simor et al., 'The Evolution of Methicillin-resistant Staphylococcus Aureus in Canadian Hospitals: 5 Years of National Surveillance', *Canadian Medical Association Journal* 165, 1 (10 July 2001): 21–31.

81. Sepali Guruge, Gail J. Donner, and Lynn Morrison, 'The Impact of Canadian Health Care Reform on Recent Women Immigrants and Refugees', in Gustafson, ed., *Care and Consequences*, 222–42.

82. *Hotline* #4.

83. Carolyn Abraham, 'Early Release of Newborns Linked to Health Problems', *Globe and Mail*, 10 Aug. 1999, A1–2.

84. In Helen Henderson, 'Home Alone', *Toronto Star*, 16 July 1994, H5.

85. Bezanson et al., *Costs, Closures and Confusion*, 10.

86. Pat Armstrong and Olga Kits, *One Hundred Years of Caregiving*. Report prepared for the Law Commission of Canada, 2001.

87. See Pat Armstrong, 'Closer to Home; More Work for Women', in Pat Armstrong et al., *Take Care: Warning Signals for Canadian Health Care* (Toronto: Garamond, 1994).

88. Interview conducted in Montreal in 1989, with support from the Social Sciences and Humanities Research Council of Canada. The research team included Hugh Armstrong, Pat Armstrong, Susan Gottheil, and Shirley Pettifer. Hereafter cited as Montreal interviews.

89. National Forum on Health, *Canada Health Action: Building on the Legacy*, vol. 2, *Synthesis Reports and Issues Papers*, 'Values Working Group Synthesis Report' (Ottawa: Minister of Public Works and Government Services, 1997), 16.

90. Marcus Hollander and Angela Tessaro, *Evaluation of the Maintenance and Preventive Function of Home Care* (Ottawa: Home Care/Pharmaceuticals Division, Policy and Communication Branch, Health Canada, Mar. 2001), 17.

91. *Hotline* #1.

92. Hotline interview.

93. Laura Sky, *Lean and Mean Health Care: The Creation of the Generic Worker and the Deregulation of Health Care*. Health Research Project Working Paper 95-3 (Toronto: Ontario Federation of Labour, June 1995).

94. *Hotline* #9.

95. 'Voices from the Ward'.

96. CIHI, *Hospital Report 2001*.

97. 'Voices from the Ward'.

98. Sky, *Lean and Mean Health Care*.

99. Bezanson et al., *Costs, Closures and Confusion*, 10.

100. Barbara Markham and Jonathan Lomas, 'Review of Multi-Hospital Arrangements Literature: Benefits, Disadvantages and Lessons for Implementation', *Health Care Management Forum* (Fall 1995). See also Astrid Brouselle, Jean-Louis Denis, and Ann Langley, *What Do We Know About Hospital Mergers? A Selected Bibliography* (Ottawa: Canadian Health Services Research Foundation, Dec. 1999).

101. Armstrong et al., '*Heal Thyself*', 75.

102. Sky, *Lean and Mean Health Care*.

103. Armstrong et al., '*Heal Thyself*', 121–2.

104. Ibid., 91.

105. Heather Mains, 'Caring Person Beats Machine', *Toronto Star*, 2 Aug. 1994, A16.

106. Armstrong et al., *'Heal Thyself'*, 121.

107. *Hotline #6*.

108. Sky, *Lean and Mean Health Care*.

109. Testimony of Josephine Flaherty in *Ontario Nurses Association v. Women's College Hospital, Sunnybrook Hospital and North York General Hospital*, Ontario Pay Equity Tribunal, 1991.

110. Armstrong et al., *'Heal Thyself'*, 102.

111. *Hotline #6*.

112. Sky, *Lean and Mean Health Care*.

113. *Hotline #3*.

114. Sky, *Lean Mean Health Care*.

115. Armstrong et al., *'Heal Thyself'*, 141.

116. Quoted in Arlene Babad, 'Financial Implications of Understaffing', *ONA Newsletter* (Aug. 1988): 14.

117. Steffie Woolhandler et al., 'Administrative Costs in U.S. Hospitals', *New England Journal of Medicine* (Aug. 1993): 400.

118. Brendan Martin, *In the Public Interest? Privatisation and Public Sector Reform* (London: Zed Press, 1993), 87.

119. 'Hospital Worker Scolded for Kindness', *The Leader* (Mar. 1987): 1.

120. Sky, *Lean and Mean Health Care*.

121. Canadian Union of Public Employees Research, *Cooking Up a Storm: Part II* (Ottawa: CUPE, June 1998), 8.

122. National Union of Provincial and General Employees, *Medical Lab Services: Private vs Public Delivery Systems* (Nepean, Ont.: May 1997).

123. See Paul Leduc Browne, *Unsafe Practices: Restructuring and Privatization in Ontario's Health Care* (Ottawa: Canadian Centre for Policy Alternatives, 2000), 51–3.

124. The president of CSL Hospital Services quoted in Bethany Keddy, 'Hospitals Cite Pros, Cons in Contracting Out Services', *Hospital News* (Dec. 1988): 22.

125. Sky, *Lean and Mean Health Care*.

126. 'Voices from the Ward'.

127. HMRI, *Comparative Analysis of the HMRI Database* (Don Mills, Ont.: HMRI, 1992), 1. HMRI has recently merged with three other agencies, including components of Health Canada and Statistics Canada, to form the new Canadian Institute for Health Information. CIHI is also a non-profit, non-governmental agency.

128. Ibid., 8.

129. Ibid., 3.

130. Ibid., 2.

131. Institute for Clinical Evaluative Sciences, *Patterns of Health Care in Ontario*, C. David Naylor, Geoffrey M. Anderson, and Vivek Goel, eds (Ottawa: Canadian Medical Association, 1994).

132. Philip Hassen, *Rx for Hospitals: New Hope for Medicare in the Nineties* (Toronto: Stoddart, 1993), 68.

133. For an excellent discussion of the importance of context, see Blake Poland et al., 'Wealth, Equity and Health Care: A Critique of the "Population Health" Perspective on the Determinants of Health', *Social Science and Medicine* 46, 7 (1998): 785–98.

134. Spitzer, '"They Don't Listen to Your Body"', 103.

135. *Hotline #7*.

136. For a further discussion of these issues, see Pat Armstrong, 'Evidence-Based Health-Care Reform: Women's Issues', in Pat Armstrong, Hugh Armstrong, and David Coburn, eds,

Unhealthy Times: Political Economy Perspectives on Health and Care in Canada (Toronto: Oxford University Press, 2001), 121–45.

137. Hollander and Tessaro, *Evaluation of the Maintenance and Prevention Function*, 27.

138. James C. Robinson 'The End of Managed Care', *Journal of the American Medical Association* 285, 20 (23/30 May 2001): 1–26.

139. Harvey Simmons, *Unbalanced: Mental Health Policy in Ontario, 1930–1989* (Toronto: Wall and Thompson, 1990) ch. 9.

140. Quoted ibid., 160.

141. Referenced ibid., 170.

142. Doreen Duchesne, *Giving Freely: Volunteers in Canada* (Statistics Canada Cat. no. 71–535) (Ottawa: Supply and Services Canada, 1989), Table 16.

143. See Pat Armstrong and Hugh Armstrong, *The Double Ghetto: Canadian Women and Their Segregated Work*, 3rd edn (Toronto: McClelland & Stewart, 1993), ch. 3.

144. Calculated from Statistics Canada, *Residential Care Facilities—Aged* (Cat. no. 82–003S18) and *Residential Care Facilities—Mental* (Cat. no. 83–238) (Ottawa: Ministry of Industry, Science and Technology, 1993).

145. Browne, *Unsafe Practices*, 60.

146. James Struthers, 'Reluctant Partners: State Regulation of Private Nursing Homes in Ontario, 1941–72', in Raymond B. Blake, Penny E. Bryden, and J. Frank Strain, eds, *The Welfare State in Canada: Past, Present and Future* (Concord, Ont.: Irwin, 1997), 181.

147. Vera Ingrid Tarman, *Privatization and Health Care* (Toronto: Garamond, 1990), 32.

148. Browne, *Unsafe Practices*, 61.

149. Pat Armstrong and Irene Jansen, with Erin Connell and Mavis Jones, *Assessing the Impact of Restructuring and Work Reorganization in Long-Term Care: Workers' Health Issues.* Report published by CUPE and NNEWH, Sept. 2001.

150. In Tarman, *Privatization and Health Care*, 76.

151. Sky, *Lean and Mean Health Care*.

152. Ibid.

153. 'Voices from the Ward'.

154. Armstrong et al., *Assessing the Impact of Restructuring and Work Reorganization in Long-Term Care*.

155. Ibid.

156. Colleen Fuller, *Home Care: What We Know and What We Need* (Ottawa: Canadian Health Coalition, May 2001), ii.

157. Royal Commission on Health Services (Hall Commission Report*)* (Ottawa: Queen's Printer, 1964), 19.

158. Quoted in Fuller, *Home Care*, 54.

159. National Forum on Health, *Canada Health Action: Building on the Legacy*, vol. 1, *Final Report* (Ottawa: Minister of Public Works and Government Services, 1997), 22.

160. Canadian Home Care Association in collaboration with l'Association des CLSC et CHSLD du Québec, 'Portrait of Canada: An Overview of Public Home Care Programs', Background Information Prepared for the National Conference on Home Care, Ottawa, Feb. 1998, 1.

161. Evelyn Shapiro, *The Cost of Privatization: A Case Study of Home Care in Manitoba* (Ottawa: Canadian Centre for Policy Alternatives, Dec. 1997), 13.

162. Ross Sutherland, *The Costs of Contracting Out Home Care: A Behind the Scenes Look at Home Care in Ontario* (Ottawa: Canadian Union of Public Employees, Feb. 2001), 12.

163. Health Canada, *Provincial and Territorial Home Care Programs: A Synthesis for Canada* (Ottawa: Health Canada, June 1999), Table 1.

164. Canadian Home Care Association et al., 'Portrait of Canada', 1.

165. National Evaluation of the Cost Effectiveness of Home Care, *Newsletter* 1, 1 (2001): 3.

166. Quoted in Nona Glazer, 'The Home as Workshop: Women as Amateur Nurses and Medical Care Providers', *Gender and Society* 4, 4 (Dec. 1990): 486.

167. Marika Morris et al., *The Changing Nature of Home Care and Its Impact on Women's Vulnerability to Poverty* (Ottawa: Status of Women Canada, 1999).

168. Prithi Yelaja, 'Home Care Getting Worse, Report Says', *Toronto Star*, 2 Aug. 2001, A3.

169. National Evaluation of the Cost Effectiveness of Home Care, *Newsletter* 1, 1 (2001): 2.

170. Hollander and Tessaro, *Evaluation of the Maintenance and Preventive Function of Home Care*, viii.

171. Care Watch Phoneline, *Behind Closed Doors: Home Care Stories from the Community* (Toronto, May 1999).

172. Hollander and Tessaro, *Evaluation of the Maintenance and Preventive Function of Home Care*, ix.

173. Helen Henderson, 'Group Wants To Do Something About Seniors Who Are Released From Hospital Too Early', *Toronto Star*, 16 July 1994, H5.

CHAPTER 4

1. George M. Torrance, 'Socio-Historical Overview: The Development of The Canadian Health System', in David Coburn, Carl D'Arcy, Torrance, and Peter New, eds, *Health and Canadian Society*, 2nd edn (Markham, Ont.: Fitzhenry & Whiteside, 1987), 14.

2. Veronica Strong-Boag, 'Canada's Women Doctors: Feminism Constrained', in S.E.D. Shortt, ed., *Medicine in Canadian Society: Historical Perspectives* (Montreal and Kingston: McGill-Queen's University Press, 1981), 207–37.

3. Ontario Ministry of Health, *Report to Public Hospitals in Ontario on the 1985 Hospital Workforce Survey and Employment Equity Initiatives in 1985/86* (Toronto: Ministry of Health, 1987).

4. John A. Price, 'Canadian Indian Families', in K. Ishwaran, ed., *The Canadian Family* (Toronto: Gage, 1983), 77.

5. H.H. Loughton, *A Gentlewoman in Upper Canada* (Toronto: Clarke, Irwin, 1964), 67, 157.

6. Ladies of Toronto and Chief Cities and Towns in Canada, *The Canadian Home Cook Book* (Toronto: Hunter, Rose and Company, 1970 [1877]), 15.

7. Grandma Nichols, *The Great Nineteenth Century Medicine Manual* (Toronto: Coles, 1978), unpaginated.

8. Ontario Pay Equity Tribunal, *Ontario Nurses Association, Applicant v. Regional Municipality of Haldimand-Norfolk*, (0001–89) (P.E.H.T.), 29 May 1991, 7–8.

9. Ontario Pay Equity Commission, *Ontario Nurses Association, Applicant v. Women's College Hospital et al.*, (0008–89; 0011–89; 0018–89; 0029–89; 0034–89; 0036–89) (P.E.H.T.), 4 Aug. 1992, 18.

10. For a review of this literature, see Miriam Stewart, *Integrating Social Support in Nursing* (London: Sage, 1993), esp. ch. 2.

11. For documentation of this process, see Dianne Dodd and Deborah Gorham, eds, *Caring and Curing* (Ottawa: University of Ottawa Press, 1994).

12. Nicky James, 'Care, Work and Carework: A Synthesis', in Jane Robinson, Alastair Gray, and Ruth Elkin, eds, *Policy Issues in Nursing* (Bristol: Open University Press, 1992), 102.

13. Statistics Canada, *1996 Census: Occupation, Industry and Class of Workers* (Cat. no. 93F0027XCB960049). Statistics Canada Web site, accessed 25 Mar. 2001.

14. Janet Ross Kerr, 'A Historical Approach to the Evolution of University Nursing Education in Canada', in Kerr and Janetta MacPhail, *Canadian Nursing* (Toronto: McGraw-Hill Ryerson, 1988), 238.

15. Ibid.; Judi Coburn, '"I See and Am Silent": A Short History of Nursing in Ontario, 1850–1930', in Coburn et al., eds, *Health and Canadian Society*, 441–62.

16. These figures on nursing are taken from Coburn, '"I See and Am Silent"', Table 2.

17. Deborah Gorham, "No Longer an Invisible Minority': Women Physicians and Medical Practice in Late Twentieth-Century North America', in Dodd and Gorham, eds, *Caring and Curing*, 184.

18. Nicky James, 'Care, Work and Carework: A Synthesis', in Robinson et al., eds, *Policy Issues in Nursing*, 97.

19. Kathryn McPherson, 'Science and Techniques: Nurses' Work in a Canadian Hospital, 1920–1939', in Dodd and Gorham, eds, *Caring and Curing*, 85.

20. Gorham, "'No Longer an Invisible Minority'", 184.

21. McPherson, 'Science and Techniques', 82.

22. Carol Green-Hernandez, 'Professional Nurse Caring: A Proposed Conceptual Model for Nursing', in Ruth Neil and Robin Watts, eds, *Caring and Nursing* (New York: National League for Nursing, 1991), 87.

23. College of Nurses of Ontario, *Standards of Nursing Practice* (Toronto: College of Nurses of Ontario, 1990), 8.

24. Sharon Horner, 'Intersubjective Copresence in a Caring Model', in Neil and Watts, eds, *Caring and Nursing*, 108.

25. *Ontario Nurses Association v. Regional Municipality of Haldimand-Norfolk*, 14–15.

26. *Ontario Nurses Association v. Women's College Hospital et al.*, 15–18.

27. Montreal interviews.

28. Patricia Yaros, 'The Feminist Movement and the Science and Profession of Nursing: Analogies and Paradoxes', in Neil and Watts, eds, *Caring and Nursing*, 82.

29. Pat Armstrong, 'Professions, Unions or What? Learning From Nurses', in Linda Briskin and Patricia McDermott, eds, *Women Challenging Unions* (Toronto: University of Toronto Press, 1993), 304–24.

30. Noah Meltz, *Manpower in Canada, 1931–1961* (Ottawa: Department of Manpower and Immigration, 1969), Table B3.

31. Statistics Canada, *1971 Census of Canada: Occupations* (Cat. no. 94–723, Vol. 11, Part 2) (Ottawa: Ministry of Industry, Trade and Commerce, 1975).

32. Phyllis Marie Jensen, 'The Changing Role of Nurses' Unions', in Alice Baumgart and Jenniece Larsen, eds, *Canadian Nursing Faces the Future* (Toronto: Mosby, 1988), 459–73.

33. Dorothy Meilicke and Jenniece Larsen, 'Leadership and the Leaders of the Canadian Nurses Association', in Baumgart and Larsen, eds, *Canadian Nursing Faces the Future*, 443.

34. Canadian Institute for Health Information (CIHI), *Supply and Distribution of Registered Nurses in Canada, 1999* (Ottawa, 2000), 23; CIHI, *Canada's Health Care Providers* (Ottawa, 2002), 9.

35. Statistics Canada, *1981 Census of Canada: Labour Force-Occupation Trends* (Cat. no. 92–920, vol. 1) (Ottawa: Ministry of Supply and Services Canada, 1983), Table 1.

36. Terry Wotherspoon, 'Immigration, Gender and Professional Labour: State Regulation of Nursing and Teaching', paper presented to CSAA 25th annual meeting, Victoria, May 1990, Table II; Canadian Institute for Health Information, *Supply and Distribution of Registered Nurses*, 33.

37. Wotherspoon, 'Immigration, Gender and Professional Labour', 14.

38. Tania Das Gupta, 'Anti-Black Racism in Nursing in Ontario', *Studies in Political Economy* 51 (Fall 1996): 97–116.

39. Trudy Richardson, *Patient Focused Care* (Edmonton: United Nurses of Alberta, 1994), 5.

40. See, for example, Janet M. Lum and A. Paul Williams, 'Professional Fault Lines: Nursing in Ontario after the *Regulated Professions Act*', in Diana L. Gustafson, ed., *Care and Consequences: The Impact of Health Care Reform* (Halifax: Fernwood, 2000), 49–71.

41. Statistics Canada, *1991 Census: Occupation* (Cat. no. 93–327) (Ottawa: Ministry of Industry, Science and Technology, 1993), Table 1.

42. Statistics Canada, *1996 Census: Occupation, Industry and Class of Workers.*

43. Statistics Canada, *Hospital Annual Statistics 1989–90* (Cat. no. 83–242, Part 5) (Ottawa: Ministry of Industry, Science and Technology, 1993), Table 58.

44. Statistics Canada, *Occupational Trends 1961–1986* (Cat. no. 93–151) (Ottawa: Supply and Services Canada, 1988), Table 2.

45. Louise Lemieux-Charles, Michael Murray, Catherine Aird, and Jan Barnsley, *Careers in Health Care Management: Results of a National Survey* (Toronto: University of Toronto, Hospital Management Research Unit, 1993), Table 4.

46. Louise Lemieux-Charles, Michael Murray, Catherine Aird, and Jan Barnsley, 'Careers in Health Care Management, Part 1: Attainment, Expectations and Aspirations', *Health Management Forum* 7, 2 (Summer 1994): 41.

47. Jerry White, *Hospital Strike* (Toronto: Thompson, 1990), 47.

48. Ibid.

49. Laura Sky, *Lean and Mean Health Care: The Creation of the Generic Worker and the Regulation of Health Care.* Health Research Project Working Paper 95–3 (Toronto: Ontario Federation of Labour, June 1995).

50. Gerard Anderson and Peter Sotir Hussey, 'Comparing health System Performance in OECD Countries', *Health Affairs* (May–June 2001): 219–32.

51. CIHI, *Supply and Distribution of Registered Nurses*, 24.

52. Ibid., Tables 10.0a and 10.0b.

53. Registered Nurses Association of Ontario, *Ensuring the Care Will Be There: Report on Nursing Recruitment and Retention in Ontario*, Submitted to the Ontario Ministry of Health and Long-Term Care (Toronto, Mar. 2000), 53.

54. CIHI, *Supply and distribution of Registered Nurses*, 25.

55. Eva Ryten, *A Statistical Picture of the Past, Present and Future of Registered Nurses in Canada* (Ottawa: Canadian Nurses Association, 1997), 9.

56. Canadian Health Services Research Foundation, 'Commitment and Care: The Benefits of a Healthy Workplace for Nurses, Their Patients and the System'. Available at: <http:/www.chsrf.ca/english/document-library/psescomcare_e.html>. Accessed July 2001.

57. 'Voices from the Ward'.

58. Montreal interviews.

59. 'Voices from the Ward'.

60. Montreal interviews.

61. Ibid.

62. 'Voices from the Ward'.

63. Frederick Winslow Taylor, *The Principles of Scientific Management* (New York: Norton, 1911).

64. For a full discussion of Taylor's approach, see Harry Braverman, *Labor and Monopoly Capital* (New York: Monthly Review Press, 1974).

65. Lise-Marie Audette, Jocelyne Carle, Angelina Simard, Charles Tilquin, et collaborateurs, *Guide de l'Usager de la Formule d'Evaluation du Niveau des Soins Infirmières Requis par le Beneficiaire* (Montréal: Université de Montreal, 1978), viii.

66. Ibid., 1.

67. Ibid., 1, 3.

68. Montreal interviews.

69. Pat Armstrong et al., *'Heal Thyself': Managing Health Care Reform* (Toronto: Garamond, 2000), 104.

70. Montreal interviews.

71. Pat Armstrong and Irene Jansen, with Erin Connell and Mavis Jones, *Assessing the Impact of Restructuring and Work Reorganization in Long-term Care. Workers' Health Issues.* Report published by CUPE and NNEWH, Sept. 2001.

72. Carol Helmstadter, 'Staffing as a Quality of Worklife Factor', mimeo, 1994, 8.

73. Montreal interviews.

74. 'Voices from the Ward'.

75. Ibid.

76. Montreal interviews.

77. CIHI, *Health Care in Canada: A First Annual Report* (Ottawa, 2000), 25.

78. Duncan Hunter and Namrata Bains, 'Rates of Adverse Events Among Hospital Admissions and Day Surgery in Ontario from 1992 to 1997', *Canadian Medical Association Journal* 160, 11 (1 June 1999): 1585–6.

79. Lisa Priest, 'Assaults by Patients Soaring, Hospitals Say', *Toronto Star*, 18 May 1993, A1, A27; CIHI, *Canada's Health Care Providers*, 91.

80. Canadian Health Services Research Foundation, 'Commitment and Care', 2.

81. 'Voices from the Ward'.

82. Armstrong et al., *Assessing the Impact*.

83. Donald Berwick, Blanton Godfrey, and Jane Roessner, *Curing Health Care* (San Francisco: Jossey-Bass, 1990).

84. Ontario Premier's Council on Health Strategy, *Achieving the Vision: Health Human Resources* (Toronto, 1991), 6.

85. Philip Hassen, *Rx for Hospitals: A New Hope for Medicare in the 90s* (Toronto: Stoddart, 1993), 63.

86. John Price, 'Total Quality Management Threatens Medicare', *Canadian Dimension* 28, 1 (Jan./Feb. 1994): 15–20.

87. Hassen, *Rx for Hospitals*, back cover.

88. Edward Deming, *Out of the Crisis* (Cambridge, Mass.: MIT-CAES, 1986).

89. Berwick et al., *Curing Health Care*, 41.

90. Working Group on Health Services Utilization (WGHSU), *When Less Is Better: Using Canada's Hospitals Efficiently* (Ottawa, 1994), 16.

91. Berwick et al., *Curing Health Care*, 11.

92. Sara Dimers, 'Total Quality Management—A Strategy for Success', *Housecall* (Women's College Hospital) (1992): 10.

93. Hassen, *Rx for Hospitals*, 168, 94, 97, 94, 63.

94. Trudy Richardson, *Total Quality Management Programs: More Work for Less Pay* (Edmonton: United Nurses of Alberta, 1993), 49.

95. CIHI, *Supply and Distribution of Registered Nurses*, Table 1.

96. 'Voices from the Ward'.

97. Ibid.

98. Registered Nurses Association of Ontario, *Earning Their Return: When and Why Ontario RNs Left Canada and What Would Bring Them Back* (Toronto: RNAO, Feb. 2001), Chart 5.

99. Richardson, *Total Quality Management Programs*.

100. Armstrong et al., 'Heal Thyself', 117.

101. Ibid., 153.

102. 'Voices from the Ward'.

103. Ibid.

104. Berwick et al., *Curing Health Care*; Hassen, *Rx for Hospitals*.

105. Hassen, *Rx for Hospitals*, 135.

106. Ibid., 105–28.

107. John Anderson, *Total Quality Management: Should Unions Buy Into TQM?* (Toronto: Ontario Federation of Labour, 1993), 18.

108. Hassen, *Rx for Hospitals*, 135.

109. Anderson, *Total Quality Management*, 19.

110. 'Voices from the Ward'.

111. Armstrong et al., *Assessing the Impact*.

112. Richardson, *Patient Focused Care*, 17.

113. Hassen, *Rx for Hospitals*.

114. These quotes are from 'Voices from the Ward'.

115. Ibid.

116. WGHSU, *When Less Is Better*, 24.

117. Ibid., 21–2.

118. 'Voices from the Ward'.

119. Ibid.

120. See, for example, Merck Frosst Canada, *Health Care in Canada: A National Survey of Health Care Providers and Users* (Montreal, 2000), 15–17.

121. Jane Aronson, 'Giving Consumers a Say in Policy Development: Influencing Policy or Just Being Heard', *Canadian Public Policy* 19, 4 (1993): 374.

122. 'Voices from the Ward'.

123. In Ontario, patient satisfaction surveys indicated that 31 per cent of patients were not pleased with how promptly their call bells were answered. CIHI, *Hospital Report 2001: Acute Care* (Ottawa, 2001), 19.

124. Richardson, *Patient Focused Care*, 29.

125. WGHSU, *When Less Is Better*, 11.

126. Ibid.

127. Ibid.

128. See, for example, Neena Chappell, 'Implications of Shifting Health Care Policy for Caregivers in Canada', *Journal of Aging and Social Policy* 5, 12 (1993): 39–55; Haya Ascher-Svanum and Teri Sobel, 'Caregiving of Mentally Ill Adults: A Woman's Agenda', *Hospital and Community Psychiatry* 40, 8 (Autumn 1989): 843–5; Joan Anderson and Helen Elfert, 'Managing Chronic Illness in the Family: Women as Caretakers', *Journal of Advanced Nursing* 14 (1989): 735–43; Carol Baines, Patricia Evans, and Sheila Neysmith, eds, *Women's Caring* (Toronto: McClelland & Stewart, 1991); Karen Whalley Hammell, 'The Caring Wife: The Experience of Caring for a Severely Disabled Husband in the Community', *Disability, Handicap and Society* 7, 4 (1992): 349–62; Judith MacBride, *Work and Family: Employment Challenge of the '90s* (Ottawa: Conference Board of Canada, 1990); H. Pizurski, A. Butter, and L. Ewart, *Women as Providers of Health Care* (Geneva: World Health Organization, 1988); Robyn Stone, Gail Lee Cafferata, and Judith Sangi, 'Caregivers of the Frail Elderly: A National Profile', *The Gerontologist* 27, 5 (1987): 616–26; Parnel Wickham-Searl, 'Careers in Caring: Mothers of Children with Disabilities', *Disability, Handicap and Society* 7, 1 (1992): 5–17; Marika Morris et al., *The Changing Nature of Home Care and Its Impact on Women's Vulnerability to Poverty* (Ottawa: Status of Women Canada, 1999).

129. Ontario Ministry of Health, *Building Partnerships in Long Term Care: A New Way to Plan, Manage and Deliver Services and Community Support* (Ontario: Queen's Printer for Ontario, May 1993), 7.

130. National Forum on Health, *Canada Health Action: Building on the Legacy*, vol. 2, *Synthesis Reports and Issues Papers* (Ottawa: Public Works and Government Services, 1997).

131. Canadian Home Care Association (in collaboration with L'Association des CLSC et des CHSLD du Québec), *Portrait of Canada: An Overview of Public Home Care Programs* (Ottawa: Health Canada, 1998); Morris et al., *The Changing Nature of Home Care*.

132. Canadian Home Care Association (in collaboration with L'Association des CLSC et des CHSLD du Quebec), *Portrait of Canada*, 2.

133. Ibid. With very recent changes in BC, the contrast has become less stark.

134. R. Bacovsky, *Federal, Provincial and Territorial Government Sponsored Drug Plans and Drug Databases: Background Information Prepared for the Conference on National Approaches to Pharmacare*, 1997.

135. H. Trottier et al., 'Living at Home or in an Institution: What Makes the Difference for Seniors?', *Health Reports* 11, 4 (2000): 49.

136. J.M. Keefe and P. Fancey, 'Financial Compensation or Home Help Services: Examining Differences among Program Recipients', *Canadian Journal on Aging/La Revue Canadienne du Vieillissement* 16, 2 (1997): 254–78.

137. J. Jenson and S. Jacobzone, *Care Allowances for the Frail Elderly and Their Impact on Women Care-Givers* (Paris: OECD, Directorate for Education, Employment, Labour, and Social Affairs, 2000), 26.

138. Keefe and Fancey, 'Financial Compensation or Home Help Services', 256.

139. Ibid., 275.

140. Ontario Ministry of Community and Social Services, *Redirection of Long-Term Care and Support Service in Ontario* (Toronto: Queen's Printer for Ontario, 1991), 210; M. Denton, 'The Linkages between Informal and Formal Care of the Elderly', *Canadian Journal on Aging/La Revue Canadienne du Vieillissement* 16, 1 (1997); I.A. Connidis, 'Living Arrangement Choices of Older Residents', *Canadian Journal of Sociology/Cahiers canadiens de sociologie* 8 (1983): 359–75.

141. C.J. Rosenthal and L.O. Stone, *How Much Help Is Exchanged in Families? Towards an Understanding of Discrepant Research Findings*, SEDAP Research Paper No. 2, McMaster University, 1999, 9.

142. G. Dalley, *Ideologies of Caring: Rethinking Community and Collectivism* (Basingstoke: Macmillan Education, 1988); S. Neysmith, *Restructuring Caring Labour: Discourse, State Practice, and Everyday Life* (Toronto: Oxford University Press, 2000); J. Finch and D. Groves, *A Labour of Love: Women, Work, and Caring* (London: Routledge & Kegan Paul, 1983).

143. C.J. Rosenthal and A. Martin-Matthews, *Families as Care-Providers Versus Care-Managers? Gender and Type of Care in a Sample of Employed Canadians*, SEDAP Research Paper No. 4, McMaster University, 1999; N. Chappell and A. Blandford, 'Informal and Formal Care: Exploring the Complementarity', *Ageing and Society* 11, 3 (1991): 299–317; M.J. Penning, 'Self-, Informal and Formal Care: Partnerships in Community-Based and Residential Long-Term Settings', *Canadian Journal on Aging/La Revue Canadienne du Vieillissement* 19, Supp. 1 (2000): 75–100; Keefe and Fancey, 'Financial Compensation or Home Help Services'.

144. M. Denton, 'The Linkages between Informal and Formal Care of the Elderly', 30.

145. K. Wilkins and M.P. Beaudet, 'Changes in Social Support in Relation to Seniors' Use of Home Care', *Health Reports* 11, 4 (2000): 45.

146. B. Morrongiello and B. Gottlieb, 'Self-Care among Adults', *Canadian Journal on Aging/La Revue Canadienne du Vieillissement* 19, 1 (2000): 38–9.

147. Employment Insurance Act, S.C. 1996, c. 23.

148. Treasury Board of Canada, Agreement between the Treasury Board and the Professional Institute of the Public Service of Canada, 2000. Available at: <http://www.tbs.sct.gc. ca/Pubs_pol/hrpubs/coll_agre/sh_e.html >.

149. B.M. Blakley and J. Jaffe, 'Coping as a Rural Caregiver: The Impact of Health Care Reforms on Rural Women Informal Caregivers', 1999, 3. Available at: <http://www.pwhce. ca/swan.htm >.

150. D. Cloutier-Fisher and A.E. Joseph, 'Long-Term Care Restructuring in Rural Ontario: Retrieving Community Service User and Provider Narratives', *Social Science and Medicine* 50, 7–8 (2000): 1043.

151. N. Buchignani and C. Armstrong-Esther, 'Informal Care and Older Native Canadians', *Ageing and Society* 19, 1 (1999): 3–32.

152. N. Chubachi, 'Geographies of Nisei Japanese Canadians and Their Attitudes Towards Elderly Long-Term Care', MA thesis (Queen's University, 1999), 1.

153. Rosenthal and Martin-Matthews, *Families as Care-Providers*.

154. K. Cranswick, 'Help Close at Hand: Relocating to Give or Receive Care', *Canadian Social Trends* (Winter 1999): 11–12.

155. Chappell and Blandford, 'Informal and Formal Care'.

156. J.A. Frederick and J.E. Fast, 'Eldercare in Canada: Who Does How Much?', *Canadian Social Trends* (Autumn 1999): 27–30; L.D. Campbell and A. Martin-Matthews, 'Caring Sons: Exploring Men's Involvement in Filial Care', *Canadian Journal on Aging/La Revue Canadienne du Vieillissement* 19, 1 (Spring 2000): 57–79; Morris et al., *The Changing Nature of Home Care*.

157. D. Taylor, 'Making Care Visible: Exploring the Healthwork of People Living with HIV/AIDS in Ontario', forthcoming.

158. Morris et al., *The Changing Nature of Home Care*, vi.

159. C. Fuller, *Reformed or Rerouted? Women and Change in the Health Care System* (Vancouver: British Columbia Centre of Excellence for Women's Health, 1999); K. Wilson and J. Howard, *Missing Links: The Effects of Health Care Privatization on Women in Manitoba and Saskatchewan* (Winnipeg: Prairie Women's Health Centre of Excellence, 2000); P. Armstrong and H. Armstrong, *Women, Privatization and Health Care Reform: The Ontario Case* (Toronto: National Network on Environments and Women's Health, 1999); J. Bernier and M. Dallaire, *What Price Have Women Paid for Health Care Reform? The Situation in Quebec* (Montreal: Le Centre d'excellence pour la santé des femmes—Consortium Université de Montréal, 2000); M. Gurevich, *Privatization in Health Reform from Women's Perspectives: Research, Policy and Responses* (Halifax: Maritime Centre of Excellence for Women's Health, 1999). Revised versions of these reports are in Pat Armstrong et al., *Exposing Privatization: Women and Health Care Reform in Canada* (Aurora, Ont.: Garamond, 2001).

160. K.M. King and P.M. Koop, 'The Influence of the Cardiac Surgery Patient's Sex and Age on Care-Giving Received', *Social Science and Medicine* 48, 12 (1999): 1735–42.

161. M. Stewart, *Chronic Conditions and Caregiving in Canada: Social Support Strategies* (Toronto: University of Toronto Press, 2000).

162. The Roeher Institute, *Personal Relationships of Support between Adults: The Case of Disability* (Toronto, 2001).

163. Blakley and Jaffe, 'Coping as a Rural Caregiver', 5.

164. N.C. Keating et al., *Eldercare in Canada: Context, Content and Consequences*. (Ottawa: Statistics Canada, Housing, Family, and Social Statistics Division, 1999), 17.

165. C. Lindsay, 'Seniors: A Diverse Group Aging Well', *Canadian Social Trends* (Spring 1999): 24–6.

166. Ibid., 25; R. Robb et al., 'Valuation of Unpaid Help by Seniors in Canada: An Empirical Analysis', *Canadian Journal on Aging/La Revue Canadienne du Vieillissement* 18, 4 (1999): 430–46.

167. J. Chen and R. Wilkins, 'Seniors' Needs for Health-Related Personal Assistance', *Health Reports* 10, 11 (1998): 39–50.

168. Rosenthal and Martin-Matthews, *Families as Care-Providers*; Campbell and Martin-Matthews, 'Caring Sons'.

169. M.A.M. Gignac, E.K. Kelloway, and B.H. Gottlieb, 'Impact of Caregiving on Employment: A Mediational Model of Work-Family Conflict', *Canadian Journal on Aging/La Revue Canadienne du Vieillissement* 15, 4 (1996): 525–42.

170. King and Koop, 'The Influence of the Cardiac Surgery Patient's Sex and Age'; J. Aronson and S. Neysmith, 'The Retreat of the State and Long-Term Provision: Implications for Frail Elderly People, Unpaid Family Carers and Paid Home Care Workers', *Studies in Political Economy* 53 (Summer 1997): 37–66; Morris et al., *The Changing Nature of Home Care*; Keefe and Fancey, 'Financial Compensation or Home Help Services'.

171. Pat Armstrong and Hugh Armstrong, *The Double Ghetto: Canadian Women and Their Segregated Work*, 3rd edn (Toronto: McClelland & Stewart, 1993).

172. Rosenthal and Martin-Matthews, *Families as Care-Providers*, 7.

173. For research on Japanese Canadians, see Chubachi, 'Geographies of Nisei Japanese Canadians'. For research on Italians, Japanese, and Anglo seniors, see M. Dorazio-Migliore, 'Eldercare in Context: Narrative, Gender, and Ethnicity', Ph.D. thesis (University of British Columbia, 1999).

174. National Forum on Health, *Synthesis Reports and Issues Papers*, 19.

175. Morris et al., *The Changing Nature of Home Care*.

176. Campbell and Martin-Matthews, 'Caring Sons'.

177. For US research in this area, see K. McCann and E. Wadsworth, 'The Role of Informal Carers in Supporting Gay Men Who Have HIV Related Illness', *AIDS Care* 4, 1 (1992): 25–34. Also see Taylor, 'Making Care Visible'; Campbell and Martin-Matthews, 'Caring Sons'.

178. Buchignani and Armstrong-Esther, 'Informal Care and Older Native Canadians'.

179. K. Cranswick, 'Help Close at Hand: Relocating to Give or Receive Care', *Canadian Social Trends* (Winter 1999): 12.

180. K.M. Kobayashi, *The Nature of Support from Adult Sansei (Third Generation) Children to Older Nisei (Second Generation) Parents in Japanese Canadian Families*, SEDAP Research Paper No. 18, McMaster University, 2000, 15.

181. S. Dhawan, 'Caregiving Stress and Acculturation in East Indian Immigrants: Caring for Their Elders', Ph.D. thesis (Queen's University, 1998).

182. S. Brotman, 'The Incidence of Poverty among Seniors in Canada: Exploring the Impact of Gender, Ethnicity and Race', *Canadian Journal on Aging/La Revue Canadienne du Vieillissement* 17, 2 (1998): 166–85.

183. Buchignani and Armstrong-Esther, 'Informal Care and Older Native Canadians'.

184. Blakley and Jaffe, 'Coping as a Rural Caregiver'.

185. G.M. Gutman, *Literature Review: Characteristics, Service Needs and Service Preferences of Younger Adults with Severe Physical Disabilities* (Burnaby, BC: Simon Fraser University, Gerontology Research Centre, 1995), 26.

186. Ibid., 26–7 .

187. Blakley and Jaffe, 'Coping as a Rural Caregiver'.

188. Dorazio-Migliore, 'Eldercare in Context'.

189. Cranswick, 'Help Close at Hand', 12.

190. H. Moore, 'Caregiving in Parkinson's: A Qualitative Study of the Perceived Impacts on and Needs of Parkinson's Caregivers', M.Sc. thesis (Queen's University, 1997), 66.

191. C. Ward-Griffin, 'Negotiating the Boundaries of Eldercare: The Relationship between Nurses and Family Caregivers', Ph.D. thesis (University of Toronto, 1998), ii.

192. C. Ward-Griffin and P. McKeever, 'Relationships between Nurses and Family Caregivers: Partners in Care?', *Advances in Nursing Science* 22, 3 (2000): 101.

193. Ibid.

194. J.J. Cochrane, P.N. Goering, and J.M. Rogers, 'The Mental Health of Informal Caregivers in Ontario: An Epidemiological Survey', *American Journal of Public Health* 87, 12 (1997): 1.

195. G. Meshefedjian et al., 'Factors Associated with Symptoms of Depression among Informal Caregivers of Demented Elders in the Community', *Gerontologist* 38, 2 (1998): 247–53.

196. Dhawan, 'Caregiving Stress and Acculturation in East Indian Immigrants', 25.

197. Ibid.

198. Statistics Canada, 'Who Cares? Caregiving in the 1990's', *The Daily*, 19 Aug. 1997.

199. MacBride-King, *Caring About Caregiving: The Eldercare Responsibilites of Canadian Workers and the Impact on Employers* (Ottawa: Conference Board of Canada, 1999).

200. Cranswick, 'Help Close at Hand', Table 5.

201. M.A.M. Gignac, E.K. Kelloway, and B.H. Gottlieb, 'Impact of Caregiving on Employment: A Mediational Model of Work-Family Conflict', *Canadian Journal on Aging/La Revue Canadienne du Vieillissement* 15, 4 (1996): 525–42; Rosenthal and Martin-Matthews, *Families as Care-Providers*.

202. N. O'Rourke et al., 'Relative Contribution of Subjective Factors to Expressed Burden among Spousal Caregivers of Suspected Dementia Patients', *Canadian Journal on Aging/La Revue Canadienne du Vieillissement* 15, 4 (1996): 592.

203. H. Echenberg, *Income Security and Support for Persons with Disabilities: Future Directions* (Ottawa: Canadian Labour Congress, 1998); Roeher Institute, *Personal Relationships of Support between Adults*.

204. MacBride-King, *Caring About Caregiving*.

205. J. Aronson, 'Women's Perspectives on Informal Care of the Elderly: Public Ideology and Personal Experience of Giving and Receiving Care', in D. Coburn, C. D'Arcy, and G.M. Torrance, eds, *Health and Canadian Society: Sociological Perspectives* (Toronto: University of Toronto Press, 1998), 399–416.

206. C. Spencer, M. Ashfield, and Vanderbijl, *Abuse and Neglect of Older Adults in Community Settings: An Annotated Bibliography* (Burnaby, BC: Simon Fraser University, Gerontology Research Centre, 1996).

207. J.-P. Lavoie, 'Support Groups for Informal Caregivers Don't Work! Refocus the Groups or the Evaluations?', *Canadian Journal on Aging/La Revue Canadienne du Vieillissement* 14, 3 (1995): 580–603; A. Colantonio, C. Cohen, and S. Corlett, 'Support Needs of Elderly Caregivers of Persons with Dementia', *Canadian Journal on Aging/La Revue Canadienne du Vieillissement* 17, 3 (1998): 330–45.

208. J. Aronson, 'Old Women's Experiences of Needing Care: Choice or Compulsion?', *Canadian Journal on Aging/La Revue Canadienne du Vieillissement* 9, 3 (1990): 244.

209. Ibid.

210. Ibid., 245.

211. Aronson, 'Women's Perspectives on Informal Care of the Elderly'.

212. S. Crompton and A. Kemeny, 'In Sickness and in Health: The Well-Being of Married Seniors', *Canadian Social Trends* (Winter 1999): 26.

213. C.A. Cott and M.A.M. Gignac, 'Independence and Dependence for Older Adults with Osteoarthritis or Osteoporosis', *Canadian Journal on Aging/La Revue Canadienne du Vieillissement* 18, 1 (1999): 13.

214. ARA Consulting Group, *Volunteer Caregiving: Meeting the Challenges of the New Reality* (Toronto: Ministry of Citizenship, 1994), 2.

215. Josephine Rekart, *Public Funds, Private Provision* (Vancouver: University of British Columbia Press, 1993), 60.

216. Leroy Stone, *Family and Friendship Ties Among Canada's Seniors* (Cat. no. 89–508) (Ottawa: Supply and Services Canada, 1988), 46.

217. Statistics Canada, *National Survey of Giving, Volunteering and Participating* (Ottawa, 1997, 2000).

218. Doreen Duchesne, *Giving Freely—Volunteers in Canada* (Statistics Canada Cat. no. 71–535) (Ottawa: Supply and Services Canada, 1989), Table 16.

219. Anita Fochs Heller, *Health and Home: Women as Health Guardians* (Ottawa: Canadian Advisory Council on the Status of Women, 1986), 43.

220. Henry Pold, 'The Gift of Time', *Perspectives on Labour and Income* 2, 2 (Summer 1990): 44.

221. Rekart, *Public Funds, Private Provision*, 114.

222. Ibid.

223. Ibid., 118.

224. Eric Shragge, 'Community Based Practice: Political Alternatives or New State Forms?', in L. Davis and Shragge, eds, *Bureaucracy and Community* (Montreal: Black Rose Books, 1990), 134–78.

CHAPTER 5

1. Leonard Marsh, *Report on Social Security for Canada* (Toronto: University of Toronto Press, 1975), 9.

2. Ibid., 10.

3. Malcolm Taylor, *Health Insurance and Canadian Public Policy* (Montreal and Kingston: McGill-Queen's University Press, 1987), 235.

4. Ibid., 328.

5. Nova Scotia Provincial Health Council, *Toward Achieving Nova Scotia's Health Goals: An Initial Plan of Action for Health Care Reform* (Halifax: Provincial Health Council, 1992), 5.

6. Douglas E. Angus, 'A Great Canadian Prescription: Take Two Commissioned Studies and Call Me in the Morning', in Raisa Deber and Gail Thompson, eds, *Restructuring Canada's Health Services System* (Toronto: University of Toronto Press, 1992), 55.

7. Calculated from Canadian Institute for Health Information (CIHI), *Drug Expenditures in Canada 1985–2000* (Ottawa: CIHI, 2001), Table A.2, Part 2. 'Real' spending is established by eliminating the effects of inflation.

8. Dominion Bureau of Statistics, *Canada 1957* (Ottawa: Queen's Printer, 1957), 264–5.

9. See Nicholas Regush, *Condition Critical* (Toronto: Macmillan, 1987), 28.

10. In 1957, the year state hospital insurance was introduced, provinces were spending 16 per cent of their budgets on health and the federal government was spending 1.2 per cent. See Dominion Bureau of Statistics, *Canada 1957*, 50, 53.

11. Lee Soderstrom, *The Canadian Health System* (London: Croom Helm, 1978), 129.

12. Ibid., 164.

13. Geoffrey York, *The High Price of Health* (Toronto: Lorimer, 1987), 78.

14. National Council of Welfare, *Funding Health and Higher Education: Danger Looming* (Ottawa, 1991), 16–17.

15. Edison Stewart, 'Ontario Health, Social Net Takes $1 Billion Cut', *Toronto Star*, 28 Feb. 1995, A9.

16. 'A Framework to Improve the Social Union for Canadians', 4 Feb. 1999.

17. Working Group on Health System Financing in Canada, *Toward a New Consensus on Health Care Financing in Canada* (Ottawa: Canadian Medical Association, 1993), 30.

18. William G. Tholl, 'Health Care Spending in Canada: Skating Faster on Thinner Ice', in Ake Blomqvist and David M. Brown, eds, *Limits To Care* (Ottawa: C.D. Howe Institute, 1994), 83–4.

19. CIHI, 'Private Sector Spending in Canada', *National Health Expenditure Trends, 1975–1998* (Ottawa: CIHI, 1998), 31.

20. CIHI, *Drug Expenditures in Canada 1985–2000*, Table A.2, Part 2.

21. British Columbia, *Closer to Home*, vol. 2 (1991), 3.

22. Taylor, *Health Insurance*, 234.

23. Statistics Canada, 'Health care services—recent trends', *Health Reports* 11, 3 (Winter 1999).

24. Taylor, *Health Insurance*, 176–8.

25. Philip Enterline, Allison McDonald, J. Corbett McDonald, and Nicholas Steinmetz, 'The Distribution of Medical Services Before and After "Free" Medical Care', *Medical Care* 11, 4 (July–Aug. 1973): 285.

26. Statistics Canada, 'Health care services—recent trends', 91.

27. The same, of course, cannot be said of health services outside medicare. In the Statistics Canada study, only 39 per cent of low-income Canadians, for example, had contacted a dentist/orthodontist in the previous 12 months, as against 79 per cent of high-income Canadians. Significant inequalities were also reported in dental insurance coverage, drug insurance coverage, and contact with alternative/complementary practitioners such as chiropractors. Statistics Canada, 'Health care services—recent trends'.

28. Taylor, *Health Insurance*, 253.

29. Philip Enterline et al., 'Effects of "Free" Medical Care on Medical Practice—The Quebec Experience', *New England Journal of Medicine* 288, 22 (1 May 1973): 1152–5.

30. David U. Himmelstein, James P. Lewontin, and Steffie Woolhandler, 'Who Administers? Who Cares? Medical Administrative and Clinical Employment in the United States and Canada', *American Journal of Public Health* 86, 2 (Feb. 1996). One US doctor we recently interviewed revealed that his three-physician group practice employs 10 administrative staff, in large measure to handle billing. When we have repeated this report to other US health professionals and policy analysts, none has found it at all surprising. For more discussion of comparative administrative costs, see Pat Armstrong and Hugh Armstrong with Claudia Fegan, *Universal Health Care: What the United States Can Learn from the Canadian Experience* (New York: New Press, 1998), esp. 113–17.

31. Arnold Relman, 'Salaried Physicians and Economic Incentives', *New England Journal of Medicine* 319, 12 (Sept. 1988): 784.

32. Jerry White, *Hospital Strike!* (Toronto: Thompson, 1990), 41.

33. See ibid.; Pat Armstrong, Jacqueline Choiniere, and Elaine Day, *Vital Signs* (Toronto: Garamond, 1993).

34. Donald Swartz, 'The Politics of Reform: Conflict and Accommodation in Canadian Health Policy', in David Coburn et al., *Health and Canadian Society*, 2nd edn (Richmond Hill, Ont.: Fitzhenry & Whiteside, 1987), 568–89.

35. World Economic Forum, *World Competitiveness Report 1991* (Lausanne, Switzerland: Institut pour l'étude des méthodes de direction de l'entreprise, 1992).

36. David U. Himmelstein and Steffie Woolhandler, *The National Health Program Book* (Monroe, Maine: Common Courage Press, 1994), 40.

37. Dawn Walton, 'Ontario close to overtaking Michigan as car capital', *Globe and Mail*, 30 Nov. 1999, A5.

38. Douglas Angus, Ludwig Auer, J. Edan Cloutier, and Terry Albert, *Sustainable Health Care for Canada* (Ottawa: Queen's University of Ottawa Economic Projects, 1995), 43.

39. OECD, *OECD Health Systems: Facts and Trends 1960–1991*, vol. 1. Health Policy Studies No. 3 (Paris: OECD, 1993), Table 3.2.6. By 1997 the Canadian rate had dropped to 6 per 1,000 live births. World Health Organization, *The World Health Report* (Geneva: WHO, 1998), Table A1.

40. Angus et al., *Sustainable Health Care*, 43.

41. Statistics Canada, *Historical Statistics of Canada*, 2nd edn (Ottawa: Supply and Services Canada, 1983), Series B59–64.

42. OECD, *OECD Health Systems*, Table 3.2.3.

43. Taylor, *Health Insurance*, 173–4.

44. Quoted in Tim Harper, 'Medicare Under the Knife', *Toronto Star*, 11 Mar. 1995, B1.

45. Angus et al., *Sustainable Health Care*.

46. Statistics Canada, *Historical Statistics of Canada*, 2nd edn, Series B514–516.

47. Dennis Guest, *The Emergence of Social Security in Canada*, 3rd edn (Vancouver: University of British Columbia Press, 1997), ch. 4.

48. OECD, *OECD Health Systems*, Table 4.2.1.

49. Angus et al., *Sustainable Health Care*, 8.

50. Malcolm Brown, *Health Economics and Policy* (Toronto: McClelland & Stewart, 1991), 34.

51. Bernard Blishen, *Doctors in Canada* (Toronto: University of Toronto Press, 1991), Table 3.7; 'Canada's Physicians Aging: CIHI Report', *CIHI Directions* (Oct./Nov. 2000): 3.

52. Statistics Canada, *91 Census: Employment Income By Occupation* (Cat. no. 93–332), Table 1.

53. Taylor, *Health Insurance*, 42.

54. See B. Singh Bolaria and Rosemary Bolaria, eds, *Racial Minorities in Medicine and Health* (Halifax: Fernwood, 1994).

55. Harper, 'Medicare Under the Knife'.

56. Robert Evans, 'Health Care Reform: "The Issue From Hell"', *Policy Options* (July–Aug. 1993): 37.

57. CIHI, *National Health Expenditure Trends, 1975–1998* (Ottawa: CIHI, 1998), Table 2.

58. CIHI and Statistics Canada, *Health Care in Canada 2001* (Ottawa: CIHI, 2001), 71–2.

59. CIHI, *Drug Expenditures in Canada 1985–2000*, Table A.2, Part 2.

60. Evans, 'Health Care Reform', 37 (emphasis in original).

61. Calculated from ibid.

62. CIHI and Statistics Canada, *Health Care in Canada 2001*, 75.

63. OECD, *OECD Health Systems*, Table 5.2.8.

64. Ibid., Table 5.2.7.

65. 'What happens to patient care when you reduce the number of hospital beds in a big city?', *Quid Novi?* Canadian Health Services Research Foundation newsletter 2, 4 (Winter 1999): 4.

66. Health Services Utilization Working Group, *When Less Is Better: Using Canada's Hospitals Efficiently*. A Report to the Federal/Provincial/Territorial Deputy Ministers of Health (Ottawa, 1994), 52.

67. Health Services Restructuring Commission, *Ottawa Health Services Restructuring Report* (Toronto: HSRC, Feb. 1997), 29–32.

68. CIHI and Statistics Canada, *Health Care in Canada 2001*, 75.

69. CIHI, *Health Care in Canada 2001*, 75–6.

70. CIHI, *Drug Expenditures in Canada 1985–2000*, 4.

71. Calculated from ibid., Table A.2, Part 2.

72. Health Canada, *National Health Expenditures in Canada, 1975–1993* (Ottawa: Supply and Services Canada, 1994), Table 8A.

73. OECD, *OECD Health Systems*, Table 5.

74. CIHI, *Drug Expenditures in Canada 1985–2000*, Table A.2, Part 2.

75. Bernie Loeppky, 'Made in Canada Health Reform', *Leadership* 3, 2 (Mar.–Apr. 1995): 13.

76. Tholl, 'Health Care Spending in Canada', 56.

77. Health Services Utilization Working Group, *When Less Is Better*.

78. Ralph Sutherland and Jane Fulton, *Spending Smarter and Spending Better* (Ottawa: The Health Group, 1994).

79. Synthesis Report of the Cost-Effectiveness of the Canadian Health Care System Project, Executive Summary, *Sustaining Health Care for Canada* (Ottawa: mimeo, 1995), 6.

80. Health Canada, *National Health Expenditures*, Table 6C.

81. Milton Terris, 'Lessons from Canada's Health Program', *Technology Review* (Feb.–Mar. 1990): 31.

82. Miro Certenig and Robert Matas, 'BC can't limit where MDs set up practices, court rules', *Globe and Mail*, 2 Aug. 1997, A1, A7.

83. Richard Mackie, 'Project not helping ease MD shortage', *Globe and Mail*, 9 July 2001, A7; Vanessa Lu, 'Billing seen as obstacle to health reform', *Toronto Star*, 9 July 2001, A4.

84. C. David Naylor, Geoffrey M. Anderson, and Vivel Goel, *Patterns of Health Care in Ontario* (Toronto: Institute for Clinical Evaluative Services, 1994).

85. *Hotline* #14, 27–8.

86. Allen R. Myerson, 'Helping Health Insurers Say No', *New York Times*, 20 Mar. 1995, Business Day. This firm, Milliman and Robertson, was subsequently hired by Ontario's Health Services Restructuring Commission to provide the technical support for its proposals on reforming primary care.

87. See, for example, Robert Evans, *Strained Mercy: The Economics of Canadian Health Care* (Toronto: Butterworths, 1984), 149–50; J. McPhee, 'Further Discussion on Saskatchewan

CHA Clinics Evaluation', *Canadian Medical Association Journal* 110, 2 (1974); York, *The High Price of Health*, 110–13.

88. York, *The High Price of Health*, 113–17; Stan Rands, *Privilege and Policy* (Saskatoon: Community Health Cooperative Federation, 1994); Marc Renaud, 'Reform or Illusion? An Analysis of the Quebec State Intervention in Health', in Coburn et al., *Health and Canadian Society*, 590–614.

89. York, *The High Price of Health*, 186.

90. Lisa Wright, 'Door Opens for U.S. Health Firms', *Toronto Star*, 2 Dec. 1995. A3.

91. John Eyles et al., 'A Needs-based Methodology for Allocating Health Care Resources in Ontario, Canada: Development and an Application', *Social Science and Medicine* 33, 4 (1991): 490. See also Pat Armstrong and Hugh Armstrong, *Primary Health Care Reform: A Discussion Paper* (Ottawa: Canadian Health Coalition, 2001).

92. CIHI, *Health Care in Canada 2001*, 75.

93. Michael Rachlis and Carol Kushner, *Strong Medicine* (Toronto: HarperCollins, 1994), 170.

94. Ibid., 171.

95. New York State Department of Health, 'Your Rights as a Hospital Patient in New York State', mimeo, n.d.

96. 'DRGs–Making Them Work for You', *Nursing* (1985).

97. Robert Sherrill, 'Medicine and the Madness of the Market', *The Nation* (9–16 Jan. 1995): 50.

98. Melinda Mitchell et al., 'Determining Cost of Direct Nursing Care by DRGs', *Nursing Management* (Apr. 1984): 29–32.

99. Letty Roth Piper, 'Accounting for Nursing Functions in DRGs', *Nursing Management* (Nov. 1983): 7–8.

100. Dave Lindorff, *The Rise of the For-Profit Hospital Chains* (New York: Bantam, 1992), 159.

101. Sherrill, 'Medicine and the Madness', 50.

102. Lindorff, *The Rise*, 25.

103. Phillip Hassen, *Rx for Hospitals: New Hope for Medicare in the Nineties* (Toronto: Stoddart, 1993), 2.

104. See Loeppky, 'Made in Canada', 13.

105. Statistics Canada, *Hospital Annual Statistics 1991–92* (Cat. no. 83–242, Part 4) (Ottawa: Minister of Industry, Science and Technology, 1994), Table 18. This kind of breakdown is no longer available. The Statistics Canada publication has been discontinued.

106. Ibid., Table 19.

107. Statistics Canada, *1991 Census: Industry and Class of Worker* (Cat. no. 93–326) (Ottawa: Minister of Industry, Science and Technology, 1993), Table 1.

108. Calculated from CIHI, *Canada's Health Care Providers* (Ottawa: CIHI, 2001), 9.

109. Arlene Billinkoff, 'NDP Attack Warns McCrae', *Winnipeg Free Press*, 9 Nov. 1993, editorial.

110. Ibid.

111. Eva Ryten, *A Statistical Picture of the Past, Present and Future of Registered Nurses in Canada* (Ottawa: Canadian Nurses Association, 1997), Table 6.

112. This percentage is calculated for 1999 from CIHI, *Supply and Distribution of Registered Nurses in Canada* (Ottawa: CIHI, 2000), Table 10.0.a.

113. Statistics Canada, *Hospital Annual Statistics*, 1993 and 1994, Table 19.

114. Peter Bergmanis, 'Total Quality Improvement: Continuous Quality Improvement. Implications for Patient Care and the Management of Health Care Resources. A Submission to "A Picture of Health"', Ontario Federation of Labour Public Forum, London, Ont., 1994, 8.

115. 'APM: "Operation Excellence" or Operation Extinction?', *California Nurse* (June 1994): 7.

116. Pat Armstrong et al., *Pay Equity in Predominately Female Establishments: Health Care Sector*. Prepared for the Pay Equity Commission, Ontario, 1988, 129–31.

117. Health and Welfare Canada, *Privatization in the Canadian Health Care System: Assertions, Evidence, Ideology and Options* (Ottawa, 1985), 42.

118. Quoted in Jim Carr, 'Consultant Brews Trouble, American Nurse Warns', *Winnipeg Free Press*, 6 June 1993, editorial.

119. Bergmanis, 'Total Quality Improvement'.

120. Quoted in Robert Goodall, 'Continuous Quality Improvement Revisited', *Leadership* 2, 3 (May–June 1993): 7.

121. CIHI, *Health Care in Canada 2001*, 27.

122. Unpublished membership data from the Canadian Association of Occupational Therapists.

123. Art Chamberlain, 'Rehabilitation on a roll', *Toronto Star*, 12 Sept. 1994.

124. Statistics Canada, *Hospital Annual Statistics 1991–92*, Part 5, Table 15.

125. Price Waterhouse Management Consultants, quoted in CUPE Research Department, *False Savings, Hidden Costs: Calculating the Costs of Contracting Out and Privatization* (Ottawa, n.d.), 20.

126. CUPE Research Department, *The Americanization of Health Care*, Research paper no. 5 (Ottawa, n.d.), 10.

127. The number of acute-care beds per capita in Ontario is about 75 per cent of the national average. David McKinnon (CEO, Ontario Hospital Association), 'Safeguarding Patient Care: Notes for Remarks to the Federal Standing Committee on Finance', 16 Oct. 2001, 2.

128. John Ibbitson, 'Just how many beds does Ontario need to reform the system?', *Globe and Mail*, 6 Jan. 2000, A6.

129. Ontario Ministry of Health, *Annual Report, 1992–93* (Toronto: Ministry of Health, 1994), 5. See also 'Safeguarding Patient Care'.

130. William G. Tholl, in Scott Feschuk and Edward Greenspon, 'Canada's Hidden Care System', *Globe and Mail*, 28 May 1994, D1, D5.

131. See *Notice to patients* from Canadian Medical Laboratories Limited, 4 Apr. 1994.

132. In Dorothy Lipovenko, '"Core" Services For Elderly Urged', *Globe and Mail*, 2 May 1995, A3.

133. Lisa Priest, 'Fourteen Hospitals' Budgets Rejected', *Toronto Star*, 28 Apr. 1995, A1.

134. Statistics Canada, *Hospital Annual Statistics 1991–92*, part 5, Tables 15 and 16.

135. Lisa Priest, 'Sunnybrook to Privatize Lab and Sell Services to U.S.', *Toronto Star*, 24 Feb. 1995, A2.

136. Art Chamberlain, 'Healthy Profits for Lab Partners', *Toronto Star*, 2 May 1995, D1.

137. Caroline Mallen and Valerie Lawlon, 'Second Ontario hospital gets a private touch', *Toronto Star*, 8 Dec. 2001, A37.

138. Priest, 'Sunnybrook to Privatize Lab', A2.

139. Chamberlain, 'Healthy Profits', D1.

140. Katherine Harding and Vanessa Lu, 'Private cancer centre under fire', *Toronto Star*, 14 Dec. 2001, A1, A26.

141. Calculated from CIHI, *National Health Expenditure Trends, 1975–2000*, accessed at <www.cihi.ca/facts/nhex2000/table_A.3.1_part1>, 15 May 2001; and from Conference Board of Canada, *The Future Cost of Health Care in Canada, 2000 to 2020* (Ottawa: Conference Board, 2001), Table 1. These cuts to hospital spending do not appear to be sustainable. Using the CIHI and Conference Board estimates, we calculate that hospital spending will increase on a real per capita basis by an anticipated 5.39 per cent between 1998 and 2000.

142. Lisa Priest, 'Should We Rate Our Hospitals?', *Toronto Star*, 11 Apr. 1995, A20.

143. Judy Haiven, 'Mediscare', *Mother Jones* (Mar.–Apr. 1991): 51–69.

144. Feschuk and Greenspon, 'Canada's Hidden Care System', D5.

145. Sedgewick Noble Lowndes, *Health Care Alert. OHIP Cuts Back—Sedgewick Noble Lowndes Has the Answer*, pamphlet, June 1994.

146. See 'Health Update', *Maclean's*, 26 Sept. 1994, an advertising feature from MIT appearing in the issue.

147. See, for example, Canada, Senate, Standing Senate Committee on Social Affairs, Science and Technology (Kirby Committee), *The Health of Canadians—The Federal Role*, vol. 4, *Issues and Options* (Ottawa, 2001), 62–3.

148. Greg Stoddart, Morris Barer, Robert Evans, and Vanda Bhatia, *Why Not User Charges? The Real Issues* (Toronto: Premier's Council on Health, Well-Being and Social Justice, 1993). The other titles in the series, all prepared by members of this team and published by the Premier's Council in 1993 and 1994, are: *The Truth about User Fees*; *Who Are the Zombie Masters, and What Do They Want?*; *Charging Peter to Pay Paul: Accounting for the Financial Effects of User Charges in Health Care*; *It's Not the Money, It's the Principle: Why User Charges for Some Services and Not for Others?*; *The Remarkable Tenacity of User Charges*; and *User Charges, Snares and Delusions: Another Look at the Literature*. See also Canadian Health Services Research Foundation, *Myth: User Fees Would Stop Waste and Ensure Better Use of the Health System*, Mythbuster series (Ottawa: CHSRF, 2001).

149. Barer et al., *The Remarkable Tenacity of User Charges*, 8.

150. Ibid., 27.

151. Stoddart et al., *Why Not User Charges?*, 7.

152. Stoddart et al., *User Charges, Snares and Delusions*, 25.

153. Quoted in Stoddart et al., *Why Not User Charges?*, 7.

154. Evans et al., *Charging Peter to Pay Paul*, 2.

155. Ibid., 3.

156. Stoddart et al., *Why Not User Charges?*, 20.

157. Evans et al., *Charging Peter to Pay Paul*, 2.

158. Evans et al., *Who Are the Zombie Masters?*, 12.

159. Harvey G. Simmons, *Unbalanced: Mental Health Policy in Ontario, 1930–1989* (Toronto: Wall and Thompson, 1990), 160.

160. Ibid.

161. Ibid., 164.

162. Ibid., 200.

163. Sue Gilbert, 'Community versus Hospital: The Costs of Caring for Level III Patients', *Leadership* 1, 5 (Sept.–Oct. 1992): 19.

164. For a sampling of the recent literature on the impacts of increased reliance on home care for paid and volunteer providers, see Jane Aronson and Sheila Neysmith, 'The Work of Visiting Homemakers in the Context of Cost Cutting in Long Term Care', *Canadian Journal of Public Health* 87, 6 (Nov.–Dec. 1996): 422–5; Neysmith and Aronson, 'Working Conditions in Home Care: Negotiating Race and Class Boundaries in Gendered Work', *International Journal of Health Services* 27, 3 (1997): 479–99; Roberta Robb et al., 'Valuation of Unpaid Help by Seniors in Canada: An Empirical Analysis', *Canadian Journal on Aging* 18, 4 (1999): 430–46; Jane Jenson and Susan D. Phillips, 'Distinctive Trajectories: Homecare and the Voluntary Sector in Québec and Ontario', in Keith G. Banting, ed., *The Nonprofit Sector in Canada: Roles and Relationships* (Kingston: School of Policy Studies, Queen's University, 2000), 29–67; Denise Cloutier-Fisher and Alun E. Joseph, 'Long-term care restructuring in rural Ontario: retrieving community service user and provider narratives', *Social Science and Medicine* 50 (2000): 1037–45.

165. Quoted in Dennis Bueckert, 'Victorian Order of Nurses faces bleak future', *Toronto Star*, 28 Dec. 2000, A3.

166. Ontario, Health Industries Advisory Committee to the Ministry of Health, *Healthy and Wealthy* (Toronto: Queen's Printer for Ontario, 1994), iii.

167. Ibid., iv.

168. Evans et al., *Who Are the Zombie Masters?*, 6.

169. See Matthew Sanger, *Reckless Abandon: Canada, the GATS and the Future of Health Care* (Ottawa: Canadian Centre for Policy Alternatives, 2001).

170. Quoted in Joyce Nelson, 'Dr Rockefeller will see you now: The Hidden Players Privatizing Canada's Health Care System', *Canadian Forum* (Jan.–Feb. 1995): 7.

171. Quoted in Health Canada, *National Health Expenditures in Canada*, 11.

172. Quoted in Health and Welfare Canada, *Privatization in the Canadian Health Care System*, 19.

173. Ibid., 18.

174. Ibid., 23.

175. Ibid., 52.

CHAPTER 6

1. Nova Scotia, Provincial Health Council, *Toward Achieving Nova Scotia's Health Goals: An Initial Plan of Action for Health Care Reform* (Halifax, 1992), 53.

2. Alberta, Premier's Commission on Future Health Care for Albertans, *The Rainbow Report: Our Vision For Health* (Edmonton, 1989), 6.

3. British Columbia, Ministry of Health and Ministry Responsible for Seniors, *New Directions for a Healthy British Columbia* (Victoria, 1993), 13.

4. Robert Evans, 'Health Care Reform: "The Issue From Hell"', *Policy Options* (July–Aug. 1993): 37.

5. Ralph Sutherland and Jane Fulton, *Spending Smarter and Spending Less* (Ottawa: Canadian Hospital Association Press, 1994), 5.

6. Merck Frosst Canada, *Health Care in Canada: A National Survey of Health Care Providers and Users* (Montreal, 2000), 15.

7. Michael O'Neill, 'Community Participation in Quebec's Health System: A Strategy to Curtail Community Empowerment', *International Journal of Health Services* 22, 2 (1992): 290.

8. Ibid., 291.

9. Joan Eakin, 'Survival of the Fittest? The Democratization of Hospital Administration in Quebec', in David Coburn et al., eds, *Health and Canadian Society*, 2nd edn (Markham, Ont.: Fitzhenry & Whiteside, 1987), 515.

10. Ibid., 530.

11. Quoted in O'Neill, 'Community Participation', 291.

12. Sharmila Mhatre and Raisa Deber, 'From Equal Access to Health Care to Equitable Access to Health: A Review of Canadian Provincial Health Commissions and Reports', *International Journal of Health Services* 22, 4 (1992): 651.

13. Pat Armstrong and Hugh Armstrong, 'Women, Privatization and Health Care Reform: The Ontario Case', in Pat Armstrong et al., eds, *Exposing Privatization: Women and Health Reform in Canada* (Aurora, Ont.: Garamond, 2001).

14. Canada, *Task Force Report on the Costs of Health Services in Canada* (Willard Report) (Ottawa: Queen's Printer, 1969).

15. Peg Folsom, Jodey Porter, Don Richmond, Ron Saddington, and Joy Warkentin, *Devolution of Health and Social Services in Ontario: Refocusing the Debate* (Toronto: Premier's Council on Health, Well-Being and Social Justice, 1994), Executive Summary.

16. Ibid., 1.

17. Ibid., 11.

18. See Peg Folsom, Jodey Porter, Don Richmond, Ron Saddington, and Joy Warkentin, *A Framework for Evaluating Devolution* (Toronto: Premier's Council on Health, Well-Being and Social Justice, 1994).

19. Donna Wilson, 'Regional Health Planning and Delivery in Alberta: A Basic Cost Benefit Analysis in Response to a Health System Performance Issue', 2000, quoted in C.M Scott, T. Horne, and W.E. Thurston, eds, 'The Differential Impact of Health Care Privatization on Women in Alberta', in Armstrong et al., eds, *Exposing Privatization*.

20. W.E. Thurston, C.M. Scott, and B.A. Crow, 'Social Change, Policy Development and the

Influence on Women's Health', Synthesis Paper for the Fifth National Health Promotion Conference, Halifax, July 1997, 17–18.

21. John Church and Tom Noseworthy, 'Fiscal Austerity Through Decentralization', in Daniel Drache and Terry Sullivan, eds, *Health Reform: Public Success, Private Failure* (New York: Routledge, 1999), 199.

22. Ibid., 189.

23. Barry Appleton, 'International Agreements and National Health Plans: NAFTA', in Drache and Sullivan, eds, *Health Reform*; 87–104.

24. Mhatre and Deber, 'From Equal Access', 664.

25. Cited in Jocelyne Bernier and Marlène Dallaire, 'The Price of Health Care Reform for Women: the Case of Quebec', in Armstrong et al., eds, *Exposing Privatization*.

26. O'Neill, 'Community Participation', 289.

27. Ibid., 292.

28. Frederic Lesemann, *Services and Circuses* (Montreal: Black Rose, 1984), 245–6.

29. J. Godbout, 'Is Consumer Control Possible in Health Care Services? The Quebec Case', *International Journal of Health Services* 11 (1981): 151–67.

30. Mirielle Tremblay, quoted in Bernier and Dallaire, 'The Price of Health Care Reform for Women'.

31. Godbout, 'Is Consumer Control Possible?'.

32. Quoted in Marilyn Ferdinand, 'Regionalization: Canadian-style Integrated Networks', *Journal of Health Care Resource Management* (January 1995): 14.

33. Lesemann, *Services and Circuses*, 195.

34. For a discussion of this process in hospitals, see Doris Grinspun, 'Taking Care of the Bottom Line: Shifting Paradigms in Hospital Management', in Diana L. Gustafson, ed., *Care and Consequence: The Impact of Health Care Reform* (Halifax: Fernwood, 2000), 25–48.

35. Josephine Rekart, *Public Funds: Private Provision* (Vancouver: University of British Columbia Press, 1993), 102.

36. Ibid., 114.

37. Regroupement Intersectoriel des Organismes Communautaires de Montréal, 1998, cited in Bernier and Dallaire, 'The Price of Health Care Reform for Women'.

38. National Forum on Health, *Canada Health Action: Building on the Legacy*, vol. 2, *Synthesis Reports and Issues Papers*, 'Creating a Culture of Evidence-Based Decision-Making' (Ottawa: National Forum on Health, 1997), 5.

39. Ibid., 11.

40. British Columbia, Royal Commission on Health Care and Costs, *Closer to Home: A Summary Report* (Victoria, 1991), 12.

41. Carol Kushner and Michael Rachlis, 'Civic Lessons: Strategies to Increase Consumer Involvement in Health Policy Development', in National Forum on Health, *Evidence and Information: Papers Commissioned by the National Forum on Health*, vol. 5 (Ottawa: National Forum on Health, 1998), 306.

42. Stewart Ranson and John Stewart, 'Citizenship and Government: The Challenge for Management in the Public Domain', *Political Studies* 37, 1 (1989): 5–24.

43. John Ralston Saul, 'Health Care at the End of the Twentieth Century: Confusing Symptoms for Systems', in Margaret A. Sommerville, ed., *Do We Care? Renewing Canada's Commitment to Health*, Conference Proceedings, Directions for Canadian Health Care (Montreal and Kingston: McGill-Queen's University Press, 1999). 14.

44. In Sutherland and Fulton, *Spending Smarter and Spending Less*, 77.

45. Ibid.

46. Dave Lindorff, *Marketplace Medicine: The Rise of the For-Profit Hospital Chains* (New York: Bantam, 1992), 24.

47. Joel Lexchin, *The Real Pushers: A Critical Analysis of the Canadian Drug Industry* (Vancouver: New Star Books, 1984); Lexchin, 'Pharmaceuticals: Politics and Policy', in Pat Armstrong,

Hugh Armstrong, and David Coburn, eds, *Unhealthy Times: Political Economy Perspectives on Health and Care in Canada* (Toronto: Oxford University Press, 2001).

48. Lesemann, *Services and Circuses*, 249.

49. Nona Glazer, *Women's Paid and Unpaid Labor* (Philadelphia: Temple University Press, 1993), 133.

50. Ibid., 111.

51. See, for example, Lexchin, *The Real Pushers*; Andrew Chetley, *A Healthy Business: World Health and the Pharmaceutical Industry* (London: Zed Books, 1990).

52. Lindorff, *Marketplace Medicine*, 28.

53. See Pat Armstrong et al. *Medical Alert: New Work Organization in Health Care* (Toronto: Garamond Press,1997); Gina Feldberg and Robert Vipond, 'The Virus of Consumerism', in Drache and Sullivan, eds, *Health Reform*, 48–64, for further discussion of the use of the term 'consumer' in health care.

54. Quoted in Lesemann, *Services and Circuses*, 145.

55. Lindorff, *Marketplace Medicine*, 25.

56. Walt Bogdanich, *The Great White Lie: Dishonesty, Waste and Incompetence in the Medical Community* (New York: Touchstone, 1991).

57. In Robert Sherrill, 'Medicine and the Madness of the Market', *The Nation* (9–16 Jan. 1995): 53.

58. Cathy Charles, Mary Gould, Larry Chambers, Bernie O'Brien, R. Brian Heynes, and Roberta Labelle, 'How Was Your Hospital Stay? Reports about Their Care in Canadian Hospitals', CHEPA Working Paper 94–3 (Hamilton, Ont.: McMaster University, 1994).

59. Lindorff, *Marketplace Medicine*, 18.

60. Glazer, *Women's Paid and Unpaid Labor*, 113.

61. Lindorff, *Marketplace Medicine*, 18.

62. Quoted in Joyce Nelson, 'Dr Rockefeller Will See You Now: The Hidden Players Privatizing Canada's Health Care System', *Canadian Forum* (Jan.–Feb. 1995): 8.

63. Colleen Fuller, *Free Trade and Canadian Health* (Vancouver: Health Sciences Association of British Columbia, 1994).

64. See Paul Leduc Browne, *Unsafe Practices: Restructuring and Privatization in Ontario Health Care* (Ottawa: Canadian Centre for Policy Alternatives, 2000); Colleen Fuller, *Caring for Profit: How Corporations Are Taking Over Canada's Health Care System* (Ottawa: Canadian Centre for Policy Alternatives, 1998).

65. Lesemann, *Services and Circuses*, 138–9.

66. Ibid., 182–3.

67. Ibid., 184–5.

68. See Bernard Blishen, *Doctors in Canada* (Toronto: University of Toronto Press, 1991).

69. Carolyn Tuohy, 'Medicine and the State in Canada', *Canadian Journal of Political Science* 21 (1988): 267–96.

70. The Institute for Clinical Evaluative Sciences began with a general practice atlas and has moved on to examine patterns in the treatment of specific conditions.

71. B.H. Gray and M.J. Field, eds, *Controlling Costs and Changing Patient Care: The Role of Utilization Management* (Washington: National Academy Press, 1989).

72. Health Services Utilization Working Group, *When Less Is Better: Using Canada's Hospitals Efficiently* (Ottawa, 1994), 9.

73. 'MD Exodus Threatens Health Care, MPs Told', *Toronto Star*, 11 May 1995, A13.

74. Canadian Health Services Research Foundation, 'Canadian Doctors are Leaving for the United States in Droves', *Mythbusters* (2001).

75. Raisa Deber, Sharmila Mhatre, and G. Ross Baker, 'A Review of Provincial Initiatives', in Ake Blomqvist and David M. Brown, eds, *Limits to Care* (Ottawa: C.D. Howe Institute,

1994), 117.

76. Pat Armstrong and Hugh Armstrong, *The Double Ghetto: Canadian Women and Their Segregated Work*, 3rd edn (Toronto: McClelland & Stewart, 1994).

77. Pat Armstrong, Jacqueline Choiniere, and Elaine Day, *Vital Signs: Nursing in Transition* (Toronto: Garamond, 1993).

78. Pat Armstrong, 'Professions, Unions, or What? Learning from Nurses', in Linda Briskin and Patricia McDermott, eds, *Women Challenging Unions* (Toronto: University of Toronto Press, 1993), 304–42.

79. Heather Clemenson, 'Unionization and Women in the Service Sector', *Perspectives on Labour and Income* 1, 2 (Autumn 1989): Table 3.

80. Pat Armstrong and Hugh Armstrong, 'Limited Possibilities and Possible Limits for Pay Equity: Within and Beyond the Ontario Legislation', in Judy Fudge and Patricia McDermott, eds, *Just Wages* (Toronto: University of Toronto Press, 1991), 110–21.

81. Premier's Council on Health Strategy, *Achieving the Vision: Health Human Resources* (Toronto, 1991), 5.

82. Laura Sky, *Lean and Mean Health Care: The Creation of the Generic Worker and the Deregulation of Health Care*. Health Research Project Working Paper 95–3 (Toronto: Ontario Federation of Labour, June 1995), 21.

83. Ibid., 26.

84. Ibid., 7.

85. Hugh Armstrong, 'The Health Reform Agenda and Industrial Relations Under Social Democratic Regimes', Working Paper 95–1, Health Research Project, Ontario Federation of Labour, 1995.

86. Sheila Neysmith and Barbara Nichols, 'Working Conditions in Home Care: Comparing Three Groups of Workers', *Canadian Journal on Aging* 13, 3 (1994): 180.

87. Susan Sherwin, *No Longer Patient: Feminist Ethics and Health Care* (Philadelphia: Temple University Press, 1992), 7.

88. Winifred Wallace Hunsburger, *One Mother to Another* (Saskatoon: Fifth House Publishers, 1992).

89. Ann Oakley, *The Captured Womb* (Oxford: Basil Blackwell, 1984).

90. Hunsburger, *One Mother to Another*, 57.

91. Blishen, *Doctors in Canada*, 153.

92. Ontario, Ministry of Citizenship, 'The Advocacy Act. A General Overview', pamphlet, 1994.

93. *Hotline* #13.

94. Elaine Carey, 'Elderly Abused at Home, Study Finds', *Toronto Star*, 13 May 1995, A3.

95. *Family Impact Study*. A study prepared for the Victorian Order of Nurses (Grey-Bruce Branch) by Rigbey & Associates, Owen Sound, Ont., 1994.

96. Ruth Lundy, speaking at an Ontario Public Service Employees Forum on Health Care, Toronto, 25 May 1995.

Bibliography

Abraham, C. 1999. 'Early Release of Newborns Linked to Health Problems', *Globe and Mail*, 10 Aug., A1–2.

Achterberg, J. 1991. *Woman as Healer*. Boston: Shambhala.

Agnew, G.H. 1974. *Canadian Hospitals, 1920 to 1970: A Dramatic Half Century*. Toronto: University of Toronto Press.

Aiken, L.H. et al. 2001. 'Nurses' Report on Hospital Care in Five Countries', *Health Affairs* (May–June 2001): 43–53.

Allahan, A.L., and J.E. Cote. 1998. *Richer and Poorer: The Structure of Inequality in Canada*. Toronto: Lorimer.

Almberg, B.E., M. Grafstrom, et al. 2000. 'Caregivers of Relatives with Dementia: Experiences Encompassing Social Support and Bereavement', *Aging & Mental Health* 4, 1: 82–9.

Anderson, C.S., J. Linto, et al. 1995. 'A population-based assessment of the impact and burden of caregiving for long-term stroke survivors', *Stroke* 26, 5: 843–9.

Anderson, G., and P.S. Hussey. 2001. 'Comparing Health System Performance in OECD Countries', *Health Affairs* (May–June 2001): 219–32.

Anderson, J. 1993. *Total Quality Management: Should Unions Buy Into TQM?* Toronto: Ontario Federation of Labour.

———— and H. Elfert. 1989. 'Managing Chronic Illness in the Family: Women as Caretakers', *Journal of Advanced Nursing* 14: 735–43.

Angus, D.E. 1992. 'A Great Canadian Prescription: Take Two Commissioned Studies and Call Me in the Morning', in R. Deber and G. Thompson, eds, *Restructuring Canada's Health Services System*. Toronto: University of Toronto Press, 49–62.

————, L. Auer, J.E. Cloutier, and T. Albert. 1995. *Sustainable Health Care for Canada*. Ottawa: Queen's-University of Ottawa, Economic Projects.

Appleton, B. 1999. 'International Agreements and National Health Plans: NAFTA', in D. Drache and T. Sullivan, eds, *Health Reform: Public Success, Private Failure*. New York: Routledge.

ARA Consulting Group. 1994. *Volunteer Caregiving: Meeting the Challenges of the New Reality*. Toronto: Ministry of Citzenship.

Armstrong, P. 1993. 'Professions, Unions or What? Learning from Nurses', in L. Briskin and P. McDermott, eds, *Women Challenging Unions*. Toronto: University of Toronto Press, 304–24.

————. 1994. 'Closer to Home: More Work for Women', in Armstrong et al. (1994).

————. 1997. 'The Welfare State as History', in Blake et al. (1997: 52–73).

———— and H. Armstrong. 1990. *Theorizing Women's Work*. Toronto: Garamond.

———— and ————. 1991. 'Limited Possibilities and Possible Limits for Pay Equity: Within and Beyond the Ontario Legislation', in J. Fudge, eds, *Just Wages*. Toronto: University of Toronto Press, 110–21.

———— and ————. 1994. *The Double Ghetto: Canadian Women and Their Segregated Work*, 3rd edn. Toronto: Oxford University Press.

———— and ————, with C. Fegan. 1998. *Universal Health Care: What the United States Can Learn from the Canadian Experience*. New York: New Press.

———— and ————. 1999. *Women, Privatization and Health Care Reform: The Ontario Case*. Toronto: National Network on Environments and Women's Health.

———— and ————. 2000. *Primary Health Care Reform: What Are the Issues and Why Should We Care?* Ottawa: Canadian Health Coalition.

————, ————, J. Choiniere, G. Feldberg, and J. White. 1994. *Take Care: Warning Signals for Canada's Health System*. Toronto: Garamond Press.

——, ——, and D. Coburn, eds. 2001. *Unhealthy Times: Political Economy Perspectives on Health and Care in Canada*. Toronto: Oxford University Press.

——, J. Choiniere, G. Feldberg, and J. White. 1994. 'Voices from the Ward', in Armstrong et al. (1994: 53–94).

——, J. Choiniere, and E. Day. 1993. *Vital Signs: Nursing in Transition*. Toronto: Garamond Press.

—— and P. Connelly. 1999. *Feminism, Political Economy and the State: Contested Terrain*. Toronto: Canadian Scholars Press.

—— and I. Jansen, with E. Connell and M. Jones. 1999. 'Assessing the Impact of Restructuring and Work Reorganization in Long Term Care'. Workers Health Issues. Toronto: National Networks for Environmental and Women's Health.

—— and O. Kits. 2001. *One Hundred Years of Caregiving*. Report prepared for the Law Commission of Canada.

—— et al. 1988. *Pay Equity in Predominately Female Establishments: Health Care Sector*. Ontario: Pay Equity Commission.

—— et al. 1997. *Medical Alert: New Work Organization in Health Care*. Toronto: Garamond.

—— et al. 2000. *'Heal Thyself': Managing Health Care Reform*. Aurora, Ont.: Garamond Press.

—— et al. 2001. *Exposing Privatization: Women and Health Care Reform in Canada*. Toronto: Garamond.

Arno, P.S., C. Levine, et al. 1999. 'The economic value of informal caregiving', *Health Affairs* 18, 2: 182–8.

Aronson, J. 1990. 'Old women's experiences of needing care: choice or compulsion?', *Canadian Journal on Aging/La Revue Canadienne du Vieillissement* 9, 3: 234–47.

——. 1993. 'Giving Consumers a Say in Policy Development: Influencing Policy or Just Being Heard', *Canadian Public Policy* 19, 4: 367–78.

——. 1998. 'Women's Perspectives on Informal Care of the Elderly: Public Ideology and Personal Experience of Giving and Receiving Care', in D. Coburn, C. D'Arcy, and G. Torrance, eds, *Health and Canadian Society: Sociological Perspectives*, 3rd edn. Toronto: University of Toronto Press, 399–416.

——. 2000. 'Restructuring Older Women's Needs: Care Giving as a Site of Struggle and Resistance', in Neysmith (2000).

—— and S. Neysmith. 1996. 'The Work of Visiting Homemakers in the Context of Cost Cutting in Long Term Care', *Canadian Journal of Public Health* 87, 6: 422–5.

—— and ——. 1997. 'The retreat of the state and long-term provision: implementations for frail elderly people, unpaid family carers and paid home care workers', *Studies in Political Economy* 53 (Summer): 37–66.

Ascher-Svanum, H., and T. Sobel. 1989. 'Caregiving of Mentally Ill Adults: A Woman's Agenda', *Hospital and Community Psychiatry* 40, 8 (Autumn): 367–78.

Audette, L.M., J. Carle, A. Simard, C. Tilquin, et collaborateurs. 1978. *Guide de l'Usager de la Formule d'Evaluation du Niveau des Soins Infirmières Réquis par le Bénéficiaire*. Montréal: Université de Montréal.

Avison, W.R. 1998. 'The Health Consequences of Unemployment', in National Forum on Health, ed., *Determinants of Health: Adults and Seniors*. Sainte-Foy, Que.: Editions MultiMondes.

Babad, A. 1988. 'Financial Implications of Understaffing', *ONA Newsletter* (Aug.): 14.

Babson, J.H., and P. Brackstone. 1973. 'The Canadian Health Care System: Its History, Current Status and Similarities with the U.S. Health Care System', *Journal of Comparative Sociology* 1, 3: 1113–26.

Bacovsky, R. 1997. Federal, Provincial and Territorial Government Sponsored Drug Plans and Drug Databases: Background Information Prepared for the Conference on National Approaches to Pharmacare.

Baines, C.T., P.M. Evans, and S.M. Neysmith, eds. 1991. *Women's Caring: Feminist Perspectives on Social Welfare*. Toronto: McClelland & Stewart.

Baker, M. 1996. *Reinforcing Obligations and Responsibilities between Generations: Policy Options from Cross-national Comparisons.* Ottawa: Vanier Institute of the Family.

Baker, S., M. Sudit, et al. 1998. 'Caregiver burden and coping strategies used by informal caregivers of minority women living with HIV/AIDS', *ABNF Journal* 9, 3: 56–60.

Baldock, C.V. 1999. 'Seniors as Volunteers: An International Perspective on Policy', *Ageing and Society* 19, 5: 581–602.

Barer, M., V. Bhatia, G. Stoddart, and R. Evans. 1994. *The Remarkable Tenacity of User Charges.* Toronto: The Premier's Council on Health, Well-Being and Social Justice.

———, R. Evans, et al. 1995. 'Avalanche or Glacier? Health Care and the Demographic Rhetoric', *Canadian Journal on Aging* 14, 2: 218.

——— and G. Stoddart. 1991. 'Toward Integrated Medical Research Policies for Canada', Federal/Provincial/Territorial Conference of Deputy Ministers of Health.

Barlow, M., and D. Robinson. 1995. 'How the Liberals are Unravelling the Social Safety Net', *Globe and Mail*, A19.

Basen, G., M. Eichler, and A. Lippman, eds. 1993. *Misconceptions.* Hull, Que.: Voyageur Publishing.

Bauer, B., ed. 1992. *Conceptual and Methodological Issues in Family Caregiving Research: Proceedings of the Invitational Conference on Family Caregiving Research June 21–22, 1990, Toronto.* Toronto: Faculty of Nursing, University of Toronto.

Bauman, A., L.L. O'Brien-Pallas, et al. 2001. *Commitment and Care: The Benefits of a Healthy Workplace for Nurses, Their Patients and the System.* Ottawa: Canadian Health Services Research Foundation.

Baumgart, A. 1988. 'The Nursing Workforce in Canada', in Baumgart and Larson (1988).

——— and J. Larson, eds. 1988. *Canadian Nursing Faces the Future: Development and Change.* Toronto: C.V. Mosby.

Bégin, M. 1987. *Medicare: Canada's Right to Health.* Ottawa: Optimum.

Beland, F., and A. Lemay. 1995. 'Many Dilemmas, Many Values for a Long-Term Care Policy', *Canadian Journal on Aging/La Revue Canadienne du Vieillissement* 14, 2: 263–93.

Belcher, J. 1988. 'Mothers Alone and Supporting Chronically Mentally Ill Adult Children: A Greater Vulnerability to Children', *Women and Health* 14, 2: 79–86.

Bellemare, D., L.P. Simon, et al. 1995. 'Aging, Employment, and Early Retirement: The Factors Influencing Firms' Management of Aging Human Resources', *Relations industrielles/Industrial Relations* 50, 3: 483–515.

Bergmanis, P. 1994. 'Total Quality Improvement: Continuous Quality Improvement. Implications for Patient Care and the Management of Health Care Resources'. Submission to *A Picture of Health.* London, Ont.: Ontario Federation of Labour Public Forum.

Bernier, J., and M. Dallaire. 2000. *What Price Have Women Paid for Health Care Reform? The Situation in Quebec.* Montréal: Le Centre d'excellence pour la sante des femmes—Consortium Université de Montréal.

Bertin, O. 1994. 'Health Care Good Medicine for Ailing Firms', *Globe and Mail*, 14 Mar., B2.

Berwick, D., B. Godfrey, and J. Roessner. 1990. *Curing Health Care.* San Francisco: Jossey-Bass.

Beuckert, D. 2000. 'Victorian Order of Nurses Faces Bleak Future', *Toronto Star*, 28 Dec., A3.

Bezanson, K., and L. Noce, with the assistance of the Speaking Out team. 1999. *Costs, Closures and Confusion: People in Ontario Talk About Health Care.* Toronto: Caledon.

Bhatia, V., G.L. Stoddart, M. Barer, and R. Evans. 1994. *User Charges in Health Care: A Bibliography.* Toronto: Premier's Council on Health, Well-Being and Social Justice.

Billinkoff, A. 1993. 'NDP Attack Warns McCrae', *Winnipeg Free Press*, 9 Nov., editorial.

Bilson, G. 1981. 'Canadian Doctors and the Cholera', in S.E.D. Shortt, ed., *Medicine in Canadian Society.* Montreal and Kingston: McGill-Queen's University Press.

Birke, L. 1986. *Women, Feminism and Biology.* Brighton: Harvester.

Blake, R.B., P.E. Bryden, and J.F. Frank, eds. 1997. *The Welfare State in Canada: Past, Present and Future.* Concord, Ont.: Irwin.

Blakley, B.M., and J. Jaffe. 1999. 'Coping as a rural caregiver: the impact of health care reforms on rural women informal caregivers'. Available at: <www.pwhce.ca/swan.htm>.

Blendon, R.J., et al. 2001. 'Physicians' Views on Quality of Care: A Five-Country Comparison', *Health Affairs* (May–June): 233–43.

Blishen, B. 1991. *Doctors in Canada*. Toronto: University of Toronto Press.

Blomqvist, A., and D.M. Brown, eds. 1994. *Limits to Care*. Ottawa: C.D. Howe Institute.

Boaz, R.F. 1996. 'Full-time employment and informal caregiving in the 1980s', *Medical Care* 34, 6: 524–36.

―――― and C.F. Muller. 1992. 'Paid work and unpaid help by caregivers of the disabled and frail elders', *Medical Care* 30, 2: 149–58.

Bogdanich, W. 1991. *The Great White Lie: Dishonesty, Waste and Incompetence in the Medical Community*. New York: Touchstone.

Bolaria, B.S., and R. Bolaria, eds. 1994. *Racial Minorities in Medicine and Health*. Halifax: Fernwood.

―――― and H.D. Dickinson. 1988. *Sociology of Health Care in Canada*. Toronto: Harcourt Brace Jovanovich.

―――― and ――――, eds. 1994. *Health, Illness, and Health Care in Canada*. Toronto: Harcourt Brace.

Bond, J. 1992. 'The Politics of Caregiving: The Professionalisation of Informal Care', *Ageing and Society* 12, 1: 5–21.

Borysenko, J. 1985. *Minding the Body, Mending the Mind*. Don Mills, Ont.: Addison-Wesley.

Botting, I., with support from B. Neis, L. Kealey, and S. Solberg. 2001. 'Health Restructuring and Privatization from Women's Perspective in Newfoundland and Labrador', in Armstrong et al. (2001: 49–94).

Boychuk, T. 1999. *The Making and Meaning of Hospital Policy in the United States and Canada*. Ann Arbor: University of Michigan Press.

Boyle, T. 1992. 'Busy MDs Prescribe More Drugs Study Says', *Toronto Star*, 27 May, A2.

――――. 2001. 'New rules cause chaos for audiologists', *Toronto Star*, 7 July, A27.

Brady, E., and C. Schoonover. 1986. 'Patterns of Parent-care when Adult Daughters Work and When They Do Not', *The Gerontologist* 26, 4: 372–81.

Braithwaite, V. 1996. 'Understanding Stress in Informal Caregiving: Is Burden a Problem of the Individual or of Society?', *Research on Aging* 18, 2: 139–74.

Braverman, H. 1974. *Labor and Monopoly Capital*. New York: Monthly Review Press.

Bravo, G., D. Girouard, et al. 1995. 'Further validation of the QUALCARE Scale', *Journal of Elder Abuse and Neglect* 7, 4: 29–48.

Breckenridge, J. 1994. 'Unorthodox . . . or Incompetent?', *Globe and Mail*, 2 July, A4.

Bridges, J., and M.J. Lynam. 1993. 'Informal Careers: A Marxist Analysis of Social, Political and Economic Forces Underpinning the Role', *Advances in Nursing Science* 15, 3: 33–48.

British Columbia, Ministry of Health and Ministry Responsible for Seniors. 1993. *New Directions for a Healthy British Columbia*. Victoria.

British Columbia Royal Commission on Health Care and Costs. 1991. *Closer to Home: A Summary Report*. Victoria.

Brody, E.M., S.J. Litvin, et al. 1995. 'Marital Status of Caregiving Daughters and Co-Residence with Dependent Parents', *The Gerontologist* 35, 1: 75–85.

Brouwer, W.B., N.J. van Exel, et al. 1999. 'The Valuation of Informal Care in Economic Appraisal: A Consideration of Individual Choice and Societal Costs of Time', *International Journal of Technology Assessment in Health Care* 15, 1: 147–60.

Brown, M. 1991. *Health Economics and Policy*. Toronto: McClelland & Stewart.

Browne, P.L. 2000. *Unsafe Practices: Restructuring and Privatization in Ontario Health Care*. Ottawa: Canadian Centre for Policy Alternatives.

Buchignani, N., and C. Armstrong-Esther. 1999. 'Informal care and older Native Canadians', *Ageing and Society* 19, 1: 3–32.

Bugge, C.R.N.M., H.P. Alexander, et al. 1999. 'Stroke Patients' Informal Caregivers: Patient, Caregiver, and Service Factors That Affect Caregiver Strain', *Stroke* 30, 8 (Aug.): 1517–23.

Burton, L., J. Kasper, et al. 1995. 'The Structure of Informal Care: Are There Differences by Race?', *The Gerontologist* 35, 6: 744–52.

California Nurse. 1994. 'APM: Operation Excellence or Operation Extinction?' (June).

Campbell, L.D., and A. Martin-Matthews. 2000. 'Caring Sons: Exploring Men's Involvement in Filial Care', *Canadian Journal on Aging/La Revue Canadienne du Vieillissement* 1 (Spring): 57–79.

Campbell, M. 1988. 'Management as "Ruling": A Class Phenomenon in Nursing', *Studies in Political Economy* 27 (Autumn): 29–52.

Canada. 1969. *Task Force Report on the Costs of Health Services in Canada.* Ottawa: Queen's Printer.

———, Royal Commission on Health Services. 1964. *Report*, vol. 1. Ottawa: Queen's Printer.

———, Health Services and Promotion Branch. 1990. *Mental Health Services in Canada, 1990.* Ottawa: Health Services and Promotion Branch, Health and Welfare Canada.

———, Library of Parliament, Research Branch. 1996. *Disability: Socio-economic Aspects and Proposals for Reform.* Ottawa: Library of Parliament Research Branch.

———, Senate, Standing Senate Committee on Social Affairs, Science and Technology (Kirby Committee). 2001. *The Health of Canadians—The Federal Role*, vol. 4, *Issues and Options.* Ottawa.

Canadian Health Coalition. 1998. *Transition = Abdication: A Citizens' Guide to the Health Protection Branch Consultation (HPB Transition).* Ottawa.

Canadian Health Services Research Foundation. 1999. 'What happens to patient care when you reduce the number of hospital beds in a big city?', *Quid Novi?* 2, 4 (Winter): 4.

———. 2001. 'Myth: Canadian doctors are leaving for the United States in droves', *Mythbusters* (Summer).

———. 2001. 'Myth: User fees would stop waste and ensure better use of the health system', *Mythbusters* (Fall).

Canadian Home Care Association, in collaboration with L'Association des CLSC et des CHSLD du Québec. 1998. *Portrait of Canada: An Overview of Public Home Care Programs.* Ottawa: Health Canada.

Canadian Institute for Health Information (CIHI). 1998. *National Health Expenditure Trends, 1975–1998.* Ottawa: CIHI.

———. 2000. *Health in Canada 2000: A First Report.* Ottawa: CIHI.

———. 2000. *Supply and Distribution of Registered Nurses in Canada, 1999.* Ottawa: CIHI.

———. 2000. *National Health Expenditure Trends, 1975–2000.* Ottawa: CIHI.

———. 2001. *Drug Expenditures in Canada 1985–2000.* Ottawa: CIHI.

———. 2001. *Hospital Report 2001: Acute Care.* Toronto: CIHI.

———. 2001. *Health in Canada 2001.* Ottawa: CIHI.

———. 2001. *Canada's Health Care Providers.* Ottawa: CIHI.

Canadian Press and Reuters. 1994. 'Breast Cancer Researcher Falsified Data in Major Study', *Globe and Mail*, 14 Mar., A2.

Canadian Union of Public Employees (CUPE). n.d. 'False Savings, Hidden Costs: Calculating the Costs of Contracting Out and Privatization'. Ottawa, mimeo.

——— and Reuters Department. n.d. 'The Americanization of Health Care', Research Paper No. 5. Ottawa, mimeo.

Carey, E. 1995. 'Elderly Abused at Home, Study Finds', *Toronto Star*, 13 May, A3.

Caro, F.G., and A.L. Stern. 1995. 'Balancing Formal and Informal Care: Meeting Needs in a Resource-constrained Program', *Home Health Care Services Quarterly* 15, 4: 67–81.

Carr, J. 1993. 'Consultant Brews Trouble, American Nurse Warns', *Winnipeg Free Press*, 6 June, editorial.

Carr-Hill, R. 1995. 'Editorial: Welcome? to the Brave New World of Evidence Based Medicine', *Social Science and Medicine* 41, 11: 1467–8.

Carriere, Y. 1998. 'The Impact of Demographic Aging on Social and Health Services Directed at the Elderly Losing Their Autonomy: Institutionalization and Care at Home', Université de Montréal.

——— and J. Legare. 2000. 'Unmet Needs for Assistance with ADLs and IADLs: A Measure of Healthy Life Expectancy', *Social Indicators Research* 51, 1: 107–23.

Carruthers, G., T. Goldberg, H. Segal, and E. Sellers. 1987. *Drug Utilization: A Comprehensive Review*. Toronto: University of Toronto Faculty of Medicine.

Carton, H., R. Loos, et al. 2000. 'A quantitative study of unpaid caregiving in multiple sclerosis', *Multiple Sclerosis* 6, 4: 274–9.

Cayley, D. 1985. *Doctoring the Family*. Montreal: CBC.

CCOHTA. 1998. 'Spotlight . . . BMS vs CCOHTA', *Connections* 1: 2.

Certenig, M., and R. Matas. 1997. 'B.C. Can't Limit Where MDs Set Up Practices, Court Rules', *Globe and Mail*, 2 Aug., A1, A7.

Chamberlain, A. 1994. 'Rehabilitation on a Roll', *Toronto Star*, 2 May.

———. 1994. 'Doctor, Drug Firm Ties Coming Into Question', *Toronto Star*, 10 May, C1, C4.

———. 1995. 'Who's Smiling Now?', *Toronto Star*, 26 Mar., D4, D5.

———. 1995. 'Healthy Profits for Lab Partners', *Toronto Star*, 2 May, D1.

Chambers, L.W., P. Tugwell, et al. 1990. 'Impact of home care on recently discharged elderly hospital patients in an Ontario community', *Canadian Journal on Aging/La Revue Canadienne du Vieillissement* 9, 4: 327–47.

Chappell, N.L. 1987. 'Interface among three systems of care: self, informal, and formal', paper presented at State University of New York, Albany.

———. 1991. 'Living arrangements and sources of caregiving', *Journal of Gerontology* 46, 1: S1–8.

———. 1992. *Social Support and Aging*. Toronto: Butterworths.

———. 1993. 'Implications of shifting health care policy for caregiving in Canada', *Journal of Aging and Social Policy* 5, 1–2: 39–55.

———. 1995. 'Health and Health Care', in R. Brym, ed., *New Society: Sociology for the 21st Century*. Toronto: Harcourt Brace Jovanovich.

——— and A. Blandford. 1991. 'Informal and formal care: exploring the complementarity', *Ageing and Society* 11, Part 3: 299–317.

——— and M. Penning. 1996. 'Behavioural Problems and Distress among Caregivers of People with Dementia', *Ageing and Society* 16, 1: 57–73.

——— and M.J. Prince. 1997. 'Reasons Why Canadian Seniors Volunteer', *Canadian Journal on Aging/La Revue Canadienne du Vieillissement* 16, 2: 336–53.

———, A. Segall, et al. 1990. 'Gender and Helping Networks among Day Hospital and Senior Centre Participants', *Canadian Journal on Aging/La Revue Canadienne du Vieillissement* 9, 3: 220–33.

Charles, C., et al. 1994. 'How Was Your Hospital Stay? Reports about Their Care in Canadian Hospitals', Working Paper 94–5. Hamilton: Centre for Health Economics and Policy Analysis, McMaster University.

Chen, J., and W.J. Millar. 2000. 'Are recent cohorts healthier than their predecessors?', *Health Reports* 11, 4: 9–23.

——— and R. Wilkins. 1998. 'Seniors' needs for health-related personal assistance', *Health Reports* 10, 11: 39–50.

Chetley, A. 1990. *A Healthy Business: World Health and the Pharmaceutical Industry*. London: Zed Books.

Choiniere, J. 1993. 'A Case Study Examination of Nurses and Patient Information Technology', in Armstrong et al. (1993: 59–88).

Christie, N. 2000. *Engendering the State: Family, Work, and Welfare in Canada*. Toronto: University of Toronto Press.

Chubachi, N. 1999. 'Geographies of Nisei Japanese Canadians and their attitudes towards elderly long-term care', MA thesis, Queen's University.

Church, J., and T. Noseworthy. 1999. 'Fiscal Authority Through Decentralization', in D. Drache and T. Sullivan, eds, *Health Reform: Public Success, Private Failure*. New York: Routledge.

Clark, P.G. 1991. 'Geriatric Health Care Policy in the United States and Canada: A Comparison of Facts and Values in Defining the Problems', *Journal of Aging Studies* 5, 3: 265–81.

Clark, S., and A. Harvey. 1976. 'The Sexual Division of Labour: The Use of Time', *Atlantis* 2, 1: 46–65.

Clarke, E. 1998. 'Toward a Triadic Exchange Relationship in Long-Term Care', paper presented at International Sociological Association meetings, Toronto.

Clarke, P.J., V.W. Marshall, et al. 2000. 'Well-Being in Canadian Seniors: Findings from the Canadian Study of Health and Aging', *Canadian Journal on Aging/La Revue Canadienne du Vieillissement* 2 (Summer): 139–59.

Clemenson, H. 1989. 'Unionization and Women in the Service Sector', *Perspectives on Labour and Income* 1, 2: 30–44.

Cloutier-Fisher, D., and A.E. Joseph. 2000. 'Long-Term Care Restructuring in Rural Ontario: Retrieving Community Service User and Provider Narratives', *Social Science and Medicine* 50, 7–8: 1037–45.

Clyburn, L.D., M.J. Stones, et al. 2000. 'Predicting caregiver burden and depression in Alzheimer's disease', *Journal of Gerontology* 55B, 1 (Jan.): 2–13.

Coburn, D., C. D'Arcy, G.M. Torrance, and P. New, eds. 1987. *Health and Canadian Society*, 2nd edn. Markham, Ont.: Fitzhenry & Whiteside.

———— et al., eds. 1998. *Health and Canadian Society*, 3rd edn. Toronto: University of Toronto Press.

Coburn, J. 1987. '"I See and I Am Silent": A Short History of Nursing in Ontario, 1850–1930', in D. Coburn et al. (1987: 39–61).

Cochrane, J.J., P.N. Goering, et al. 1997. 'The mental health of informal caregivers in Ontario: an epidemiological survey', *American Journal of Public Health* 87, 12: 2002–7.

Cohen, G. 1992. 'Hard at Work', *Perspectives on Labour and Income* 4, 1 (Spring): 8–14.

Cohen, M.G., and Ontario Institute for Studies in Education, Centre for Women's Studies in Education. 1986. *The Invisible Hand, Is It Around Our Throats? Women and Economics*. Toronto: Centre for Women's Studies in Education, OISE.

Colantonio, A., C. Cohen, et al. 1998. 'Support needs of elderly caregivers of persons with dementia', *Canadian Journal on Aging/La Revue Canadienne du Vieillissement* 17, 3: 330–45.

College of Nurses of Ontario. 1990. *Standards of Nursing Practice*. Toronto: College of Nurses of Ontario.

Colt, H.G., and A.P. Shapiro. 1989. 'Drug-Induced Illnesses as a Cause of Admission to a Community Hospital', *Journal of the American Geriatric Society* 37: 323–6.

Confederation des syndicats nationaux. n.d. *Choisir*. Montréal: CSN.

Conference Board of Canada. 2001. *The Future Cost of Health Care in Canada, 2000 to 2020*. Ottawa: Conference Board.

Consumer Reports. 1992. 'Health Care Dollars', (July): 436.

Coward, R. 1989. *The Whole Truth: The Myth of Alternative Therapies*. London: Faber and Faber.

Crane, D. 1999. 'Beware profit motive in food, drug research', *Toronto Star*, 20 July, C2.

Cranswick, K. 1999. 'Help close at hand: Relocating to give or receive care', *Canadian Social Trends* (Winter): 11–12.

Crellin, J.K. 1994. *Home Medicine: The Newfoundland Experience*. Montreal and Kingston: McGill-Queen's University Press.

Crichton, A. 1997. *Health Care: a Community Concern? Developments in the Organization of Canadian Health Services*. Calgary: University of Calgary Press.

Crompton, S. 2000. 'Health', *Canadian Social Trends* (Winter): 12–17.

—— and A. Kemeny. 1999. 'In Sickness and in Health: The Well-being of Married Seniors', *Canadian Social Trends* (Winter): 22–7.

Cusack, S. 1996. 'Isolated Elders Closer to Home Demonstration Project: A Descriptive Evaluation', Simon Fraser University, Gerontology Research Centre.

Das Gupta, T. 1996. 'Anti-Black Racism in Nursing in Ontario', *Studies in Political Economy* 51 (Fall): 97–116.

Dautzenberg, M.G.H., J.P.M. Diederiks, et al. 1999. 'Multigenerational Caregiving and Well-Being: Distress of Middle-Aged Daughters Providing Assistance to Elderly Parents', *Women and Health* 29, 4: 57–74.

David, L., and E. Schragge, eds. 1990. *Bureaucracy and Community*. Montreal: Black Rose Books.

Davies, L., J.A. McMullin, et al. 2001. *Social Policy, Gender Inequality and Poverty*. Ottawa: Status of Women in Canada.

Davies, M. 1995. 'Institutionalizing Old Age: Residential Accommodation for the Elderly in British Columbia, 1920–1960', Ph.D. thesis, McGill University.

Davis, A. 1980. 'Disability, Home Care and the Care-Taking Role in Family Life', *Journal of Advanced Nursing* 5: 475–84.

Davis, S.M., Queen's University, School of Public Administration., et al. 1992. *Health Care: Innovation, Impact and Challenge*. Kingston: School of Policy Studies/School of Public Administration, Queen's University.

Day, S., G. Brodsky, et al. 1998. *Women and the Equality Deficit: The Impact of Restructuring Canada's Social Programs*. Ottawa: Status of Women Canada.

Deber, R., S. Mhatre, and G.R. Baker. 1994. 'A Review of Provincial Initiatives', in Blomqvist and Brown (1994: 91–124).

—— and G. Thompson, eds. 1992. *Restructuring Canada's Health Services System*. Toronto: University of Toronto Press.

Deming, E. 1986. *Out of the Crisis*. Cambridge, Mass.: MIT-CAES.

Denton, F.T., C.H. Feaver, et al. 1998. 'The Future Population of Canada, Its Age Distribution and Dependency Relations', *Canadian Journal on Aging/La Revue Canadienne du Vieillissement* 17, 1: 83–109.

—— and B.G. Spencer. 1995. 'Demographic Change and the Cost of Publicly Funded Health Care', *Canadian Journal on Aging/La Revue Canadienne du Vieillissement* 14, 2: 174–92.

Denton, M. 1997. 'The Linkages between Informal and Formal Care of the Elderly', *Canadian Journal on Aging/La Revue Canadienne du Vieillissement* 16, 1: 30–50.

Dhawan, S. 1998. 'Caregiving Stress and Acculturation in East Indian Immigrants: Caring for their Elders', Ph.D. thesis, Queen's University.

Dimers, S. 1992. 'Total Quality Management—A Strategy for Success', *Housecall* (Toronto, Women's College Hospital).

Djulbegovic, B., et al. 2000. 'The uncertainty principle and industry-sponsored research', *Lancet*: 635–8.

Dodd, D.E., and D. Gorham, eds. 1994. *Caring and Curing: Historical Perspectives on Women and Healing in Canada*. Ottawa: University of Ottawa Press.

Dominion Bureau of Statistics. 1957. *Canada 1957*. Ottawa: Queen's Printer.

Dorazio-Migliore, M. 1999. 'Eldercare in Context: Narrative, Gender, and Ethnicity', Ph.D. thesis, University of British Columbia.

Dowler, J.M., D.A. Jordan-Simpson, et al. 1992. 'Gender inequalities in care-giving in Canada', *Health Reports* 4, 2: 125–36.

Drache, D., and W. Clement, eds. 1985. *The New Practical Guide to Canadian Political Economy*. Toronto: James Lorimer.

Drake, D., and M. Uhlman. 1993. *Making Medicine, Making Money*. Kansas City: Andrews and McKeel.

Duchesne, D. 1989. *Giving Freely: Volunteers in Canada* (Cat. no. 71–535). Ottawa: Supply and Services Canada.

Dumas, J., and A. Belanger. 1994. *Report on the Demographic Situation in Canada 1994* (Cat. no. 91–209E). Ottawa: Minister of Industry, Science and Technology.

Duncanson, J.L. 1998. '"For Better or for Worse": The Impact of Multiple Sclerosis on the Marital Relationship', Ph.D. thesis, University of Regina.

Dunlop, M. 1990. 'Home Care', *Toronto Star*, 19 Oct., C1.

———. 1994. 'New In Medicine', *Toronto Star*, Toronto 11 June, K2.

Duran-Aydintug, C., C.C. Torres, et al. 1995. 'The Home Care Allowance Program: A Change in Policy and Implications for Elder Clients', *Home Health Care Services Quarterly* 15, 4: 19–31.

Eakin, J.M. 1987. 'Survival of the Fittest? The Democratization of Hospital Administration in Quebec', in Coburn et al. (1987: 515–32).

———. 1987. 'Stroke Patients in a Canadian Hospital', in Coburn et al., (1987: 533–44).

Easty, T. 1994. Speech at 'Women in Health Care Technology' conference, McMaster University, Hamilton, Ont.

The Economist. 1993. 'Smelling a Rat in Medical Research', *Globe and Mail*, 22 Mar., A7.

Edelman, P., and S. Hughes. 1990. 'The impact of community care on provision of informal care to homebound elderly persons', *Journal of Gerontology* 45, 2: S74–84.

Enterline, P., A. McDonald, J.C. McDonald, and N. Steinmetz. 1973. 'The Distribution of Medical Services Before and After "Free" Medical Care', *Medical Care* 11, 4 (July–Aug.): 269–86.

———, J.C. McDonald, A. McDonald, L. Davignon, and V. Salter. 1973. 'Effects of "Free" Medical Care on Medical Practice: The Quebec Experience', *New England Journal of Medicine* 288, 2.

Epp, J. 1986. *Achieving Health for All: A Framework for Health Promotion*. Ottawa: Supply and Services Canada.

Esteves, E. 2000. 'The New Wageless Worker: Volunteering and Market-guided Health Care Reform', in Gustafson (2000: 154–76).

Ettner, S.L. 1995. 'The impact of "parent care" on female labor supply decisions', *Demography* 32, 1: 63–80.

Evans, P.M., and G.R. Wekerle. 1997. *Women and the Canadian Welfare State: Challenges and Change*. Toronto: University of Toronto Press.

Evans, R. 1984. *Strained Mercy: The Economics of Canadian Health Care*. Toronto: Butterworths.

———. 1993. 'Health Care Reform: "The Issue from Hell"', *Policy Options* (July–Aug.): 35–41.

———, M. Barer, and G. Stoddart. 1991. *Charging Peter to Pay Paul: Accounting for the Financial Effects of User Charges*. Toronto: Premier's Council on Health, Well-Being and Social Justice.

———, ———, ———, and V. Bhatia. 1994. *Who Are the Zombie Masters and What Do They Want?* Toronto: Premier's Council on Health, Well-Being and Social Justice.

———, ———, ———, and ———. 1994. *It's Not the Money, It's the Principle: Why User Charges for Some Services and Not Others?* Toronto: Premier's Council on Health, Well-Being and Social Justice.

Eyles, J. 1991. 'A Needs-Based Methodology for Allocating Health Care Resources in Ontario, Canada: Development and an Application', *Social Science and Medicine* 33, 4: 489–500.

Faber, H. 1996. 'Partnerships meeting the challenges of informal caregiving', *Journal of Gerontological Nursing* 22, 1: 7.

Fancey, J. 1997. 'Financial Compensation or Home Help Services: Examining Differences Among Program Recipients', *Canadian Journal on Aging/La Revue Canadienne du Vieillissement* 16, 2: 254–78.

Fawcett, G., Canadian Council on Social Development, et al. 1996. *Living with Disability in Canada: An Economic Portrait*. Hull, Que.: Human Resources Development Canada Office for Disability Issues.

Federal Centre for AIDS (Canada). 1989. *Caring Together: The Report of the Expert Working Group on Integrated Palliative Care for Persons with AIDS.*

Feeny, D. 1986. 'Introduction: Health Care Technology', in Feeny, G. Guyatt, and P. Tugwell, eds, *Health Care Technology: Effectiveness, Efficiency and Public Policy.* Montreal: Institute on Public Policy.

Feldberg, G., and R. Vipond. 1999. 'The Virus of Consumerism', in D. Drache and T. Sullivan, eds, *Health Reform: Public Success, Private Failure.* New York: Routledge.

Ferdinand, M. 1995. 'Regionalization: Canadian-Style Integrated Networks', *Journal of Health Care Resources Management* (Jan.): 14–20.

Feschuk, S., and E. Greenspon. 1994. 'Canada's Hidden Health Care System', *Globe and Mail*, 28 May, D1, D5.

Finch, J., and D. Groves. 1983. *A Labour of Love: Women, Work, and Caring.* London: Routledge & Kegan Paul.

Findlay, D., and L. Miller. 1994. 'Through Medical Eyes: The Medicalization of Women's Bodies and Women's Lives', in Bolaria and Dickinson (1994: 276–306).

Florio, E.R., and R. Raschko. 1998. 'The Gatekeeper Model: Implications for Social Policy', *Journal of Aging & Social Policy* 10, 1: 37–55.

Folsom, P., J. Porter, D. Richmond, R. Saddington, and J. Warkentin. 1994. *A Framework for Evaluating Devolution.* Toronto: Premier's Council on Health, Well-Being and Social Justice.

———, ———, ———, ———, and ———. 1994. *Devolution of Health and Social Services in Ontario: Refocusing the Debate.* Toronto: Premier's Council on Health, Well-Being and Social Justice.

Frankel, B.G., M.R.S. Speechley, et al. 1996. *The Sociology of Health and Health Care: A Canadian Perspective.* Toronto: Copp Clark.

Frederick, J., and J. Fast. 1998. 'Applications of the 1996 Canadian Survey on Social and Community Support', paper presented at International Sociological Association meetings, Toronto.

——— and ———. 1999. 'Eldercare in Canada: who does how much?', *Canadian Social Trends* (Autumn): 27–30.

Fredriksen, K.I. 1996. 'Gender Differences in Employment and the Informal Care of Adults', *Journal of Women & Aging* 8, 2: 35–53.

———. 1999. 'Family caregiving responsibilities among lesbians and gay men', *Social Work* 44, 2: 142–55.

Fuller, C. 1994. *Free Trade and Canadian Health.* Vancouver: Health Sciences Association of British Columbia.

———. 1998. *Caring for Profit: How Corporations Are Taking Over Canada's Health Care System.* Ottawa: Canadian Centre for Policy Alternatives.

———. 1999. *Reformed or Rerouted? Women and Change in the Health Care System.* Vancouver: British Columbia Centre of Excellence for Women's Health.

———. 2001. *Home Care: What We Know and What We Need.* Ottawa: Canadian Health Coalition.

———. 2001. 'The Information Gap: The Impact of Health Care Reform on British Columbia Women', in Armstrong et al. (2001).

G. Allan Roeher Institute. 1995. *Disability and Vulnerability: A Demographic Profile.* North York, Ont.: Roeher Institute.

Gee, E.M. 1999. 'Ethnic identity among foreign-born Chinese Canadian elders', *Canadian Journal on Aging/La Revue Canadienne du Vieillissement* 18, 4: 415–29.

———. 2000. 'Living arrangements and quality of life among Chinese Canadian elders', *Social Indicators Research* 5, 3: 309–29.

Gignac, M.A.M., C. Cott, et al. 2000. 'Adaptation to chronic illness and disability and its relationship to perceptions of independence and dependence', *Journal of Gerontology* Series B: Psychological Sciences and Social Sciences 55B, 6: 362–72.

————, E.K. Kelloway, et al. 1996. 'Impact of caregiving on employment: a mediational model of work-family conflict', *Canadian Journal on Aging/La Revue Canadienne du Vieillissement* 15, 4: 525–42.

Gilbert, S. 1992. 'Community Versus Hospital: The Costs of Caring for Level III Patients', *Leadership* 1, 5 (Sept.–Oct.): 17–20.

Gillett, G. 1989. *Reasonable Care*. Bristol: Bristol Press.

Gingras, G., and E.D. Sherman, eds. 1977. *Human Rights for the Physically Handicapped and Aged*. Montreal: Rehabilitation Institute of Montreal.

Glazer, N. 1990. 'The Home as Workshop: Women as Amateur Nurses and Medical Care Providers', *Gender and Society* 4, 4 (Dec.): 479–99.

————. 1991. *Women's Paid and Unpaid Labour*. Philadelphia: Temple University Press.

Glouberman, S., and H. Mintzberg. 1999. 'Managing the Care of Health and the Cure of Disease. Part I: Differentiation', mimeo (Jan.).

Godbout, J. 1981. 'Is Consumer Control Possible in Health Care Services? The Quebec Case', *International Journal of Health Services* 11: 151–67.

Goodall, R. 1993. 'Continuous Quality Improvement Revisited', *Leadership* 3, 3 (May–June): 6–11.

Gordon, S., and P.E. Benner, eds. 1996. *Caregiving: Readings in Knowledge, Practice, Ethics, and Politics*. Philadelphia: University of Pennsylvania Press.

Gorham, D. 1994. 'No Longer an Invisible Minority: Women Physicians and Medical Practice in Late Twentieth-Century North America', in Dodd and Gorham (1994: 183–211).

Gottlieb, B. 1990. *The Family Support Project: Feedback Report*. Guelph, University of Guelph, Department of Psychology.

Gough, I. 1979. *The Political Economy of the Welfare State*. London: Macmillan.

Grant, K.R., and N.L. Chappell. 1983. 'What Is Reasonable Is True: Life Satisfaction and Functional Disability among Day Hospital Participants', *Social Science and Medicine* 17, 2: 71–8.

Gray, B.H., and M.J. Fields, eds. 1989. *Controlling Costs and Changing Patient Care: The Role of Utilization Management*. Washington: National Academy Press.

Greaves, G., and P. Lewis. 1998. 'The experience of clients and informal caregivers with community health care services', *Healthcare Management Forum* 11, 4: 33–9.

Green-Hernandez, C. 1991. 'Professional Nurse Caring: A Proposed Conceptual Model for Nursing', in Neil and Watts (1991: 85–96).

Grinspun, D. 2000. 'Taking Care of the Bottom Line: Shifting Paradigms in Hospital Management', in Gustafson (2000).

Growe, S.J. 1991. *Who Cares? The Crisis in Canadian Nursing*. Toronto: McClelland & Stewart.

Guest, D. 1997. *The Emergence of Social Security in Canada*, 3rd edn. Vancouver: University of British Columbia Press.

Gurevich, M. 1999. *Privatization in Health Reform from Women's Perspectives: Research, Policy and Responses*. Halifax: Maritime Centre of Excellence for Women's Health.

Guruge, S., G.J. Donner, and L. Morrison. 2000. 'The Impact of Canadian Health Care Reform on Recent Women Immigrants and Refugees', in Gustafson (2000).

Gustafson, D.L., ed. 2000. *Care and Consequences: The Impact of Health Care Reform*. Halifax: Fernwood.

Gutman, G.M. 1995. 'Literature Review: Characteristics, service needs and service preferences of younger adults with severe physical disabilities', Gerontology Research Centre, Simon Fraser University.

Habib, M. 1994. 'Giving Up On Breastfeeding', *Toronto Star*, 16 June, B7.

Haddad, T., and L. Lam. 1988. 'Canadian Families—Men's Involvement in Family Work: A Case Study of Immigrant Men in Toronto', International Journal of Comparative Sociology 29, 3–4: 269–81.

Haiven, J. 1991. 'Mediscare', *Mother Jones* (Mar.–Apr.): 51–69.

Hall, M., and Statistics Canada. 1998. *Caring Canadians, Involved Canadians: Highlights from the 1997 National Survey of Giving, Volunteering and Participating*. Ottawa: Statistics Canada.

Hallman, B.C., and A.E. Joseph. 1999. 'Getting There: Mapping the Gendered Geography of Caregiving to Elderly Relatives', *Canadian Journal on Aging/La Revue Canadienne du Vieillissement* 18, 4: 397–414.

Hamilton, N. 2001. 'Aging and Health Care Reform', *Health Policy Research Bulletin* (Mar.): 3–4.

Hammel, K.W. 1992. 'The Caring Wife: The Experience of Caring for a Severely Disabled Husband in the Community', *Disability, Handicap and Society* 7, 4: 349–62.

Hanley, R.J., J.M. Wiener, et al. 1991. 'Will paid home care erode informal support?', *Journal of Health Politics, Policy & Law* 16, 3: 507–21.

Harding, J. 1986. 'Mood-Modifiers and Elderly Women in Canada: The Medicalization of Poverty', in K. McDonnell, ed., *Adverse Effects*. Toronto: Women's Press.

Harding, K., and V. Lu. 2001. 'Private cancer centre comes under fire', *Toronto Star*, 14 Dec., A1, A26.

Harlton, S.-V., et al. 1998. 'Defining eldercare for policy and practice: perspectives matter', *Family Relations* 47, 3 (July): 281–8.

Harman, L.D. 1989. *When a Hostel Becomes a Home: Experiences of Women*. Toronto: Garamond Press.

Harper, T. 1995. 'Medicare under the Knife', *Toronto Star*, 11 Mar., B1.

Harrow, B.S., S.L. Tennstedt, et al. 1995. 'How costly is it to care for disabled elders in a community setting?', *The Gerontologist* 35, 6: 803–13.

Harvey, A., K. Marshall, and J. Frederick. 1991. *Where Time Goes* (Cat. no. 11–612E). Ottawa: Supply and Services Canada.

Hashizume, Y.R.N.M.S. 2000. 'Gender Issues and Japanese Family-Centered Caregiving for Frail Elderly Parents or Parents-in-Law in Modern Japan: From the Sociocultural and Historical Perspectives', *Public Health Nursing* 17, 1(Jan.–Feb.): 25–31.

Hassen, P. 1993. *Rx for Hospitals: New Hope for Medicare in the Nineties*. Toronto: Stoddart.

Health and Welfare Canada. 1985. *Privatization in the Canadian Health Care System: Assertions, Evidence, Ideology and Options*. Ottawa: Health and Welfare Canada.

Health Canada. 1994. *National Expenditures in Canada, 1975–1993*. Ottawa: Supply and Services Canada.

———. 1994. *National Health Expenditures in Canada*. Ottawa: Health Canada, Policy and Consultation Branch.

———. 1998. 'Recent news about drug risks: application to Canadians', *Canadian Adverse Drug Reaction Newsletter* 8, 4: 1.

———. 1999. *Provincial and Territorial Home Care Programs: A Synthesis for Canada*. Ottawa: Health Canada.

———. 2000. *Canada Health Act 1999–2000*. Ottawa: Minister of Public Works and Government Services Canada.

———. 2001. *Health Care in Canada, 2001*. Ottawa: Canadian Institute for Health Information.

Health Services. 1970. *Task Force Report on the Cost of Health Services in Canada*. Ottawa: Queen's Printer.

Health Services Restructuring Commission (Ontario). 1997. *Ottawa Health Services Restructuring Report*. Toronto: HSRC.

Health Services Utilization Working Group. 1994. *When Less Is Better: Using Canada's Hospitals Efficiently*. Ottawa: HSUWG.

Heeney, H., and S. Charters. 1995. *Life Before Medicare: Canadian Experiences*. Toronto: Ontario Coalition of Senior Citizens Organizations.

Helmstadter, C. 1994. 'Staffing as a Quality of Worklife Factor', mimeo.

Henderson, H. 1994. 'Home Alone', *Toronto Star*. 16 July, H5.

————. 1994. 'Group Wants to Do Something About Seniors Who Are Released From Hospital Too Early', *Toronto Star*, 16 July, H5.

Hicks, C. 1988. *Who Cares?* London: Virago.

Hills, G., et al. 1998. 'Caregivers of the Elderly: Hidden Patients and Health Team Members', *Topics in Geriatric Rehabilitation Caregivers of the Elderly: Issues for Health Professionals* 14, 1 (Sept.): 1–11.

Himmelstein, D.U., and S. Woolhandler. 1994. *The National Health Program Book*. Monroe, Maine: Common Courage Press.

————, J.P. Lewontin, and S. Woolhandler. 1996. 'Who Administers? Who Cares? Medical Administrative and Clinical Employment in the United States and Canada', *American Journal of Public Health* 86, 2 (Feb.): 172–8.

Holicky, R. 1996. 'Caring for the Caregivers: The Hidden Victims of Illness and Disability', *Rehabilitation Nursing* 21, 5: 247–52.

Hollander, M., and A. Tessaro. 2001. *Evaluation of the Maintenance and Preventive Function of Home Care*. Ottawa: Home Care/Pharmaceuticals Division, Policy and Communication Branch, Health Canada.

Horner, S. 1991. 'Intersubjective Copresence in a Caring Model', in Neil and Watts (1991: 107–15).

Hospital Medical Records Institute (HMRI). 1992. *Comparative Analysis of the HMRI Database*. Don Mills, Ont.: HMRI.

House, J., K. Landis, and D. Umberson. 1990. 'Social Relationships and Health', in House, Landis, and Umberson, *The Sociology of Health and Illness: Critical Perspectives*. New York: St Martin's Press.

Howe, A.L., H. Schofield, et al. 1997. 'Caregiving: a common or uncommon experience?', *Social Science and Medicine* 45, 7: 1017–29.

Hunsburger, W.W. 1992. *One Mother to Another*. Saskatoon: Fifth House Publishers.

Hurst, L. 1994. 'The Lure of Instant Therapy', *Toronto Star*, 27 Mar., F3.

Ibbitson, J. 2000. 'Just how many beds does Ontario need to reform the system?', *Globe and Mail*, 6 Jan., A6.

Illich, I. 1976. *Limits to Medicine*. London: Penguin.

The Institute for Clinical Evaluative Sciences. 1994. *Patterns of Health Care in Ontario*, vol. 1. D. Naylor, G.M. Anderson, and V. Goel, eds. Ottawa: Canadian Medical Association.

James, N. 1992. 'Care, Work and Carework: A Synthesis', in J. Robinson, A. Gray, and R. Elkan, eds, *Policy Issues in Nursing*. Bristol: Open University Press, 97–111.

Jensen, P.M. 1988. 'The Changing Role of Nurses' Unions', in Baumgart and Larson (1988: 459–73).

Jenson, J., S. Jacobzone, et al. 2000. *Care Allowances for the Frail Elderly and Their Impact on Women Care-givers*. Paris: OECD.

———— and S.D. Phillips. 2000. 'Distinctive Trajectories: Homecare and the Voluntary Sector in Québec and Ontario', in K. Banting, ed., *The Nonprofit Sector in Canada: Roles and Relationships*. Kingston: School of Policy Studies, Queen's University.

Jin, R.L., C.P. Shah, and T.J. Svoboda. 1995. 'The Impact of Unemployment on Health: A Review of the Evidence', *Canadian Medical Association Journal* 153, 5 (1 Sept.): 529–40.

Jutras, S., and F. Veilleux. 1991. 'Informal Caregiving: Correlates of Perceived Burden', *Canadian Journal on Aging/La Revue Canadienne du Vieillissement* 10, 1: 40–55.

Kaden, J., and S.A. McDaniel. 1990. 'Caregiving and Care-Receiving: A Double Bind for Women in Canada's Aging Society', *Journal of Women & Aging* 2, 3: 3–26.

Kane, R.L. 1992. 'Lessons in long-term care: the benefits of a northern exposure', *Health Economics* 1, 2: 105–14.

Karp, D.A., and D. Watts-Roy. 1999. 'Bearing Responsibility: How Caregivers to the Mentally Ill Assess Their Obligations', *Health* 3, 4: 469–91.

Kaufert, P., and P. Gilbert. 1987. 'Medicalization and Menopause', in Coburn et al. (1987: 172–84).

Keating, N.C., J. Fast, et al. 1999. *Eldercare in Canada: Context, Content and Consequences*. Ottawa: Statistics Canada, Housing, Family and Social Statistics Division.

———, ———, et al. 1997. 'Bridging policy and research in eldercare', *Canadian Journal on Aging* 16, Supp. (Spring): 22–41.

Keddy, B. 1988. 'Hospitals Cite Pros, Cons in Contracting Out Services', *Hospital News*: 1.

Keefe, J.M., and P. Fancey. 1997. 'Financial compensation or home help services: examining differences among program recipients', *Canadian Journal on Aging/La Revue Canadienne du Vieillissement* 16, 2: 254–78.

Kennedy, M. 1997. 'Fears raised over cuts to health protection', *Montreal Gazette*, 15 Sept.

Kerr, J.R. 1988. 'A Historical Approach to the Evolution of University Nursing Education in Canada', in Kerr and J. MacPhail, eds, *Canadian Nursing*. Toronto: McGraw-Hill Ryerson, 237–58.

Kieval, Y.M.H. 2000. *Organizational Democracy: A Quality Mandate for Health Care Organizations*. Miami: University of Miami.

King, K.M., and P.M. Koop. 1999. 'The Influence of the Cardiac Surgery Patient's Sex and Age on Care-Giving Received', *Social Science and Medicine* 48, 12: 1735–42.

Kobayashi, K.M. 2000. *The Nature of Support from Adult Sansei (Third Generation) Children to Older Nisei (Second Generation) Parents in Japanese Canadian Families* (SEDAP Research Paper No. 18). Hamilton: McMaster University.

Koivusalo, M., and E. Ollila. 1997. *Making a Healthy World*. London: Zed Books.

Krishnan, V. (1989). 'Attitudes of Adult Daughters toward Custodial Care to Parents', *International Review of Modern Sociology* 19, 2: 29–54.

Kunisch, J. 1992. 'Electronic Fetal Monitors: Marketing Forces and the Resulting Controversy', in K.S. Ratcliff, ed., *Healing Technology: Feminist Perspectives*. Ann Arbor: University of Michigan Press, 41–60.

Kurian, G. 1972. 'Social and Financial Provisions for the Elderly in Canada—A Case-Study in the City of Calgary', *Indian Journal of Social Research* 13, 2: 119–26.

Kushner, C., and M. Rachlis. 1998. 'Civic Lessons: Strategies to Increase Consumer Involvement in Health Policy Development', in National Forum on Health, *Evidence and Information: Papers Commissioned by the National Forum on Health*, vol. 5. Ottawa: National Forum on Health.

Ladies of Toronto and Chief Cities and Towns in Canada. 1970. *The Canadian Home Cook Book*. Toronto: McGraw-Hill Ryerson.

Laino, C. 1994. 'Blood Test Could Eliminate Need for Amniocentesis, Doctors Say', *Toronto Star*, 16 May, D3.

Lalonde, M. 1974. *A New Perspective on Health for Canadians*. Ottawa: Minister of Supply and Services.

LaPerrière, B., Health Canada, Policy and Consultation Branch and Health System and Policy Division. 1997. *Proceedings of the Invitational Symposium on Palliative Care: Provincial and Territorial Trends and Issues in Community-Based Programming*. Ottawa, 23–4 Mar. 1997.

Lapierre, L. 1992. 'Measures of outside care given and received by seniors', *Health Reports* 4, 4: 355–66.

Lavoie, J.-P. 1995. 'Support groups for informal caregivers don't work! Refocus the groups or the evaluations?', *Canadian Journal on Aging/La Revue Canadienne du Vieillissement* 14, 3: 580–603.

The Leader. 1987. 'Hospital Worker Scolded for Kindness' (Mar. 1987): 1.

Lefley, H. 1989. 'Family Burden and Family Stigma', *American Psychologist* 44, 3: 556–60.

Lemieux-Charles, L., M. Murray, C. Aird, and J. Barnsley. 1993. *Careers in Health Care Management: Results of a National Survey*. Toronto: University of Toronto Hospital Management Research Unit.

———, ———, ———, and ———. 1994. 'Careers in Health Care Management, Part 1: Attainment, Expectations and Aspiration', *Health Management Forum* 7, 2 (Summer): 38–45.

Lépine, L., Health and Welfare Canada, Policy Planning and Information Branch. 1982. *Palliative Care in Canada*. Ottawa: Policy Planning and Information Branch, National Health and Welfare.

Lesemann, F. 1984. *Services and Circuses*. Montreal: Black Rose Books.

———— and C. Martin. 1993. *Home-based Care, the Elderly, the Family, and the Welfare State: An International Comparison*. Ottawa: University of Ottawa Press.

Levesque, L., et al. 1995. 'Multidimensional examination of the psychological and social well-being of caregivers of a demented relative', *Research on Aging* 17, 3 (Sept.): 332–60.

———— et al. 2000. 'Community services and caregivers of a demented relative: users and those perceiving a barrier to their use', *Canadian Journal on Aging* 19, 2: 186–209.

Lexchin, J. 1984. *The Real Pushers: A Critical Analysis of the Canadian Drug Industry*. Vancouver: New Star Books.

————. 1994. 'Profits First: The Pharmaceutical Industry in Canada', in Bolaria and Dickinson (1994: 700–20).

Lindorff, D. 1992. *Marketplace Medicine: The Rise of the For-Profit Hospital Chains*. New York: Bantam.

Lindsay, C. 1999. 'Seniors: A diverse group aging well', *Canadian Social Trends* (Spring): 24–6.

Lipovenko, D. 1995. '"Core" Services for Elderly Urged', *Globe and Mail*, 2 May, A3.

Lippman, A. 1993. 'Worrying—and Worrying About the Geneticization of Reproduction and Health', in G. Basen, M. Eichler, and Lippman, eds, *Misconceptions*. Hull, Que.: Voyageur Publishing, 39–65.

Loeppky, B. 1994. 'Made in Canada Health Reform', *Leadership* 3, 2 (Mar.–Apr.): 12–13.

Loughton, H.H. 1964. *A Gentlewoman in Upper Canada*. Toronto: Clarke, Irwin.

Lu, V. 2001. 'Billing seen as obstacle to health reform', *Toronto Star*, 9 July, A4.

Lum, J.M., and A.P. Williams. 2000. 'Professional Fault Lines: Nursing in Ontario After the Regulated Professions Act', in Gustafson (2000).

Lupi, E. 1991. 'Fathers in Transition: The Case of Dual-Earner Families in Canada', in J. Veevers, ed., *Continuity and Change in Marriage and Family*. Toronto: Holt, Rinehart and Winston.

Lux, A. 1983. 'The Aging of Quebec: Perspectives for the Twenty-First Century', *Recherches Sociographiques* 24, 3: 325–77.

Luxton, M. 1980. *More Than a Labour of Love*. Toronto: Women's Press.

Lynham, M.J. 1992. 'Towards the Goal of Providing Culturally Sensitive Care: Principles upon which to Build Nursing Curricula', *Journal of Advanced Nursing* 17, 1: 149–57.

MacBride, J. 1990. *Work and Family: Employment Challenge of the '90s*. Ottawa: Conference Board of Canada.

MacBride-King, J.L. 1999. *Caring About Caregiving: The Eldercare Responsibilities of Canadian Workers and the Impact on Employers*. Ottawa: Conference Board of Canada.

McDaniel, S.A., and A.L. McKinnon. 1993. 'Gender differences in informal support and coping among elders: findings from Canada's 1985 and 1990 General Social Surveys', *Journal of Women and Aging* 5, 2: 79–98.

McDonald, P.L., J.P. Hornick, G.B. Robertson, and J.E. Wallace. 1991. *Elder Abuse and Neglect in Canada*. Toronto: Butterworths.

MacDougall, H. 1990. *Activists and Advocates: Toronto's Health Department 1883–1983*. Toronto: Dundurn Press.

McIntosh, G. 1992. 'Ottawa Overlooked Implant Concerns, Documents Indicate', *Globe and Mail*, 18 June, A9.

McIsaac, W., D.C. Naylor, G.M. Anderson, and B.J. O'Brien. 1994. 'Reflections on a Month in the Life of the Ontario Drug Benefit Plan', *Canadian Medical Association Journal* 150, 4.

McKeown, T. 1979. *The Role of Medicine: Dream, Mirage or Nemesis*. Princeton, NJ: Princeton University Press.

————. 1981. 'Medical Technology and Health Care', in M.S. Straum and D.E. Larson, eds, *Doctors, Patients and Society*. Waterloo, Ont.: Wilfrid Laurier University Press.

McKibbon, J., L. Genereux, et al. 1996. 'Who cares for the caregivers?', *Canadian Nurse* 92, 3: 38–41.

Mackie, R. 2001. 'Project not helping to ease MD shortage', *Globe and Mail*, 9 July, A7.

McKinnon, D. 2001. 'Safeguarding Patient Care: Notes for Remarks to the Federal Standing Committee on Finance', 16 Oct.

Maclean's. 1994. Health update (advertising feature from MIT), 26 Sept.

McPhee, J. (1974). 'Further Discussion on Saskatchewan CHA Clinics Evaluation', *Canadian Medical Association Journal* 110, 2.

McPherson, K. 1991. 'Looking at Caring and Nursing Through a Feminist Lens', in Neil and Watts (1991).

———. 1994. 'Science and Techniques: Nurses' Work in a Canadian Hospital, 1920–1939', in Dodd and Gorham (1994: 71–101).

McQuaig, L. 1993. *The Wealthy Banker's Wife*. Toronto: Penguin.

McRae, J., and F. Tapon. 1994. 'Prices, Patents, and R&D Location in the Canadian Pharmaceutical Industry', in Blomqvist and Brown (1994).

Mains, H. 1994. 'Caring Person Beats Machine', *Toronto Star*, 2 Aug., A16.

Makover, M.E. 1998. *Mismanaged Care: How Corporate Medicine Jeopardizes Your Health*. New York: Prometheus.

Mallen, C., and V. Lawlon. 2001. 'Second Ontario hospital gets a private touch', *Toronto Star*, 8 Dec., A37.

Manitoba Centre for Health Policy and Evaluation. 1999. *Winnipeg Hospital Bed Closures: Problem or Progress?* Winnipeg, Feb.

Marchand, A., F. Beland, et al. 1994. 'The Burden of Caring for Aged Parents Living in an Institution', *Canadian Journal on Aging/La Revue Canadienne du Vieillissement* 13, 1: 79–95.

Marsh, L. 1975. *Report on Social Security for Canada*. Toronto: University of Toronto Press.

Marshall, K. 1993. 'Employed Parents and the Division of Housework', *Perspectives on Labour and Income* 5, 3 (Autumn): 23–30.

Martens, L.A. 1999. 'The Psychological Well-being of Family Members of Individuals with Schizophrenia', MA thesis, University of Calgary.

Martin, B. 1993. *In the Public Interest? Privatisation and Public Sector Reform*. London: Zed Press.

Marzouk, M.S. 1991. 'Aging, Age-Specific Health Care Costs and the Future Health Care Burden in Canada', *Canadian Public Policy/Analyse de Politiques* 17, 4: 490–506.

Masi, R., L.L. Mensah, et al. 1993. *Health and Cultures*. Oakville, Ont.: Mosaic Press.

Mathews, G. 1990. 'Sociology and Demographic Problems', *Cahiers de recherche sociologique* 14 (Spring): 111–15.

Matthews, S.H. 1990. 'Canada and the United States: Fertile Ground for Cross-Cultural Research', *Journal of Cross-Cultural Gerontology* 5, 3: 293–9.

Mays, N. 1994. 'Family Care May Not Be Enough for Elderly Patients', *Today's Seniors* (Mar.).

Medical Tribune News Service. 1994. 'Allergy Drugs Cancer Suspects', *Toronto Star*. 18 May, A18.

Meilicke, D., and J. Larson. 1988. 'Leadership and the Leaders of the Canadian Nurses Association', in Baumgart and Larson (1988: 421–57).

Meissner, M., E. Humphreys, S. Meiss, and W. Sheu. 1975. 'No Exit for Wives: Sexual Division of Labour and the Culmination of Household Demands', *Canadian Review of Sociology and Anthropology* 12, 4: 424–39.

Meltz, N. 1969. *Manpower in Canada, 1931–1961*. Ottawa: Department of Manpower and Immigration.

Merck Frosst Canada. 2000. *Health Care in Canada: A National Survey of Health Care Providers and Users*. Montreal.

Merrill, D.M. 1993. 'Daughters-in-Law as Caregivers to the Elderly: Defining the In-Law Relationship', *Research on Aging* 15, 1: 70–91.

Meshefedjian, G., J. McCusker, et al. 1998. 'Factors associated with symptoms of depression among informal caregivers of demented elders in the community', *The Gerontologist* 38, 2: 247–53.

Mhatre, S.L., and R.B. Deber. 1992. 'From Equal Access to Health Care to Equitable Access to Health: A Review of Canadian Provincial Health Commissions and Reports', *International Journal of Health Services* 22, 4: 656.

Michelson, W. 1985. *From Sun to Sun: Daily Obligations and Community Structure in the Lives of Employed Women and Their Families*. Ottawa: Rowan and Allenheld.

Michols, D. 1997. Drugs and Medical Devices Programme: Quality Initiative Bulletin 2. Questions and Answers: Who is our client? Drugs Directorate, Health Protection Branch, memo.

———. 2000. 'Can the Therapeutic Products Programme Keep Up?', *Health Policy Forum* (Summer): 11.

Mimoto, H., and P. Cross. 1991. 'The Growth of the Federal Debt', *Canadian Economic Observer*: 1–17.

Mitchell, M., et al. 1984. 'Determining Cost of Direct Nursing Care by DRGs', *Nursing Management* (Apr.: 29–32).

Moen, P., J. Robison, et al. 1995. 'Caregiving and women's well-being: a life course approach', *Journal of Health & Social Behavior* 36, 3: 259–73.

Moore, E.G., and D.L. McGuinness. 1997. 'Adjustments of the Elderly to Declining Health: Residential Moves and Social Support', *Canadian Studies in Population* 24, 2: 163–87.

Moore, H. 1997. Caregiving in Parkinson's: A qualitative study of the perceived impacts on and needs of Parkinson's caregivers, MA thesis, Queen's University.

Moore, T., et al. 1998. 'Time to act on drug safety', *Journal of the American Medical Association* 279, 19: 1571–3.

Mori, M. 1991. 'Palliative care of the elderly: An overview and annotated bibliography', Gerontology Research Centre, Simon Fraser University.

Morris, M., J. Robinson, et al. 1999. *The Changing Nature of Home Care and Its Impact on Women's Vulnerability to Poverty*. Ottawa: Status of Women Canada.

Morrongiello, B., and B. Gottlieb. 2000. 'Self-care among adults', *Canadian Journal on Aging/La Revue Canadienne du Vieillissement* 19, 1: 32–57.

Moskop, J.C. 1981. 'The Nature and Limits of Physician Authority', in M.S. Straum and D.E. Larson, eds, *Doctors, Patients and Society*. Waterloo, Ont.: Wilfrid Laurier University Press.

Myerson, A.R. 1995. 'Helping Health Insurers Say No', *New York Times*, 20 Mar., Business Day.

National Council of Welfare. 1991. *Funding Health and Higher Education: Danger Looming*. Ottawa: National Council of Welfare.

National Council of Women in Canada. 1975. *Women of Canada: Their Life and Work*. Ottawa: NCWC.

National Evaluation of the Cost Effectiveness of Home Care. 2001. *Newsletter* 1, 1: 1–4.

National Forum on Health. 1997. *Canada Health Action: Building on the Legacy*, vol. 1, *Final Report*. Ottawa: Public Works and Government Services.

———. 1997. *Canada Health Action: Building on the Legacy*, vol. 2, *Synthesis Reports and Issues Papers*. Ottawa: Public Works and Government Services.

———. 1998. *Determinants of Health: Adults and Seniors*. Sainte-Foy, Qué.: Éditions MultiMondes.

Naylor, D. 1986. *Private Practice, Public Payment*. Montreal and Kingston: McGill-Queen's University Press.

———, G.M. Anderson, and V. Goel, eds. 1994. *Patterns of Health Care in Ontario*, vol. 1. Ottawa: Canadian Medical Association.

Neal, M.B. 1993. *Balancing Work and Caregiving for Children, Adults, and Elders*. Newbury Park, Calif.: Sage Publications.

Neil, R., and R. Watts, eds. 1991. *Caring and Nursing: Explorations in Feminist Perspectives*. New York: National League for Nursing.

Nelson, J. 1995. 'Dr. Rockefeller Will See You Now: The Hidden Players Privatizing Canada's Health Care System', *Canadian Forum* (Jan.–Feb.): 7–11.

Neufeld, A., and M.J. Harrison. 1998. 'Men as caregivers: reciprocal relationships or obligation?', *Journal of Advanced Nursing* 28, 5: 959–68.

New York State Department of Health. n.d. Your Rights as a Hospital Patient in New York State, mimeo.

Neysmith, S.M., ed. 2000. *Restructuring Caring Labour: Discourse, State Practice, and Everyday Life.* Toronto: Oxford University Press.

———— and J. Aronson. 1997. 'Working Conditions in Home Care: Negotiating Race and Class Boundaries in Gendered Work', *International Journal of Health Services* 27, 3: 479–99.

———— and B. Nichols. 1994. 'Working Conditions in a Home-Care Company—Three Groups of Workers', *Canadian Journal of Aging* 13, 3: 169–86.

Ng, R., and J. Ramirez. 1981. *Immigrant Housewives in Canada.* Toronto: Immigrant Women's Centre.

Nichols, G. 1978. *The Great Nineteenth Century Medicine Manual.* Toronto: Coles.

Nichols, M. 1994. 'Questioning Prozac', *Maclean's*, 23 May, 36–41.

Nijboer, C., M. Triemstra, et al. 1999. 'Determinants of caregiving experiences and mental health of partners of cancer patients', *Cancer* 86, 4: 577–88.

Northcott, H.C. 1994. 'Public Perceptions of the Population Aging "Crisis"', *Canadian Public Policy/Analyse de Politiques* 20, 1: 66–77.

Nova Scotia Provincial Health Council. 1992. *Toward Achieving Nova Scotia's Health Goals: An Initial Plan of Action for Health Care Reform Report.* Halifax: Provincial Health Council.

Nursing. 1985. 'DRGs—Making Them Work for You'.

Oakley, A. 1984. *The Captured Womb.* Oxford: Basil Blackwell.

O'Connor, J. 1973. *The Fiscal Crisis of the State.* New York: St Martin's Press.

Oderkirk, J. 1993. 'Disabilities Among Children', *Canadian Social Trends* (Winter): 21–4.

O'Neill, M. 1992. 'Community Participation in Quebec's Health System: A Strategy to Curtail Community Empowerment', *International Journal of Health Services* 22, 2: 287–301.

Ontario Health Industries Advisory Committee to the Ministry of Health. 1994. *Healthy and Wealthy.* Toronto: Queen's Printer for Ontario.

Ontario Human Rights Commission. 2000. *Discrimination and Age.* Toronto: Human Rights Commission.

Ontario Ministry of Citizenship. 1987. *The Advocacy Act: A General Overview.* Toronto: Ministry of Citizenship.

Ontario Ministry of Community and Social Services. 1991. *Redirection of Long-Term Care and Support Service in Ontario.* Toronto: Queen's Printer for Ontario.

Ontario Ministry of Health. 1987. *Report to Public Hospitals in Ontario on the 1985 Ontario Hospital Work Force Survey and Employment Equity Initiatives in 1985/86.* Toronto: Ministry of Health.

————. 1991. Graph prepared for and distributed to members of the Research Steering Committee of the Ontario Premier's Council on Health, Well-Being and Social Justice.

————. 1992. Working Document: Goals and Strategic Priorities. Toronto.

————. 1993. *Building Partnerships in Long Term Care: A New Way to Plan, Manage and Deliver Services and Community Support.* Toronto: Queen's Printer for Ontario.

————. 1994. *Annual Report 1992–93.* Toronto: Ministry of Health.

————. 2000. *The Long-Term Care Facility System in Ontario.* Toronto.

Ontario Pay Equity Tribunal. 1991. *Ontario Nurses Association v. Women's College Hospital, Sunnybrook Hospital and North York General Hospital.* Toronto: Ontario Pay Equity Tribunal.

————. 1992. *Ontario Nurses Association, Applicant v. Regional Municipality of Haldimand-Norfolk, Respondent.* Toronto: Ontario Pay Equity Tribunal.

Ontario Premier's Council on Health Strategy. 1991. *Achieving the Vision: Health Human Resources*. Toronto.

———. 1991. *Nurturing Health: A Framework on the Determinants of Health*. Toronto.

———. 1991. *A Vision of Health: Health Goals for Ontario*. Toronto.

Organization for Economic Co-operation and Development (OECD). 1993. *OECD Health Systems Facts and Trends 1960–1991*, vol. 1. Paris: OECD.

O'Rourke, N., B.E. Havercamp, et al. 1996. 'Relative contribution of subjective factors to expressed burden among spousal caregivers of suspected dementia patients', *Canadian Journal on Aging/La Revue Canadienne du Vieillissement* 15, 4: 583–96.

Overall, C., ed. 1989. *The Future of Human Reproduction*. Toronto: Women's Press.

Pappert, A. 1986. 'The Rise and Fall of the IUD', in K. McDonnell, ed., *Adverse Effects, Women and the Pharmaceutical Industry*. Toronto: Women's Press, 167–71.

Paterson, G.R. 1967. 'Canadian Pharmacy in Pre-Confederation Medical Legislation', *Journal of the American Medical Association* 200, 10 (5 June): 849–52.

Pauch, W.G. 1996. 'Mother's care: A study of the caregiving responsibilities of women with schizophrenic adult children', Ph.D. thesis, University of Manitoba.

Pedlar, D.J., and D.E. Biegel. 1999. 'Impact of family caregiver attitudes on the use of community services for dementia care', *Journal of Applied Gerontology* 18, 2 (June): 201–21.

Penning, M.J. 2000. 'Self-, informal and formal care: partnerships in community-based and residential long-term settings', *Canadian Journal on Aging/La Revue Canadienne du Vieillissement* 19 (Supp. 1): 75–100.

——— and N.L. Chappell. 1990. 'Self-care in relation to informal and formal care', *Aging and Society* 10, pt. 1 (Mar.): 41–59.

Pharmaceutical Inquiry of Ontario. 1990. *Rx: Prescriptions for Health*. Toronto: Ministry of Health.

Phillips, J. 1995. *Working Carers: International Perspectives on Working and Caring for Older People*. Avebury, Aldershot.

Pilote, L., N. Racine, and M. Hlatky. 1994. 'Differences in the Treatment of Myocardial Infarction in the United States and Canada', *Archives of Internal Medicine* 154, 10 (23 May): 1090–7.

Piper, L.R. 1983. 'Accounting for Nursing Functions in DRGs', *Nursing Management* (Nov.): 7–8.

Pizurski, H., A. Butter, and L. Ewart. 1988. *Women as Providers of Health Care*. Geneva: World Health Organization.

Poland, B., et al. 1998. 'Wealth, Equity and Health Care: A Critique of the "Population Health" Perspective on the Determinants of Health', *Social Science and Medicine* 46, 7: 785–98.

Pold, H. 1990. 'The Gift of Time', *Perspectives on Labour and Income* 2, 2 (Summer).

Porter, J. 1965. *The Vertical Mosaic*. Toronto: University of Toronto Press.

Prasil, S. 1993. 'Seniors 75+ Lifestyles', *Canadian Social Trends* (Autumn).

Premier's Commission on Future Health Care for Albertans. 1989. *The Rainbow Report: Our Vision for Health*. Edmonton.

Price, J. 1994. 'Total Quality Management Threatens Medicare', *Canadian Dimension* 28, 1 (Jan.–Feb.): 15–20.

Price, J.A. 1983. 'Canadian Indian Families', in K. Ishwaran, ed., *The Canadian Family*. Toronto: Gage.

Price, W. 1988. *Direct Nursing Requirements of Extended Care Residents in Homes for the Aged and Nursing Homes in Ontario*. Toronto: Price Waterhouse.

Priest, L. 1992. 'Labour-Halting Drug Called Ineffective and Risk to Health', *Toronto Star*. 31 July, C1.

———. 1993. 'Assaults on Patients Soaring, Hospitals Say', *Toronto Star*, 18 May, A1, A27.

———. 1995. 'Should We Rate Our Hospitals?', *Toronto Star*, 1 April, A20.

————. 1995. 'Fourteen Hospitals' Budgets Rejected', *Toronto Star*, 28 April, A2.

————. 1995. 'Sunnybrook to Privatize Lab and Sell Services to the U.S.', *Toronto Star*, 24 Feb., A2.

Proctor, E. 1993. 'Adequacy of Informal Care for Elderly Patients Going Home From the Hospital: Discharge Planners Perspectives', *Journal of Applied Gerontology*.

Pryke, K.G. 1988. 'Poor Relief and Health Care in Halifax, 1827–1849', in W. Mitchinson and J.D. McGinnis, eds, *Essays in the History of Canadian Medicine*. Toronto: McClelland & Stewart, 39–61.

Québec Commission d'Étude sur les Services de Santé et les Services Sociaux (Clair Commission). 2000. *Les Solutions Émergentes*. Québec: Ministere de la Santé et les Services Sociaux.

Quinn, S.B. 1995. 'Maintaining Stability: the process within the key caregiver of the person with schizophrenia', MA thesis, Dalhousie University.

Rachlis, M. 2000. *Modernizing Medicare for the Twenty-First Century*. Victoria: Ministry of Health and Ministry Responsible for Seniors.

————, R.G. Evans, et al. 2000. *Revitalizing Medicare: Shared Problems, Public Solutions*. Vancouver: Tommy Douglas Research Institute.

———— and C. Kushner. 1994. *Strong Medicine*. Toronto: HarperCollins.

Rands, S. 1994. *Privilege and Policy*. Saskatoon: Community Health Co-operative Federation.

Ranson, S., and J. Stewart. 1989. 'Citizenship and Government: The Challenge for Management in the Public Domain', *Political Studies* 37, 1: 5–24.

Rasmussen, L., L. Rasmussen, C. Savage, and A. Wheeler. 1976. *A Harvest Yet to Reap*. Toronto: Women's Press.

Registered Nurses Association of Ontario. 2000. *Ensuring the Care Will Be There: Report on Nursing Recruitment and Retention in Ontario*. Toronto: Ontario Ministry of Health and Long-Term Care.

Regush, N. 1987. *Condition Critical*. Toronto: Macmillan.

————. 1993. *Safety Last: The Failure of the Consumer Health Protection System in Canada*. Toronto: Key Porter Books.

Rehner, J. 1989. *Old Myths, New Meanings*. Toronto: Second Story Press.

Rekart, J. 1993. *Public Funds, Private Provision: The Role of the Voluntary Sector*. Vancouver: University of British Columbia Press.

Relman, A. 1973. 'Salaried Physicians and Economic Incentives', *New England Journal of Medicine* 288, 22 (1 May): 1152–5.

Renaud, M. 1987. 'Reform or Illusion? An Analysis of the Quebec State Intervention in Health', in Coburn et al. (1987).

Reuters News Agency. 1993. 'Drug That Delays Labour May Harm Fetus, Study Finds', *Globe and Mail*, 25 Nov., A4.

Richardson, T. 1993. *Total Quality Management Programs: More Work for Less Pay*. Edmonton: United Nurses of Alberta.

————. 1994. *Patient Focused Care*. Edmonton: United Nurses of Alberta.

Rigbey & Associates. 1994. *Family Impact Study*. A study prepared for the Victorian Order of Nurses (Grey-Bruce Branch). Owen Sound, Ont.: Victorian Order of Nurses.

Robb, R., M. Denton, et al. 1999. 'Valuation of Unpaid Help by Seniors in Canada: An Empirical Analysis', *Canadian Journal on Aging/La Revue Canadienne du Vieillissement* 18, 4: 430–46.

Robinson, J.C. 2001. 'The End of Managed Care', *Journal of the American Medical Association* 285, 20 (23–30 May): 1–26.

Romanow, R. 2001. 'Romanow Outlines Mandate for Commission'. Available at: <www.healthcarecommission.ca>.

Roos, N.P., P. Montgomery, et al. 1987. 'Health Care Utilization in the Years Prior to Death', *Milbank Quarterly* 65, 2: 231–54.

Rootman, I., and J. Raeburn. 1994. 'The Concept of Health', in A. Pederson, M. O'Neill, and Rootman, eds, *Health Promotion in Canada*. Toronto: W.B. Saunders.

Rosenberg, M.W., and E.G. Moore. 1997. 'The Health of Canada's Elderly Population: Current Status and Future Implications', *Canadian Medical Association Journal* 157: 1025–32.

Rosenthal, C.J., and A. Martin-Matthews. 1999. 'Families as care-providers versus care-managers? Gender and type of care in a sample of employed Canadians' (SEDAP Research Paper No. 4). Hamilton, Ont.: McMaster University.

———— and L.O. Stone. 1999. 'How much help is exchanged in families? Towards an understanding of discrepant research findings' (SEDAP Research Paper No. 2). Hamilton, Ont.: McMaster University.

Rouleau, J.L., et al. 1993. 'A Comparison of Management Patterns after Acute Myocardial Infarction in Canada and the United States', *New England Journal of Medicine* 328, 11 (18 Mar.): 779–84.

Royal Commission on Health Services (Hall Commission). 1964. *Report*. Ottawa: Queen's Printer.

Ryten, E. 1997. *A Statistical Picture of the Past, Present and Future of Registered Nurses in Canada*. Ottawa: Canadian Nurses Association.

Salvatori, P., M. Tremblay, et al. 1998. 'Aging with an intellectual disability: a review of Canadian literature', *Canadian Journal on Aging/La Revue Canadienne du Vieillissement* 17, 3: 249–71.

Sanborn, B., and S. Bould. 1991. 'Intergenerational Caregivers of the Oldest Old', *Marriage and Family Review* 16, 1–2: 125–42.

Sanger, M. 2001. *Reckless Abandon: Canada, the GATS and the Future of Health Care*. Ottawa: Canadian Centre for Policy Alternatives.

Saskatchewan Commission on Directions in Health Care. 1990. *Future Directions for Health Care in Saskatchewan*. Regina.

Saul, J.R. 1999. 'Health Care at the End of the Twentieth Century: Confusing Symptoms for Systems', in Margaret Somerville, ed., *Do We Care? Renewing Canada's Commitment to Health*. Conference Proceedings, Directions for Canadian Health Care. Montreal and Kingston: McGill-Queen's University Press.

Schragge, E. 1990. 'Community Based Practice: Political Alternatives or New State Forms?', in L. David and Schragge, eds, *Bureaucracy and Community*. Montreal: Black Rose Books.

Scotton, L. 1995. 'Spring Tune-Up', *Toronto Star*, 21 Apr., C1.

Sedgewick Noble Lowndes. 1994. *Health Care Alert . . . OHIP Cuts Back—Sedgewick Noble Lowndes Has the Answer*. Toronto: Sedgewick Noble Lowndes.

Shah, C.P. 1998. *Public Health and Preventive Medicine in Canada*. Toronto: University of Toronto Press.

Shapiro, E. 1997. *The Cost of Privatization: A Case Study of Home Care in Manitoba*. Ottawa: Canadian Centre for Policy Alternatives.

Sherrill, R. 1995. 'Medicine and the Madness of the Market', *The Nation*, 9–16 Jan., 45–72.

Sherwin, S. 1992. *No Longer Patient: Feminist Ethics and Health Care*. Philadelphia: Temple University Press.

Shorter, E. 1985. *Bedside Manners: A Troubled History of Doctors and Patients*. New York: Simon and Schuster.

Simmons, H. 1990. *Unbalanced: Mental Health Policy in Ontario, 1930–1989*. Toronto: Wall and Thompson.

Simor, A.E. 2001. 'The Evolution of Methicillin-Resistant Staphylococcus Aureus in Canadian Hospitals: 5 Years of National Surveillance', *Canadian Medical Association Journal* 165 (10 July): 21–31.

Sinclair, P., and L. Felt. 1992. 'Separate Worlds: Gender and Domestic Labour in an Isolated Fishing Region', *Canadian Review of Sociology and Anthropology* 29, 1 (Feb.): 55–71.

Singleton, J. 2000. 'Women Caring for Elderly Family Members: Shaping Non-Traditional Work and Family Initiatives', *Journal of Comparative Family Studies* 31, 3: 367–75.

Sky, L. 1995. *Lean and Mean Health Care: The Creation of the Generic Worker and the Deregulation of Health Care*. Health Research Project Working Paper 95–3. Toronto: Ontario Federation of Labour, June.

——— and S. Ericksen. 1992. *Keep Medicare Healthy: It Might Not Be There When You Need It.* Ottawa: Canadian Union of Public Employees.

Smith, D., and S. David, eds. 1975. *Women Look at Psychiatry.* Vancouver: Press Gang.

Soderstrom, L. 1978. *The Canadian Health System.* London: Croom Helm.

Spencer, C., M. Ashfield, et al. 1996. 'Abuse and neglect of older adults in community settings: An annotated bibliography', Gerontology Research Centre, Simon Fraser University.

Spitzer, D.L. 2000. '"They Don't Listen To Your Body": Minority Women, Nurses and Childbirth Under Health Reform', in Gustafson (2000).

Statistics Canada. 1975. *1971 Census of Canada: Occupations.* Ottawa: Ministry of Industry, Trade and Commerce.

———. 1979. *Canada's Elderly.* Ottawa: Statistics Canada.

———, S. Fletcher, et al. 1981. *Aspects of Population Aging In Canada: A Chartbook.* Ottawa: Statistics Canada.

———, Business, Provincial and Municipal Relations Division and Toronto Regional Office Advisory Services. 1982. *Statistics Canada's Bibliography of the Elderly.* Ottawa: Statistics Canada.

———. 1983. *Historical Statistics of Canada.* Ottawa, Minister of Supply and Services Canada.

———. 1983. *1981 Census of Canada: Labour Force - Occupation Trends.* Ottawa: Minister of Supply and Services Canada.

———. 1984. *The Elderly in Canada.* Ottawa, Supply and Services Canada.

———. 1987. *Health and Social Support, 1985.* Ottawa: Statistics Canada.

———. 1988. *Canada's Seniors.* Ottawa: Statistics Canada.

———. 1988. *The Daily.*

———. 1988. *Occupational Trends 1961–1986.* Ottawa: Supply and Services Canada.

———. 1989. *Statistics Canada Data on Seniors: A Bibliography.* Toronto: Statistics Canada.

———, Housing, Family and Social Statistics Division. Target Group Data Bases. 1990. *A Portrait of Seniors in Canada.* Ottawa: Statistics Canada.

———, Family and Community Supports Division. 1991. *Caring Communities: Proceedings of the Symposium on Social Supports.* Ottawa: Statistics Canada.

———. 1992. *Labour Force Annual Averages 1990.* Ottawa: Ministry of Industry, Science and Technology.

———. 1993. *Hospital Annual Statistics 1989–90.* Ottawa: Ministry of Industry, Science and Technology.

———. 1993. *Labour Force Annual Averages 1991.* Ottawa: Ministry of Industry, Science and Technology.

———. 1993. *91 Census Employment Income by Occupation.* Ottawa: Ministry of Industry, Science and Technology.

———. 1993. *91 Census Industry and Class of Worker.* Ottawa: Ministry of Industry, Science and Technology.

———. 1993. *91 Census Occupation.* Ottawa: Ministry of Industry, Science and Technology.

———. 1993. *Residential Care Facilities - Aged.* Ottawa: Ministry of Industry, Science and Technology.

———. 1993. *Residential Care Facilities - Mental.* Ottawa: Ministry of Industry, Science and Technology.

———. 1994. *Hospital Annual Statistics, 1991–92.* Ottawa: Minister of Industry, Science and Technology.

———. 1994. *Labour Force Annual Averages 1993.* Ottawa: Minister of Industry, Science and Technology.

———. 1994. *Nursing in Canada 1993: Registered Nurses.* Ottawa: Ministry of Industry, Science and Technology.

———. 1994. *Report on the Demographic Situation in Canada 1994; Current Demographic Analysis; The Sandwich Generation: Myths and Reality*. Ottawa: Statistics Canada.

———. 1995. *Labour Force Annual Averages 1994*. Ottawa: Minister of Industry, Science and Technology.

———. 1997. 'Who cares? Caregiving in the 1990's', *The Daily*, 19 Aug.

———. 1999. 'Health care services – recent trends', *Health Reports* 11, 3 (Winter).

———, Housing, Family and Social Statistics Division, et al. 1999. *A Portrait of Seniors in Canada*, 3rd edn. Ottawa: Statistics Canada.

———. 2000. *Women in Canada 2000*. Ottawa: Ministry of Industry.

———. 2001. *96 Census: Occupation, Industry and Class of Workers*. Ottawa: Statistics Canada.

Steele, R.G., and M.I. Fitch. 1996. 'Coping strategies of family caregivers of home hospice patients with cancer', *Oncology Nursing Forum* 23, 6: 955–60.

Stewart, C. 1994. 'Putting the Weakest at Risk', *Toronto Star*, 6 Jan., C1.

Stewart, E. 1995. 'Ontario Health, Social Net Takes $1 Billion Cut', *Toronto Star*. 28 Feb., A9.

Stewart, M. 1993. *Integrating Social Support in Nursing*. London: Sage.

———. 2000. *Chronic Conditions and Caregiving in Canada: Social Support Strategies*. Toronto: University of Toronto Press.

Stoddart, G., M. Barer, and R. Evans. 1994. *User Charges, Snares and Delusions: Another Look at the Literature*. Toronto: Premier's Council on Health, Well-Being and Social Justice.

———, ———, ———, and V. Bhatia. 1993. *Why Not User Charges? The Real Issues*. Toronto: The Premier's Council on Health, Well-Being and Social Justice.

Stoffman, D. 1988. 'Losing Patience. Are Hospitals Killing the Taxpayer?', *Canadian Business* (Nov.).

Stoller, E.P. 1989. 'Formal Services and Informal Helping: The Myth of Service Substitution', *Journal of Applied Gerontology* 8, 1: 37–52.

Stone, L. 1988. *Family and Friendship Ties among Canada's Seniors: An Introductory Report of Findings from the General Social Survey*. Ottawa: Supply and Services Canada.

Stone, R., G.L. Cafferata, et al. 1987. 'Caregivers of the Frail Elderly: A National Profile', *The Gerontologist* 27, 5: 616–26.

——— and P.F. Short. 1990. 'The competing demands of employment and informal caregiving to disabled elders', *Medical Care* 28, 6: 513–26.

Strong-Boag, V. 1981. 'Canada's Women Doctors: Feminism Constrained', in S.E.D. Shortt, ed., *Medicine in Canadian Society: Historical Perspectives*. Montreal and Kingston: McGill-Queen's University Press.

Struthers, J. 1997. 'Reluctant Partners: State Regulation of Private Nursing Homes in Ontario, 1941–72', in S. Raymond et al., eds, *The Welfare State in Canada: Past, Present and Future*. Concord, Ont.: Irwin, 171–92.

Sunter, D. 1993. 'Working Shift', *Perspectives on Labour and Income* 5, 1: 16–23.

Sustaining Health Care for Canada. 1995. *Synthesis Report of the Cost-Effectiveness of the Canadian Health Care System Project*, Executive Summary. Ottawa.

Sutherland, R. 2001. *The Costs of Contracting Out Home Care: A Behind the Scenes Look at Home Care in Ontario*. Ottawa: Canadian Union of Public Employees.

——— and J. Fulton. 1994. *Spending Smarter and Spending Less*. Ottawa: The Health Group.

Swartz, D. 1987. 'The Politics of Reform: Conflict and Accommodation in Canadian Health Policy', in Coburn et al. (1987: 568–89).

Tamblyn, R.M., et al. 1994. 'Questionable Prescribing for the Elderly', *Canadian Medical Association Journal* 150, 11: 1801–9.

Tarman, V.I. 1990. *Privatization and Health Care*. Toronto: Garamond.

Tausig, M., G.A. Fisher, et al. 1992. 'Informal systems of care for the chronically mentally ill', *Community Mental Health Journal* 28, 5: 413–25.

Taylor, D., et al. forthcoming. 'Making Care Visible: Exploring the Healthwork of People Living with HIV/AIDS in Ontario'.

Taylor, F.W. 1911. *The Principles of Scientific Management.* New York: Norton.

Taylor, M. 1987. *Health Insurance and Canadian Public Policy.* Montreal and Kingston: McGill-Queen's University Press.

Taylor, P. 1994. 'Busiest MDs Prescribe the Most Drugs', *Globe and Mail,* 15 Mar., A1.

——— and R. Mickleburgh. 1992. 'Breast Implant Sales Suspended', *Globe and Mail,* 8 Jan., A4.

Temple, L., et al. 2001. 'Defining Disease in the Genomics Era', *Science* 293 (3 Aug.): 807–8.

Terris, M. 1990. 'Lessons from Canada's Health Program', *Technology Review* (Feb.–Mar.): 27–34.

Tholl, W.G. 1994. 'Health Care Spending in Canada: Skating Faster on Thinner Ice', in Blomqvist and Brown (1994: 54–89).

Thomas, D. 2000. 'Participation in Voluntary Associations by the Elderly: The Case of the Abitibi-Temiscaminque Region', Ph.D. thesis, Université de Montréal.

Thompson, B., F. Tudiver, et al. 2000. 'Sons as sole caregivers for their elderly parents: How do they cope?', *Canadian Family Physician* 46: 360–5.

Thurston, W.E., C.M. Scott, and B.A. Crow. 1997. *Social Change, Policy Development and the Influence on Women's Health.* Halifax: Synthesis Paper for the Fifth National Health Promotion Conference, July.

Toronto Star. 1995. 'MD Exodus Threatens Health Care, MPs Told', *Toronto Star,* 11 May, A3.

Torrance, G.M. 1987. 'Hospitals as Health Factories', in Coburn et al. (1987: 497–500).

———. 1987. 'Socio-Historical Overview: The Development of the Canadian Health System', in Coburn et al. (1987: 6–32).

Toughill, K. 1992. 'Doctors Charging Extra Fees Up Front', *Toronto Star,* 27 May, A2.

Transitional Council of the College of Midwives. 1993. Policy Documents. Toronto.

Trottier, H., L. Martel, et al. 2000. 'Living at home or in an institution: What makes the difference for seniors?', *Health Reports* 11, 4: 49–61.

Tully, P., and E. Saint-Pierre. 1997. 'Downsizing Canada's hospitals, 1986/87 to 1994/95', *Health Reports* 8, 4: 33–9.

Tuohy, C. 1988. 'Medicine and the State in Canada', *Canadian Journal of Political Science* 21: 267–96.

Van Dijk, J. 1997. 'Ethnicity, Aging and Support among Dutch Canadians: A Study of Community in Two Generations of Catholics and Calvinists', MA thesis, McMaster University.

Vatri Boydell, K.M. 1996. 'Mothering adult children with schizophrenia: the hidden realities of caring', Ph.D. thesis, York University.

Walton, D. 1999. 'Ontario Close to Overtaking Michigan as Car Capital', *Globe and Mail,* 30 Nov., A5

Warburton, R., and W.K. Carroll. 1994. 'Class and Gender in Nursing', in Bolaria and Dickinson (1994: 556–69).

Ward-Griffin, C. 1998. 'Negotiating the boundaries of eldercare: the relationship between nurses and family caregivers', Ph.D. thesis, University of Toronto.

——— and P. McKeever. 2000. 'Relationships between nurses and family caregivers: partners in care?', *Advances in Nursing Science* 22, 3: 89–103.

Waring, M. 1988. *If Women Counted: A New Feminist Economics.* San Francisco: HarperCollins.

Waxler-Morrison, N., J. Anderson, and E. Richardson, eds. 1990. *Cross-Cultural Caring.* Vancouver: University of British Columbia Press.

Weissert, W.G. 1992. 'Cost-effectiveness of home-care', in R.B. Deber and G.G. Thompson, eds, *Restructuring Canada's Health Services System: How Do We Get There from Here?* Toronto: University of Toronto Press, 89–98.

White, J. 1990. *Hospital Strike!* Toronto: Thompson.

Whittaker, J.A. 1984. 'The Search for Legitimacy: Nurses' Registration in British Columbia, 1913–1935', in B. Latham and R. Pazdro, eds, *Not Just Pin Money*. Victoria: Camosun College.

Wickham-Searl, P. 1992. 'Careers in Caring: Mothers of Children With Disabilities', *Disability, Handicap and Society* 7, 1: 5–17.

Wilkins, K., and M.P. Beaudet. 2000. 'Changes in social support in relation to seniors' use of home care', *Health Reports* 11, 4: 39–47.

——— and E. Park. 1998. 'Home care in Canada', *Health Reports* 10, 1: 29–37.

Willis, E. 1983. *Medical Dominance*. Sydney: George Allen and Unwin.

Wilson, D. forthcoming. 'Regional Planning and Delivery in Alberta: A Basic Cost Benefit Analysis in Response to a Health System Performance Issue'.

Wilson, K., and J. Howard. 2000. *Missing Links: The Effects of Health Care Privatization on Women in Manitoba and Saskatchewan*. Winnipeg: Prairie Women's Health Centre of Excellence.

Wolfe, S. 1991. 'Ethics and Equity in Canadian Health Care: Policy Alternatives', *International Journal of Health Services* 21, 4: 673–80.

Wolfson, C., R. Handfield-Jones, et al. 1993. 'Adult children's perceptions of their responsibility to provide care for dependent elderly parents', *The Gerontologist* 33, 3: 315–23.

Woolhandler, S., et al. 1993. 'Administrative Costs in U.S. Hospitals', *New England Journal of Medicine* (Aug.).

Working Group on Health Services Utilization. 1994. 'When Less Is Better: Using Canada's Hospitals Efficiently', Conference of Federal/Provincial/Territorial Deputy Ministers of Health.

Working Group on Health System Financing. 1993. *Toward a New Consensus on Health Care Financing in Canada*. Ottawa: Canadian Medical Association.

World Economic Forum. 1992. *World Competitiveness Report 1991*. Lausanne, Switzerland: Institut pour l'Etude des Méthodes de Direction de l'Entreprise.

World Health Organization (WHO). 1986. *Ottawa Charter for Health Promotion*. Ottawa: Canadian Public Health Association.

———. 1990. *Consultation on the Place of In Vitro Fertilization on Infertility Care*. Copenhagen.

———. 1998. *The World Health Report*. Geneva: WHO.

Wotherspoon, T. 1991. 'Immigration, Gender and Professional Labour: State Regulation of Nursing and Teaching', paper presented to the Canadian Sociology and Anthropology Association annual meeting, Victoria.

Yalnizyan, A. 1998. *The Growing Gap: A Report on Growing Inequality between the Rich and the Poor in Canada*. Toronto: Centre for Social Justice.

Yamashita, M. 1998. 'Family coping with mental illness: a comparative study', *Journal of Psychiatric & Mental Health Nursing* 5, 6: 515–23.

Yaros, P. 1991. 'The Feminist Movement and the Science and Profession of Nursing: Analogies and Paradoxes', in Neil and Watts (1991: 77–83).

Yelaja, P. 2001. 'Home Care Getting Worse, Report Says', *Toronto Star*, 2 Aug., A3.

Index